AHEAD OF HIS AGE

AHEAD OF HIS AGE

BISHOP BARNES OF
BIRMINGHAM

by

JOHN BARNES

COLLINS
St James's Place, London
1979

William Collins Sons & Co Ltd
London · Glasgow · Sydney · Auckland
Toronto · Johannesburg

The photograph opposite p. 289 is reproduced by courtesy of
BBC Publications (Radio Times Hulton Picture Library).
The cartoon on p. 329 by David Low is reproduced by courtesy of the
Low Trustees, the London Express News and Feature Service and the
London School of Economics; the cartoon on p. 330 is reproduced by
permission of *Punch*; the cartoon on p. 411 by Osbert Lancaster
is reproduced from *Sign of the Times* by Osbert Lancaster,
published by John Murray, London

First published 1979
© John Barnes 1979
ISBN 0 00 216087 0
Set in 11pt Monotype Times
Made and printed in Great Britain by
William Collins Sons & Co Ltd, Glasgow

To
various embodiments
of the
Barnes genes

CONTENTS

CONTENTS

FOREWORD

Whether my father would have wanted a life of him written or not, he would not have wanted his son to write it. One can hear him say: 'Don't waste your time, dear boy.' Perhaps that is why it has waited twenty-five years to be written.

Some will say that a son should not write about his father. They may be right. It is not easy to strike a balance between affection and objectivity. Slavish adulation and unseemly criticism are both out of place.

But he was an unusual person. One could not live in his orbit and be indifferent to him. He did not wait upon events; he made them happen. With a strong analytical mind, he asked less 'What do I think about this?' than 'What should I do about it?' What is more, his mind was not fixed on either/or, but on both/and. He touched life at many points and sought to find a relation between them all. On no subject could he not have a view. He was not just an ecclesiastic, still less a conventional ecclesiastic, and he cannot have just a conventional ecclesiastical biography. Unluckily, only he himself could do justice to all the many subjects in which he was interested and knowledgeable.

Biography is not history. But nor, one hopes, is it altogether a tale told by an idiot. If history records the march of events, biography records how man marched with or against events. My father, perhaps as much as many men of his generation, seemed to march ahead of events. John Bright declared in Birmingham for peace, retrenchment and reform. My father, in Birmingham and elsewhere, worked for peace, reconciliation and progress.

My thanks are due to many people. His Grace the Archbishop of Canterbury has given me personal encouragement; he and the Trustees of Lambeth Palace Library have kindly allowed me to make use of material in their possession. I am grateful to the Right Honourable James Callaghan for his personal interest and official help. The

9

Council of Trinity College, Cambridge, have permitted me to consult their minutes and Dr R. Robson, Fellow of the College, has been notably generous with advice and assistance. The Master and Fellows of Magdalene College, Cambridge, have allowed me to see Arthur Benson's diaries and Dr David Newsome, the Headmaster of Christ's Hospital, made this extremely easy for me, not least through the index which he has compiled. The authorities of the Public Record Office, the Cambridge University Library and the Birmingham Reference Library have all been patient and helpful. Mr Richard Ekin, the Registrar, and Mr John Watson, the Secretary, of the Diocese of Birmingham made their time and information freely available to me.

Several people who knew my father at Cambridge, in London, at Birmingham or elsewhere have responded nobly to my importunate appeals for their memories of him, and among them I am particularly grateful to Bishop Michael Parker, Dr J. S. Boys-Smith, Dr R. D. Richardson, Professor J. C. Burkill and Canon R. S. O. Stevens. Dame Mary Cartwright has valiantly done her best to help me conceal my total ignorance of mathematics.

The work would not have been possible without the use of my father's papers, systematically classified as a labour of love by his long-time secretary, Mrs Edward Parker, formerly Miss N. M. V. Owen, to whom he himself owed so much.

Nor could I possibly have worked with so little difficulty, or indeed so agreeably, but for the facilities generously put at my disposal by Messrs N. M. Rothschild & Sons, Limited, in particular by Lord Rothschild and Mr Evelyn de Rothschild.

May I specially record my thanks to David Lasocki, who has laboured long on the typewriter to make my text intelligible?

I have been undeservedly lucky in the help and encouragement received from my publishers, notably Lady Collins herself and Mrs Michèle Byam.

My brother William has given me astringent advice from a better memory than mine.

Had it not been for the example and the precept of my mother, when she was alive, this book would never have been written. Not only was she insistent that there should be such a book. She also over many years compiled in huge albums and in labelled packages all the information on which is based any backbone which it may possess.

10

But, above all, as in everything else in life, my dearest debt is to my wife, without whose constant help and encouragement I should never have had the brashness to begin, the courage to continue or the energy to end this book.

JOHN BARNES
Hurstpierpoint
May 1979

CHAPTER I

BIRMINGHAM
1874-1892

Boyhood Brilliance

The boy who was born on 1 April 1874 might have been forgiven later for thinking that he had been fooled.

All the barometers seemed set fair in the world which faced him. It was the heyday of the Victorian Era, when ever-increasing material progress was accepted by the majority of Englishmen as the natural order of divine providence. At home, the political scene was marked by tranquil stability, at least in comparison with the previous generation of Reform and Chartism. Liberals and Conservatives decorously succeeded each other in power. Abroad, thanks to her navy and her currency, the position of Britain and her world-wide empire went well-nigh unchallenged. Indeed, apart from the aberrations of the Crimea and the Indian Mutiny, already largely forgotten, she had enjoyed peace for two generations and no war cloud the size of a white man's hand showed on any horizon. Meanwhile, even though the rapid advance of science and technology suggested that man was already mastering his environment, Christianity was still the accepted philosophy, and indeed morality, of civilization in the northern hemisphere, and in England the established Church still enjoyed a position of predominant privilege.

But the spirit of change was already in the air, or at least fermenting under the surface. The Reform Act of 1867 had again widened the franchise, and Robert Lowe had delivered himself of his famous quip that 'now we must educate our masters'. Indeed, the Education Act of 1870 had ushered in a national system of elementary education.

The previous generation had seen Shaftesbury's industrial reforms, culminating in a Factory and Workshops Act of 1871. Now the trade unions were strengthening their organization in the moves which led to the Trades Union Acts from 1871 to 1876. Keir Hardie and John Burns, who were to be among the first Labour members of Parliament, with Burns the first working-man to sit in a British cabinet, had been born in 1856 and 1858 respectively. In the field of ideas, Darwin had published the *Origin of Species* in 1859, and the *Descent of Man* in 1871, while *Das Kapital* appeared in 1867 and in 1869 Huxley had invented the word 'agnostic' as a challenge to dogmatic religion. The shock of Darwin was immediate; the impact of Marx was delayed. More ominously, in international affairs, the adventurism of Louis Napoleon and the expansionism of Bismarck had once again disturbed the concert of Europe, and the formation of the German Empire in 1871, with its annexation of Alsace-Lorraine, was to inaugurate the ding-dong conflict of Gaul and Teuton for three generations to come.

Indeed, all these forces rapidly gathered momentum. The eighty years from 1874, which spanned Barnes's lifetime, were to see Britain involved in one colonial and two world wars. She was to be relegated, at best, to the second division of the world power league. The pound sterling and the Royal Navy were both to topple from their pedestals. Throughout the world, conflict grew more familiar than confidence. At home, the rise of the Labour Party broke up the pattern of politics. Not only for this reason and not only in Britain, the class struggle was sharpened. Darwin's pioneer work was left far behind by new discoveries in science, particularly in nuclear physics, which shattered assumptions on the nature of the world and came near to shattering the world itself. Neo-positivism and materialism in various forms grew to undermine faith in Christian belief and the Christian ethic. There was to be a massive drift from the churches.

All this could have led to total disillusion. The intellectual could have withdrawn into the ivory tower of scholarship. The moralist could have despaired of influencing his generation for the better. The churchman could have confined himself to the arid wastes of administration. The Englishman could have gathered rosebuds while he might in his national garden, heedless of wars and rumours of wars. But this was not to be the response of Ernest William Barnes to the challenges of his time. Progress is a process of challenge and response, and throughout his long life he never ceased to believe in progress

14

or to champion the causes, intellectual, political, social, scientific and religious, which he held to be just and true. For he came of sturdy stock.

Family lore has it that his branch of the Barnes tribe, artisans in the cotton trade, were descended from the Lancashire witches. This is an intriguing thought, in view of the marked aversion from anything smacking of magical practices which Bishop Barnes showed in later life. Certainly, the name of Barnes crops up in Lancashire history, and one Thomas Barnes, Doctor of Divinity, achieved a certain reputation as Principal of the Manchester Academy towards the end of the eighteenth century. He is said to have been a man of liberal religious principles and, according to Baines's *History of Lancashire*, 'he could not endure to see irregularity and disorder prevailing in an institution under his management, which it was not in his power to correct'. There are obvious parallels with the state of affairs in the Birmingham diocese after 1924. But unluckily no family connection can be traced.

A more interesting echo of the witches occurs in the name of the Bishop's father, who was christened Starkie. Now a certain other Starkie, born in 1584, had at the age of ten been one of seven people reported as possessed of evil spirits at Whalley in Lancashire. He and the others were purged of their devils by preachers of an unspecified religious persuasion. It is therefore perhaps not surprising to find the same John Starkie as one of the two magistrates before whom the second group of seventeen witches of Pendle Forest were arraigned in 1633. They were luckier than the first group, of whom seven had been executed in 1612, since, although Starkie and his colleagues condemned them all to death, they were given a free pardon by order of Charles I. But here again no direct link can be found between John Starkie of the seventeenth century and Starkie Barnes, who in later life called himself John Starkie Barnes, in the nineteenth, although it is tempting to surmise that John was added in conscious recollection. It would be even more tempting, in view of his eldest son's later career, to trace a connection with Thomas Starkey, a contemporary of Thomas More, whose most famous published work was an *Exhortation to Christian Unity, or Treatise against Papal Supremacy*; but that would be still more far-fetched.

Starkie, as he was baptized, was born at Manchester Road, Haslingden, on 13 June 1843, the son of John Barnes and his wife Betty, née Smith, who could not write her name and signed the baptismal register with a cross. Even so, these names could hardly be less revealing, and little or nothing can be found further back. Smith, it is true, sometimes means gypsy stock. The etymology of Barnes is varied. One theory is that it is a corruption of bairns, which could give it a Scottish connotation. In another view, it is a Welsh patronymic derived from Ap Arns. Scots, Welsh and gypsies were no doubt all present in the Lancashire melting-pot of the industrial revolution in the early nineteenth century. But the rest is speculation. Again, according to family tradition, John Barnes owed his survival to having had three elder brothers, called, not too originally, Matthew, Mark and Luke. 'Cotton was bad' in Lancashire at the time, as often before and since, and the first three brothers had all emigrated to Australia. Things did not improve, and their father, perhaps recalling his inheritance from the witches, spent a night alone in an empty haunted house to ask the resident spirit if John should join his brothers in the antipodes. The spirit replied to the effect that the things you know of are better than the things you know not of, and John stayed in Lancashire, where he was at first apparently a cotton power-loom weaver, but by the time of his son's birth had become a warehouseman. The ship in which he would have sailed was never heard of again.

Starkie had three brothers, James, Smith and Howarth. There was obviously some ability in the family, as James was manager of a mill by the time he was thirty and later had his own mill at Hyndburn, while Smith also founded his own weaving firm of Barnes and Rothwell, which still exists. But Starkie seems to have been the only member of the family with academic ambitions. He appears to have been largely self-educated and then to have taught at various schools in England and Scotland. At some stage he enrolled at London University, presumably for correspondence courses, and he also studied Latin, Greek, French and Mathematics for a time at Owens College, Manchester, of which, strangely enough, his eldest son's father-in-law was to be Principal. By the early 1870s he had emerged as headmaster of the Derby Road School at Nottingham and here he met his wife.

Jane Elizabeth Kerry was the fourth of five children of the village shoemaker at Charlbury in Oxfordshire. William Kerry, her father, combined his roles as cobbler, smallholder and special constable with that of itinerant Wesleyan preacher. Some of his sermon notes have survived, but his grandson had reluctantly to admit that he

16

could discern no great theological scholarship in them. The family background was, without doubt, strongly religious. As Jane Kerry was to record towards the end of her long life:

> We were always taught to recognize the good in others, whatever their belief. We always had family prayers directly after breakfast, of which to my mind they were an integral part. My father read a few verses of scripture, offered a short earnest prayer for guidance during the day and finished with the Lord's Prayer.

Her eldest son was to continue the habit of family prayers throughout his life. William Kerry was also superintendent of the Sunday School when he was not away preaching in a nearby village. Sunday School took place soon after breakfast, followed by Chapel itself at 10.30, then home to Sunday dinner at noon, after which Sunday School again until four o'clock. After tea the choir came in for half an hour's practice until evening service, which the children also attended, coming home for a light supper and bed by nine o'clock. It sounds a strenuous observance of the Lord's Day, but the children enjoyed it. Although they were brought up on strictly teetotal lines, and attended a weekly meeting of the Band of Hope, their father carried his tolerance into this field too, once publicly championing, against an itinerant American temperance orator, the agricultural labourer who often had to travel far afield to his work and naturally included a can of beer with his day's sustenance of bread and cold bacon.

As another example of William Kerry's tolerance, he once took a day off from work to go with his daughter to hear the Bishop of Oxford, 'Soapy Sam' Wilberforce, preach in the village church. As she recalled:

> I was much more interested in his dress than his discourse, and especially admired his lovely white muslin sleeves. If anyone had told me that one of my own sons would one day preach from that pulpit and dress in similar garb, well I simply should not have believed it.

That this intensive religious education bore fruit can be seen from another of her anecdotes:

> This episode I do not remember but it was a household joke for some time. Our Minister was paying us a pastoral visit and took me on his knee. Wishing, I suppose, to conquer my shyness, he asked me 'Did I

17

go to chapel yesterday?' A very shy 'Yes.' 'Did I hear him preach?' 'Yes.' 'Did I know what he preached about?' Then taking my courage in both hands I breathlessly repeated 'Go send men to Joppa and call for one Simon whose surname is Peter and he shall tell thee things whereby thou mayest be saved.' My people said the look of astonishment on the good man's face was one to be remembered.

But life was not all so scriptural. They had 'penny readings' once a week in the winter months, when each member paid a penny, and anyone was free to read, recite, play or sing for the benefit of the rest. There were walks with their father through Wychwood Forest. There was skating at Cornbury Park, where the Churchills made the public free of their lake. On a rare occasion there was a haunch of venison from Lord Dillon at Ditchley. Clearly, although work was continuous and hard, and money was scarce, this was a self-contained and generally happy rural community.

Jane, or Lizzie as her husband later called her, was evidently a bright child, who at the age of five went to the village school at Charlbury, then financed by the Quakers and directed single-handed by Jesse Clifford. The school later passed under public control and while she was there was inspected by Matthew Arnold, cousin of her future daughter-in-law. In 1862, when she was only twelve, and overriding her father's objection that, if she spent all her young days in school, she would never learn to run her own house properly, she became an assistant teacher at the infants' school next door, at the princely salary of £5 a year, with annual rises of £1. Some six years later she spent two years training as a teacher at Stockwell College in London, where she was again inspected by Matthew Arnold, although there is nothing to show whether he saw any special ability in her. It was from here, where incidentally she was for the first time confronted by gaslight, that she was appointed headmistress of the girls' school at Derby Road, Nottingham. Her lifelong partnership with Starkie Barnes had begun.

They were married in 1873 and soon moved to Manchester, where Starkie took over another headmastership. They lived at Altrincham in Cheshire and here their two elder sons were born in 1874 and 1875, in a small, mid-nineteenth-century house at 1, Wellington Place. But in 1876 Starkie became headmaster of the Elkington Street school in Birmingham. Thus started the long connection with Birmingham.

They became citizens of no mean city. Birmingham was at a high point in its history. Its advance in the industrial revolution had been due primarily to its position as a centre of minerals and communications. But religious principle, notably that of the Nonconformists, and social mobility with few class barriers had also tempered the winds of economic change to the victims of industrial progress. The population had grown by geometric progression, from 70,000 in 1801 to 144,000 in 1831 and 344,000 in 1871. The years from 1870 to 1873, in particular, had seen the biggest boom of the century, from which Birmingham was already well placed to gain a lion's share. This boom was the economic basis on which Joseph Chamberlain founded the civic progress of the years of his mayoralty from 1873 to 1876. The historian of Birmingham has called these years 'the golden age of the social gospel' and said that 'it was during the '60s and '70s that the centre of Birmingham began to take something like its present shape'. Joe Chamberlain is now chiefly remembered as a ruthless politician on the national and imperial stage. It is true that he founded his power on machine politics in Birmingham of a new kind in British local government. But, like other ambitious men, he began life as a reformer and as a pioneer in the municipalization of social services, notably gas, water and housing. It was due to him above all others that by 1890 an American could describe Birmingham as 'the best governed city in the world'. Chamberlain had set an example of Unitarian devotion to social service by resigning altogether from business in 1874. The boom years were, it is true, followed in 1875–6 by a depression, caused largely by the exhaustion of iron deposits, by their replacement by steel, and by foreign competition. But Birmingham was already well on its way to claiming the title of 'the workshop of the world'. It was already called 'the city of 1500 trades'. It was thus a natural centre of attraction, particularly for a young Non-conformist making his way in the world.

The Non-conformists, in fact, seem to have contributed much more to the development of Birmingham than did the Church of England, even in the nineteenth century when the national Church still held such a predominant position in the national life and was only slowly and reluctantly loosening its hold on positions of political and academic power and privilege. Indeed, the Church's attention was still focused more on those corridors of power and those groves of academe than on the dark, satanic mills of the new cities. It is barely an exaggeration to say that the national Church ministered to the gentry and peasantry while the Dissenters ministered to the cities and their suburbs. The Church, in fact, had not yet caught up with the industrial revolution. This was partly because its interests had been elsewhere. After the worldliness of the eighteenth century, when the bishops were still territorial magnates and the inferior clergy were squarsons, there had come the spiritual reaction of the Evangelical revival, which had itself, *par esprit de contradiction*, given rise to the Oxford Movement. Then the Oxford Movement in its turn, by looking too much over its shoulder at a medieval golden age, had provoked the revival of rationalism, expressed in such divers ways as the publication of *Essays and Reviews* in 1860 and the utterances of Bishop Colenso. This series of challenges and responses had caused the Church increasingly to turn in on itself and on the niceties of doctrinal controversy, at the expense of pastoral activity. The Christian Socialism of men like Kingsley and Maurice still spoke with quite a small voice. High Churchmen, when they were not resident at universities, were more likely to be found, like Pusey and Manning, in country vicarages than in the slum parishes of large cities. The days of Dolling were yet to come. Missionary endeavour was concentrated on darkest Africa rather than the Black Country of the English Midlands. Thus it was that Birmingham still comprised a few urban parishes in the huge rural diocese of Worcester and the driving force in civic life came largely from the Non-conformists.

Not only was the centre of the city transformed during the 'golden age'; new housing areas had arisen, both to serve new industrial areas and to allow businessmen and workers alike to escape from the furnace at the city centre. It was in these new outlying suburbs that the Barnes family were to find their successive homes. They lived briefly at Bevington Road, Aston, and then in another new housing area at 20, Gladstone Road, Sparkbrook. Sparkbrook has been described about this time as 'rows and rows of anaemic looking houses, depressingly uniform in pattern, effacing the picturesque delights of lane and meadow'. Similarly, it has been said of Moseley, where they later lived, that, having been 'a pretty little village with a green, low-roofed, old-fashioned houses, and a parish church tower dominating the landscape, it changed . . . into an exclusive suburb with large villas of red brick, regular train services into Birmingham, and trams'. None the less, to begin with, Starkie Barnes and his young family were no doubt only too happy to live on the fringes of the city rather than in its central grime.

While they were at Sparkbrook, Starkie was appointed in 1879 to be Clerk of the King's Norton School Board, and then in January, 1882, Inspector of Schools for Birmingham. This was the height of his ambition and his achievement and he held the post until he retired in 1908. Two more sons were born to them in Sparkbrook, in 1879 and 1881, and the family was now complete. The recurring predominance of male children is interesting, and the next generation also was to consist only of boys, as Ernest was the only one of Starkie and Lizzie's sons to marry.

The family later moved to Sparkhill and in about 1890 to 65, Alcester Road, Moseley, until in 1911 their second son found them more spacious quarters in the house where he himself also lived, at Westcroft, 122, Anderton Park Road, Moseley. Here Starkie was to die on 1 December 1922, and here his widow lived on until her own death at the age of eighty-eight on 24 October 1938.

Starkie Barnes never earned more than £500 a year. But as is shown by the testimonials which he presented for his appointment as an Inspector of Schools, he was a methodical man who had prepared himself conscientiously for his profession. Not only had he studied classics, French and mathematics at London and Manchester; he had passed examinations in science and held certificates for drawing and singing. He also wrote the article on Birmingham for the 1880 edition of Chambers's Encyclopaedia, describing it as 'the chief town in Britain for metallic manufactures'. Despite these attainments he does not seem to have left any impression of great intellectual power or interests. In religion he was a Baptist, of a reputedly rather militant kind. His main recreation was in long walks, although in 1887 he also acquired a bicycle. His wife did not try to follow him on these excursions.

Against this background it is hard to explain the academic prowess of all four of his sons. Three of them won scholarships to Cambridge and the fourth at Birmingham. The eldest became a fellow of his college and a bishop; the second was the leading physician in Birmingham and a neurologist of national repute; the third was called to the Bar with first-class honours and would have gone far in the Civil Service if he had not died of cancer before the age of forty; and the youngest son was knighted as Deputy Secretary to the Admiralty. As Ernest was to say in his Gifford Lectures many years later, 'unless a boy has inherited some mathematical ability, it will be impossible to make a mathematician of him'. There are, it is true, some intriguing possibilities. Two Thomas Starkies, father and son, of Twiston in Lancashire, were Senior Wranglers at Cambridge in 1771 and 1803 respectively; and the Starkies of Huntroyde, who called themselves Le Gendre Starkie from the late eighteenth century onwards, were said to have taken the Le Gendre from the famous French mathematician of that name. But, as no connection can be traced between these landed Starkies and the Barnes artisans, only surmise is possible. Certainly, according to the Haslingden census of 1841, John and Betty Barnes were near neighbours of an older couple, John and Mary Starkie, with whom lived Alice Smith. If Alice and Betty Smith were sisters, they could by their ages have been daughters, presumably illegitimate, of Mary Starkie before she married John. Could John Starkie himself have been a scion, again perhaps on the wrong side of the blanket, of one of the Starkie county families? Perhaps a girl in service there could have attracted a young son of the house. Was this how the mathematical ability of the Starkies was transmitted? All this is sheer conjecture, however, and by the four Barnes boys' own admission, by far the greater influence in their childhood seems to have been their mother. Writings of Jane Kerry's which remain, especially the fragment of her reminiscences, show that she had wit, style and character, as indeed she must have had to become a headmistress, even of an infant school, at the age of twenty-one in the then state of feminine education. She had no academic background and no great educational achievements. It is true that her grandmother was reputed in the family to be an expert in mental arithmetic; but even if the standard of judgement is sound, this hardly explains a mastery of gamma functions three generations later. Nevertheless, it seems just as likely that the mathematical skills came from the Kerry as the Barnes side and that, from whatever source, Jane Kerry carried the genes which flourished in all four of her sons and to those genes she certainly added the determination and the encouragement on which their success was built. Not for her to wrap her talent in a napkin. In a sermon in 1911, her eldest son was to give special praise to lessons learned at one's mother's knee. As further evidence of this, a charming note survives in four childish hands:

20 Gladstone Road
28 June 1888

Dear Mother,
We wish you many happy returns of your birthday and hope you may

be long spared to us in health and strength. With very best love we are
your affectionate sons,

E. W. Barnes
S. Barnes
A. E. Barnes
Sidney Barnes

The eldest son, Ernest William, was born in the vintage year of
1874. It saw the birth of Churchill, Weizmann, Hoover and Mackenzie
King among politicians, Marconi for the scientists, Hewlett Johnson,
the Red Dean, as another not inappropriate churchman, Shackleton
and Howard Carter as different breeds of explorer, and in the world
of the arts, G. K. Chesterton, Robert Frost, Holst, Maugham and
Gertrude Stein. For good measure, it also gave birth to Houdini
and is said to have been the best champagne vintage of the century.
Ernest William's own birth took place on 1 April 1874, at
Altrincham, but the family moved to Birmingham two years later.
According to a letter from his mother to his wife over forty years
later, he was a strong-willed baby, refusing to lie down when required
or to wear shoes or socks; the child is the father of the man, as he
later only took to gaiters with reluctance. It is not known why he
was given his Christian names. His mother's father was called
William, it is true, but there is no trace of an Ernest on either side of
the family. His next brother claimed, somewhat improbably for the
son of an allegedly militant Baptist and an admittedly liberal-
minded Wesleyan, to have been called Stanley after the Dean of
Westminster, Arthur Penrhyn Stanley. Yet there is no obvious
Ernest of ecclesiastical or political distinction at the time who could
have rendered the same service to the eldest boy. In the light of later
events it is enticing to recall that Ernest Renan's *Vie de Jésus* had been
published in 1863, but any link would indeed be *tiré par les cheveux*.
A more prosaic explanation is that Ernest had for some time been
a recognized Evangelical Christian name; for example, in 1835, in
The Way of All Flesh, Samuel Butler had the Reverend Theobald
Pontifex christen his son Ernest since 'the word "earnest" was just
beginning to come into fashion'. Starkie Barnes may have had the
same idea. If so, his hopes were justified.
Ernest's first school was at Clifton Road, King's Norton. But his
father seems to have disapproved of this institution and moved him
in 1882 to the Tindal Street school, under a headmaster, whom he

23

knew well, called William White. Here he was taught the piano by a Miss Bell, but then, as in later life, showed no affinity for music. In September 1883, not yet ten years old, he was accepted as a foundation scholar at Camp Hill Grammar School, where the headmaster was Arthur Jamson Smith. It is recorded that the precocious boy was thought too young to enter the school at once and was sent away for a cooling-off period of some months with his mother's family at Charlbury. In a sermon delivered at Westminster Abbey in April 1919, he was to recall the experience in a passage which illustrates not only his lifelong love of nature but also his early interest, natural or inculcated, in matters religious:

When I was a small boy, some eight years old, I was sent for a summer to run wild in Oxfordshire. On Sundays, I was taken indifferently to Church or Chapel. There were some queer fonts and old stained-glass windows to make Church attractive, but I liked Chapel best because though bare and gaunt, it was more alive. In Chapel on Sunday I heard a sermon about the Kingdom of Heaven, a happy country where all was sunshine and joy, and the peace of a glorious summer afternoon. For days after I wondered where that land could be and how one could get there, and gradually I persuaded myself that I knew the way. One went up the hill past old Hickory's cottage, a ruin where sour plums still grew on a tree in the old-time garden, and then you walked on to where the old Roman road ran, grass-grown, wide and straight, beside the moss-covered walls of a great park. It always seemed sunny on the Roman road: there were partridge nests to be found there and great rabbit-warrens to wonder at. But one could never go far along the road, for one always had to get back for meal-times. Yet it seemed certain that, if one could only follow it to the top of the distant rise, just below the crest there would certainly lie the Kingdom of the Chapel preacher, the land of one's hopes and dreams. Cautiously and shyly, I asked a cowman where the old highway led. 'That be the road to Chipping Feilden Farm', he said. I did not dispute his knowledge, but I did not believe him. And for years the instinct persisted that along that grass-grown Roman road, just out of reach, lay the country that I wished to discover.

The only other recorded story of his early schooldays, as told by himself seventy years later, is that at a performance of *A Midsummer Night's Dream* he played the part of a fairy in tights; apparently, the headmaster was not amused by the costume, but as R. W. Dale, the leadng Congregational minister in Birmingham applauded, the headmaster had to hold his peace, and the fairy escaped censure.

Jamson Smith was in close touch with A. R. Vardy, the headmaster of King Edward VI Grammar School, then as now the leading school of the city, and in January 1886, Ernest entered it at New Street, again as a foundation scholar. In the family's financial circumstances, it was essential for the boys to win their way by scholarships, and they all did so.

At King Edward's, Ernest soon came under the eye of Rawdon Levett, the mathematics master, who must have been an inspired teacher, as others of his pupils have testified. Barnes himself was to say twenty years later: 'I went by chance to a school where there was the greatest mathematical teacher of his generation. Privately he showed me the way to the fountain of life.' In an eloquent obituary notice in *The Times* in February 1923, he also paid tribute to his forward-looking teacher, crediting him among other things with 'the abolition of Euclid'. It was through Levett that Barnes developed the mathematical bent which was to carry him to Cambridge and ultimately to a Fellowship of the Royal Society. Levett himself took a close interest in his gifted pupil; in a letter of 26 February 1919, he wrote to him:

Dear old Barnes,
You will always be 'dear old Barnes' in my memory. Whether you are FRS, or Master of the Temple, or Archbishop of Canterbury, or Pope of Rome, or other great personage, that pleasant smile or quick look of intelligence as you took a point in the old days in Set Al room will be 'Barnes' for me.

Ever yours affectionately
R. Levett

King Edward's was also a school with a strong Church of England tradition, *alma mater* of Edward White Benson, Archbishop of Canterbury, Joseph Barber Lightfoot and Brooke Foss Westcott, successive Bishops of Durham, who were all three in the school together, and more recently and directly J. F. Bethune-Baker, Professor of Divinity at Cambridge, and C. F. Andrews, friend of Tagore, Gandhi and Indian independence. Although Ernest's parents were a Baptist and a Wesleyan, they seem to have allowed the boy to go his own way, or possibly the intellectual influence of the school was stronger. A more likely influence is the feeling, to which he often gave expression in later life, that the Church of England, with its broad tradition of variety and tolerance, was the Christian body best suited to the religious temper of the British people and particularly to their genius for compromise. Moreover, as he said in a sermon of 1916, 'the Free Churches fail sufficiently to emphasize the sacramental principles of Christianity'; this also may well have been a factor in his decision. Even at this early stage too he may have felt, with the critical enthusiasm of youth, that the Church of England was not active enough in absorbing and responding to the mathematical and scientific facts which he had been learning at school, and perhaps even that he himself had something to contribute on this score, in the search for truth and the pursuit of progress. In later life, he told a story of those days:

> Outside one of the great markets of Birmingham sat an old dame selling oranges at four a penny. She held four oranges piled up in her hand. 'Turn them over, mother,' said a realist schoolboy friend, as we passed her, to receive in turn a volley of abuse. She resented the insinuation that her stock was mouldy, the more fiercely because the insinuation was true.

He used the analogy to illustrate the reaction of old-fashioned churchmen to new ideas. While at King Edward's he was confirmed, at the church of St John's, Sparkhill, and thereafter worshipped there, alone of his family. He was already ploughing his lonely furrow in matters spiritual.

Little is recorded of his other interests at this stage. He seems to have taken part conscientiously in school games, but without any particular aptitude or enthusiasm. Many years later, he told a school audience: 'I still remember the acute pleasure it gave me to contort myself round a horizontal bar, and if I had to choose between the gymnasium and the playing-fields I always voted for the former.' At the same time he admitted: 'When I was at King Edward's, some of us in the sixth form spent many happy hours in the library, often to the neglect of our regular work. But I think we were laying the basis of a good education.' Although in later life he enjoyed long walks, there is no evidence that he acquired this taste by accompanying his father. King Edward's was also the school of Edward Burne-Jones, and Barnes retained a liking for the Pre-Raphaelites all his life. But pictorial art was never a ruling passion for him, and his taste tended to be guided by moral or even religious preferences.

26

As a boy he seems not to have frequented the theatre, from lack either of interest or of money; but the family saw Buffalo Bill at the Aston Lower Grounds and enjoyed the transformation scenes at the Curzon Hall. At work, he did not confine himself to mathematics: in a sermon he once recalled translating the New Testament from the Greek at school and having some doubts even then about some of St Paul's ideas. He also related how he had been inspired at school to practise chemistry at home, so that his father was obliged to build a shed to contain him and his enthusiasms. He won the school prizes for English essay and verse, was Secretary of the Debating Society, acted in French and Latin plays in his last year, passed the Higher School Certificate with distinction in various subjects, and, on leaving, was awarded not only the Benson Exhibition of £14 9s 0d for one year at Oxford or Cambridge but also a School Exhibition worth £50 a year for four years at either university. Yet his energies were clearly concentrated on his mathematics, in which in 1892 he won a major open scholarship at Trinity College, Cambridge, the only non-resident scholar on a list which also included Bertrand Russell.

CHAPTER II

CAMBRIDGE
1892-1915

Scholarship into Sermons

Cambridge, and Trinity in particular, opened a new world for Barnes. For the first time, the boy from a narrowly restricted home and background found himself in a society which was drawn from many widely differing walks of life and which, although academic prowess was still ostensibly its *raison d'être*, was open to many other influences and interests. Preaching for the first and, it seems, the only time at the annual service of Commemoration of Benefactors on 11 December 1906, he bore eloquent witness to his love for the College:

> When we recall those undergraduate days when first we realized that these historic buildings were to be for three or more brief years our dwelling-place, when first we grasped that we too shared to some extent the hoarded treasures of this time-worn sanctuary, the glamour of it all shines with vivid glory before our mental gaze. We can realise that which makes this our College and our home one of the places of pilgrimage of the English-speaking world. We can see once again with wondering eyes undimmed by familiarity and age the beauty of the buildings where we live, the splendour of our corporate treasures. We can see the Hall lit for us for the first time by the morning sun and we catch the beauty of the roof beams and the Jacobean moulding of the screen. We can once again stand in memory for the first time on the threshold of Wren's great library perfect in its classic simplicity. Once again we look with eager curiosity at Grinling Gibbons's carving and once again

the long line of busts draws us to the mysterious beauty of Thorwaldsen's statue. Once again curious treasures are exhibited: mementoes of the great whose names are indissolubly associated with our walls: once again we eagerly, laughingly or sadly gaze on these chance relics of the giants of the past. We recall how for the first time we saw the massive display of College plate, the feelings with which we first held Nevile's great cup in eager tremulous hands and saw in its polished bowl, as in some magic mirror, visions of the spacious days of Whitgift and Essex, Bacon and Coke. Memory brings back once more the day when, timorous freshmen, the pictures of the Lodge for the first time met our sight, when we saw those grave faces which look down from the walls of the dining-room, till we forgot our awe of the Master of the present in dreaming of the Masters of the past.

Later in the same sermon, he gave his personal testimony:

May one who as so many have done came from a home where the burden of narrow means was rendered tolerable by family affection and from a school not undistinguished by the roll of its alumni but touched by the commerce of the great city in whose centre it is placed, may such a one add his tribute of reverence to the torch with which this College lighted his fate? He came here 'and youth's ardour and emprise burst into life before him'. He found brilliant teachers who were sympathetic friends. He realised some of the beauty of study and research. He saw men guided by the principle that money is a secondary consideration in life, who used their corporate wealth as a sacred trust. He began to understand that great traditions can be an inspiration and not a burden, to feel the pride of possession of great artistic treasures. He saw that life could be splendid and compassionate, that a certain stately magnificence could be associated with personal simplicity. He saw, as Bishop Andrewes put it, 'a Power from on High transforming into sanctity from without and invisibly, yet with inward efficacy and evident tokens' and came by slow degrees to know something of the compassion, the patience and the love of One who died that we might inherit Eternal Life.

It was in this spirit that Barnes embarked on what was to be a new sea of high adventure but also of high achievement. In his academic career the achievement is incontestable. In the mathematical schools, he carried virtually all before him. The only major entrance scholar of his year at Trinity, he was awarded a resident major scholarship after his first year's work. In 1896 he was bracketed Second Wrangler, although he had no doubt hoped for the Senior Wrangler's place.

The Master of Trinity wrote to him: 'you will never really regret the bracket', and the *Cambridge Review* was later to comment that 'as everyone knows' the Second is always better than the First. Indeed, little was heard thereafter of that year's Senior Wrangler. But the failure, in his own valuation, may have rankled; certainly he became one of the leading advocates of the reform of the Mathematical Tripos in 1910, whereby the Wranglers in order of merit were abolished in favour of a single collective First Class. However that may be, in 1897 he refuted any criticism, even his own, by being placed in the First Division of the First Class in Part II of the Tripos and, in May 1898, winning the First Smith's Prize, the blue riband of Cambridge mathematics. Later that year, his work on gamma functions won him his Fellowship at Trinity, when the Master, in his congratulations, wrote that 'the mathematical examiners speak in very high terms of your dissertation and lead us to hope that you will have fresh light to throw on abstruse subjects'. Also elected Fellows in 1898 were G. M. Trevelyan and G. E. Moore; so again it was a vintage year. In the context of vintage, his friend Figgis wrote in congratulation: 'Don't get drunk out of a rejoicing heart; but, if you do, do so on claret.'

Only the experts can properly assess his mathematical work. This has been done comprehensively and with authority by Sir Edmund Whittaker and Professor W. N. Bailey in their obituary notices of Barnes for the Royal Society and the London Mathematical Society respectively. To the ordinary reader, his work is mainly of interest for what it reveals of the character of the man. He had come to Trinity at a time when English and, in particular, Cambridge mathematicians were beginning to pay much more attention to the pure mathematics being produced on the Continent and indeed claimed to have taken over the lead in their field from the French, who had set the pace in the earlier years of the nineteenth century. Barnes's own tutor, Rouse Ball, in his *Short History of Mathematics*, writes that 'the French school, which had occupied so prominent a position at the beginning of this century, ceased for some years to produce much new work'. He goes on to show how they had, in particular, developed the modern theory of functions. The torch was first taken up in Cambridge by A. R. Forsyth, of whom the *Dictionary of National Biography* records that:

he had for some time realised, as no one else did, the most serious deficiency in the Cambridge school, namely its ignorance of what had been and was being done on the continent of Europe. He determined to reform this state of things and with this aim published in 1893 his *Theory of Functions*, a book which had a greater influence on British mathematics than any work since Newton's *Principia*. From the day of its publication, the face of Cambridge was changed: most of the pure mathematicians who took their degrees in the next twenty years became function-theorists.

Although this comment, and indeed Rouse Ball's verdict too, may in the light of later knowledge seem over-generous to Forsyth and over-critical of French mathematicians, such as Hadamard, at the end of the nineteenth century, Barnes certainly saw himself as one of Forsyth's earliest disciples and indeed remained his friendly admirer even after marital troubles had driven Forsyth from Cambridge. Apart from sitting at the feet of Forsyth and others in Trinity itself, he was coached, as was the habit of those days, by R. R. Webb of St John's and E. W. Hobson of Christ's. Hobson himself specialized in functions. Barnes's own particular interest came to be in asymptotic formulae or expansions giving precise information about the functions concerned, as the complex variable on which they depend tends to infinity. In layman's language, he was interested in extreme extensions of mathematical thought, and it is perhaps not entirely fanciful to suggest that this interest in extremes was to show itself in other disciplines and causes with which he was later to associate himself. For the time being, however, he was above all concerned with expressing mathematical truths in the most elegant possible generalizations. As Barnes was to write in his Gifford Lectures, 'there is an aesthetic element in scientific theory. The mathematician shapes his symbols and polishes his formulae until they take to themselves a satisfying beauty'. A friend recorded him as saying in 1910 that mathematics was a high kind of poetry and was struck by his sense of artistic beauty about it; he described Barnes speaking of functions 'as a naturalist might speak of observing the habits of bright and beautiful birds' and saying that 'they made him believe in the unknown world'. This is an area in which form and style are almost as important as substance. It must provide an excellent discipline both for the mind and the character.

Barnes himself described his mathematical work as being concerned with four main groups of subjects:

31

(a) the theory of gamma functions;
(b) the theory of asymptotic expansions of functions defined by Weierstrassian products;
(c) the theory of linear difference equations;
(d) the theory of functions defined by Taylor's series.

Much of his work was in fact on functions which arise in the theory of mathematical physics. The subjects in which he specialized were all fields of international study at the time. He himself has recorded how mathematicians in other countries were obtaining similar results at much the same time and on one occasion he was challenged by one of them for using his work without due acknowledgement. Barnes, however, insisted that his own work had priority in what he called 'the more general functions of multiple sequence'. He took evident pride in his original research and was unwilling to pull down his flag if he believed it rightly hoisted. But he was generous too. Writing of his work on functions defined by Taylor's series, he says:

> My own investigations which in such a wide field were naturally lengthy had yielded the fundamental results when unfortunately a paper by Hardy containing the beginning of the theory was submitted to me as referee. I suggested that Hardy could extend his theory as if to agree with my own developments, and thought it best to continue on my own lines, allowing him to have priority of publication of such ideas as were similar to the two investigations.

Not only was he generous to younger men. It is clear that he was also an influential teacher of them. Indeed, in this field as later in life, he was among the pioneers in recognizing and supporting new ideas. He had come up to Cambridge at a time when the mathematical physicists dominated Cambridge mathematics and he had set himself to obtain as much completely accurate information as he could about certain functions, many of them arising in mathematical physics. These he treated by rigorous mathematical methods. At the same time, he knew enough about work being done elsewhere, especially on the continent of Europe, to recognize and encourage men working outside his own immediate field. Among them, G. H. Hardy and J. E. Littlewood, who were born in 1877 and 1885 respectively, and who collaborated for many years, are probably recognized as the greatest pure mathematicians of the first half of the twentieth century. Of Hardy, the *Dictionary of National Biography* records that 'he started his career at a time when the theory of functions, the creation of the great European mathematicians, was only just beginning to be known in England. He made this one of the chief mathematical studies in English universities'. In reviewing Hardy's Collected Papers for the London Mathematical Society, J. C. Burkill has stated that 'clearly Hardy was initially influenced by Barnes'. Littlewood himself has acknowledged his own debt. In his *A Mathematician's Miscellany*, writing of the start of his mathematical research, he says:

> My director of studies (and tutor) E. W. Barnes suggested the subject of integral functions of order 0. The first idea was to find asymptotic formulae for functions with simple given zeros like $a_n = e^n$; the analytic methods he had been using with success for non-zero order were not working.

After relating how he dealt with the problem, Littlewood continues: 'Barnes was now encouraged to suggest a new problem: prove the Riemann Hypothesis'. Littlewood, no doubt with some irony, describes this as an 'heroic suggestion'. In the context of Hardy and Littlewood, Barnes always said that perhaps his own most brilliant pupil was Srinivasa Ramanujan, the young Indian whom Hardy claimed with justice to have discovered and who flashed like a meteor across the mathematical sky, but went back to India to die at the tragically early age of thirty-three, shortly after the First World War; C. P. Snow has told Ramanujan's story in his foreword to Hardy's *Mathematician's Apology*. It was on the joint recommendation of Barnes, Hardy and Littlewood that Ramanujan was awarded an exhibition at Trinity. Thus, although Barnes's reputation as a whole no longer rests solely on his early mathematical work, it is evident that he was an influential figure in a new world of English thought, where few men could expect to have the ability to hold their own. To quote Bailey, 'there is no doubt that, if he had remained a professional mathematician, his contribution to mathematics would have been even greater than it is'. As it was, 'Barnes's lemma' was for many years a household word among mathematicians. Until the end of his life, mathematicians still sought his comments and advice in fields where he had blazed the trail half a century before. Even after his death, in 1959, the *Quarterly Journal of Mathematics* printed an article on two of Barnes's unpublished manuscripts on Legendre functions.

The picture which emerges is of a powerful but austere, fastidious and lonely mind, self-confidently conscious of its own strength but also perfectionist and intolerant of error or weakness. Already he was grappling with transcendental verities and determined to use logic to distil truth and order out of a part of the mathematical mash. Certainly he was soon to earn the respect and recognition of the authorities. He first published, in 1897 and 1899, in the *Messenger of Mathematics*. But in 1899 his work also appeared in the *Quarterly Journal of Mathematics* and in 1900 not only in the *Proceedings of the London Mathematical Society* but also in the *Proceedings of the Royal Society*. He was to continue to publish through these and other bodies until 1907, when other work left him little time for further original research.

His work brought him various distinctions in his chosen field and he became a member of the London Mathematical Society and a Fellow of the Cambridge Philosophical Society at the end of 1898 and, in the spring of 1899, a Fellow of the Royal Astronomical Society. These distinctions came by invitation. Much more significant were the award in 1906 of a Doctorate of Science and in 1909 the coveted Fellowship of the Royal Society, at the age of thirty-five.

With this academic record it is not surprising that he was soon in demand as a teacher. In the autumn of 1898, with his examinations behind him, he seems to have thought of reading for the Bar; his old mathematics master at Birmingham, Rawdon Levett, whom he had presumably consulted, strongly advised him to do so. Instead of this, however, he accepted a post as Instructor at the Royal Military Academy at Woolwich. In view of his later attitude to warlike arts and the military establishment, this seems an astonishing choice. Perhaps his experiences at Woolwich helped to form that later attitude. Within a year he resigned from his post there, giving ill-health as his reason. That this was not just an excuse is borne out by his own later statement that his work after 1898 on asymptotic expansions was hampered by ill-health. In 1899 he came back into residence at Trinity and resumed his research work. But already in that year he was asked to examine for entrance awards to Trinity and was taking pupils at Newnham College. By 1901 he was also asked to coach at Girton. These are interesting assignments, incidentally, since in 1897, while still an undergraduate, he had played

34

a leading part in resisting degrees for women. It is not clear if he had already changed his mind or if he believed that women should have the inward and intellectual grace, even if they were not permitted the outward and visible gown. In 1903 he was appointed first to be Assistant Lecturer and then full Lecturer at Trinity and in May 1905, he became Director of Mathematical Studies for the college.

He continued to lecture until 1915 on a wide range of subjects, including analysis, algebra, conics and theory of equations, differential equations and integral calculus. One of his pupils of those days has recorded that

> as a lecturer in Mathematics he really was first-class. Few of the people who lectured . . . were so good: most of them somehow gave the impression that they were not greatly interested . . . His great merit was that he took the trouble to go at a reasonable speed and to be entirely clear.

As a director of studies at Trinity, he was no doubt fortunate in his material, as the college was the mathematical Mecca of his day. Even so, out of seventy-six pupils from 1905 to 1913, thirty-three of them won firsts. Although he had more students after 1913, many of them did not finish their courses after the outbreak of war. This was to leave him some bitter memories. In a sermon towards the end of the war, he reflected: 'Of my pupils at Cambridge at least one-half, and practically all the best, have been killed or maimed for life; the work that I did has been for the most part wasted.'

One of his students, G. P. Thomson, afterwards the distinguished nuclear physicist, has written:

> My first call on Barnes is perhaps worth recording, for it could hardly have gone as it did anywhere but in Cambridge. In assigning me to my lectures Barnes included those of G. H. Hardy, then the leading mathematician in the country and of world-wide fame. I asked to be excused and had the impudence to say that I did not like Hardy's mathematics. I had read an introduction to pure mathematics he had recently published, which used in a simple form some of the more rigorous methods of proof till then little considered in British mathematical teaching, though common abroad. Barnes replied with his characteristic slow smile: 'Well, you need not go to Hardy's lectures if you don't want, but you will regret it', as indeed I have.

Another pupil later to achieve great distinction was A. V. Hill, whom Barnes, according to his register of pupils, thought of at one time as a possible candidate for Holy Orders and who has recalled:

> He used to get me to write essays, very bad ones I think, and he criticized them. We got on very well; and I was really quite familiar with him. One day he blew into my room and said: 'Hill, will you teach me to ride a motor-bicycle?' That was not what you would have expected of him at all. So I gave him a book about motor-bicycles and told him to read it. He came back a few days later and asked me now to show him how to drive a motor-bicycle. I took him out in my motor-bicycle and sidecar and, when he'd learned about that sufficiently, he then borrowed one of his own. He was much intrigued by this; and when he had driven it for a bit and had got used to it he came in and said to me: 'Hill, it is a funny thing, the faster you go, the nicer it is.' I said: 'You know, Barnes, a lot of your pupils have observed the same thing and have been in the police courts because of it.'

The story has a sadder end:

> He came to me one day and said that he wanted to go to the region of the Roman Wall in Northumberland and to drive a friend in the sidecar. I said: 'Are you going to drive your sidecar all the way from Cambridge?' He said no, that he was going to hire it in Newcastle-on-Tyne. 'Well,' I said to him, 'Barnes, you don't know much about human nature if you think a motor-bicycle agent in Newcastle, with a completely unknown stranger turning up and saying he wants to borrow a motor-bicycle and sidecar, will lend you a reliable one.' He didn't take any notice of it; he had too high an opinion of human nature, in spite of what he said about it, and they started off. Before they'd been very many miles, his motor-bicycle and sidecar came in two pieces and ran into a wall and they both had to go to hospital. That was the end of his motor-bicycling.

It is a pity that history does not relate who the friend was. This episode may also have sown the seeds of a marked dislike of fast driving later in life.

So life at Trinity was not all mathematics and the pursuit of learning. It was an education in life in a community of great variety and distinction. The Master of the College, during all the time when Barnes was at Trinity, was Henry Montagu Butler, formerly Headmaster of Harrow and Dean of Gloucester. The reposeful portrait by Orpen at Trinity does not do him justice. While he seems to have had no great interest in administration as such, he took infinite pains with the human relations of the society over which he presided. His handwritten notes to a younger man are models of felicitous prose and of kindly understanding. While he had been Senior Classic himself, his second wife had in 1887 actually been placed above the Senior Classic. Mrs Butler, a sister of the Duchess of Atholl who became a Conservative Minister, was a Christian Scientist, who did not greatly endear herself to her friends, when her children appeared to have some infectious disease, by sending them out to play with the friends' children, as if nothing was the matter with them. However, her sons survived this treatment; of them, Jim became Vice-Master of Trinity and Regius Professor of Modern History and Nevile Ambassador at Rio de Janeiro and The Hague.

Trinity was full of other characters, some of whom were to become friends of Barnes's bachelor days. According to one source, as an undergraduate he wrote in French 'a rather undesirable novel'; but, even if his French was up to it, there is no corroboration of the story, on the face of it improbable, and no trace of the novel itself. But apart from his mathematical work, the main interest of his student days seems to have been in debating. He joined the Magpie and Stump, the Trinity Debating Society, soon after going up, becoming one of its Auditors by 1897. He was also soon to become a successful and popular speaker at the Union, where he made his maiden speech in January 1894, and was duly elected Vice-President for the Easter Term and finally President for the Michaelmas Term of 1897. He was the first President of the Union ever to come from King Edward's, Birmingham, and indeed most of his contemporaries and rivals in the Cambridge debates would seem to have come from what would normally be classed as grander schools. They included such men as C. F. G. Masterman, F. W. Pethwick-Lawrence and Edward Hilton-Young, later Lord Kennet, all to become Cabinet Ministers, and St John Basil Wynne Wilson, who became Bishop of Bath and Wells but who, after he married a tobacco heiress, was known as Bishop of Bath and Wills.

The views which Barnes defended in debate do not always seem consistent with those he advocated in later life. It is not surprising to find him in 1896 opposing a motion that 'this House would sympathize with an Anglo-French alliance'. Again in 1898 it seems natural for him to oppose a motion that 'the Government found a university in Ireland to meet the special needs of Irish Roman Catholics'. Similarly, it is consistent that in 1902 he should have seconded G. M. Trevelyan's motion that 'the execution of our captured enemies is in the highest degree impolitic' and earlier opposed a motion that 'England is bound by her past conduct to interfere more actively than she has done in the Eastern question'. But it is not altogether clear why he should in 1897 have opposed a motion that 'this House would disapprove of increased aid to Voluntary Schools', and in view of his later support for many feminist causes and for progressive ideas in general, it is astonishing that, as an undergraduate, he was one of the leading opponents of Cambridge degrees for women. He seems to have shared a general view that the admission of women to degrees would drive male students away from the University. After the decision went his way, he even went to defend it at the Oxford Union, where his main antagonist was John Simon, the future Foreign Secretary and Lord Chancellor, whom he was to come to know well in later years at the Temple. But he was not a consistent anti-feminist: he also opposed a motion that 'to be a misogynist should be every man's ambition'. There may perhaps have been some personal antagonism in his choice of policies, as he seems regularly to have found himself on opposite sides to T. F. R. McDonnell, and there is some evidence to suggest that, as President of the Union, he organized the voting so as to exclude McDonnell from the succession. Certainly, this was the way things went. He was never a great admirer of the Celts. But Barnes was obliquely criticized in the Cambridge press for arranging the election, unusually at the time, on party lines and adopting what were stigmatized as Tammany tactics. Perhaps it was partly for this reason that, a few years later, he was to be described as 'fond of affairs and intrigues, with an odd, perverse and malicious humour, which often gives pain to his friends'. But at the time this was no doubt all good clean fun and it will certainly have helped to sharpen his talents for controversy. Yet none of it prevented his speeches from earning regular praise. Thus in 1896 the *Granta* recorded, on the Anglo-French treaty, that Mr Barnes, 'whose smile will, we fancy, always hold its own, was in great form and he delivered the speech of the evening. Being a mathematician, he divided the said speech into four parts, and he tore the treaty to fragments every time he passed from one to the other'. In June 1897, the Oxford *J. C. R.* reported that he 'was quite out of sympathy with the claims of women at the present day:

but he made quite the lightest and most interesting speech of the evening'. Giving him a profile as President of the Union in October 1897, the *Granta* wrote that

> as a speaker, Mr Barnes excels in subtle persuasiveness and dialectical niceties. He speaks with a slow deliberation, and a certain hesitation of pronunciation that adds great effect to his epigrams. He is one of the cleverest debaters that this Union has had for some time. His extempore efforts are not less effective than his more elaborate speeches. He has an airy easiness, a fund of humour and versatility of knowledge that make him an admirable conversationalist. In fact, after hearing him talk one realises with difficulty that he is a brilliant mathematician.

The same article contained the prophetic phrase: 'the more one thinks and the more one's dream forms itself, the more fascinating is the idea of Bishop Barnes'. But, after these oratorical triumphs, it is not surprising that he toyed with the idea of going to the Bar.

Nor is it surprising that he was soon in demand for college office. In 1901 he became Treasurer of the College Mission and in 1906 he was made Junior Dean, rather against his will, it seems, because the College authorities would not agree to impose penalties for absence from chapel, so that Barnes had to rely on moral suasion to secure a congregation. Results were meagre; one morning there were only seven undergraduates in chapel and a friend suggested to Barnes that he should read vespers to them in his rooms instead. In 1908, therefore, he was probably delighted to be appointed a Tutor. Trinity at this time had four Tutors, each of whom was responsible for the welfare and discipline of between 150 and 200 men *in statu pupillari* at any given time. He could also be in charge of their studies if these were in his own subject. When Barnes became Tutor, the senior Tutor was W. C. Dampier-Whetham; he was born Whetham, changed his name to Dampier, his initials were W. C., he lived at Upwater Lodge, and it was said of him that he was one damp thing after another. Barnes took great pains over his pupils, the details of whose Cambridge careers were all carefully recorded in minuscule handwriting in a special ledger. One of them remembers meeting him thirty years later, when he at once said 'You are So-and-so and you read history'. Another was mainly impressed by the silent but clear way in which his tutor indicated that each interview was at an end. One pupil recalls him mainly for preaching a sermon on the text 'You are full of new wine'. This undergraduate remembered the text better than the sermon itself. Another pupil, R. M. Wright, who went down from Trinity in 1912 and later became Second Master at Winchester, was delighted to write to his old tutor's wife in 1930: 'It is curious that after your husband did his best some twenty years ago to disuade me from becoming a schoolmaster, I should now be entrusted with the care of his son.'

Barnes himself used to tell two stories in particular of his tutorship. One of his pupils, by the name, later more familiar in a different spelling, of Chrouschoff, was a nephew of Pobedonostsev, Procurator of the Holy Synod, which is those days ran the Russian Orthodox Church from St Petersburg in the name of the Tsar and was reported to be enormously corrupt. Barnes was able to save the young man from some scrape, whereupon his uncle and guardian sent his tutor several cases of Imperial Tokay. Barnes disapproved of the Holy Synod but approved in moderation of the Tokay, several bottles of which were in fact to survive him. The other story was of a young man of great possessions, or rather, great expectations. He went to his tutor more than once to ask for a week-end's leave of absence as he was meeting a group of friends with a view to taking Holy Orders. Barnes, being in orders himself, could hardly refuse this virtuous request. But on the young man's twenty-first birthday, a gang of obvious crooks, including one who seemed to be acting as chaplain, appeared in Barnes's rooms and claimed that the boy had undertaken to bestow a large sum of money on them. Now that he was of age, they expected him to redeem his promise. Barnes apprehensively consulted the boy's guardian, who gleefully told him that the young man did not inherit his fortune until he was twenty-five. The gang had shown their hand too early and their knavish trick was frustrated. This story had a sequel: in 1932 Barnes had to appear as an assessor in the Court which was trying Harold Davidson, the notorious Rector of Stiffkey, and he was intrigued to find that Davidson was none other than the chaplain of the gang which had appeared in his Cambridge rooms twenty years or so earlier.

Barnes also served more than one stint as a member of the College Council, the elected executive which actually ran the College on behalf of the whole corpus of Fellows, who would have formed much too unwieldy a body. This was perhaps his first experience of corporate administration, of which he was to have his fill in later life and at which, although he always professed to dislike it, he showed marked capacity. But life at Trinity was not all work and no play. For most of his time as a Fellow, Barnes occupied a fine set of rooms on A staircase at the north-west corner of Great Court, between the Master's Lodge and the Chapel, in which, to his own satisfaction and the gratitude of his successors, he early installed a bathroom. He made friends easily at that time of his life. From about 1902 onwards, a small dining club had been formed, with Barnes, Arthur Benson, F. J. Foakes Jackson, Gaillard Lapsley and R. V. Laurence as its permanent core of members, who invited others to dine with them. Benson, son of the Archbishop of Canterbury and later Master of Magdalene, was one of Barnes's closest Cambridge allies and was to become his elder son's godfather. Despite the recurrent depressions from which he suffered, like other members of his family, he had a highly successful career as Eton housemaster, Cambridge don and writer of *belles lettres*. Rumour has it that he also had a posthumous success: a great diner-out, he was much in demand to write obituaries of Cambridge men for *The Times*. These he used to write after dining with them, and it seems that his assessment of the man tended to depend on the quality of the dinner. For some years after Benson's death, vitriolic notices were appearing of his acquaintances who had not come up to his culinary standards. A Christian rather than a churchman and a shrewd but generous observer of the human scene, Benson probably had as much influence as anyone on the development of Barnes's ideas. Although Benson's diaries contain some critical references to Barnes, he obviously admired the younger man's ability and liked him too, calling him excellent company, often taking walks and bicycle rides with him and inviting him to his family home; he would also give him shrewd and frank advice.

Foakes Jackson, like Benson some years older than Barnes, was at this time a theological don at Jesus, but left Cambridge for the Union Theological Seminary at New York in the First World War and, although he used to write Barnes witty letters, compounded of ecclesiastical learning and cynical comment on contemporary men and events, they saw little of each other after that. Lapsley crossed the Atlantic in the other direction. Born an American, a friend of Henry James and Edith Wharton, he taught English Constitutional History at Cambridge and gave Lucullan dinners until the Second World War. Generations of Trinity men will remember the horrendous snorts with which he accompanied his witty conversation. Laurence was probably Barnes's best friend and indeed they spent several holidays in Italy together. Said to be Acton's favourite pupil, Laurence never fulfilled his early promise and, like his master, failed to publish any important book and died quite young. He seems to have been a clever, if malicious, conversationalist, who became a *bête noire* of Lytton Strachey. Strachey held Laurence responsible for turning him down for a Trinity Fellowship and once called him 'wicked as usual'. Strachey's biographer, who describes Laurence as Strachey's 'enemy from Trinity', asserts that Laurence became an alcoholic before he died, and drink was certainly, by all accounts, a factor in the picture; but, as he also characterizes him in another passage as 'that rather prim and austere Irishman', it is hard to know ust where the truth lies. Barnes later recorded that Laurence, who was the grandson of an Irish Archbishop, had been a keen Anglo-Catholic when they first knew each other and, certainly, Laurence was held in high enough respect to become Senior Tutor of Trinity and in that capacity after the First World War to be appointed tutor to the Dukes of York (later King George VI) and Gloucester, when they were at Trinity, and to be made a CVO for his pains. Other close friends, though not apparently regular members of the same dining club, were D. A. Winstanley, the historian of Cambridge who was later godfather to Barnes's younger son, and A. E. Housman, of Shropshire Lad fame, whose private character, by common consent of those who knew him, belied his cantankerous public reputation. The immense esteem which Housman's poetry enjoyed in the 1930s has since been largely forgotten. Barnes remained an admirer and, when Housman died, recalled how he had once asked him why he had used the title 'A Shropshire Lad', and Housman had replied that for him, as a boy at the Lickey Hills, Shropshire was the land of the sunset, the Golden West, the Eldorado, to which he looked out across valleys, woods and ridges towards the high-reared head of Clee. Barnes also remembered how, when once he was preaching the University Sermon at Cambridge, Housman the agnostic had appeared in the procession; twitted on this, he had answered 'The Anglo-Catholics have given you such a bad reputation that no one will think that I have been converted to Christianity'.

Life for these Cambridge bachelor dons was easy and pleasant at the beginning of the century. They could afford to travel and, if they cared, to do themselves well. Barnes used to remember with Protestant glee how Father Nolan, the University Catholic chaplain with dining-rights at Trinity, would appear in Hall during Lent and of necessity eat sparingly, but as the decanter came round would help himself liberally, remarking: 'Augh, and there's no fast on the drink.' Another Trinity story was of Tennyson dining at High Table and when offered the best port, then the 1834, leaning across and pouring water in it, as if it was *vin ordinaire* at a French *estaminet*. After that, it was said that no Fellow of Trinity would ever read a line of Tennyson again. But that did not prevent Barnes from preaching an eloquent sermon on Tennyson's religious influence in Trinity Chapel on 24 October 1909, after the poet's statue had been unveiled there. He took as his text 'Who prophesied with a harp to give thanks and to praise the Lord' (I Chronicles xxv, 3) and, while criticizing Tennyson for some worldly valuations, praised his 'lofty patriotism and stately chivalry of thought' and emphasized his belief not only in human progress but also in the immortality of the soul.

In those years Barnes certainly acquired a discriminating palate for wine. But he remained abstemious all his life. Indeed, in his middle and later years he never drank spirits and never took a drink before a meal. The pleasures of the table or of travel were never allowed to interfere with the constant flow of administration, reading, reflecting, writing and speaking. Indeed, the dangers of excessive indulgence in luxury and the need for self-denial were to become constant themes of his preaching.

So far, then, this is the record of a traditional *cursus honorum academicorum*, crowned with success at virtually every point. Had he wished, Barnes could no doubt have gone on to other academic posts at Cambridge or elsewhere. Indeed, in 1907 he was sounded for a headmastership, and was at first inclined to let his name go forward. At one time there was even a suggestion that he might go as Principal to Hong Kong University. During these years he had already become a Governor of his old school at Birmingham. But there were two turning-points which can be seen as diverting him from a conventional career as teacher or academic administrator. The first was his ordination and the second the complex of circumstances under which he was to leave Cambridge.

By the beginning of the twentieth century, ordination was by no means as normal a procedure for a university don as it had been a generation or more earlier. George Trevelyan has written of the Victorian era that 'the whole period was marked by interest in religious questions'. But since the Test Act of 1871, it was no longer even necessary for a member of the University to be a member of the Church of England. Indeed, in those post-Darwinian and neo-positivist days, mathematicians and scientists in particular were growing less and less likely to be adherents, let alone ministers, of the Christian religion. In the obituary notice on Barnes in the *Old Edwardian Gazette* of December 1953, it is recorded that 'he lived, to quote the recollections of the late C. F. G. Masterman, "in an atmosphere hostile to all accepted religious beliefs". Barnes, he says, at the gatherings where this hostility revealed itself, questioned rather than asserted'. A typical example of this Trinity atmosphere was McTaggart, the philospher, between whom and Barnes there was little sympathy and who is described in the *Dictionary of National Biography* as 'an atheist who believed in human immortality'. But Barnes was to tell a friend in later years that from his earliest youth 'all things seen and heard had appeared to him as the symbols and signs of mystery and power' and certainly he had always followed his own bent in matters religious, notably when, while still a schoolboy, he had broken away from his family's Non-conformism and was confirmed into the Church of England. This could have been an adolescent emotion, influenced by the Anglican tradition of King Edward's, Birmingham. But his brothers at the same school were unaffected, and he himself continued steadfastly on his chosen course. What is more, despite the sceptics, there was a strong tradition of churchmanship at Trinity itself. The Master himself was in orders. So were several of the senior Fellows, by no means all of them in the Faculty of Divinity; they included, for example, William Cunningham, the pioneer economic historian who became Archdeacon of Ely. Of Barnes's own older clergyman friends, who may have consciously or unconsciously influenced him, were Foakes Jackson at Jesus and J. N. Figgis of St Catherine's, the historian of Church and State, who later became a member of the Mirfield Community of the Resurrection. Although Figgis and Barnes probably disagreed on almost all matters ecclesiastical, and many political too, and although Barnes mistrusted Figgis in university affairs, they were personally friendly and, when Figgis died at the early age of fifty-three, Barnes wrote a humorously affectionate envoi to him in the *Challenge*. He always said that Figgis was the untidiest man he ever met.

These contacts apart, it may have been that the South African war was one catalyst which helped Barnes to make up his mind. Not only, after years of virtually unbroken peace, had England suddenly found herself involved in a war leading to numerous casualties among Barnes's own contemporaries. To many on the liberal side of politics it was also an unjust colonial war, damaging to Britain's image abroad. Campbell-Bannerman, for example, used the phrase 'methods of barbarism', which Barnes later often quoted, about Kitchener's concentration camps in South Africa. In many ways, though perhaps less intensely, the same questions were aroused, the same divisions created, as by the Suez crisis of 1956. The Boer War must thus have stirred his religious feelings and sown the seed of that Christian pacifism which became one of the strongest features of his later thinking and teaching. But there is no direct evidence of this in his writings. Indeed, he was later to praise the national spirit during the South African war and, catalyst or not, it cannot have been the prime cause of his movement towards ordination. Never one to wear his heart on his sleeve, he himself left few clues to his spiritual pilgrimage. But in a sermon to Girton College as early as November 1902, on the text 'There are diversities of gifts but the same spirit' (I Corinthians xii, 4), which is basically concerned with the need for education to go beyond utilitarian learning, he says that he wants to speak of 'the importance of recognizing this Divine Factor in yourselves' and goes on:

You must think within yourselves, read to yourselves, question frankly, to the verge of irreverence as we moderns term it, if you like; struggle till for sheer weariness you turn thankfully to purely intellectual or mechanical work. And then you may find yourselves: you may determine your just relationship to God and Christ. I trust and believe that you may find yourselves with a living belief not only in God but in that religion under whose auspices we are met together tonight.

Then he adds: 'I am more confident of that, for personally it is the end of my own struggle.' That was said less than six months after his ordination. He may also perhaps have been thinking of himself when, writing many years later of conversion, he said:

Conversion usually takes place during that period of strain and stress known as adolescence. The growing boy or girl begins to realise life's perplexities, difficulties and dangers . . . Suddenly, all is changed. Help from on high has come. Discords are harmonized. The period of storm and stress ends . . . Of course, conversion does not always occur during adolescence. Sometimes, as with St Paul, the spiritual crisis happens at a more mature stage of life. But it always ends a period of spiritual struggle and brings escape from some inward tension.

The problem of temptation and the story of Christ's temptation in the desert are also recurrent themes of his earliest sermons. So is the need for self-denial and self-discipline. It is perhaps significant that he often returns to the text 'What is a man profited if he gain the whole world and lose his own soul?'. It seems clear that he saw himself to have conquered temptation. Despite his remarks on conversion, this does not seem to be just the usual Victorian preoccupation with the sins of the flesh, although in preaching to the young he constantly refers to the dangers of 'vice' in the sense of sexual licence, and the need for purity is a regular theme of his addresses. What seems likely is that he had also seen how easily he could use his intellectual gifts for worldly self-advancement at others' expense, that he had been tempted, like Becket in T. S. Eliot's *Murder in the Cathedral*, to do the right thing for the wrong reasons, to accept suffering for self-glorification, and that he had had to struggle to subdue those unworthy motives. Indeed, he more than once took the 'Temptations of Success' as the subject of a sermon. Another passage in a sermon, as late as May 1914, may also be self-revealing:

A man must have found, as the opportunities of his career have opened before him, that life is beautiful by what one gives and not for what one takes; he must have seen a vision of the Christ, must have found purification through suffering, humility through sin, and in striving he must have learned to have pity for those weaker than himself who have fallen in the battle of life.

Already in 1905 he had spoken of 'those who, like myself, are frankly mystics', and he came back in his sermons time and time again to the dominant need for and reality of personal spiritual experiences. If, since his change of ecclesiastical allegiance in his teens, or even before, he had been engaged in some such struggle as these passages suggest, then it is natural that this quest should have ended in ordination.

For, over and above his academic background, and his determination to acquire knowledge of truth for itself and to impart it to others, there shines through his deep personal conviction of spiritual reality and his belief that, in the last resort, religious truth can only be apprehended by personal experience. He pays repeated tribute to the mystics, not only those of past centuries like Thomas à Kempis and Julian of Norwich, but also his own contemporaries, above all Evelyn Underhill. Indeed, he was confident that he had had similar experiences himself, although he rarely spoke of them privately or publicly.

Another, later but parallel, glimpse of his view of the clergyman's function is to be found in a letter to his future wife written on New Year's Day, 1915, in which he says, speaking of 'the dull and outwardly worthy life I lead',

> Yet somehow I never think of it in your phrase as 'doing the work of a priest of God'. I have always shrunk from the impersonal authoritativeness involved in the priestly idea: the democratic equality of struggle suggested by minister is more applicable. Life is always a search, a quest for truth, for knowledge of God, for further understanding of Christ. In idea, the priest seems to know all – to be the channel of revelation and grace alike. I know that I don't know: there are just glimmerings and flashes and intuitions.

Then self-deprecatingly he ends: 'This is an odd gossipy sort of letter for a man to write on New Year's Day to the woman with whom he is in love.'

As Fellow of a Cambridge college, he was entitled to present himself for orders without the need to follow a course of theological study or to take examinations, although he was required to present a thesis to the Bishop's examining chaplain. What is surprising in this situation is that he did not seek ordination, as was usual for a Cambridge don, from the Bishop of Ely but from the new Bishop of London, Arthur Foley Winnington-Ingram. In later life, Barnes was not one of Ingram's greatest admirers, although their personal relations always remained friendly. But at that time Ingram had just been appointed Bishop of London at the early age of forty-three, after a great success in the East End of London as head of Oxford House at Bethnal Green and then Bishop Suffragan of Stepney. Although later his thoughts tended to crystallize in a conservative mould, Ingram must at that time have appeared to Barnes, as to others, a progressive and socially constructive figure in the Church. To those who wanted to identify themselves with a cause, Ingram looked then like a leader.

So on Trinity Sunday, 25 May 1902, he was ordained deacon by the Bishop of London at Fulham Palace and, as he wrote to his mother on 3 June:

> I preached my first sermon on Sunday evening last in St Sepulchre's Church near the Old Bailey: and was able in the course of it to tell the congregation that peace had been declared. Stanley was present: so you can find out from him what it was like.

The same letter contains some revealing details both about his attitude to his career and his relations with his family. After some comments on people he has met and on his duties as an examiner, he goes on:

> This week I have about a dozen duty invitations to give and receive. It is portentously dull: but one has to mix with the people one lives among and it seems wise to entertain pupils at times. Only the latter costs money that I can ill afford.
>
> I wish you could get Father to let me know more in detail what he does with the money I send him. He seems to think that I save it quickly and easily and that I am indifferent to what becomes of it. Do he and you not realise that I am sacrificing more than I ought to make it? I ought to be doing a lot of scientific work and preaching. I ought to publish a book that should make me known. All these things I put on one side just to have some money to help tide me over the next ten years. The more I think over things the more I see that if I have no money of my own to back me up I shall fail.
>
> No doubt it seems to Father that I ought to be able to live on £100 a year. But I cannot and see anything of people of importance and stand out from the ruck.
>
> If I get on the staff here I shall for some years have money enough to live on comfortably and time enough to make a name. If I don't my time for mathematical work is at an end. And it will be touch and go whether, with money worries, I make any mark otherwise.
>
> Money for itself I do not want a bit. But for the leisure which it will give and the way it will help me in externals it is all important. And I cannot go on trying to make it in the present way – so slowly – without losing all vigour and elasticity.
>
> You see it is a different game from the one you and Father played when you were young. And the wider arena needs a big change in the point of view. I do not think I am becoming luxurious. I try not to: I had much rather wear old clothes and no collar as I do at Dunwich

than go to the Bishop of London's tailor and pay heavy prices for good and well-cut clothes. But it has to be done. By the way, I have a lot of old clothes. Would you like them to give to anyone? They are too old for my brothers. I have given Alfred my nearly new frock coat suit. If you like, I will send you them.

This letter, which was accompanied by a reproachful note to his father enclosing £100 for which Starkie Barnes had asked, may sound rather worldly from a young man newly ordained. But it also shows quite touchingly the worries confronting a poor boy who had moved on to a much more spacious stage than any on which he had walked before. Perhaps he was more worried than he need have been. His abilities were to stand him in good stead. He was soon appointed to the College staff and established himself on terms of friendship and mutual respect with men of widely differing background. There seems to have been little social snobbery at Trinity in those days. It was an aristocracy of brains, not of birth.

Moreover, while Barnes clearly felt at this time some impatience with his father, he evidently thought he owed his mother a detailed explanation of his hopes and fears. He also stayed on friendly terms with all his brothers and stood ready, as the letter quoted shows, to lend a helping hand, particularly to the younger two, who followed him to Trinity as undergraduates when he was already a Fellow. Alfred won his debating spurs at the Magpie and Stump and took a first-class degree in Classics before passing into the Local Government Board. Sidney seems at this time to have been of a more literary bent, being an acquaintance of Lytton Strachey, who read to a Cambridge Society a now lost work called *Colloquies of Senrab*, Barnes's name in reverse, in reply to a paper by Sidney, called 'Intellectual Snobs', directed against Strachey and his friends. Sidney too, with a first in Mathematics, joined the Civil Service, in his case at the Admiralty, where he was soon to become Private Secretary to Prince Louis of Battenberg as First Sea Lord.

Ernest, meanwhile, with his ordination had added a new dimension to his academic activities. He preached regularly in the College chapel, even before becoming Junior Dean, and as early as 1905 he was for the first time invited to preach the University Sermon at Great St Mary's. Thereafter he was increasingly in demand as a preacher in various parts of the country. In 1906 he was appointed an examining chaplain by the Bishop of Llandaff, J. P. Hughes. In the words he had used in his letter after his ordination, he was already beginning to stand out from the ruck.

At this time of his life, Barnes does not seem to have belonged to any particular school of churchmanship. The nature and development of his ideas can be traced through a study of over sixty of his sermons from 1902 to 1915, from his ordination to the end of his time at Cambridge. At the very start he was content to rely on notes. But within months he had adopted what was to be his regular practice thereafter of writing out a full text in longhand, often in pencil, often on the back of mathematical calculations. These texts were on occasion used more than once again, but, if so, carefully revised to take account of changes in time, place and circumstances, so that in the end they resembled veritable palimpsests. Then, and often even in their original state, he must have found it hard to use them as a basis for delivery. Indeed, in expounding the art of preaching to ordinands, he would claim that he did not read verbatim from them. He described his method in this way:

> The preacher most to be envied is he who, having laboriously written and polished his sermon, can go to the pulpit and repeat it without a note. I confess that this gift is not mine; I would it were. I like to have the full manuscript beneath my eyes. I do not read from it as a rule. It is usually illegible, a mass of erasures and corrections, but a few words give me a whole sentence, and if mind will not supply the exact word or the right turn of phrase, the eye can pick it out.

None the less, the texts themselves, with the care obviously devoted to finding just the right words, indicate that he must have adhered to them more closely than he thought, especially as time went on and he became more and more fully reported in the press. In later years, reporters were to complain that his addresses were so carefully articulated, with every word counting, that one could not summarize them, but had to report them verbatim. The first drafts were obviously written rapidly, as befits a clear-headed mathematical thinker, in an elegant but, as he admitted, often well-nigh illegible handwriting, which, for example, makes 'missions' indistinguishable from 'minions' and 'views' from 'vices', which allows 'persuasion' to become 'possession' or even 'perversion', and which indiscriminately confuses 'devices' and 'desires', 'right' and 'might' or even 'conversion' and 'communism'. Only the context helps, and matters are not made easier by some strange but recurrent spelling mistakes. Then on re-reading he made amendments to clarify the arguments, simplify the language, or add new illustrations, and sometimes to insert quotations, usually from nineteenth-century poets, of whom his favourites seem to have been Browning and Russell Lowell. Every sermon, of course, has its text, and increasingly, as time went by, they began to be given subject titles too, although it was not until the end of this period that he began to have them typed and occasionally printed for private circulation. Sometimes, in a moment of self-criticism, a text would be marked 'Bad Sermon'. Sometimes, too, but rarely, it is evident from the appearance of a second hand that he consulted friends on subjects outside his own immediate range or on points where he was anxious about the effect he would make. For, although he was clearly confident in both his intellectual powers and his spiritual insight, he was even now anxious not to give needless offence and at pains to be scrupulously honest. This leads to the occasional quaint or immature banality, as when, in a sermon to the Trinity Mission in East London, devoted mainly to the need for hard work in this world as preparation for the next, he suddenly emphasizes the importance of girls going to cookery classes. Time and again, moreover, his sermons are couched in the form of putting questions or objections into the mouths of his audience and then carefully expounding his own answer. This Socratic method would have been particularly well adapted to academic audiences, especially of young people. His addresses to schoolboys seem rather less inspired, perhaps because he himself had matured early in religious consciousness and had probably never really entered into the mentality of the ordinary schoolboy. But, despite their overwhelming earnestness, in the spirit of nineteenth-century evangelicalism, and their strong academic content, the sermons are rich with natural imagery and reflect that love of the country, both in Italy and above all in England, to which he was to return again and again throughout his life.

In the content of his sermons almost the full range of interests which were to gain his attention throughout his life is already apparent: Christology, mysticism, the relationships between religion, science and philosophy, miracles, human behaviour, sin and the problem of evil, other political and social problems arising from inequalities of wealth and status, international questions and, of course, peace. On many of these subjects, particularly those which might be called applications of his Christian beliefs, his thought not surprisingly develops. But the basis of his Christian faith itself remains totally consistent. So much has been written about his views that it is as well to be sure just what they were. To those who see him as a destructive critic, what will be surprising is that there are no surprises. He believed in an omnipotent God the Father, transcendent and immanent at once, the creator of the world; in Jesus Christ, the perfect and sinless man, who was the incarnation of God and the saviour of the world; in the Holy Spirit working continuously in the world; and in the immortality of the soul in the world to come. This was the pure doctrine of the Christian Church. His acceptance of it, indeed his assertion of it, could be illustrated from countless passages. While he emphasizes God the creator, teaching that 'both life and matter are subject to and informed by some all-powerful mind that we call God' and referring in a single phrase to 'the purpose of God in making the world, his scheme for giving to us salvation through Christ and the larger hope of immortality', the guiding light of his thought is devotion to the person of Jesus. As he says, 'It is the life and teaching of Jesus Christ which is, which has always been and which must continue to be the inspiration of Christians,' and he asserts that 'the founder of the Eucharist . . . who showed the possibility of life without sin, was no mere man but the divine force of the universe incarnate, that being to whom death is unthinkable'. He thus synthesizes his view of the triune God:

> We have not begun to understand the Incarnation if Jesus is merely a teacher, 'a prophet of a distant time and another clime'. The Christian affirms that He lives in us and is therefore a living example to us, that He is one who can lift us to God because He is God. The Trinity too is a meaningless theological dogma, unless we see that the mystical presence who is always with us and the historical Jesus who fires us by His teaching and His love are both one with the living Father who directs the world.

These may seem pious platitudes of no unusual interest. But, in the light of later criticism of his work, their very orthodoxy is interesting and his language was often striking. There is indeed testimony from a contemporary that 'his sermons were really impressive, that he gave the impression of real depth and sincerity and that there was nothing negative in what he said'.

Beyond the constant emphasis on mystical intuition as ultimately the only sure approach to knowledge of God, he always also laid weight on the intellectual foundation of belief. He was convinced that emotional Christianity was not safe without an intellectual background. 'You must know and not only accept the truths of the Christian religion.' He comes back many a time to the Pauline theology of body, mind and spirit, and in one sermon draws an elaborate analogy with wisdom, power and love as aspects of Christianity representing Christ in Calvin's categories as prophet, king and priest respectively. His own detailed knowledge of the Bible was remarkable in one for whom theology was not his academic discipline, and he had already made some study of biblical criticism, making himself particularly familiar with the problem of the dating, authorship and historicity of the books of both the Old and New Testaments. He accepted the spiritual inspiration of the Bible as a guide to human conduct, but not its literal inspiration as a historical narrative or scientific treatise. Here, as in other aspects of his theology, he was at pains always to distinguish between the essence and the accident in the philosophical sense. He taught the need to take account of the nineteenth-century discoveries which in geology, for example, had shown that Genesis was myth not history, in evolutionary theory had demonstrated the unity of nature, and in anthropology had revealed the parallel developments of religious consciousness. But, despite these advances of science, he asserted that 'Some, and I am one of them, think that the essence of our faith will be changed not one whit'.

In this context can be seen his attitude at that time to miracles. He concerned himself with this problem from early days, and in May 1914 brought his thoughts together in a series of three lectures, entitled 'The Nature of Miracles', 'The Possibility of Miracles' and 'The Truth and Falsehood of Christian Miracles'. Here again he may be thought remarkably conservative. Indeed, some of his Cambridge friends seem to have thought that his position was not worthy of a man of his intellectual ability. He starts from the premise that miracles are revelations of God, and that it is thus not the fact of an event but our interpretation of it which makes it miraculous. Indeed, the ordinary course of nature is often miraculous in this sense, and the performance of miracles is not an argument for divine gifts, since, and here the mathematician speaks, no fact can ever

53

prove anything but itself. He accepts too that 'the miraculous events recorded in the New Testament make men sceptical of the truth of the Gospel records and so hinder rather than advance the cause for which older apologists regarded them as the most cogent arguments'. Nevertheless, recognizing the omnipotence of an immanent God, he asserts that miracles, in the sense of interference with the laws of science, are possible but that, if so, they must take place for a very exceptional purpose. Thus he is more inclined to look for miracles of that kind in the great past events of the Christian religion than in men's daily lives today. At an earlier stage, in a sermon of 1904, he was claiming that 'if Christ be not the son of God risen from the dead then is our faith vain and all the teaching of the Christian Church from the time of St Paul to our own day is based on a delusion'; and in another sermon of 1913 he suggests that St Luke may have heard the story of the Virgin Birth authenticated by Mary herself. In 1914 he summed it up categorically:

That parthenogenesis should be a commonplace of biology and yet impossible in the Birth of Christ I cannot accept. The other super-natural miracles associated with the life of Jesus I do not find incredible . . . I am compelled to accept the Resurrection as a literal fact and the empty tomb causes me no difficulty . . . My own imagination, my own sense of the infinite power of God and the unique personality of Christ lead me to find no difficulty in the supernatural miracles of the Gospel.

This interest in the miraculous is also reflected in his thoughts on sacramental religion. While as early as 1905 he was rejecting transub-stantiation in the sense of any physical or chemical change in the consecrated elements, he stated his conviction of a Real Presence, in a spiritual sense, which could be recognized and felt by a sincere approach to the Eucharist. As he put it in 1909, 'The Eucharist is a perpetual miracle, not because it is contrary to nature, though its explanation lies outside the field of the natural sciences, but because God working through nature gives us in it a special revelation of Himself'; and already in 1905 he had numbered himself among those who, recognizing

that we can never hope to understand the spiritual significance of our actions, because we can never probe the ultimate secrets of the universe, shrink from the idea that baptism is little more than the sign of ad-mission to the Church, just as we shrink from the idea that the bread and wine in the Holy Communion are merely commemorative symbols of Christ's body and blood . . . The grace of God, and the peace of God, come, we know not how.

The need to link modernism, of which he was already speaking in 1914, with mystical devotion was one of his strong and constant convictions. Already too he was regretting what he saw as the conversion of the Gospel into a mystery-religion by St Paul and wishing that the purer mysticism of St John could have proved the stronger.

Another traditional, not to say almost archaic, aspect of his thought at this time lies in his attitude to sin. To him sin is real and indeed he sees it as a necessary corollary of the evolutionary process that man is born with the potentiality of sin. Moreover, this is an element of human freewill, which he regards as essential if we are to understand anything of the otherwise insoluble problem of evil. If there is no freewill, how can the really evil man be explained? Indeed, many of Barnes's statements in his sermons of this period appear to imply that he still regards the Devil as a real power independent of God. This at least seems to underlie the thought of some of his frequent early utterances on the theme of temptation, where the conquest of sin is continually taught as an essential preliminary to consciousness of God. As he put it in 1908, 'to attempt to Christianize people without preaching God's vengeance against their vices is as futile as to attempt to feed the higher carnivore on vegetable matter'. It is not surprising that, when that classic study of devilish temptation, C. S. Lewis's *The Screwtape Letters*, appeared in 1942, Barnes took a lively interest in it: for the Devil the problem of evil was inverted into the problem of good. The conquest of sin, moreover, could for him only be achieved, not just by resisting the temptations of the devil, but by deliberate pursuit of positive goodness. He reiterates time and again the need for moral earnestness and 'wholesome' behaviour, the need to be sober, industrious and honest oneself and to practise the Christian virtues of pity and kindness to others. None of these are very exciting virtues, perhaps. But they are pre-eminently the virtues of nineteenth-century evangelicalism, which, in a book of that name, has been described as 'the call to seriousness'. Indeed, Barnes is often explicit in his praise for the nineteenth century in England, particularly when compared with the laxity and levity of the eighteenth, which, to

some extent, he attributed to reaction against the excesses of religious
zeal in the seventeenth. He was a puritan rather than a Puritan.

But, even at this period, he was not just a docile recipient of
conventional wisdom. For example, he early developed strong views
on the place of the Church in society and on the relative merits
of the different denominations. From the start, the emphasis of his
teaching is on action. He is not enamoured of the individual saving
his own soul in solitude. As he was to say in 1915, 'it is not through
monasteries that the world will be saved but by the acknowledgement
of those living in the world that they are bound by Christ's teaching'.
Indeed, ten years later he would go further and say that 'the monastic
life is contrary to the will of Christ. We were meant to live in the
world and take part in its improvement'. But in 1902 he focused his
thought less on the world than on the nation and on the Church of
England within it. In a powerful sermon of July 1903, he praised
Pope Leo XIII, who had just died, as a just and good man, a liberal
champion of Christian democracy. He also paid consistent tribute to
Acton and von Hügel, Catholic laymen whose thoughts and teaching
transcended the boundaries of their own Communion. But at the
same time he denounced the Church of Rome as such for its continued obscurantism and attachment to worldly power. He remained
convinced that the Church of England was the best form of Christianity for the English people and that it was Rome which must
change if reunion were to be possible. This reflects the national self-
confidence of Englishmen of that epoch. But from 1913 on he was
already active in the Anglican Fellowship, founded by his own
Cambridge pupil and fellow Fellow of Trinity, A. C. Turner, with
annual meetings at Swanwick, as a movement to reform the Church
of England from within. Indeed, while he was particularly suspicious
of the Roman Catholic Church in alliance with the State, where
what he called clerico-military parties exercised power to suppress
liberal opinion, he was equally critical of any Church which amassed
wealth, as the practice of Christian virtues such as thrift tended to
make easy, and then allied itself with the forces of property and
thus of reaction. There is, for example, a scathing denunciation of
Cardinal Mercier giving absolution at the funeral of King Leopold
II of the Belgians in 1909. Without actually quoting Acton's dictum
on power and corruption, he obviously had it in mind. From this
early stage he was conscious of the difference between the primitive
Church, with what he called in 1912 'the magnificent socialism of

Christianity', and the ecclesiastical corporations of the twentieth century. As he put it in 1914:

> A Christian Church should preach Christ: its members should endeavour to mould their lives by His life and teaching and if they have a sincere belief that His Kingdom is finally to prevail, they can accept with equanimity the chances and changes of political fortune and triumph over the passions of enemies by that strongest of all weapons, true beauty of character.

However, it was not only the Church which he aimed to influence, but rather the nation as a whole. From the beginning he was concerned with social problems, although at first he was quite prepared to abide by the existing social framework. With something approaching *naïveté*, typical of his generation and of its social Darwinism, he accepted, approved and admired the pre-eminent position of England and the English people. In his eyes, not only the Latin Europeans but other members of the Anglo-Saxon race lacked the full benefits of social and political wisdom. England, as befitted her wealth and power, had a duty to set an example, the equivalent of America's 'manifest destiny'. Within England, too, there was a dominant class with a similar duty. Class distinctions were deplorable but they existed. There would always be a rich man in his castle and a poor man at his gate. All the more need for the rich man not only to set the poor man an example but to help him too. In these early days he totally condemned anarchism and, almost as strongly, socialism in its current political manifestation; he was suspicious of the influence of trade unions who might advise their members to withdraw their labour. For at all times he preached the sin of sloth and the value of hard work as part of man's preparation for his immortal destiny. Above all, when he spoke to public schoolboys and undergraduates, whom he openly addressed as members of the 'upper classes' and 'English gentlemen', he taught them never to build lives of ease and idleness on the labour of others. He believed in the dignity of labour and he condemned waste of money, above all because it was a waste of other people's labour. Gambling, in particular, he denounced not only for its effect on the gambler's own character, but for the temptation which it put in the way of others less able to afford it. Indeed, a sermon on this is a strange mixture of morals and expediency, as when he denounces sexual vice because of its effect on the health. His whole attitude to money, in fact, shows a certain ambivalence. The Edwardian era has become a byword for conspicuous consumption and materialistic complacency. As one historian of the Church of England says, 'There has seldom existed a generation of English people which more needed and less desired the Christian redemption.' This was said of the propertied classes, and Barnes too at this time is strong in his attacks on luxurious extravagance. But he is always careful to admit that there can be no objection to making money or even to investing it to provide the necessities of life, or indeed for legitimate pleasures. Yet like the Christian Church throughout the ages, as R. H. Tawney has brilliantly shown in his study of usury in *Religion and the Rise of Capitalism*, Barnes obviously finds it hard to draw a clear line between the good and the bad, the legitimate and the excessive. As he often remarks, it is the motive which matters.

But, as the years passed, he began increasingly to question the established social order. His University Sermon of June 1907 is almost a revolutionary tract, denouncing luxury with the accents of a Savonarola. 'Christianity, wherever it has been true to itself, has been a social science', although he makes clear that, while the Church cannot be indifferent to the problems of the day, it should not usurp the functions of the state and should confine itself to principles rather than judgements. This in fact was to be the theme of William Temple's *Christianity and Social Order* nearly forty years later. By the time of his University Sermon of 1909, Barnes is calling for industrial reform, which by now he also links with the need for disarmament. For he has come already to see money and power as the forces jointly making not only for materialism but for military aggression. All this to him is a sign of the advance of a new paganism, which he associates particularly with the malign influence of Nietzsche and the doctrine of the Superman, a gospel couched in exclusively human terms. It is to this that he opposes the need to follow the example and precepts of Jesus Christ.

Now he is beginning to concern himself more with international questions. From the start, he had preached the need for missionary work. But he had set it in the context of a recognized hierarchy of nations and races. He spoke of the higher and the lower races in an essentially paternalistic vein, as if a great gulf were eternally fixed between Britain and the rest of the Empire for which she was responsible. Through all his words at this time runs an intense patriot-

58

ism, a love of country and a feeling of England's innate superiority, which spurs him on to remove such warts as still disfigure her face. Even when in 1912 he is castigating the luxury and vice of the international rich on the Riviera, he contrasts it with the prevailing spirit of Christian England. But rights engender duties, and as early as 1903 he was laying weight on the interdependence of nations, a phrase which was hardly to become fashionable until the 1960s.

These views were of course to be intensified by the outbreak of the First World War. In his first wartime sermon, at a Royal Artillery camp near Cambridge, in August 1914, he sounds almost like an army chaplain.

> We shall, I believe, win, but we shall not win easily . . . On the efforts of the British army and navy and of the whole British people during the next few months the future not only of our children but of our children's children depends . . . We believe that never has this country entered into a war with right more clearly on our side . . . No other course was possible . . . War was inevitable . . . We are fighting not only for our national existence . . . but also for the sanctity of treaties and the freedom of small nations . . . The British army and the British people are one and indivisible.

But the course of events soon gave him furiously to think. He was to speak later of his agony of mind in the first two months of the war, and as he told the Church Assembly years later:

> My conversion to extreme pacifism dates to the latter part of August 1914. The war had broken out, men had flocked to the colours, and a camp had been established in Cambridge, where I was then a don. I was asked to speak to some of these men on a Sunday morning. I accepted without hesitation and then began to write out my address. I wrote it once, then I went back to Christ's teaching and tore it up. I did the same a second and third time, and then I ventured an address which seemed to me ludicrously inadequate. I still have that address but I have never since spoken in favour of war.

By October 1914, he was preaching in Trinity Chapel on the text 'Love your enemies'. This of itself at that time must have made his hearers sit up and take notice. But while he continued to praise the heroism of those who had gone to war, while he continued to speak of and hope for our victory, while he constantly depicted Prussian militarism as the main villain of the piece, he began more and more to say things which few thought, let alone said, and which must have grated on the ears of more conventional patriots:

There is no Christian God of battles: he is a pagan illusion.

While the majority of Christians in all ages have thought it right to bear arms at the command of the authorities of the state, they have only done so because a chain of evil circumstances has forced them to ignore Christ's teaching.

All war is contrary to the mind of Christ.

War will brutalize our people.

The interaction of dynamic civilization and the idea of nationalism has inevitably produced the conflagration.

When we should be glad that all men of every nation are brothers in a common civilization through the sacrifice of Jesus, the citizens of Europe are using every devilish instrument of war to exterminate their fellows.

Only the soldiers of Christ can disband the armies of the world and only at the foot of the Cross can a permanent treaty of peace be signed.

This was not the sort of stuff which many of the Fellows of Trinity expected or wanted to hear from one of their number. It was probably not made any more palatable for them because Barnes attributed to all governments, including Britain, which had aroused German jealousy, a measure of responsibility for the war and included the organized Church in this condemnation. Moreover, he contrasted official policy with the 'essentially Christian comradeship' of the 'artisan organizations' of Europe and looked forward, after the war, to a time of international brotherhood and a peaceful federation of great states. Thus, in the eyes of his critics, to the sin of pacifist indifference between one country and another was added the offence of egalitarianism between social classes.

Through it all, however, he himself continued to preach and, when he could, to practise tolerance. This lay at the heart of his approach to international questions. In ecclesiastical affairs, too, while he attacked the Roman Catholic Church as an ally of the politico-military establishment, he always held out the hand of friendship to individual Roman Catholics. He sat lightly to ritual and, as Dean of Trinity, even officiated at a Sung Eucharist in Chapel in 1913, although, despite assiduous coaching, his lack of a musical ear led him to intone the Gloria in place of the Creed. 'Toleration' was indeed the title of a powerful sermon preached in Westminster Abbey on St Bartholemew's Day, 1913, in which he advocated toleration rather than persecution for such a mixed bag of recipients as Nonconformist schools, divorce reformers, the Welsh Church in its disendowment, suffragettes and those who wanted to change the creeds of the Anglican Church. This, like his pacifism, derived essentially from the need to love your enemies and to accept that 'we are members one of another'.

Barnes's eventual departure from Cambridge was occasioned by the interaction of three factors: his pacifism, the offer of a position in London, and his wish to marry.

Trinity in the First World War was not a comfortable place for pacifists. Not only, it seems, did the College share the prevailing war fever at a temperature remarkable for an academic institution. This was partly a conservative reaction, particularly among the older Fellows, against the presence in their midst of colleagues of less chauvinistic views, some of whom expressed those views in a pretty provocative way. Barnes understandably came to be counted among this number. The older members of the College therefore feared that Cambridge, and Trinity in particular, might gain a reputation as a pacifist stronghold. There was thus also a motive of self-interest, since they were afraid that, after the war, this reputation might deter patriotic parents from sending their sons to Trinity. This was the atmosphere which led to the College's extrusion of Bertrand Russell. The story of that extrusion, which took place in two stages, has often been told, notably by Russell's strong supporter, G. H. Hardy, in a pamphlet printed privately in 1942. It need not be retold, except in so far as Barnes's part in it is concerned.

Despite the obvious differences of background and personality, there are constantly surprising parallels between the careers, outlooks and utterances of Russell and Barnes. It is true that Russell was a scion of the Whig aristocracy, while Barnes came of poor, provincial, Non-conformist stock. To apply Beatrice Webb's definition, Russell could be called aristocratic, anarchic and artistic; Barnes's origins were bourgeois, bureaucratic and benevolent. It is true, too, that Russell's pacifism was spasmodic and relative while Barnes's was constant and absolute. It is also the case that Russell led a turbulent private life, while Barnes remained the faithful husband of one wife, with no other attachments discernible at any stage. But, none the less, many of the statements by or about Russell, particularly in the standard biography of him, could equally well have been applied to Barnes. Of course, they were of the same generation, born within two years of each other, and their lives spanned and were influenced by the same events. The main domestic influence on the childhood of each was a woman, Barnes's mother and, after the early death of Russell's parents, his grandmother. Both were brought up in an atmosphere of hereditary liberalism and Low Church piety. Neither went to a public school, so that they both escaped the snobbish and conventional pressures of those institutions in those days. Both responded warmly to Trinity. Russell was to say, 'Cambridge holds a great part of my affection; I should be homesick if I were shut out from it'. Barnes would have echoed that sentiment. Mathematics gave both men their first intellectual stimulus. Russell described mathematics as the very sternest and most austere of all the gods. Both turned to more metaphysical speculations later. Whitehead and Russell's *Principia Mathematica* is described as having 'whole pages without a single word of English'; the same is true of Barnes's *Scientific Theory and Religion*. To Russell is attributed a puritan distaste for all things Gallic and a description of Italy as 'the most perfect country ever invented'. Within the limits of his English patriotism, Barnes shared the same prejudices. When Russell speaks of the 'need to search for certain truth in an uncertain world', when his incurable optimism is mentioned, or his belief that the conventional order of things was there to be felled, when he himself speaks of his soul burning with patriotism, despite all his difficulties with the national powers that be, or when his biographer speaks of him as 'liberal in sympathies, rational in outlook and with a vigorous mistrust of all established religion and most political orthodoxies', one can easily recognize Barnes's approach as well. Even some of the criticisms have a familiar ring. Russell's biographer refers to a mixture of genius and folly; he talks of Russell 'pulling a hypothesis from the air by a process as much artistic as scientific and only then searching about for its justification'; and he mentions 'not only the spirit of questioning and dissent, but also its extension, the natural and slightly bloody-minded reaction of being perverse for perversity's sake'. The same barbs, not always in more moderate terms, were aimed at Barnes. Two other judgements in Russell's biography are also apposite. In his biographer's words, 'Beneath Russell's critical, analytical intellect, there lay the mind of a romantic manqué, forever tempted to look out at events through the rosiest of spectacles and see there, not the real landscape, but a scene of his own imagining'. Or, as a writer in the *Yorkshire Post* put it in 1962, Russell 'lays down the law as if the world were peopled by potentially rational, honourable, selfless human beings just waiting to be taught by good example, instead of by fundamentally blind, selfish, deceitful, crafty fools'. Barnes had some of the same defects of his own qualities.

Apart from such similarities of temperament and mentality, the two men certainly shared some similar experiences. Both found themselves in the courts for their convictions: Russell for civil disobedience during the First and after the Second World War, and Barnes, although, unlike Russell, he never went to prison, when he was ordered to institute an unwelcome incumbent in the 1920s and again when he was sued for libel by the cement companies in the Second World War. Both were put under pressure to resign their positions but refused to do so: Russell in 1940 when his appointment to the City College in New York was attacked on moral grounds, and Barnes during the row over his *Rise of Christianity* in 1947. Russell then defined his position *vis-à-vis* his opponents in terms which, *mutatis mutandis*, Barnes could have endorsed:

If I had retired, I should have robbed them of their *casus belli* and tacitly assented to the proposition that substantial groups should be allowed to drive out of public office individuals whose opinions, race or nationality they find repugnant. This would appear to be immoral.

In retrospect it is amusing that in 1916 the *Manchester Guardian*, commenting on the Russell case at that time, wrote: 'The dismissal of a leader of thought like Mr Russell has the same sort of effect as the degradation of a bishop would have in the Church.'

But this is to anticipate events. In 1915 both men were members of Trinity, Barnes as Fellow and Tutor, Russell as Lecturer but not at that time a Fellow. According to Hardy, Barnes took the lead in urging that a lecturer of Russell's distinction should also be a Fellow. In February 1915 the College Council showed itself ready to accept this view and appoint Russell to a Fellowship in the following October. But when, in May that year, Russell asked for leave of absence for what was known, but not admitted by him, to be political activity, the Council decided, in effect, that this would debar him from a Fellowship. Only Barnes and Winstanley voted against this decision, while Stanton, the Regius Professor of Divinity, abstained.

It was natural for Barnes to support Russell. Apart from their affinities of interest and ideals, both men were active members of the Union of Democratic Control, the organization founded by E. D. Morel shortly after the start of the war, primarily to advocate liberal peace aims, but soon to acquire a pacifist label. It had other distinguished members, including Ramsay MacDonald, Philip Snowden, Arthur Henderson, Charles Trevelyan and Norman Angell. It is of incidental interest in this context that Russell attributed his own pacifism to the South African War, which, as has been seen, may have had a partly similar effect on Barnes, and have been one factor leading him, unlike Russell, to ordination. It was Russell's prominence in the Union, and the support of other Fellows for it, which led Trinity first to ban meetings of the Union in the College and then to block Russell's Fellowship. Barnes, too, had been prominent in the Union, taking the chair at the first public meeting of its Cambridge branch on 4 March 1915, when Russell and Morel also spoke, and arguing in his chairman's address for policies which would prevent another war.

But although these activities had not endeared Barnes to his more conservative colleagues at Trinity, he had not challenged the authorities so sharply nor made himself so nationally notorious as Russell, who had after all a birthright of national notoriety. Yet he became Russell's chief champion in the College, challenging the position of the Council both on banning the UDC and on debarring Russell from his Fellowship. By the time, in July 1916, after Russell's conviction for prejudicing the recruitment and discipline of the forces, when the College Council decided actually to remove him from his lectureship, Barnes had left Cambridge. But on 27 July of that year he wrote the following letter to Russell:

64

Private

Dear Russell,

This is just a line to say that after reading the account of your trial on June 5 I agree with the comments of the 'Manchester Guardian' of July 15. I deeply regret the action of this College Council in depriving you of your lectureship. We disagree fundamentally on many questions but because of that disagreement I write these few words. Do not reply and, if possible, do not grieve. When the war is over men's attitudes will change and some at least of present wrongs will be righted.

Sincerely yours,
E. W. Barnes.

Barnes's own comment on Hardy's pamphlet of 1942 was:

After these resolutions [of May 1915] had been passed I put before Russell the suggestion that I should bring the issue before a College meeting. He replied that the animus against him was due to his pacifism and that my proposal was equivalent to conflict on his behalf. I felt – and still feel – that his refusal to allow even such a form of war was true Christianity.

Russell would hardly have welcomed this description. It is a pity that the myth has arisen that he was dismissed in a context not of pacifism but of atheism. This was because in his *Sceptical Essays* (1928) he complained that he was not offered a Fellowship because 'the clerical party did not wish to add to the anti-clerical vote'. Hardy, in his pamphlet, assumed that this referred to the events of 1915; but Russell then told him, as he related in a postscript, that he had in mind the original offer of a lectureship without a Fellowship in 1910. But the myth had taken root. Even in the 1930s Winstanley used to object that Russell had complained of the clerical party, whereas in fact the Fellows who had voted for him were Stanton, Professor of Divinity, Barnes, who was also in holy orders, and Winstanley himself, a practising High Churchman, none of whom was obviously an adherent of the anti-clerical vote.

It must thus be doubted whether the guardians of orthodoxy who removed Russell would ever have gone so far as to take an initiative for Barnes's extrusion too. In fact, events played into their hands. Barnes was offered by the Prime Minister the Mastership of the Temple in London. What then took place is best recorded in his own words. Writing in 1942 he said:

The bitterness of College feeling in 1915 against those of us who were pacifists was such that even now I do not like to recall it. When Asquith offered me the Mastership of the Temple, he knew that further service for a very few years would entitle me to a life fellowship. So his letter ran:

Confidential   17 Sept 1915

My dear Sir,

The Mastership of the Temple has become vacant by the death of Dr Woods. I should be glad if you would allow me to propose to the King that you should be his successor. I may say that the appointment is not incompatible with the performance of outside duties at the University or elsewhere.

Yours faithfully,
H. H. Asquith

I communicated the terms of the letter privately to Jackson [then Vice-Master of Trinity] and Parry [then Senior Dean] and some two months later received from Innes as Secretary of the Council the following letter:

15 November 1915

Dear Barnes,

I think I ought to let you know at once that I have received notice of the following motion for next Friday's Council.

'That Dr Barnes's tenure of the Mastership of the Temple is inconsistent with his retention of a qualifying office after the end of the present term.'

Yours sincerely,
H. McLeod Innes

Privately I was informed that it was Jackson who had given notice of the resolution – and that on the Council a majority for it had been secured. Moreover, I was told that my continued presence in the College was not desired . . . I am sure that I was right in making no protest or appeal . . . At the Temple my pacifism was not liked, but I met with extraordinary generosity. I have often wondered why the College should have so far fallen short of the two great legal Societies.

This restrained and factual account was written in the context of Russell's case, and Barnes was concerned to show that both men had decided that as pacifists they should not contest their opponents' actions. He resigned his tutorship and lectureship, and his seat on

66

the College Council was thus automatically declared vacant.
He added 'one other footnote to Hardy's record':

After Russell's sentence of imprisonment in the second division in 1918, I was asked by some of my legal friends whether I would, with others, testify as to his 'character' when the appeal for first division treatment was made. Of course, I assented at once: but it was subsequently learned that the request would be granted without such testimony.

In fact, Barnes had also agreed to a request from Gilbert Murray to appear as a character witness at the trial itself, but defence counsel had decided to call no such witnesses but to argue Russell's case on legal grounds only. In writing to thank him, Murray not only described the magistrate, Wallace, as 'a very good and level-headed man', but expressed immense relief at Russell's sentence:

a nominal fine would have been sufficient, but I am not sure that six months imprisonment in the first division, with all facilities for reading and writing, may not bring a certain element of comfort with it. I suppose it is difficult to judge without trying.

Nevertheless, although Barnes did not contest the Council's decision in his own case, the affair rankled deeply. Not only did he, as he said, have only a comparatively short time to serve before he would have been qualified for a life fellowship. In normal times, it would have been possible, even if complicated, for his colleagues to arrange for him, as a mark of respect and affection, to retain a College office qualifying him for a life fellowship. Asquith's offer had indeed held out this possibility: formally at any rate, duties at the Temple were restricted to Sundays and he could, if desired, have spent the rest of the week at Cambridge. But the times were not normal. The emotions of wartime prevailed and, after over twenty years of service to the College, Barnes was allowed, indeed pressed, to leave it, unhonoured and unsung. It was a long time before he could bring himself easily to go back to Trinity. Indeed, as late as 1945, when he was asked to preach there, he wrote to the Dean to refuse because he was 'still the same convinced pacifist whose opinions gave rise to so much annoyance thirty years ago'.

But a happier note was struck when, in April 1974, on the hundredth anniversary of his birth, a service of commemoration was held in the College Chapel. The Master attended; the Dean of Chapel, Bishop

John Robinson, who had inherited some of Barnes's theological attitudes, officiated; Dr Alec Vidler, a former 'rebel' in the Birmingham diocese, gave the address; and several Fellows of First World War vintage were present, including Littlewood, aged nearly ninety, whom few could remember ever seeing in Chapel before. All of Barnes's living descendants were also at the service.

But, even without the complications of the manner in which he left Trinity, the move from Cambridge to London was not a straightforward matter. It is interesting that Asquith should at this juncture of the war have selected, for a prominent pulpit in the capital, a man who had openly expressed doubts about the war and his government's conduct of it. But this was in the Prime Minister's character. An intellectual himself, he had a respect for academic excellence and took trouble to secure men of quality for his ecclesiastical appointments. His letter to Barnes, for example, was written in his own hand. He was, moreover, liberal not only by party affiliation but in his personal convictions. His biographers record Gilbert Murray's account of his approach to Asquith through the Prime Minister's PPS and Murray's brother-in-law, Geoffrey Howard, about the sufferings of a particular conscientious objector and of Asquith's immediate reaction of indignation and determination to have justice done. In the light of this incident, it is less surprising that he should have chosen to send a known pacifist to the Temple. He knew that the Benchers would form a critical but respectful congregation for a talented preacher and had, no doubt, in his usual way, taken care to satisfy himself of Barnes's capacities in this respect. Perhaps too he may have taken a mischievous glee in putting a youngish and liberal kitten among those elderly and, some of them, conservative pigeons. The offer seems in fact to have been instigated by Arthur Benson, who had suggested the idea to Davidson some time before and who commented that it would be a fine appointment, adding that 'Barnes is a very incisive and intelligent preacher and has graceful manners, if he is not ruffled. He is sick of Cambridge and ought to spread his wings.' Benson, too, obviously expected Barnes to keep his fellowship and, when the appointment was announced, noted that 'this has been one of my most successful plots'.

Barnes was certainly attracted by the offer. It gave him the chance, for which he had long sought to prepare himself, to make his mark on a wider world. It would give him the entrée, not only into the

Temple itself, where he could match himself against some of the best brains of the kingdom, but into the City of London as a whole and, through both, into the more general life of the nation. Moreover, life at Trinity cannot have been easy for him at this time. Indeed, for some time past he seems to have struck his friends as stale and pessimistic, not only on public affairs. As early as 1912, he had confided to Benson that 'he regarded Cambridge as in no sense a home, just living in college as a sort of club and office combined, and that his real life only began when he went off'. The war had increased his depression: early on in it he told Benson that 'the burdensome sense of life was far more constant than the pleasurable sense' and 'if he could know that he would sink into sleep tonight never to wake until he himself gave the word, he never would give the word'. By July 1915, he was telling Benson that the war had killed all talk at Trinity: people were thinking of the war all the time; they were tired of talking about it but could not talk of anything else.

But this enticing opportunity coincided with a crisis in his personal affairs. For some years, his acquaintance at Cambridge with Adelaide Ward, the only child of the Master of Peterhouse, had been ripening into love. He had been a welcome and increasingly frequent guest at Peterhouse Lodge and had met the family on holidays in Scotland and in Italy. He was determined to make Adel, as her family knew her, his wife and take her to London with him. She was deeply attracted. They were neither of them young: he was already forty-one and she was thirty-three. But they both had passionate natures and neither seems to have experienced any comparable feeling before. Indeed Benson described Barnes as shy with women who, while they were impressed by his obvious ability, could not quite make him out and seemed alarmed by him; Benson's own comment was, 'I suppose I am used to him and know that he is kinder and simpler than he seems'. In any case, now that a real attraction had come, it was to grow to be strong and lasting on both sides.

But the three Wards, parents and daughter, formed a particularly united family group. Sir Adolphus Ward and his wife, who were first cousins, had both been born in 1837 and had married late, in 1878. Their first child, a boy, had died at the age of less than four months and his mother was already at the time of life when it must have been doubtful whether she could have another baby. So Adel's birth, on 31 December 1881, had come as a particular joy to both her parents. She had responded to this and had remained close and devoted to them all her life, only leaving home for a spell of two years at Royal Holloway College, where she did not even take a degree, or for short holidays, mostly with older women friends or relations, unless with her parents themselves. By the time that Barnes wanted to marry her, she was firmly set in this way of life. Moreover, her mother, who was bronchitic and by now nearly eighty, had for years adopted an invalid existence and relied a good deal on her daughter's presence and support at home, where there naturally had to be much entertaining. This was not in any way a situation like that of Elizabeth Barrett or Beatrix Potter, and there is no suggestion that her parents put any pressure, or even moral suasion, on Adel to stay at home and reject marriage. It was more that she herself, having probably had no previous offers of marriage to pose the problem acutely for her, not only saw herself with a duty to her parents, but was, at the age of thirty-three, apprehensive of the whole idea of marriage. She immensely admired Barnes's character and abilities but was tormented by doubt whether she was capable of going beyond intellectual friendship into love of the kind which he sought from her. Although he had proposed marriage in the spring of 1914 and she had at first been ready to accept him, she then withdrew her acceptance and for eighteen months bombarded him with a stream of intensely introspective letters, in which she must have torn herself to pieces in the agony of trying to analyse her own feelings. These letters survive; most of his replies do not. But he evidently showed great patience and determination throughout, and his touch in their letters to each other at all times was lighter than hers. Indeed, although he could often in life be impatient and quick-tempered over small things, he was always remarkably patient and serene over those which really mattered. During 1914 and 1915, while not wanting to refuse Barnes, she could not bring herself to accept him. So Asquith's offer of the Temple in September 1915, brought matters to a head. Faced with her indecision and the conflict of her loyalties, Barnes made clear that if she would not go with him, he could not bring himself to leave Cambridge without her and would refuse the Temple. Realizing what this would mean to him and for his career, she at last made up her mind to marry him. From that time onwards, neither seems ever to have had any further doubts.

The appointment was announced on Michaelmas Day, 29 September 1915, the engagement two months later, and they were married, quite quietly, by the Bishop of Ely, Dr Chase, in Peterhouse Chapel by special licence on 3 January 1916. It is believed to have been the first wedding ever held in the Chapel. Stanley Barnes, in the uniform of the Royal Army Medical Corps, was best man to his pacifist brother. Rather surprisingly, the main hymn was 'Fight the good fight with all thy might', but the Lesson, the famous passage on charity in I Corinthians xiii, seems more fitting. Even this occasion was clouded for Adel by her mother asking her, when they came back from the chapel to the Lodge, if she had actually been married yet. This temporary mental blockage was perhaps the sign of a subconscious rejection of the whole idea of Adel's marriage. But, even though it did prove quite temporary, it added some unhappiness to her leave-taking. The honeymoon was spent in the somewhat improbable watering-place of Weymouth, but in wartime married couples could not go far afield. Luckily in London, where they returned to the Master's House at the Temple after their honeymoon, Ernest and Adel were not too far from Cambridge, and she, in particular, was often able to visit her parents there.

Marriage brought Barnes into relationship with a family very different from his own. Ward is perhaps an even more common name than Barnes. The records of heraldry show it scattered all over England. There are some grand branches of the species: Wards of Dudley, Wards of Capesthorne. The branch to which Adolphus William Ward belonged had mostly consisted of government servants in a modest way. In the eighteenth and early nineteenth centuries they had, from father to son, served as customs collectors, first in the Isle of Wight and then at Dover. The last of these fiscal exactors had introduced new blood into the family by marrying the sister of Thomas Arnold, the famous headmaster of Rugby, whose own family had been active in the West Indies. The eldest son in this branch of the Ward clan was traditionally called John, and the eldest son of John Ward and Martha Arnold broke away from the collection of customs dues. He first attached himself to Lord Durham, the notorious Jog Durham, so-called because he said that you could jog along all right on £40,000 a year, and he helped that pro-consul to write reports on New Zealand and Canada. But this John Ward, born in 1805, then turned aside from his first patron's paths to become an expert on Germany. Lord Palmerston said of the Schleswig-Holstein question that only three men had understood it: the Prince

71

Consort who was dead, a German Professor who had gone mad, and he himself who had forgotten it. But John Ward was also credited with a good knowledge of the problem. However that may be, the only surviving direct judgement on him by Palmerston is on a small piece of paper on which is characteristically written: 'I wish Mr Ward would write a little larger. P.'

John Ward spent most of his active career as a diplomatist in Germany, serving as consul-general in several German cities and ending as Minister to the Hansa Towns, resident at Hamburg, until Bismarck, whom he knew socially, put an end to his career in 1870 by the creation of the German Empire. John Ward, who had become a Roman Catholic, then retired to Dover, where he died in 1890.

His wife, Caroline Bullock, also belonged to a family with branches in many parts of England, particularly in East Anglia, where they had long been based at Faulkbourn and occupied the living of Radwinter. They were country gentry of the type to be found in Jane Austen's novels, whereas the Wards perhaps smacked a bit more of Trollope. John Ward and Caroline Bullock had five children, three sons, of whom Adolphus was the second, and two daughters. The eldest brother, who was of course called John, entered the Bengal Civil Service, became a judge, married the daughter of the Prussian Minister at Washington, and died in India at the age of thirty-nine; the youngest brother, William, followed in his father's footsteps, ending his career as Consul-General at Hamburg and a KCMG. Adolphus, whose first name betrays his quasi-German origin, broke away from these bureaucratic traditions and followed an academic career. He and his brothers had been brought up in Germany and to the end of their respective days corresponded with each other in German, in minuscule handwriting on postcards. Adolphus Ward himself was educated at Bury St Edmunds School and then at Peterhouse, Cambridge, where he duly won his Fellowship and, in announcing it to his mother at the age of twenty-five, proudly signed his letter 'Coll:Div:Pet:Soc:'. A historian who always said that, although he never had a date right, he was never more than two years wrong, he moved on to Manchester, where in time he became Professor of History and English Literature, Principal of Owens College and Vice-Chancellor of the new Victoria University. But throughout his long life, his historical scholarship remained of the massive German kind. He wrote copiously and

72

rotundly. His first major work was on Elizabeth, the Winter Queen of Bohemia, but he went on, after an output of astonishing range over English literature and European history, to become Acton's first lieutenant and, after his chief's death, himself principal editor of the Cambridge Modern History and, in consequence, of most of the related series of Cambridge histories. The solidity of these works reflects their Germanic links, and it is perhaps additionally significant that, at the end, his principal collaborator was George Gooch, who also had close personal and intellectual connections with Germany. But, weighty though they may have been, some of his books were still being reissued as university textbooks in the 1960s. Moreover, on family occasions, he had a felicitous talent for light verses, many of which have been preserved.

Ward's wife, his first cousin, was the daughter of his father's sister and of Thomas Burne Lancaster, rector of Grittleton in Wiltshire. Lancaster's father, R. H. Lancaster, vicar of Warnford in Hampshire, next door to Hambleden where cricket began and where his wife's hatchment could in the 1970s still be seen on a church pillar, had been a talented amateur painter, who, with his son Hume, is given honourable mention in most works on nineteenth-century English landscapists. T. B. Lancaster himself owed his middle name and the circumstances of his life to his uncle and godfather, William Way Burne, who was indeed his predecessor as rector of Grittleton, but also, somewhat incongruously for a clerk in holy orders, owner of property in a fairly dubious region of Paddington, except that, as this was before the spread of the railways, things were perhaps better then. William Way Burne's fortune, though later much divided and attenuated, helped to lubricate some academic careers which would otherwise have depended well-nigh entirely on midnight oil. Adelaide Laura Lancaster was the second of T.B.'s three daughters, of whom the third married an Irish squireen, and the eldest, after showing some talent as a pianist, retired to her bed in her teens and never left it until she died in it thirty years later. Another Jane Austen character, or almost worthy of the Brontës.

The Wards were made of sterner, more moralistic stuff. Thanks to his grandmother, Adolphus was a cousin of Matthew Arnold and this in its course meant family connections with the Trevelyans, Mrs Humphry Ward and, less directly, with many of those families whom Noel Annan has pictured as the intellectual aristocracy of Victorian and post-Victorian England. Adolphus Ward showed no particular interest in these connections or in other more worldly links. Indeed, when as Vice-Chancellor he dined with the Chancellor of his University, the Duke of Devonshire, at Chatsworth, he was the only man at table without his own manservant behind his chair. He belonged to a liberal tradition, politically and intellectually. At Manchester, apart from his academic work as teacher and administrator, he reviewed books and plays regularly for the *Manchester Guardian* and became a close friend of its great editor, C. P. Scott, the champion of Liberalism and later of Zionism. Indeed, one of Ward's appointed subordinates, Arthur Schuster, Professor of Physics, after marrying Ward's niece, Cary Loveday, became the close friend and patron of Chaim Weizmann, who went from Pinsk by way of Manchester to become the first President of modern Israel.

But in 1897, aged sixty, Ward had retired from Manchester, where his daughter Adel had been born and had attended Withington Girls' School, taken a house in Addison Road in London and prepared to devote the rest of his life to historical writing. Then in 1900 an unexpected vacancy in the Mastership of Peterhouse caused the Fellows, on Lord Kelvin's initiative, to recall him to his old College as its head. This was an appeal which he could not refuse. He served as Master for twenty-four years, writing continuously to the end of his days, but having, in the meantime, been Vice-Chancellor of the University, President of the British Academy and knighted in the Coronation Honours of 1911.

He worked hard and died in harness at the age of eighty-six. At the same time, it is true, largely thanks to Lady Ward's inheritance, the Wards lived comfortably, more comfortably perhaps than many of their academic colleagues. When they went on their annual summer holiday to Braemar, for example, it was taken as a matter of course that they would hitch a private coach to the northbound train and travel in it, complete with their own servants, animals and luggage. They were neither rich nor ostentatious. But, strange as it may now seem, this was then the accepted practice of people of their station and generation. Yet it was a far cry from Ernest William Barnes's own antecedents and upbringing.

What is more, although the Wards lived comfortably and sometimes in lovely houses like Peterhouse Lodge, they did not add much to the beauty of their surroundings. Furniture was of the variety known as *confort cossu*, heavy, ingenious and utilitarian, but without style or elegance. Things were admired more for their connections with loved ones, in an animistic way, than for their own beauty. A sale catalogue survives, showing that towards the end of the nineteenth century the Lancasters sold off all the Chippendale furniture, as worthless, from the servants' bedrooms. This reflected the taste of the inheritors of the industrial revolution, particularly in provincial England. Barnes, on the other hand, had imbibed from his colleagues at Cambridge an interest, not only in Italian art and French vintages, but also in English furniture, some of which had decorated his Cambridge rooms. He and his bride devoted a good deal of their honeymoon to spending their wedding-present cheques on some pieces of what would, before the revived vogue for Victoriana, have alone been called antiques, with which to start their new home and their new life in London.

CHAPTER III

THE TEMPLE
1915-1919

Liberal among Lawyers

The Master of the Temple is the incumbent of the Temple Church, built, like other round churches, by the Order of Knights Templars, on the model, some say, of the Church of the Holy Sepulchre, but more probably of the Dome of the Rock on the very site of Solomon's Temple at Jerusalem, as a constant reminder of the Crusaders' abiding determination to recapture and preserve the Holy City for Christendom. The church dates from the twelfth century, having been consecrated in 1185 by the Patriarch of Jerusalem in the presence, it is said, of King Henry II.

In those days the Master of the Temple deserved his title. As the direct representative in England of the Grand Master at Jerusalem, he sat in Parliament as the first baron of England, first, that is to say, among the Priors of the realm. He enjoyed lofty status as the English representative of a powerful international organization, whose revenues he administered and on whose behalf he held in trust or in sanctuary treasures of great value in money and in kind. Being at once a powerful ecclesiastic and a dedicated knight of a Christian order, under the feudal system he exercised both temporal and spiritual power and was entitled to be termed both Reverend and Valiant. Even in the twentieth century both appellations were still used by traditionalists addressing the Master.

But within little more than a century after the foundation of the Temple Church, the power and wealth of the Order had brought their own retribution. In France and England alike, the Knights Templars were broken by the secular authorities, who coveted their possessions and probably trumped up the charges of immorality and other offences brought against them. The Master of the Temple himself was condemned for heresy, and by 1312 the Order was suppressed.

Great was the fall thereof. By 1915 the official emoluments of the Master of the Temple, from the Crown which appointed him, came to only £26 3s 7d a year. Luckily the two Inns of Court to whom he ministered, the Inner and Middle Temple, each subscribed £200 a year, and on Barnes's appointment this figure was raised to £250. The Master of the Order had become the servant of two learned societies.

Most earlier holders of the office had held it in plurality with other positions in the Church, thus supplementing its meagre income. Asquith had indeed suggested that Barnes could do likewise, but the attitude of the Fellows of Trinity had made this impossible. He thus suffered quite a sharp drop in income. Throughout his life he kept meticulous accounts, recorded in his own elegant handwriting in a bound ledger, of his receipts and expenditures. This was, no doubt, partly a legacy of his early years, when he had needed to watch every penny. It was also in part due to his ability, as a mathematician, to keep his affairs in apple-pie order. But it also reflects the ambivalence throughout his life of his attitude to worldly goods. From the start he had attacked attributes of wealth, such as gambling or other luxurious living, and in later life he was to direct some of his sharpest denunciations at 'big business' and the evils of the capitalist system. But he always defended the individual's right to provide not only for the necessities of life but for modest comforts and pleasures as well; and he had begun to acquire shares in 1907 and continued throughout his life to interest himself in investments and the market, to the amusement and, indeed, irritation of his brother Stanley, who was himself a much more successful operator on the Stock Exchange and found it hard to understand what he saw as Ernest's double standard. However, the immediate point was that, in his last year of bachelor life, the new Master of the Temple had an income of £1821, of which over £1200 came from Trinity, whereas in the next year, even with an overhang of £265 from Trinity and his wife's investment income of some £300, his total receipts as a married man only came to £1605 and fell the next year, with the final loss of the

Trinity emoluments, to £1504. But he had saved some money from his Trinity days, and the drop in income seems to have weighed little in his scales against the other advantages which his new post had to offer. Even so, moreover, they started married life with four domestic servants.

Financial inducements apart, he also enjoyed a beautiful house in the centre of London and a recognized entry to the life and functions of the City. The original Master's House had been destroyed in the Great Fire of London in 1666, like all the buildings of the Temple, except the Church itself. According to tradition, it was rebuilt to designs by Christopher Wren, or at least in his style. The architecture was certainly original. Owing to the exigencies of the site, backing against Fleet Street, all the windows faced south towards the Inner Temple Library, while the staircase rose against the back wall of the house. The façade was charming but impressive, in classic late-seventeenth-century style, complete with pediment, but softened by creeper and by the frontage of a paved Dutch garden and wrought-iron entrance gates. Two hundred and fifty years later, it was bombed by Hitler's minions but has been rebuilt in its original form and is still a delight to the eye, a little corner of domesticity in the City of London.

The new Master had several distinguished predecessors. Prominent among them was Richard Hooker, the 'judicious' Hooker who wrote the *Laws of Ecclesiastical Polity* in the sixteenth century. Montagu Butler delightfully gave Barnes as a wedding-present Keble's 1841 edition of Hooker's works, inscribed 'from the Master of Trinity to the Master of the Temple'. More recent incumbents were C. J. Vaughan, also Headmaster of Harrow and Dean of Llandaff, and Alfred Ainger, friend of Tennyson and biographer of Lamb. Barnes's immediate predecessor, Dr Woods, had the reputation of being one of the dullest preachers in London and was generally regarded as 'an easy man to succeed'.

Above all, Barnes now had the chance to preach the Gospel and to spread his own convictions to a wider audience than had been possible from his comparatively narrow base at Cambridge. Writing on 2 October to the Archbishop of Canterbury, Davidson, who had had a hand in his appointment and who, like himself, came from Nonconformist stock, he said:

I will do my best by God's help to be worthy of the position which through you has been entrusted to me. It is difficult to follow the great men who have been at the Temple Church in the past. They have set a high standard of service and I can only ask that health and power will be given to me for the task that lies ahead . . . I hope to make the Master's House there a convenient centre for meetings and discussions. The Anglican Fellowship and the Student Movement have brought me into contact with many Anglican and Nonconformist laymen and with many of the younger clergy. It will, I hope, be possible to give some of the latter an opportunity of preaching to the Temple congregation. Many of them are sincere Christians, well acquainted with the results of critical scholarship and not afraid of the future. If I can get such men to put their position from the Temple pulpit it may be possible to do something to show that the Christian position can be held by the modern intellectual. In trying to do this we can, I trust, emphasize the spiritual realities without which theological discussions become lifeless. My ideal is a liberal Christianity in which liberalism is not a cloak for unbelief but an attitude of sympathy to all Christian religious experience and a positive formulation of Christian values, principles and facts.

In the first draft of the letter he had elaborated on this issue to explain that at Cambridge he had had friends ranging from Nonconformists, such as T. R. Glover, to High Churchmen at the Oratory of the Good Shepherd, all of whom were trying to serve a common Master and solve the same problems. He hoped to help bridge the gulf between, as he put it, the *Hibbert Journal* and Cuddesdon. But, on reflection, perhaps wisely, he thought it better not to enter into such Church politics with the Primate at that moment.

This was the spirit in which he embarked on his new life. He and his bride had received numerous letters on the announcements of his appointment and their engagement, one following the other in quick succession. To the conventional congratulations were added many expressions of regret that he was leaving Cambridge. Most of these were obviously sincere, but some of the commiserations, such as those of Henry Jackson, can only have been hypocritical in the light of the circumstances of his departure from Trinity. His more percipient correspondents saw his appointment as a departure from the pattern of the past and an invitation to break new ground and sow new seed. Indeed, Asquith himself, writing in his own hand to acknowledge Barnes's letter of acceptance, said, 'I am very glad that you are able to go to the Temple, where I am sure you will find a large and to some extent untilled field'. He also received a warm welcome from several Londoners, not least from the Benchers of the Temple themselves, who conveyed standing invitations to luncheon after the Sunday morning service and dinner on Sunday evenings. The only difficulty, an *embarras de richesse*, was to choose, without giving offence, between the hospitality of the Inner or the Middle Temple.

The letter which may have given him the greatest pleasure came from Birmingham:

Sep. 29 1915

My dear Ernest,

This morning's B'ham Post announces the appointment of the new Master of the Temple but is evidently unaware of his connection with Birmingham.

Well, some men are born to greatness, and some achieve it, but you belong to the third category, which should be accounted the greatest honour. It is a position of great responsibility and influence, for it will rest with you to guide and direct the thoughts of many intellectual and important people. But I know you are absolutely capable, conscientious and painstaking, so I have not the slightest fear for your success. Don't be too dogmatic. Make allowance for those who cannot see things quite so clearly, or quite from the same standpoint, remembering that people's minds and intellects are as diverse as their faces, and I believe you will exert a powerful, beneficent influence on this poor, striving and, on the whole, decent generation.

Your ever affectionate
Mother.

The Master was assisted by a Reader, fulfilling the functions of curate, and the then Reader wrote to point out, none too tactfully, that he had always regarded the Mastership as a post to which to retire, that the absolute duties of the office were confined to taking part in and preaching at the Sunday morning service, that the weekday services had fallen into abeyance, that the Sunday afternoon service was generally left to the Reader, that the arrangement of the services was controlled by a Choir committee, and that there would be plenty of leisure for literary work. This warning-off is unlikely to have coincided with Barnes's own conception of his future activity. Luckily, he found an outstanding new friend and ally in the Temple organist, Walford Davies, who welcomed him with open arms and all the warmth of a great heart and was to collaborate with him, as many letters of the next years testify, not only in beautifying many special occasions but in making the regular Sunday services moving and memorable, both to the regular congregation and to numerous visitors, including British and foreign servicemen on leave and many others who had suffered bereavement or other wartime afflictions. Davies had been organist at the Temple since 1898 and had raised the singing of the choir, which later included such star performers as the famous treble, Ernest Lough, to enjoy one of the highest reputations in London. He was, of course, to become organist of St George's Chapel at Windsor and Master of the King's Musick. He also became godfather to Barnes's younger son.

Press comment on Barnes's appointment was, on the whole, reserved. To the national newspapers he was largely an unknown quantity. *The Times* described it as 'specially interesting', but largely because the new Master was so much younger than his recent predecessors 'whose main life's work has already been done before going to the Temple'. 'But', it continued, 'Dr Barnes will receive a no less hearty welcome from the Benchers if he may be considered as beginning a new career as a religious teacher in one of the most important pulpits in London.' The *Challenge*, of which William Temple was editor, was more friendly, describing the Temple as 'the place of worship for many of the keenest-minded of the laity' and commenting that 'to guide their thought is a great opportunity and Dr Barnes is just the man to use that opportunity to the great gain of our spiritual life'. *Public Opinion* also remarked, a trifle ambiguously: 'Dr Barnes is a great mathematician, but this is not his chief qualification for the pulpit, as some papers seem to suggest.'

Certainly there was nothing leisurely in Barnes's assumption of his duties. Appointed on 29 September, he preached his first sermon at the Temple Church on 3 October. As the incumbent of that church, he now for the first time in his life had a regular pulpit, from which he was to preach on almost every Sunday while he occupied the Mastership and often on special weekday occasions too, as well as fulfilling numerous outside speaking engagements and, incidentally, having to refuse many more. He must have done a great deal of travelling in the uncomfortable conditions of wartime. Despite this pressure, as well as a heavy correspondence and no secretary, he continued to prepare a verbatim text of virtually every address and rarely preached the same sermon twice, unless with extensive adaptation, to bring it fully up-to-date, to include topical references or to adjust it to a different audience. Often he would preach a series of connected sermons, announcing the subjects in advance, and on special occasions he would have them printed and circulated to friends and others likely to be interested. But it is evident that he also made time for extensive reading, at the British Museum Reading Room as well as at home: his sermons contain constant references, not only to the latest theological literature but also to a wide range of other books. His reading of the Bible and of biblical criticism must have continued to be both profound and perceptive. Authors whom he quotes, apart from theologians, include such a mixed bag as Marcus Aurelius, Machiavelli, Burke, Pascal, Shelley, de Tocqueville, Schiller, Ruskin, Acton, Emerson, Leslie Stephen and Maynard Keynes. He was, not unnaturally, conversant with at least the broad lines of the latest scientific discoveries, and, more surprising in a mathematician, his sermons reveal a wide knowledge of history, both political and ecclesiastical. He had not wasted his conversations at the High Table at Trinity. He also kept abreast of the political and ecclesiastical news of the day, citing documents as diverse as reports of Archbishops' Committees and the War Aims Memorandum of the Labour Party. Moreover, he took advantage of his position at the heart of London to talk with men of affairs and to use in his sermons material from private conversations not to be found in the public press. Dean Inge, for example, records in his diary for 1917: 'A long walk with Barnes, who told me very interesting stories about German spies, which he had just heard from Justice Sankey.' It is perhaps not fanciful to see an autobiographical touch in one passage from a sermon of 1916, although Barnes did not overtly, or perhaps even consciously, apply it to himself:

> For years a man may find opportunity denied to his abilities: he may be in a position made impossible by circumstances and tendencies which he cannot alter; and suddenly he may be called to a new position where the discipline of years of unrequited labour is seen to have developed him with peculiar fitness for his new duties.

Certainly the cap fits.

In his first Temple sermon he presented himself to his new congregation by discussing the duties of a Christian teacher. Preaching for him would always be teaching. As he said in that first sermon:

> Personally, I would prefer to use the term 'religious teacher' rather than

82

'preacher' to suggest the ideal that is before me. At times we conceive of the preacher as one detached from his message, expounding a finished body of doctrine, occupied in presenting some perfect deposit of faith once delivered to the Church. Such a conception I would have you set aside. Christian belief is no petrified organism: it is a growing, living thing, changing its form while preserving an essential unity, adapting itself to the knowledge both physical and spiritual of successive generations of men, and becoming even more wonderfully attractive as those in whose hearts it flourishes grow in power and grace.

But he wasted little time on self-analysis or the mechanics of preaching. As he once put it:

If the personality of the preacher is obtrusive, if he subtly draws attention to himself rather than to his message, we lose rather than gain. He clearly should seek so to preach that men forget rather than admire him while he is speaking. He should lose himself in his theme and as he delivers his discourse his hearers should be drawn to the precepts and power of the Master whom he serves.

The content of his teaching at the Temple remained consistent with his earlier thinking, and many of the old themes recur time and again. But with maturity and experience, with exposure to a wider audience, came development and broadening of his thought. On one occasion in 1919, he admitted:

I turned up an old address of mine delivered some sixteen years ago. I found it precise and rigid, unimpeachable in its traditionally Anglican orthodoxy. But also I found it curiously unsatisfying. A certain hard definiteness seems to me now to carry with it the assumption that one can reap at the fullest regions of the spiritual realm with precision as of a land-surveyor. Today I should say: Christ is present, yes; but the fact means a fullness of beauty alone, which cannot be measured or really explained, because it must stretch away to the infinite beyond our comprehension if it is to link us to the divine. I am sure that in the years since I wrote that unsatisfying address I have not lost faith. I am sure, rather, that a greater spiritual certainty has come to me. In a true sense my understanding has increased and for that very reason I am less able to formulate what I feel or to accept the formulae which others have sought to impose on the minds of men.

This Socratic I-know-that-I-know-nothing approach is not mock humility. It reflects his constant preoccupation with truth and with progress and, within those parameters, with the need to absorb new knowledge and mould it into a convincing presentation of Christianity. But he also realised the need for that presentation to be positive. Preaching at the Temple towards the end of 1916, he set out his position:

> I have tried to recall the number of occasions on which I had given to you teaching which emphasized some aspect of modern biblical research, and to reflect on the attitude, so far as I could gauge it, of those who heard me. The occasions have been comparatively rare and yet they have seldom failed to evoke some kindly protest. This rarity has been deliberate. When I came here, little more than a year ago, my views were unknown and for that reason it seemed necessary to put before you my positive faith. Many knew that former work at Cambridge qualified me to speak on certain scientific questions: it was a natural deduction that the theology of one so trained would be sympathetic to modern views: and, I fear we must add, it was almost inevitable that some would suspect that my positive faith was nebulous. There is among many Churchgoers a feeling that the result, if not the object, of higher biblical and doctrinal criticism is destruction and not construction; that modern science and philosophy are, as it were, acid eating into the Faith whenever they come into contact with it. This view is false: if it were true, I should not be here. But, knowing that such fears exist, it was a primary duty to disclose a personal faith, to demonstrate how true to the facts of experience the essentials of Christianity are and so to shew that the destructive effect on Christianity of modern knowledge has been erroneously exaggerated. One has tried to be constructive and yet in positive teaching to say nothing that one does not believe to be strictly true, and to imply no assent to beliefs that modern knowledge and scholarship have rendered doubtful.

Such scrupulous honesty might have sounded like intellectual sleight-of-hand. So he went on:

> The preacher must emphasize first and foremost the joy and hope of the Christian faith . . . be always considering some new phase of Christ's personality, some instance of His wisdom, some incident of His life, some parable or miracle that shews His insight and powers . . . Such matters are largely independent of modern philosophy or biblical scholarship; they are barely touched by the conclusions which men of science have arrived at concerning the nature of the physical universe and the progressive development of man and of religion.
>
> But many older Christians cannot be persuaded that this is true. They

feel that . . . some of their old beliefs are being undermined and they ask anxiously whether there is any limit to the process of restatement or denial. They have a horror, which all right-minded people share, of the unbelieving priest . . . Now, . . . the agnostic clergyman is much more common in fiction than in real life . . . Most men who in England take orders . . . believe too much rather than too little . . . Their influence with those who accept traditional beliefs is naturally strong. Yet it is perhaps harmful with the younger men and women who are certain that some beliefs must be discarded and know not which to abandon and which to retain . . . The new knowledge has come in like a flood . . . The men and women over fifty who still attend our churches are normally . . . untouched by it. Those under thirty have almost invariably felt its influence. This difference . . . creates a gulf between the generations.

The teachers of the Church . . . must recognize the new knowledge. Their teaching cannot be adequate unless they discriminate carefully between true and false theories . . . They must admit that some old beliefs are no longer tenable and they must at the same time shew that in its essentials the revelation of God which Jesus gave to the world is true.

Faith is, as it were, a system of fortifications guarding a city. So long as the enemy held none of them, those within lived in spiritual security. Some have fallen; and men cry that the city is lost, ignorant that other and stronger trenches exist behind the old outworks. Christian teachers today have to admit the loss of the obsolete facts and to shew the strength of the new.

We need a dynamic faith, enriching itself as men grow in knowledge and experience. Christian teachers must build up a new system of belief which has behind it the authority of accurate scholarship, of intellectual honesty and of true spiritual perception. It will be new, yet strangely like the old.

When the process is finished, men will wonder why it caused such difficulties. Think of the shock to belief caused by Galileo's assertion that the earth moved . . . Today we are untroubled by the controversy. Galileo was right. So be it. Our faith is unharmed.

This quotation is more self-revealing than much in Barnes's sermons. It represents typically and faithfully his approach to his task. These preoccupations with what he called 'the new knowledge', the product of the nineteenth century which he often termed a Second Renaissance, and the need to make Christianity intelligible and acceptable to 'younger men and women' are constant and dominant themes. Not for him the cosy repetition of familiar bromides. As he put it: 'It is the business of the preacher to educate his congregation, not to flatter the prejudices of his hearers.' On another occasion, mixing his metaphors a little, he said: 'The tables of stone on which the Church's commandments are engraved get tarnished by time: the moss must be cleared away, the letters must be recut and all who share this work will justify their membership and repay their debt to those who have revealed to them the hidden things of Christ.'

But at the same time he saw his duty as teaching and leading without imposing his views on others, who must think out and experience their faith for themselves. As he said: 'Men hate second-hand religion as they hate second-hand clothes.' His sermons were always carefully articulated and it is impossible by brief summaries or by staccato quotations out of context to do justice to the substance or quality of his teaching. When he himself summarized the essential content of Christian belief, as it emerged unscathed from contact with 'the new knowledge', he did so in these words:

The Universe was made and is controlled by a single spiritual being whom we call God. By calling Him a spiritual being we mean that He is somehow comparable to that part of highly civilized man which is independent of the body. But this is only a half-truth for, in the second place, Jesus asserted that God the Creator of the Universe is good. He is best described as a loving father. Thirdly, Christ said that God had made man to achieve goodness through moral struggle. He intended men to be His sons, to shew His love. Fourthly, Christ taught 'other-worldliness': in His view the world of the spirit, which will be our home after death, is far more important than the present life. This world rightly regarded is but the preparation for the kingdom of light and love. Finally, Jesus gave us the supreme example of Himself. He showed how man must struggle and suffer to do God's will. He revealed Himself as perfect man and so is 'God in man made manifest'.

On another occasion, he formulated 'a few of the main dogmas which we all accept' in rather more factual, indeed almost credal, language:

We believe that there is one and only one God. We believe that Jesus of Nazareth was His only Son, our Saviour, our Lord and our God. We believe that in the Gospel are His commands which it is our duty to obey, that the life which they shew that He lived is the pattern life for all men. We believe that He aids and strengthens all who turn to him by the Holy Spirit, the God we perceive within our hearts. We believe that

86

the other books of the New Testament shew how His early followers were divinely guided to continue His work. We reverence the Old Testament because it contains the literature of the spiritually gifted race to which He belonged and because it shews that for centuries the great prophets of that race had expected His Advent. We believe that we are immortal and that if we make ourselves worthy we shall ultimately live with Christ. We believe that God works in the world, that He welcomes and, if it be according to His will, answers prayer. We believe in sacramental grace: that is to say that, through Baptism and the Holy Communion, God in an especial way aids those who seek his help. We believe that religion is a fellowship and that we can only realise our fellowship by belonging to a Church. And finally we believe that the Church of England so preserves the traditions of Christ's teaching and the organization adopted by His early followers that, better than any other body, it can spread His influence over this our land.

From all these passages the Personality of Christ can be seen as still central to all Barnes's thinking and teaching. He had no doubt that Christ was the Messiah, and held Himself to be the Messiah, for whom the Jewish people and their Hebrew prophets had for centuries been waiting and preparing. Nor did he doubt in any way that Jesus was not just in tune with the creative spirit of the universe, but that He actually was that Spirit incarnate in human form. To express his understanding of the Incarnation, Barnes thus comes back time and again to the prophecies, above all those of the Second Isaiah, who foreshadowed the Christian idea of righteousness, and to the mystical theology of the Fourth Gospel. He sees the Suffering Servant of Jewish prophecy and the Divine Logos of Greek philosophy combined in a single Being. For an explanation of the unique combination, as he saw it, of the Divine and human natures, which had troubled philosophers and theologians through the centuries, he was inclined, with St Paul, to favour the doctrine of κένωσις, by which Christ emptied Himself of Divine attributes to take our nature upon Him. In one sermon he used the parallel that God 'emptied Himself of some of his attributes as Creator, just as a patrician would have divested himself of power in becoming a slave'. Otherwise it would be hard to reconcile some of the sayings of the human Jesus with the omniscience of God. As Barnes put it: 'Personally I find it a help to my religious life to think of Jesus as limited in his knowledge of history or natural science or social customs.' Despite

His attested power to work miracles, Christ had, in Barnes's view, in matters of worldly knowledge the human limitations of 'a Galilean peasant-artisan'. But he was convinced that on spiritual things Christ could not have been mistaken or His whole authority for the Christian would vanish. Broadly, his argument ran that if Christ said something about the spiritual nature of the Universe, then, in view of his Divinity and his unique spiritual insight, it must be true; if therefore a saying is attributed to Christ which we are convinced cannot be true, it is essential to satisfy oneself that Christ did not say it. It was, of course, unnecessary to assume equal spiritual perception in Christ's followers, even the earliest of them. Thus, in a sermon at the end of 1919, he went to great lengths to show that Jesus' apparent prophecies of His own early Second Coming must have been interpolated by a believer in Jewish apocalyptic doctrine into Jesus' own forecast of the destruction of Jerusalem. On Barnes's own showing, it was perhaps hardly necessary for him to justify the truth of the Gospel narrative in just this way, any more than it is necessary to the Christian doctrine of the Incarnation to show that Jesus was the expected Messiah of the Jews. *Per contra*, but also on the strength of the Gospel narrative, Barnes tended at this time perhaps to exaggerate the influence of Jesus on His own generation, by quoting judgements from the New Testament which are hardly corroborated by contemporary non-Christian literature. If the evangelists could be mistaken in their records of Christ's teaching, they could also by misplaced loyalty overstate the effect of that teaching on others. The verdict of St Mark's Gospel that 'truly this was the Son of God' is a long way ahead of Tacitus's reference to 'one Christus, who had been put to death by the procurator Pontius Pilate in the reign of Tiberius'.

But, whatever may have been Christ's impact on His own times, Barnes's Christology inevitably meant that he still had to wrestle with the problem of miracles. Here he maintained but developed his earlier attitude. He accepts that God the Creator could in theory, if He so wished, interfere in the material workings of the Universe which He had made. To believe otherwise would be to accept Deism, which at one time he described as 'God as an absentee landlord'. He speaks of some scholars whom he regards as 'mistaken in so stressing the uniformity of nature as to deny the possibility of miracle' and contrasts this with 'the more conservative position to which personally I incline'. But, despite the theoretical possibility of miracles, he does not see God intervening in the natural world in normal times, except indirectly through His influence on human beings as his agents. On prayer, for example, he says: 'I see no warrant to the belief that by prayer, apart from human agency, the face of the natural world is changed.' History he sees as a process in which events are made by men, but men working under the inspiration of God. He warns against looking for miracles in contemporary life, even in the liturgy: for, as he puts it, 'popular theology always degrades the supernatural into the miraculous, the sacramental to the mechanical'. Christ Himself, as God incarnate, is however an exception to this rule, perhaps a unique exception. He was able to perform miracles, even if all those attributed to Him in the New Testament cannot necessarily be attested as true. But the problem is not, of course, solely concerned with miracles performed by Christ on others: more difficult for many to accept are the miracles involved in Christ's own Incarnation, notably the Virgin Birth and the Resurrection. Here Barnes repeatedly asserts his own continuing belief in both dogmas as facts. To him at this time the Resurrection remained supremely important as testifying to the continued presence of the Holy Spirit working in the souls of men. He described the Resurrection as 'the greatest victory the world has ever seen'. Indeed, on Easter Day, 1916, he declared that 'If you are to accept anything worthy of the name of Christianity, among your beliefs there must be the certain conviction that Christ rose from the dead on Easter Day and that you yourself will one day do likewise, and live as He lives in another state'. At the same time, he struck a note of caution, warning that 'it would be wise to base the doctrine of human immortality, as Jesus did, on the very nature of God, not on the evidence of the Resurrection, strong though this is'. On the Virgin Birth, his attitude remained similar, though arguably less committed. As before, he still regarded parthenogenesis as biologically commonplace. Preaching in 1919, he said that

> the most discussed exhibit at the Royal Society soirée this year was a frog produced by a pin-prick in an unfertilized egg. To what discoveries will such experiments lead? . . . It is possible that scientific research will, in a not distant future, demonstrate that the way in which God works in nature leaves a place for the Virgin Birth.

This, by the way, was half a century before any controversy on clones and genetic engineering. But Barnes already realised that many of his younger contemporaries were concerned lest the Virgin Birth could be seen not as adding to the stature of Christ, but as detracting from it. Even for him it was not a proof of the Divine Nature.

> Suppose that the Virgin Birth were established by the most rigid evidence and that Jesus had had the character of Nero. Would then anyone have claimed that it proved our Lord's divinity? . . . The Virgin Birth at most confirms our faith . . . Though personally I hold to it . . I deprecate forcing its acceptance on others.

His teaching in fact followed the line which Boyd Carpenter had put succinctly in a private letter of 1902:

> The Virgin Birth did not make Jesus Christ the eternal Son of God. He was wonderfully born because He was Son of God. He was not Son of God because He was wonderfully born.

It is in making this distinction between the facts of the miracles of Christ's lifetime and the unlikelihood of miracles in our own time that Barnes was led to repeated denunciations of spiritualism. He recognized the attractions, especially in wartime when many had lost those dear to them, of belief in communication with the dead. But he deprecated what he saw as 'magic and necromancy' incompatible with Christian truth: 'a sign of religious degeneration' and 'a crude type of thought which thinks of God as revealing himself in the material Universe rather than in the moral and spiritual realm'. As he saw it, 'the only . . . convincing record which we have of survival after death is that of our Lord Himself'. Indeed, so strongly did he feel about the dangers of spiritualism that in 1918 he published a pamphlet, issued by Longmans for 2/-, on *Spiritualism and the Christian Faith*. While accepting the validity of telepathy and even the existence of evil spirits, and while recognizing the present limitations of human knowledge, he saw spiritual communication as something taking place between living beings in this world and not between the living and the dead. Apart from the risks of sheer charlatanry, the idea of summoning up the spirits of the departed by means of mediums and séances cheapened the next world. It was better to find solace in the Love of God and Eternal Life with Christ. The pamphlet was quite widely noticed in the press and given a favourable reception, except, of course, by reviewers already committed to advocacy of psychical phenomena. In similar vein, he warned against the specious attractions of Christian Science, which he described as neither Christian nor scientific and which rather chauvinistically he classed among 'certain forms of belief of transatlantic origin'. Although he would have been the last to deny the supremacy of mind in the universe, it would not be achieved by pretending that matter was otherwise than it is. The same philosophy was later to underlie his approach to sacramental theology.

Thus over and again he comes back to the unique beauty of Christ's character and the perfection of His moral insight and teaching as the bedrock of his faith. But the concept of the goodness of God and of Christ as His complete revelation forced Barnes to continue to confront the problem of evil. He still often speaks of the Devil as if he believes in his independent existence and he asserts that 'the constant struggle between Good and Evil fills the whole universe'. Certainly he still believes vividly in the existence of sin and declares that 'the Antinomian heresy which denies the reality of sin is the most horrible of all perversions of Christianity'. 'Men are not good by nature: none of us now share that noble fallacy of Rousseau'. By the same token he saw no attraction in the Hindu religion and what he called allied Western philosophies, for he regarded anything smacking of pantheism as 'incompatible with our instinctive sense of sin' and as failing 'to satisfy us because there is no room for the sharp distinction between right and wrong which conscience demands'. He went further and said that 'more potent than modern science or modern criticism [as a force destructive of Christian faith] has been the influence of Eastern religious thought and the moral levity which naturally goes with Hinduism has done great harm'. In this Barnes remained typical of his generation, which saw the world sharply divided into Christian and pagan, and the function of Christian Europe as bringing light to less developed races of men. This 'Europe knows best' attitude had been characteristic of Livingstone and most of the Victorian missionaries and their supporters. But it did not prevent Barnes, partly through his friendship with C. F. Andrews, another Old Edwardian, and his admiration for Gandhi's espousal of non-violence, from becoming a sympathetic supporter of Indian self-government.

To Barnes human nature was a compound of base animal instincts, inherited by the process of evolution, and of a developed moral and spiritual consciousness enabling man to choose between good and evil and to purify his nature closer and closer to that of God, as revealed in Jesus Christ. Neither God nor Christ was to be regarded as indifferent to sin. As Barnes put it, Christ 'is too often pictured as a sort of stage curate, a good, pious, simple creature, incapable of shrewd humour or incisive command'. On the contrary, we men have free will but we are required so to exercise it as to align ourselves with the will of God. This is not an easy or even a painless process. 'Man has free will, but if he sets himself against God's purpose will suffer for it.' Life is a constant moral struggle, and redemption comes through suffering, which has a moral value of its own. 'We fight not against men only but against the power of darkness in our own souls.' As von Hügel taught, suffering was the price of spiritual health. These thoughts were particularly attuned to the circumstances of war, but they were also central to Barnes's teaching on the Atonement. As a believer in evolutionary progress he was bound to reject the traditional story of the Fall of Man, on which he thought 'a worthless superstructure' had been built. In 1919 he put it this way:

Many old theories of the Atonement seem to me to have been horrible, to have exalted the Devil and to have assailed the loving justice of God. I would abandon all ideas of a ransom paid to the Devil, all legal fictions by which Christ was thought to have been punished for our sins. He bore our sins because as man He bore the burden of human sin, just as we all, innocent or guilty, have to bear it. But He was the Lamb of God who taketh away the sin of the world, because by His steady and unfailing resistance to every force of evil He brought into the world the power of perfect righteousness.

But, as always wrestling with his own conscience to achieve truth, he adds:

It is very difficult to say how the perpetual miracle of the Atonement, for so I regard it, works. We do not know what human personality really is, nor how spiritual influences flow from soul to soul, nor how the soul receives guidance and strength from the Divine.

Or, as he puts it in another context, 'we finite beings can have no mental certainty as regards any ultimate question'. None the less, he was convinced that goodness, beauty and truth formed a single unity and should be pursued together, and that only by achieving bodily, mental and spiritual purity would man reach his ultimate destiny. God was love and was working in the world to achieve the ultimate triumph of the good in the Kingdom of Heaven. But God was also just, and evil would be punished. 'Men do not die: they pass to judgement.' While admiring the Stoic ethic, as exemplified by Marcus Aurelius, he saw it as limited and sterile without the sanction of divine judgement or the wider hope of immortality. This approach underlay Barnes's view of the next world:

> I conceive of eternal life as existence for which, not immediately but finally, all that is evil has been removed and in which all that is good has been perfected . . . At the beginning of life after death memory must persist, or there will be no continuity of human personality, worthy of the name, but our memories will be gradually strained . . . An intermediate state of purgation in which the soul is slowly fitted by discipline for perfect life with Christ may well be a sequel to life on earth . . . He who does evil on earth suffers in the life to come, but the pain will be an incidental part of the process of purification . . . Purification, not punishment, is the Divine process . . . This will be a temporal process . . . I am led to say that the future life is temporal. But I doubt if it is spatial . . . The resurrection of the body is not material. Hence the glorified body need not be spatial, for space and matter are not independent realities. But there could be no resurrection of the body in any reasonable sense of the phrase unless we continue after death to exist in time.

This belief in a process of purification after death led him to make a rather superfine distinction between purification and Purgatory, which in its Roman Catholic dogmatic form had become associated with the sale of indulgences and other abuses. In similar vein, in a sermon of January 1917, he expressed no objection to prayers for the dead, provided they did not lead on to invocation of the saints as intermediaries with God. These formulations may smack somewhat of logic-chopping and can hardly be said to be in full accord with the Thirty-Nine Articles of the Church of England. But they are certainly symptomatic of Barnes's constant striving to achieve a consistent synthesis of science and religion. Pitting himself, as he was at this time, against some of the best legal brains of the kingdom, he was determined not to gloss over intellectual problems, but to face them squarely and overcome them if he could, and the internal evidence shows that he was concerned to seek truth and justify it, not only for his hearers, but also for himself.

Above all, he was concerned with two aspects of 'the new knowledge': the impact of advances in geology and biology on our view of the physical universe and of human nature and, secondly, the impact of biblical criticism on our view of Christ's teaching and the Hebrew background to it. He saw the two processes as interacting: scientific discoveries revealed more clearly the evolutionary nature of God's action on the universe and thus shed new light on the biblical accounts, while historical criticism, with which Barnes had made himself thoroughly familiar, showed the limitations of biblical writers and thus enabled men to discard unworthy beliefs, even when they were attributed to Christ Himself. Once again, the over-riding search was for truth. A distinction must be made between the eternal spiritual truths and temporal secular opinions. Thus, it was neither necessary nor possible to believe in the literal inspiration of Holy Scripture, even though, as Barnes believed, it was a vehicle of great spiritual inspiration. But he saw Christianity as the product of evolution not revolution, the summit of what he called 'successive steps of a staircase' thus defined:

First, the nebula contracting into the incadescent globe. Then primitive life as the earth cools. Then animals with self-consciousness. Then instinctive reasoning which develops into the pursuit of knowledge. Then the moral law slowly extending its sway over human action. Finally, the spiritual sense unifying the whole process . . . Men are the unfinished products of a stream of Divine purpose: unfinished until they grow to the measure of the stature of the fullness of Christ.

Or, in another context,

'Evolution' is a slow process . . . Man is like a speck of mud on the rim of the chariot-wheel of God: as the wheel goes slowly round, the speck goes up and down, down and up, but ever its progress is forward.

Barnes dwelt at length on his theology at this time not only to emphasize its positive and conservative aspects, but also because for the first time in his life he was having to present his full case convincingly at the bar of public opinion. But, neither then nor at any time, was he only concerned with metaphysical or eschatological speculation. To him 'faith without works is dead'. 'The aim of the Christian should be to do good rather than to be good.' 'Unless we make Christianity do things we had better give it up.' He used to urge his audiences in all circumstances to ask themselves: 'What would Jesus do?' As always, he rejected the monastic approach of saving one's own soul by contracting out of the world. 'We are not ants on a dustheap . . . but pilgrims to eternity.' 'There is but one conflict in the spiritual world: it is the battle between good and evil, the eternal Armageddon of selflessness against selfishness, of those who bear others' burdens against those who would escape their own, of those who struggle for light against those who love darkness.' As R. H. Tawney said of John Ruskin, 'he was a man whose sense of the moral unity of the world was so passionate that it impelled him to verify and expound it in one human activity after another'.

Above all, his years at the Temple were the years of the First World War, and he remained preoccupied, not to say obsessed, with the problems which the war had brought to the country. As a pacifist he wished to emphasize that to the Christian no war can ever be holy. 'Let us not call this war holy: war is in its nature an evil thing.' In a powerful sermon on Good Friday, 1916, he asks, 'What would you have done on Calvary?' and goes on,

> Today another crucifixion is taking place. Europe is crucifying her young men . . . What are you doing while this awful outrage is going on? . . . Even should further courage lead to victory, Europe will not be saved thereby.

But he did not just condemn the fact of war itself. As an exponent of Christ's teaching and His injunction to 'love your enemies', Barnes argued, at the Temple as he had at Trinity, that responsibility for the war did not lie with Germany alone but with all the countries of Europe who had shared in the pre-war system. That system he saw as having been based on material greed and national rivalry for military and economic motives. Although Bismarck's empire had been founded on expansionist militarism, on blood and iron, the similarly materialistic actions of Germany's neighbours had aroused her suspicions and helped to lead to war. As he put it later, 'the supreme tragedy of the war was that among our enemies many of the best men thought that they were fighting for high ideals: that they were solely defending the fatherland in which they had known justice and love'. We were all in some measure to blame. Barnes was always critical of the practices of diplomacy, and when the Secret Treaties between Russia and her allies were published by the Bolsheviks after their revolution, showing how the Powers had planned to carve up Europe, he deployed all his invective against the old diplomacy. In a sermon of 1918 on psychological miracles, after the former German Ambassador at London had revealed some of Germany's pre-war plans, he was able to say that 'God for His own purposes can make men – even Ambassadors – throw prudence to the winds'. With hindsight and in the light of all the diplomatic documents, his judgements on the origins of the war are not so surprising today. But at that time they were rare almost to the point of idiosyncrasy, especially when contrasted with some of the tub-thumping, rabble-rousing sermons which most of Barnes's clerical colleagues were preaching. As he scathingly said at the time:

> When the war began, some of the most virulent abuse of Germany came from those who professed to follow Him who said 'Love your enemies' . . . Those who have done most to preach peace and love among the belligerents are not the Christian Churches but workmen and their leaders . . . If you wish to inflame the passions of war, do not imply that you do so as a follower of the Prince of Peace.

In similar vein, he denounced 'professing Christians' who when 'demanding reprisals . . . quote "an eye for an eye and a tooth for a tooth" as though it were not a detestably evil maxim'. Indeed, in reflective mood in 1919 he was to recall sadly that 'repeatedly during the war, when I protested against blind anger, or degrading reprisals, or denial of liberty of conscience, I found myself working with agnostics'. To his way of thinking, retaliation meant sinking to the level of German barbarism. But he was rather less than fair in his sweeping condemnation of other Churchmen. The bishops, with Davidson at their head and Gore and Talbot of Winchester in strong support, had taken a bold line and risked much unpopularity by speaking out against reprisals and the treatment of conscientious objectors. Yet it is true that some even of the bishops and many of the lesser clergy were less able or willing to swim against the tide of public opinion.

What is more, unlike those clergy who preached on the ennobling effect of war, which 'brought out the best in men', Barnes consistently pointed to its degrading effects on individuals and the nation. 'I do not agree with those who say that war purifies a nation.' Unlike Reinhold Niebuhr in his book *Moral Man and Immoral Society*, Barnes was never prepared to accept that the state could be exempt from the rules which applied to Christian conduct in its citizens. He saw moral standards lowered all round: drunkenness, extravagance, mental inertia, intolerance were all rife. At various times, he denounced such abuses, among others, as the loss of civil liberty, not least in the treatment meted out to conscientious objectors; the diversion to the production of alcohol of resources which could be more productively employed; sexual license and in particular the creation of brothels for the army in France; and the fortunes made by war-profiteers. He criticized the poor staff-work of the army and the shortage of industrial research as the products of a disregard for education before the war, when Germany had been the best-educated nation in Europe. The defence of conscientious objectors, their freedom from victimization and their early release after the war was over were causes to which he devoted particular attention, corresponding with individual objectors, supporting them before tribunals and advocating their case in public. He used regularly to compare their plight with the persecution of the early Christians for refusing to offer incense on the altar to Caesar as if to a deity. But the parallel was hardly exact, as his view of the early Christians was often probably idealized, and it cannot be said that he made much headway with public opinion. Not for the first or last time, his was a voice crying in the wilderness.

None of these opinions helped to make him popular. It is said that, after one of his pacifist sermons, the Lord Chancellor of the day was heard to comment to a fellow-Bencher: 'If I did not know it was a privileged occasion, I would have that Master of ours in gaol tomorrow.' He received occasional letters of polite remonstrance from some of his congregation and sometimes was criticized in the press. Thus the *Oxford Magazine* on 12 November 1915:

The Master of the Temple gave the University on Sunday a thorough-going pacifist sermon. It was a pity that he showed himself either quite unfamiliar with or unable to grasp the Christian objections to the views he was maintaining. It might be expected that in the University pulpit an attempt would be made to deal with a difficult subject from a philosophical point of view and not from a one-sided standpoint . . . It seems that even great mathematicians from the sister University can allow logic to be overpowered by sentiment.

As Barnes had said in the context of the Russell case, the Universities were less tolerant than the Inns of Court. But he was not deflected from his course. In comparing two other preachers, he said that 'men are inspired by the guerrilla leader rather than by the more prudent general', and this no doubt was how he saw his own function too. The interesting thing is the extent to which he was still pacifist and patriot at once. He was convinced that German militarism bore the main responsibility for the war, whatever other countries' faults; that the British Government had done more than any other to try to avert it; that the allies were fighting for freedom, and the moral supremacy lay with the free peoples; that the war had to be won and must indeed continue until it was made clear that militarism, like all evil, destroyed those who put their trust in it; and that it was incumbent on all good citizens not to impede the war effort. Thus he did not oppose the war as such; nor, unlike Russell, did he preach anything which could even remotely be construed as subversive. Moreover, he explicitly and repeatedly recognized that British democracy had stood up well to the strains of war and that the degradations which war caused were to a large extent balanced by the items on the credit side: patriotism, self-sacrifice, submergence of political conflict, absence of hysteria, generous gifts to charity, individual enterprise and hard work by both men and women in the national cause. But his constant concern was that in the physical and moral turmoil of war men should not lose sight of the specifically Christian values and virtues, that they should not only be good citizens but Christian citizens too. His powerful sermon at the Temple Church in December 1917, when Jerusalem and the site of Solomon's Temple in that city had fallen to the British, is a typical combination of patriotic satisfaction and exhortation to yet greater Christian endeavour, although his old friend Lapsley wrote from Trinity to chide him for referring to 'parliament' in the time of Henry II.

But from his earliest days at the Temple, he was already concerning himself not so much with the conduct of the war, on which he fully accepted the need not to rock the boat, but with its consequences. He realised, perhaps earlier than most, that no one would win the war, that all would have lost economically and that exhaustion and poverty could all too easily breed pessimism, despair and recklessness. In these circumstances, if men went back to what he saw as the prevailing materialism and selfishness of pre-war days, this could only lead to a renewal of conflict between nations of the world and between classes at home. From early days he was a strong advocate of the League of Nations, as a means of preventing another European or world war, and for this, despite his pacifism, he agreed at first that the League must have the teeth to impose sanctions. But he went further than many at the time in urging that it should not be a League of conquerors, but that Germany and her erstwhile allies should also be included and no indemnities should be imposed on them, if the pre-war cycle of rivalry, suspicion and conflict was not to be renewed.

Through it all he remained at bottom an optimist, a convinced believer in progress. In May 1917, he was saying:

The civilization that we knew is crumbling away ... Traditions as old as Magna Carta have been swept aside. The British Constitution as we knew it three years ago is gone ... Europe is exterminating a whole generation of young men and dissipating the accumulated wealth of a century ... There will be attempts to reconstruct the old system, with its furious discontent, its jealousies between rival nations anxious to exploit the wealth of the world, its bitter disputes between capital and labour. Men will try once again to make envy, greed and poverty the actual incentives to progress. But most certainly such attempts will fail. There will be a reversion to the ideals of the Kingdom of Heaven. The instinctive idealism of men will rise in revolt. It will show itself – already we see the process at work in Russia – in a thousand ways which will baffle statesmen and confuse all accustomed to think according to the fundamentally non-Christian standards of the era that has gone. But the best things that struggled to survive in the days before the war, humanity's respect for itself, men's happiness in seeing others happy, their reverence for self-denial, their instinct that honesty is a poor virtue without a friendly and even quixotic charity, all these things will seek to find new and more powerful expression. They will gush out like streams of living water and great will be the hissing as they fall on the embers of the present conflagration. Let us not be dismayed in spirit as we see the conflict. None of us will escape pain and loss. At Armageddon the angels of death and destruction fly through the air. But the victory rests with the Lamb of God, who taketh away the sins of the world.

The mention of Russia in this sermon is interesting in view of Barnes's later attitude to that country. While grateful for Imperial Tokay, he had long mistrusted Tsarist tyranny and the corruption of the Orthodox Church under the secular rule of Pobedonostsev and the Holy Synod. He rejoiced to see it swept away. Indeed, he welcomed the February revolution, not only as a triumph of democracy in Russia itself, but as an accretion of moral strength to the allies as a whole, since they were freed from association with a reactionary empire and could now really be seen to be fighting to destroy privilege, oppression and intolerance. But at this stage he was by no means sure that the change had been for the better. Speaking soon after the February revolution, during the period of the Provisional Government, he said:

When from this pulpit I spoke of the Russian Revolution, I warned you that, in Acton's words 'The passion for equality might make vain the hope of freedom' . . . Today we can see the process at work . . . We regret it unreservedly.

Not only did he regret that in Russia political theory had overcome discipline. But by 1918, after the October Revolution, he was speaking of Bolshevik chaos, asserting that Bolshevism had become an attempt to advance social reform by cruel methods and denouncing it as social madness. While expressing some admiration for both Tolstoy and Marx, he declared that 'masses of men, fired by the inspiration of Tolstoy and Marx, have created an anarchy which, even if, as some suggest, it is not so black as it has been painted, has nevertheless been productive of more misery and more injustice than existed under the evil government that has been overthrown'. All the same he maintained, a bit inconsistently, that a reaction in Russia would be the worst possible calamity, as Bolshevism at least did not raise the spectre of a hostile combination of Teuton and Slav against the West. It was too early for him to foresee Rapallo or the Ribbentrop-Molotov Pact. But he was percipient enough to prophesy in 1918 that 'the ultimate danger to democracy, economic perhaps more than militarist, lies in the non-European, non-Christian East'. In contrast with his views on Russia, he unreservedly welcomed America's entry into the war, which made ultimate victory certain and brought into play in allied councils the idealism of President Woodrow Wilson.

But through it all, his message was directed at his own country, whose traditions and whose destiny meant so much to him. As he put it: 'England may yet help to give such a pure ideal of national righteousness to mankind that never again will the present conflict of the nations be renewed.' It was in his determination that his own country should not fall short of that ideal that, although he said 'I believe that the British Empire has been of incalculable value to the world', he continued to denounce such blots on her overseas policies as the alleged use of forced labour in Egypt, oppressive measures in Ireland and the firing on the crowd at Amritsar.

His attention was by no means only directed at international affairs. Being disturbed by the prospect not only of international but also of class conflict, he was of course led straight into the whirlpools of domestic politics. But he maintained that the existence of an Established Church imposed 'on the ministers of the Church an obligation to criticize the policy of the state in the light of the principles of Christ'. He complained too that if a preacher 'discusses the really important developments of political life . . . angry protests are raised. He is mixing up politics and Christianity, as if you could divorce political principles from Christian morality'. So, even though at times he professed to think that the Church should confine itself to restating principles, he continued in fact to prescribe detailed remedies for national ills. He was still by no means an uncritical admirer of trade unions, especially when they led their members to strike or to go slow against the national interest, and he condemned Syndicalism, as expounded by Sorel, as 'simply class-warfare', even though, 'deplore it as we may, it is but the retort of angry men to the tyranny of the bureaucratic Leviathan'. Class-bitterness, as he saw it, seriously hampered our efforts to defeat the aggression of Germany and would also make it harder to maintain our position as a leading manufacturing nation. But he saw hope in international workers' solidarity, for 'in the Labour movement of today, in the aspirations of international socialism that even the war has not killed, there is an essentially Christian element'. This element, of course, was love for one's neighbour, the brotherhood of man; one of his favourite texts was 'We are members one of another'. Moreover, consistently with his earlier teaching that no man could righteously live off another's labour, he realised that the workers had suffered for what he called 'the despotic power at present vested in the employer' and that 'modern industrialism has made work wearisome and intense. It is wasteful of the health and efficiency of the workers to such an extent that great industrial areas are centres of race-deterioration'. As he saw it, the remedy lay in co-operation not subordination, mutual service rather than veiled antagonism. He looked with favour on

Sir William Lever's advocacy of co-partnership and declared that

> the workers must share in settling the conditions of industry . . . They must be consulted by management before wages are changed . . . All the workpeople must be represented in the Works Committees which must be an accepted feature of industry in the future . . . The business autocrat has to become the constitutional monarch.

This was thirty years before *Mitbestimmung* in Germany and sixty before the days of a government committee on industrial democracy in Britain. Even during the war, his ideas developed fast. To begin with, his approach was still essentially paternalistic: the governing classes must recognize the workers' interests, must concede their justified demands. This was a question of Christian sympathy; there was no suggestion of worker control or of public ownership of the means of production. By the end of the war, he could say that 'for three generations the middle classes have controlled the state: the skilled artisans will apparently before long take their place'. He also foresaw that

> we must expect drastic interference with the present power which a man has to dispose at death of his property as he pleases. We must expect state ownership of monopolies and the breaking-up of great private fortunes . . . A democracy must provide all men with food for their bodies, minds and souls. This means some form of state socialism.

But, with Russia in mind, he warned that here too equality could destroy liberty.

His own political sympathies were also clearly developing. Whereas in past years he had been almost a Gladstonian and certainly an Asquithian Liberal and had condemned socialism, as when he had said that 'the evil side of socialism the world over is its tendency to ignore the spiritual in seeking material comfort', by 1918 he could say, 'I have personally much sympathy with socialist ideals' and he watched with interest the rise of the Labour Party, which he saw as 'due to moral disquiet greater than any desire for violent economic change'. But he still qualified these thoughts with the warning that 'a religion whose basis is material happiness has in it grave potentialities for evil'. Indeed, with the approach of the post-war election, he was urging his congregation to

102

consider candidates' moral standards rather than the views which they may hold. A great war naturally throws up a crowd of adventurers, successful speculators, self-seeking demagogues and the like . . . As Christians let us give them no support as they will lead the nation into temptation.

Two other recurrent themes of his political thought at this time stand out from the astonishingly wide range of subjects which he covered. The first was education, which for twenty years had been his profession and in which, as one who still saw himself as a teacher, he retained an abiding interest, showing itself, incidentally, in an active connection for many years with the Student Christian Movement, where he was a willing victim of Prebendary Tissington Tatlow's relentless importuning of him for speeches and articles. He believed intensely, first, that the citizens of the future should be fully developed in body, mind and spirit and, secondly, that the educated citizens of all classes would need and demand a rational political and religious philosophy of a kind which had never been offered to them before. As he saw it, 'The most grievous source of national weakness that the war has revealed is our imperfect educational system'. By contrast, Germany was 'the best educated nation in the world'. Therefore 'our citizens must be trained to think'. While public schools should be forced to take poor boys, while the school-leaving age should be raised from thirteen to fifteen and while this should be followed by continuation schools, with free education and if necessary even payment for attendance, the objective was not just knowledge for the sake of knowledge. There must also be Christian education for Christian purposes. After the war, wasteful expenditure should be eliminated, but we should not economize on education or social reform, for, 'as we pay taxes for these purposes, we obey the precepts of Christ'. Here was another field for State action, as well as for private charity. 'Suffer little children to come unto me.'

His interest in Christian education was exemplified by his Appendix, not accepted by his colleagues, to the 1918 Report of the Archbishop's Committee on the Teaching Office of the Church, of which he was a member. Starting from the need for more and better men to serve as clergy, he argued that ordinands could no longer be drawn only from the upper and middle classes or the older universities. They should either be selected while still at school or from older men, provided they were not just misfits from other professions. In either case, they should have a secular education in some other subject before going on to theological training, so that they should not be encouraged to think of the priesthood as a separate caste. They could then go to Theological Colleges, but these colleges should in future be uniform in size and controlled and financed by a single national board, exercising supervision through local committees. The Colleges should be in university towns and linked with the local University. Their courses should be standardized, and examinations should be national to avoid inequality of standards; local diocesan examinations by each Bishop's examining chaplains would thus be abolished. This early foray into the field of ecclesiastical administration was a far-sighted plan of reform, much of which has later come to pass. But, not surprisingly, an appendix which struck at so many vested interests was not accepted by the full Committee.

Secondly, he repeatedly expressed keen interest in the new status of women. He had progressed a long way from his opposition to degrees for women at Cambridge. The Franchise Act, giving votes to women after the long agitation of the suffragettes, struck him as 'the greatest achievement of national solidarity in modern times'. He recognized that, by their education and by the service which they had given to the state in war, women had now earned an equal voice in shaping the destiny of the next generation. More than that, owing to the slaughter of young men, women would now have a disproportionate weight in public affairs, and it was vital that their energies should be given an outlet in service to the community. This did not mean that boys and girls should necessarily be educated in the same way. 'The wise man will neither wish men to do women's work nor women to do that which is natural to men.' But, apart from that still conservative sentiment, he did call not only for equal pay for equal work, but for more higher education of women, for more women, for example, as doctors, so that we could increasingly look to women 'for the maintenance of a healthy tone in public and social life'. He also advocated an order of deaconesses within the Church. Even in these practical admonitions, he bases himself on the life of Christ and the Bible. He says, for example, that 'St Luke's Gospel is the one which I prefer to any other' and 'St Luke's is primarily the woman's Gospel.' 'It alone gives us details of the Saviour's life which must have come from His mother or from the women who cared for Him and followed Him to the end'. These are unusual sentiments from one firmly rooted in Protestant theology.

But again one of his criticisms of St Paul is that 'his attitude to women, a tinge of asceticism, are defects in his preaching of the Gospel of Christ'. There was no need to prove St Paul's spiritual infallibility, even if he had wanted to do so. As Barnes saw it, 'Christ did not teach asceticism.' 'A man has no right to deprive himself or others of the common joys of humanity'.

> Asceticism, I believe, is always wrong, though the motive from which it proceeds is often entirely noble . . . Not in a violent abstinence, but in restraint and temperance do we best fulfil the law of Christ . . . They are right who criticize St Paul's depreciation of marriage . . . St Paul's views in this matter are not those of his Divine Master, whose love of children was almost unique in the ancient world.

Indeed, St Paul's 'depreciation of marriage has embedded itself in the Christian tradition largely owing to the great but, as I hold, often dangerous influence of St Augustine'. Though still a demanding moralist and a rigorous teacher of purity, in body, mind and soul alike, the married man has triumphed over the bachelor don.

Needless to say, Barnes was not concerned with the Christian leaven in the State alone. Though not yet responsible for ecclesiastical administration, he was, as a clergyman and a patriotic Englishman, intensely interested in the nature of the Church of England itself. He retained, it is true, a profound suspicion of all organized Churches. There was not only the Orthodox Church under the Holy Synod in Russia. 'Ecclesiastical Christianity has in political conflicts usually been found on the anti-democratic side.' 'The whole weight of the Catholic Church in France was thrown against Dreyfus.' 'The Church is usually half a century behind the rest of the country in its views.' Too often, as he saw it, the Church had been ranged with the powers that be, if not even the forces of reaction, military as well as financial. This, be it said, was long before the days of Christian-Democratic governments in Europe. These strictures applied pre-eminently to the Roman Catholic Church, as when he referred to 'the contrast between the solemn beauty of the Roman Mass and the deplorable political activity of the Roman Church', saying that 'in France and Italy the political and social conscience is more highly developed among non-Christians than among Catholics'. Moreover, he saw this backsliding in religion as well as in politics:

> Catholicism has so hardened into a rigid system that it cannot apparently

105

adapt itself to the changed outlook on the world which has grown up with the growth of secular knowledge since the Renaissance . . . Catholicism is at present static rather than dynamic, a self-centred, somewhat isolated system of thought, rather than one quickly responsive to the spiritual movements of the time.

He wanted to be sure that the Church of England would not go the self-same way. He saw it as essentially a comprehensive body, and such it should remain. Admittedly, 'inside the English Church the three traditional schools of thought, the High, the Broad, the Evangelical, emphasize respectively authority, intellect and free religious experience. The Church is thus harnessed to three vigorous horses and it must be admitted that they are a somewhat unruly team'. But 'the Church must recognize that unity can exist in diversity'. Englishmen resist regimentation and the Church cannot be too disciplined as, for example, the Anglo-Catholics wanted it to be. This, by the way, is almost the first reference in Barnes's teaching to Anglo-Catholicism as such. He accepted at this time that the Oxford Movement's influence on the religious life of the country had been profoundly beneficial, contrasted with the previous groups comprising only orthodox Anglicans, narrow evangelicals and critical liberals, and not least because of the social reformers in the ranks of its later followers. But 'the early Tractarians fail, notwithstanding their earnestness and devotion, because their gaze is turned to the past rather than to the future'. For 'the political tradition of the medieval Church . . . has developed into the modern Ultramontanism of the Papacy' and 'an ecclesiastical organization controlled by priests and laymen of "priestly" temper may be alike ungenerous in its action and hostile to new aspects of truth'. As always, theology for him is seen against both its intellectual and social backgrounds.

The Church of England, on the other hand,

should be the soul of this nation . . . In our own country, no problem more urgently awaits solution than that presented by the relations of the democracy to organized Christianity . . . The English Church has become a prosperous middle-class organization with the sympathies of an enlightened aristocracy.

In other words, although Barnes did not use them, the Church of England is 'the Tory Party at prayer'. Again, his remedies were exact and specific. First, to avoid the dangers of 'priestliness', the laity, men and women alike, should take, and be allowed to take, a more active part in Church affairs. 'The clergy have too much power to change the type of services to which the people are accustomed.' This, indeed, was already one of the main objects of the Life and Liberty Movement, of which William Temple was the guiding light and which culminated in the Enabling Act of 1920. Secondly, to avoid the drift of young people and workers from the churches, 'the reform of our own liturgy is long overdue: it contains too much that we can only accept in a non-natural sense'. Even so,

> reverence for the past will still leave in our liturgy many traces of ideas which we no longer accept. Must we then leave the Church? I, for one, who have thought on this problem for many years, emphatically say 'No'.

There is irony in these statements by one who ten years later was to be a leading opponent of the Revised Prayer Book. Thirdly, there must be financial reform. 'Diocesan finances should be centralized and administered by a strong body of representative laymen.' The logical link between these three proposals for reform is apparent. In the context of the third proposal, seen in retrospect, it is significant that he not only defended Bishops' incomes, arguing that their amount was not a real scandal even though they might be better presented to show the expenses inevitably incurred against them, but also condemned the sale of advowsons, calling for private patronage to be abolished and representative parishioners to be given a say in the appointment of clergy. Within a few years, he was to be the recipient of a Bishop's income and engaged in controversy with the recalcitrant private patrons of a living.

Relevant to these viewpoints is his attitude on Modernism, a label not so common in wartime as in the early post-war years and certainly not yet attached to himself. Even so, he was already concerned to analyse and, as far as he could, defend it. He started from the proposition that 'Modernism is not scepticism'. But he realised the dangers of Modernism for its own sake and the pitfalls which it would open up. Speaking in 1918, he said:

> There are two kinds of Modernism. One is that which Pius X tried to put down and of which Loisy was the ablest exponent: it sought – still seeks – to retain the Church and the sacraments while practically

ignoring the Divine Christ. The movement was agnostic and pragmatic:
I hear on good authority that recently it has infected even the Jesuit
body in France. It necessarily reduces Catholicism to the level of the
mystery-religions which since the dawn of history seem to have flourished
round the shores of the Mediterranean. Such a movement is regressive.
I believe that its ultimate failure is inevitable. But there is also a modernism which goes straight to Christ, which would reinterpret Him and His
work afresh, fearing no assured conclusion of modern science, no
honest criticism of ancient documents, no historical investigation, no
bouleversement of traditional views. It uses Him, His moral perspective
and spiritual genius, as a fact by which to test philosophic speculation.
It sees how His influence, even when obscured by other forces, has
created great institutions and modified the policy of powerful states. It
believes in Him and believes that He will still be the supreme factor in
moulding the progress of mankind. Such for me is the Christian fait h.

His sympathy for the movement is clear, but it is still the sympathy
of an outsider. Incidentally, he goes further elsewhere and says that
'the type of modernism of which Loisy was the foremost exponent
was rightly and inevitably condemned by Pius X'. He would hardly
have said as much thirty years later.

Already he was finding it easier to hold out the hand of friendship
and co-operation to the Free Churches than to the Roman Catholics.
Indeed, he constantly regretted, during his time at the Temple, that
he could not exchange pulpits with Free Churchmen, despite regular
invitations to do so. But he abode by the discipline of the Church of
England which forbade the practice.

Barnes's teaching at the Temple on this variety of subjects shows
the widening range of his interests and the breadth of his knowledge:
science, history, philosophy, theology, mysticism, international
relations, domestic politics, education, sociology, peace, patriotism,
ecclesiastical administration, even already some eugenics. Now, as
later, respect for tradition and desire for innovation go hand in
hand. Not only was he now, as always, absorbing new knowledge
and synthesizing it with the old. He was positively searching for new
ideas, seeking to bring about changes which would mould things
nearer to Christ's desire. But now for the first time too he had fully
exhibited his wares to the connoisseur. He had fashioned and
polished them with his own methods and his own style. While he
rarely repeats himself exactly, nor does he seriously contradict
himself, he usually manages to relate his message to current pre-

occupations and to crystallize it in a few lapidary phrases. He often comes back to his favourite texts: 'members one of another', 'what shall it profit a man if he gain the whole world and lose his own soul?', 'blessed are the pure in heart, for they shall see God' and Acton's dictum 'the influence of Christ in the world which He redeemed fails not but increases'. He makes much use of his favourite books of the Bible: the Second Isaiah, pre-eminent among the Hebrew Prophets; the Gospels of St Luke and St John, humanist and mystic respectively; Job, the victor over temptation; the Psalms, which he calls the hymnbook of a nation in trouble; and Daniel, where is demonstrated the value of religion in politics. Indeed, for him the prophets and the saints are his models. But they must be doers, not just seers. His saints are those who have helped to change the world about them: St Paul, St Augustine, St Catherine of Siena, St Teresa, John Wesley, David Livingstone, Elizabeth Fry, General Booth, Sister Dora of Walsall. But both prophets and saints are needed: 'it would be better if the horses of the prophets drove the saint's chariot of wisdom and love through the streets of the city'. For more modern mentors, he confesses that in spite of some disagreement he owes more to F. J. A. Hort and to F. W. Robertson of Brighton than to any other English theologians: an interesting combination of rigorous intellect and mystical devotion. Indeed, when he quotes Robertson as saying 'My tastes are with the aristocrat, my principles with the mob', he may almost be making his own apologia after twenty years at Trinity before emerging on to a wider stage. Perhaps the influence of debates at the Cambridge Union can also be seen in one logical weakness: he often defends his own views by attributing them to 'the opinion of competent critics' or 'the conclusions which practically all competent scholars accept'. This device cannot be faulted by quoting a dissentient, as the dissentient can then be dismissed for incompetence, but it none the less rests only on a subjective value judgement. This debating trick apart, and some naïve assumptions about the immediate impact of Christ and the early Christians on their contemporaries in the first century AD, his sermons of this period convey a remarkable impression of sustained power. The mental, moral and spiritual fastidiousness is not left to convince by itself. It is joined to a strongly articulated argument, in which he shows a determination not to rely just on assertion or on selected texts, but to bring logical difficulties and counter-arguments into the open, face them squarely and defeat them. It is not surprising that in this endeavour he was sometimes accused of relying too heavily on his manuscript. But to judge from both private and public reactions he was usually successful.

The sermons were regularly noticed in the press, more perhaps in newspapers directly concerned with ecclesiastical affairs than in the national organs. The *Challenge* and the *Church Family Newspaper* were particularly assiduous in asking for, and printing, the text of his addresses. Comment, though sparse, was generally favourable, except from spiritualist or rationalist mouthpieces. Thus, as early as March 1916, the *British Weekly* was saying, after a sermon at St Paul's:

> Dr Barnes is rapidly coming to the front as a London preacher. He draws round him Sunday by Sunday an intellectual and highly appreciative body of listeners. The scientific and historical allusions in his sermons are much quoted at dinner and tea tables . . . His strong, penetrating voice and careful enunciation are well suited to Cathedral preaching.

By 1919 the *Manchester Guardian* could report on

> a particularly inspiring ministry to Bench and Bar. He has certainly revived the ancient glories of the Temple Pulpit. Men and women of enlightened views find the Temple a real spiritual home, where profound scholarship has been touched by noble ideals into a ministry of genuine service during troubled years.

In October 1918, the *Church Family Newspaper* also surveyed his ministry from a rather different angle:

> The Master of the Temple sticks closely to his manuscript. He would fill higher rank as a preacher but for his rigid adherence to paper, which tends to divert his attention from the congregation to the reading-desk. This defect, however, is largely counterbalanced by the interest of his matter, the splendid voice and short words and sentences in which it is expressed. It is given to few Doctors of Science or Fellows of the Royal Society to attain such perfect simplicity of style.
>
> Neither the remoteness of a University town nor the seclusion of the Temple has narrowed his vision. Pre-eminently he is a man sensitive to the last degree to the problems and perplexities, the sorrows and anxieties which oppress his fellow-men, especially at this crisis. His heart beats with that of the multitude.

The end of the war in November 1918 changed the whole setting. Barnes has described movingly how it came to him:

I well remember how I heard the news that the slaughter was to end. I was in the country and at about 8.30 in the morning I went out to get a few more newspapers. All seemed as usual in the somewhat drab street except that suddenly one saw a child's flag tied to a child's chair and placed in a cottage doorway. It was – how shall one say? – trivial, pathetic, and yet full of meaning, pregnant with hope. It seemed to light up the whole street with its simple sincerity. It conveyed the joys of the Psalmist when he wrote: 'the valleys shall stand so thick with corn that they shall laugh and sing'. Three doors further down was the newspaper shop and the young woman in black – her husband had been killed – said in a curiously even voice: 'It's going to stop today. The air-force station on the hill picked up a wireless message and they have just sent the news down.' I was silent, trying to see the new world that had come into being: and she said, in that same even voice: 'I'm glad it's over; there's been too much killing.' I have often thought since of her words. We had won the greatest war in our history and the verdict of simple humanity was 'There's been too much killing'.

From then on Barnes's thoughts in this field were concentrated on the Peace Treaty. Here again he preached the need for reconciliation. In 1918 he had become a Vice-President of the League of Nations Society. He was as glad as anyone that the German militarists had been defeated but he realised that 'we won – God forgive us – by means of the blockade'. Without saying so in terms, he saw that the legend of a stab in the back could sow the dragon's teeth of another war. As he put it:

the society of nations must restrain and if need be punish by force a state where aggressively ambitious men get the upper hand . . . If we impose [on the Germans] conditions of peace which they think unjust, if we exclude them from the League of Nations, they will await an opportunity to strike again . . . Disarmament all round is a fundamental idea of the League. No nation must retain more troops than will suffice for police-work.

Here was by no means an absolute pacifism of non-violence. Economic sanctions would also be necessary and 'each nation must hold its tropical dependencies as a trust for which it is responsible to the Council of the League'. But Britain would have to give up control of the seas; there must be no more secret treaties; no more discriminatory trade or tariffs; old-age pensions, health and unemployment insurance should be compulsory in all countries to prevent competitive advantages occurring to the trade of countries who did not provide such benefits. Speaking of the Peace Treaty in April 1919, shortly before it was published, he said:

> Measure that document when it appears by the standards of Christian renunciation. Test it by the witness of the Spirit. It is to contain, we are told, between 150,000 and 200,000 words. How many of them will be such as could have come from the lips of Christ?

This was a high standard to set. Needless to say, the Peace Treaty did not measure up to it, and Barnes was correspondingly disappointed and critical of it.

His activities during these years were by no means confined to preaching sermons, many as he did preach all over the country. He was of course particularly in demand at gatherings of educationalists or where scientific knowledge was at a premium, as when in 1919 he preached in Birmingham on the centenary of James Watt's death. He was also naturally sought after by bodies interested in international understanding. But, quite apart from sermons, his mind and his pen were actively employed in reviewing books, mostly for the like-minded *Challenge* and *Church Family Newspaper*, although at the end of the war and increasingly thereafter he was sent books for review by *The Times Literary Supplement*, whose editor, Bruce Richmond, had close family connections with the Wards. Barnes's book reviews, like his sermons, were obviously elaborated and articulated with care, so that almost always each review is a positive essay in itself rather than just a commentary on another author's work. Many years afterwards, urging a younger colleague to follow his example and write reviews for the 'Lit. Supp.' he said: 'I was learning theology then and the reviewing helped to fix my ideas.'

Apart from serving on the Archbishop's Committee on the Teaching Office of the Church, he had played an active part in 1916 in the National Mission of Repentance and Hope, from which indeed that Committee had sprung. To anyone with his strong belief in the reality of sin and temptation and in the need for redemption through suffering, the theme of repentance came readily to hand. In wartime all men, and clergy in particular, are much acquainted with suffering; and at the Temple, Barnes was deeply and constantly involved in ministering to the care of souls, many of whom had suffered separation and bereavement. Numerous signs of gratitude and lasting friendships resulted. For the Temple was indeed a parish church, even if its congregation was functionally rather than geographically based. Barnes's life there provides the answer to those who were later to impute to him the lack of any parochial experience.

Other distinctions began to be added or offered to him. Early in his Temple days he was asked to join the Governing Body of King's College, London, and he was later elected a Fellow; but he declined to become Dean of its Theological Faculty in plurality with the Mastership of the Temple. As examining chaplain to the Bishop of Llandaff, he was often in Wales and took an active interest in the Church of Wales during the throes of its disestablishment. In 1918 he was elected to its newly-formed Governing Body. Outside the sphere of ecclesiastical affairs he served on the committee of the Oxford and Cambridge Club, and in 1916 he was elected a member of the Athenaeum under Rule II, by which distinguished men are invited to join without submitting to the purgatorial discipline of a waiting-list. In the next year too he was asked to contribute his photograph to the archives of the National Portrait Gallery.

But a new dimension came into his life with his appointment in 1919 as a Canon of Westminster. The offer came from Lloyd George and was therefore all the more welcome to Barnes: as a gesture to a pacifist from that source so soon after the war, it obviously could not be seen as a piece of political patronage. None the less, he hesitated, being reluctant to leave his unique position at the Temple to be a member of a collegiate chapter at the Abbey. The offer had been made on the understanding that the Canonry would not be compatible with staying at the Temple. Barnes asked for time to consult the Archbishop and, although no record remains, it seems that the Archbishop at first gave no definite advice. In the end, Barnes decided to accept Westminster, and Davidson then wrote warmly approving his decision and emphasizing 'that if a man is prepared to rise to the greatness of the opportunities offered by a Westminster Canonry he has notable work to do for a vast number of people of all classes. The very fact that his congregations are constantly changing widens the sphere of his possible influence'. It seems possible that one factor weighing in Barnes's decision was a hint conveyed to him from Westminster that Buckingham Palace had been given reason to believe that he would accept and had passed his name on to the Prime Minister, with a consequent risk of embarrassment all round if in the end he refused. Needless to say, Barnes obtained no explicit confirmation of this, apart from expressions of confidence, from the Palace. The King's Private Secretary wrote:

Buckingham Palace
10th December, 1918

Dear Master of the Temple,

It was very kind of you to write to me respecting the offer made to you of the vacant Canonry of Westminster.

All I did in the matter was, on behalf of the King, to urge the selection of one whom His Majesty had satisfied himself would be welcomed by the Dean and Chapter of Westminster, and who would bring to that body fresh gifts and renewed powers.

I can well imagine that you leave the Temple with many regrets; regrets which I venture to say will be shared by your very representative congregation.

Believe me,
Yours very truly,

Stamfordham

Stamfordham himself had often been in Barnes's congregation at the Temple and it may well have been at his instigation that on 29 December 1918, the King and Queen attended morning service there for what was ostensibly a thanksgiving but may also have been intended to give them the chance of hearing Barnes preach. He took as his text 'God hath given us the victory' but coupled it with a strong plea for magnanimity to the defeated.

After all this, it was somewhat of a surprise that, when the appointment was announced, it was coupled with the news that Barnes would also retain the Mastership of the Temple 'at the convenience of the Crown'. This no doubt had its compensations but meant that Barnes had to perform the duties of both posts and involved attendance at numerous meetings and functions at the Abbey, while during his periods in residence there he had to preach two sermons each Sunday or find someone else to occupy one or other pulpit. It is clear from surviving sermons that in fact he often did preach twice. But even his dynamic energies at that time of his life could not keep this up indefinitely, and in November 1919, W. H. Draper was appointed to succeed him at the Temple.

The Prime Minister's Secretary had written on 29 October to say that Lloyd George now wanted to appoint a new Master and to express 'his appreciation of your courtesy in continuing your association with the Temple for such a long period after taking over your present appointment and his sincere thanks for your services'. There had evidently been a long search for a successor. Barnes himself had hoped that Gore, who had just resigned the see of Oxford, might succeed him and was in touch with Gore about it. Archbishop Davidson also favoured this suggestion. Gore replied to Barnes that he had himself refused the Westminster canonry, as he wanted 'a year of perfect freedom'. He was at first doubtful whether he wanted any employment or whether he would be welcome to the Benchers; but he wrote again a few days later to say that if they were prepared to have him he would probably accept. Some Benchers were in fact in favour, but others apparently preferred an unidentified Canon B. In the end, the Prime Minister took neither but went his own way. Draper was essentially a littérateur, who had specialized in hymn-writing and translations from the Latin; he had lost three sons in the war. It was soon agreed between them that Barnes would continue to hold the Mastership and do the work at the Temple until early in the New Year. Barnes preached his last sermon at the Temple on 25 January 1920, and the family finally moved to Westminster.

His family life had not stood still meanwhile. His brother Alfred had died of cancer in July 1916, at the early age of thirty-seven and after a successful start to a Civil Service career. On 22 June 1917, Barnes's own first son was born and christened John by his father in the Temple Church on 29 July, at a service for which Walford Davies composed a special anthem, 'The Token of the Cross'. On 7 July, only a fortnight after the baby's birth, there was a daylight air-raid on the City of London. Barnes, who was out, rushed home and carried his wife and young son down to the safety of the cellar. On reaching his house he found the door jammed by the *Manchester Guardian* and, pushing at it in urgent impatience, swore never to read that newspaper again, a vow he did not keep. But after this he decided to remove them to the greater safety of Redhill in Surrey, where mother and child lived at Kirkgate House for several months, Barnes joining them when he could and otherwise fending for himself in London. His affection for his family was also revealed in a sermon on the League of Nations next year at St Martin-in-the-Fields, which he marked 'popular', and this may account for a choice of vocabulary unusual for him:

> At home I have a small toddler sixteen months old, just beginning to walk and talk. You can imagine what a jolly little beggar he is. I don't want him to be smashed by some high explosive shell in years to come.

It must be added that in a book review of November 1919, criticizing the sanguine optimism of an Inspector of Schools about human nature, he wrote:

> Inside ourself is a capacity for growth, but the devil is there too, has been from our earliest years. Mr Holmes must have 'inspected' thousands of school children; let him try the experiment of taking charge of a two-year-old boy for an hour. He might begin to doubt whether 'the limitlessness of the child's unrealised reserves of capacity' coincided with 'the general orientation of his nature towards good'.

In April 1919, a second son was born to them, occasioning the headline in the *Star*: 'Two Babies in the Temple: Another Little Prattler in the Master's House.' The paper pointed out that this was 'a state of things which has not existed since the latter days of the seventeenth century, when Dr William Sherlock, D.D., was Master'. The new baby was christened William, but not after Sherlock. The press report, incidentally, produced an agreeable letter from a labourer in the Victoria Docks, who said he was Sherlock's eldest lineal descendant and enclosed an impression of the seal, still in his possession, of 'Sherlock's father, Thomas', who had been Bishop of London. In fact, however, to judge from the *Dictionary of National Biography*, William, who was Master of the Temple 1685–1704, was a generation older than Thomas, Bishop of London 1748–61.

Married life and contact with the wider world had indeed released new springs within Barnes and given him greater presence and authority. Above all, he was happy and his happiness showed. Benson noted at the end of 1916 that he looked more robust and thought him 'in a way a bigger man, with much sunshine and affection about him'; although Benson went on to wonder if this was not going to make him 'a bit tyrannical' and if he had not been more sympathetic when he suffered more, he concluded by saying that he was 'very nice, able, quick, amusing and obviously knew more of the world'.

116

Others were to find him 'a bit tyrannical' later on but to succumb to his charm as well.

Now the Temple years ended, years of fulfilment but also of promise. His wife always regarded them as the high point of Barnes's career. Some time afterwards, compiling one of her many albums of letters and cuttings, she drafted in pencil, literally on the back of an envelope, the following note, which was only found after her death:

If our boys, in days to come, turn over the pages of this book, they will find that I have included the following letters – a few that have survived from the last month of three eventful years – that they may see something of the variety of their Father's activities at that time. Men's minds were tense and alert. Looking back to those anxious days of the world's history, I sh^d. like to put on record for his children some hint of the impress which their Father made. A Preacher's fame is ephemeral; his wife however critical is perhaps not impartial: yet it w^d. be idle to pretend ignorance of the thrill, and the power, which then stirred heart and mind in the Temple Church.

In that Church and at that time, the realities of life were vital as to many they had never been before. War – red and ruthless – was with us – crude and hideous for all the sacrifice that lay behind. No platitudes would serve for a congregation unknown to any other Church: ecclesiasticism was worthless at a moment when emotion and passion and sorrow and hate were bare before heart and eyes. To many your Father spoke at a moment when such blinding realities came crushing on them – men & women w^d. write, or w^d. come to have interpreted for them the meaning of the tragedy of pain or grief: young & old could stand no bargaining with truth: superficialities w^d. not serve. Toby's godfather [Walford Davies] gave us a friendship which grew out of the work and the intercourse between him and your Father – together they 'arranged' the services, sometimes almost at a moment's notice, so that words & music & hymns & silences should all carry the same thought or prayer. I do not think anyone who shared in the intimacies of that Church can ever have had a similar experience of worship. I wish you c^d. have known it: it was not sentimental: but it was an appeal – & an appeal which did not fail – to the minds & hearts of men & women. It wasn't sentimental – it just happened to be beautiful because it meant so much & was so real & because the two men who led it seemed especially inspired. I wish I c^d. give you any idea of the strain and the interest of those Sundays. I wish too that I c^d. describe to you the Temple Church – you can go & see it, of course, & remember that you were both christened at the font in the Round – & you can attend a service but you can't (and I may thank God for it) know what the Church stood for in the war years to those of us in whom it has left its mark for as long as we live.

Of course I had often been there in my early days (during Canon Ainger's Mastership) but when I went there to be introduced to the Benchers & their wives as the future wife of their new Master, I can't tell you how shy I was. That day I sat (the only time I think) in the Benchers' seats on the 'Middle' side (North) & the Master preached. I can't tell you now what the Sermon was about, but I can see him looking so 'young' & yet always so exactly suitable in the high pulpit – & I have an absurdly vivid impression of the lights in the Church shining on the white of his ample surplice & the scarlet splash of his Dr's hood.

Afterwards came the first lunch with the 'Middle' & I didn't realise (luckily) at the time that specially many 'wives' had come in order to inspect me! But I remember very clearly my sense of inadequacy & perhaps even more the inadequacy of my frock, which my 'Master' w^d. not let me say.

It was all so strange – & looking back to that first day, it is difficult to believe how soon the Sunday services became a possession of one's being.

CHAPTER IV

WESTMINSTER
1920-1924

Controversial Canon

Barnes must have known that, in going to Westminster with the evident interest of Buckingham Palace and with Davidson's encouragement to widen his influence ringing in his ears, he was bound sooner or later to be offered a Bishopric. Of the major intellectual influences in the Church of England at the time, Gore and Henson had both gone to the episcopal bench from Westminster canonries and William Temple was shortly to follow in their footsteps. It may well have been this prospect which made Barnes hesitate. Not only was he happy and successful at the Temple, comfortably lodged among an agreeable and appreciative congregation who gave him plenty of intellectual stimulus. The move to Westminster would inevitably bring him closer to the centre of the life and organization of the Church. Undoubtedly he wanted his teaching to make as wide an impact as possible and he must have realised the opportunities which the Westminster pulpit and eventual episcopal office would give him to that end.

But he had already given ample evidence of his mistrust for ecclesiastical officialdom and of his belief that, in Church as in State, power corrupts. He wanted his message to go out loud and clear, not blurred by the background noises of Church politics. Over and above these factors, he remained at heart a scholar, who wanted beyond everything else to seek truth and ensue it. This he had been able to do to his own and others' satisfaction from his study and pulpit at the Temple. Could he continue to do so at Westminster or would he there, and still more in a diocese, become enmeshed in the toils of bureaucracy and administration? It would be wrong to suggest that he preferred to be a single star at the Temple rather than to shine amid a galaxy of talent at Westminster. But it is true that he was by nature a loner. Wordsworth called Newton 'a mind, for ever voyaging through strange seas of thought, alone'. Barnes's candle glowed in the light of Newton's lamp. Just as he was a puritan without being a Puritan, so throughout his life he remained non-conformist, even though he had long since ceased to be a Non-conformist. He preferred to commune with his own soul and then, when he had chosen his path, to follow it according to the light of his own nature. He had none of the instincts or skills of the politician, whose base of action and power is the group and who seeks to achieve the highest common measure of agreement within the group, making any necessary compromises in the process.

For all these reasons, he may have hoped, with half his heart, that the cup would be taken from him. As late as 1923, he was telling Benson that he would not dream of taking a bishopric. But with the other half, he must have realised the prospect before him or, as he might well have put it to himself, the will of God. *Magna est veritas et praevalet.* He wanted desperately that truth should prevail, and he undoubtedly also wanted, and felt himself bound, to be one of the instruments by which it would prevail. To his mind, moreover, truth was not stationary. It walked hand in hand with progress. Seekers after truth must broaden their horizons, making sure that they surveyed the whole landscape and not merely its narrower confines, and they must constantly be seeking for new ways forward, if necessary hacking away the undergrowth of ignorance, fear and suspicion. The highway led forward. He could not rest on the laurels of the Temple. If he was to teach, preach and lead, he must widen his way ahead.

Here lay the prospect at Westminster. When Barnes went there, the Abbey was, perhaps more than ever before or since, the parish-church of the Empire. This of itself appealed to the traditionalist in him and he came to love the building and its associations, historical and continuing. But England, to which his patriotism was deeply attached, stood at a cross-roads of its history. The Empire had lost a million dead. But the 'war to end wars' was over. England was supposed to be 'a land fit for heroes to live in'. London was still the capital of 'the Empire on which the sun never sets'. It should have been a time of unparalleled self-confidence, with Englishmen flocking to church to thank God that they were 'not as other men are'.

And yet? In fact, this was not the spirit of the age, neither in the nation, nor in the Church. Barnes had been right in foretelling a time of restless disillusionment. The British people had lost their way. They had won the war, or so they were told. The House of Commons was full of 'hard-faced men who looked as if they had done well out of the war'. But already Britain seemed to be on the way to losing the peace. 'Squeezing Germany until the pips squeaked' may have sounded good in newspaper headlines at the breakfast table, but it did not seem to be bringing home the bacon. At home there were economic troubles and industrial unrest. The social hierarchy and class structure which had been taken for granted before the war were falling to pieces. Abroad there was continued conflict in the Ruhr, in the Near East and in Russia. America without Woodrow Wilson seemed to be turning away from the Europe which she had helped to save, but making sure that she filled her money-bags on the turn.

If in these circumstances the political formulae failed to satisfy, religious creeds seemed to many to be sheer escapism. Biblical legends not only had no practical value. To many they were simply untrue and life could not be built on a lie. To such minds the teaching of the Christian Churches had been put together by a narrow sacerdotal sect of mutually-admiring believers. If the nation was losing its courage, the Church was losing its faith. Or rather, the Church was turning in on itself and the nation was losing its faith in the Church.

To one of Barnes's temperament and convictions, here was the challenge. The younger generation, above all, men and women alike, many of them newly-enfranchised, had to be brought back to the Christian way, so that they might again infuse the nation with the Christian spirit. To that end, they must be told the truth, but told it in a form which they could both understand and accept. Never would Barnes have said, with Henri Quatre, that 'Paris vaut la messe'. Far from it. But he did hold, with all the strength of his being, that England deserved a national Church which would inspire her with the united Christian ideals of goodness, beauty and truth. He believed that he could be of service in that cause. So he took up the challenge.

121

He was again warmly welcomed at Westminster. His new colleagues formed a distinguished body of men. The Dean, Herbert Ryle, had in younger days been a learned Old Testament scholar; but, after a difficult episcopate at Winchester, his health had given way and he had retired to the comparative calm of the Abbey. But he remained a figure of dignity and charm, as was seen in his letter of welcome to Barnes, in which, echoing Davidson, he perceptively wrote:

> You will find the congregation more mixed, less well-to-do, more cosmopolitan in all probability, than at the Temple. But it is a worthy and uplifting opportunity for anyone who has a spiritual message.

Although they did not always agree, he was a source of wise advice to his younger colleague over the next few years and Barnes always called him 'an exceptionally good Dean'. The Sub-Dean was Carnegie, who had married Joseph Chamberlain's widow; but he belonged to an older generation and does not seem to have made any marked impression on his own. Archdeacon Charles, on the other hand, who was to be Barnes's neighbour and close ally on the Chapter, was possessed of immense energy and erudition, and Barnes looked up to him as 'the greatest living authority on Jewish and Christian Apocalyptic literature'. Here was a man after his own heart. Canon de Candole, who became Dean of Bristol, was more of an administrator than a scholar. But William Temple, who was to overlap with Barnes for a few months, was both in preeminent degree. He was a subtle philosopher, in later life perhaps too subtle; but no ivory tower for him. Coming to Westminster after spells as headmaster of Repton and rector of St James's, Piccadilly, he had virtually single-handed, through his editorship of the *Challenge* and his dominance of the Life and Liberty Movement, wrested self-government for the Church from Parliament and was to go on, as Bishop and Archbishop, to wear himself out in the struggle to bring Church and State into harmony. Barnes's own predecessor, Boyd-Carpenter, had been another retired Bishop from an older generation; but as Bishop of Ripon for nearly thirty years he had done much to support liberal movements in the Church and indeed had founded what was to become Ripon Hall, the Modernist theological college at Oxford which loomed large in Barnes's own later life. Finally, the Chapter was about to be completed, on the preferment

of Ernest Pearce to the see of Worcester, by the appointment of
Vernon Storr, the acknowledged intellectual leader of the Liberal
Evangelicals, who, unlike Barnes, decided to stay at Westminster
rather than accept any of the episcopal posts offered to him.

Though appointed to succeed Boyd-Carpenter, Barnes did not
follow him in his Dean's Yard house. He wanted a garden where his
children could play and chose to take over from Pearce at 3, Little
Cloisters. Little Cloisters, with its enclosed garden and central
fountain, is an oasis of peace at the heart of London. No. 3, with a
noble front-door, stood on the site of the old infirmary of the Abbey
and its garden lay where had been the infirmary chapel of St Catherine,
with the filled-in arches of the chapel as its boundary-wall and the
altar-step still rising in the middle of the lawn. The house itself was of
seventeenth-century red brick with white stone facings; but the
breakfast-room floor could be lifted to reveal the bases of Norman
pillars below. Though not unique as the Master's House at the
Temple had been, it had the quiet charm and dignity of the Abbey
precincts, while Big Ben chiming and striking overhead was a constant reminder of the great world on the doorstep. By a malign fate,
this house too was to be destroyed by bombs in the Second World
War.

He did not find his new work altogether congenial. Writing to a
friend who was having similar problems of adjustment years later,
he said:

> When I went to the Abbey I found it not easy to work with the Cathedral
> Chapter after having lived in a College society. I believe it to be essential
> to allow outside interests to absorb all one's emotional energy and
> largely to ignore the causes of friction which arise inside a Chapter. At
> the beginning one has to force oneself to pursue such a policy, and
> there are times when it seems second-best or even cowardly. In the end
> its wisdom becomes apparent if in working at outside things one
> spreads either Christian truth or Christian idealism. I fear that all these
> remarks sound like a sermon: they are, in fact, the outcome of ex-
> perience.

Accordingly, during his years at Westminster Barnes continued to
concern himself actively with political as well as theological problems.
In October 1919, for example, together with Gore and Temple, he
wrote a letter to the press, in which they urged a settlement, on the
basis of an adequate minimum wage, to avert the threatened railway

strike. This was an interesting triumvirate. Barnes and Temple were of the same generation and, at this stage of their lives, found themselves in broad agreement on the liberal side of political and ecclesiastical problems alike, although, in Barnes's eyes, Temple, like others of their colleagues, was to grow more conservative in Church matters as time went by. Significantly, Temple and Henson, the two men in whom this drift to the right of the theological spectrum was most marked, had both felt the whip of the heresy-hunter early on: Temple when the Bishop of Oxford had at first refused to ordain him and Henson in the outcry when he was nominated to the see of Hereford; perhaps, once bitten, they were both twice shy. Even Gore, though a much older man with his career now largely behind him, knew what it was to be suspected of unorthodoxy. Writing in *Lux Mundi*, which he edited in 1889, he had refused to accept the historicity of the Old Testament and asserted that Christ's references to it reflected the ignorance of His age and were thus humanly fallible. This had brought down on his head the horrified reproaches of Liddon and caused a London hostess to describe him as 'that awful Mr Gore, who doesn't believe the Bible'. He did believe strongly in the power of human reason, saw both history and science as necessary approaches to religion and rejected the verbal inspiration of the Bible. While putting great emphasis on the need for truth, he also insisted on the ethical path to faith. In all this, as in his social and international sympathies, he and Barnes were largely of one mind. Barnes used to say of Gore that he was typical of his day in needing to attach himself to a cause and that he found that cause in social justice. Gore and Barnes shared Arthur Benson's view of Englishmen of their generation: 'We are impatient, restless, unsatisfied; we cannot be happy unless we have a definite end in view.' Gore was also a scholar at heart, and in this too Barnes felt a ready affinity for him; moreover, he was a natural aristocrat and treated other scholars and colleagues with all the courtesy of his background and generation. His letters to Barnes are models of graceful consideration and Barnes repaid the compliment: during the heresy-hunt over Henson's appointment to Hereford, widely as they differed on the substance of the matter, Barnes paid public tribute to the personal generosity of Gore's attitude to Henson himself. But, despite all these grounds for sympathy, Barnes had to recognize that Gore was deeply Catholic in his theology and indeed the accepted intellectual leader of that party in the Church, much as he might disapprove of the antics of some of its younger members. Even while Gore vehemently asserted the right to freedom of speculation, his conclusions seemed increasingly to coincide with the traditional answers. The protest against his own consecration, which had been taken to the High Court in 1902, was directed at too much rather than too little orthodoxy. When he did become a bishop, he was to persuade one Birmingham vicar to resign for preaching sermons which impugned the validity of certain miracles. Gore's whole conception of the Church's structure, sustained by the rigid pillars of creeds, sacraments and priesthood, was totally different from Barnes's own; and Barnes's later experience was to make him more conscious of the differences than the affinities. Even so, for many years and in many utterances, he often seems to be conducting an unspoken dialogue with Gore; and as late as 1931, he sent an indirect message to Gore that 'the more he preaches in Birmingham the better shall I be pleased'.

Ironically enough, there were to be few people in the Church of England of the second quarter of the twentieth century who championed progressive causes in both Church and State. Those who devoted themselves most actively to the welfare of the poor and needy, like Gore himself or Dolling, for example, tended to be High Churchmen, partly from conviction and partly perhaps because they realised the attractions of ritual in brightening the drabness of slum parishes in days of poverty and depression. Barnes's own allies and supporters in what came to be known as the Modernist party, on the other hand, were almost all staunch conservatives in politics. Typical examples can be found in Inge, who wrote for the Beaverbrook press and kept in touch with the ex-Kaiser, or H. D. A. Major, as Editor of the *Modern Churchman* the chief publicist of Modernism, who stood well to the political right, or Foakes-Jackson who, while a radical in biblical criticism, could say 'I hate Labour' and write from America of 'so hypocritical a scoundrel as this verminous Wilson'. Apart from Barnes himself, only a handful of men, such as Charles Raven, Dick Sheppard or Hewlett Johnson, were to be found on both the political and theological barricades to the left of the street. Even of these, some were moved more by generous enthusiasm than by intellectual analysis.

But all that was to come. It was in an exclusively theological controversy that Barnes now first attracted wide public attention, as a result of what came to be known as his 'monkey sermons'. On 29

August 1920, he preached to members of the British Association for the Advancement of Science in Cardiff Parish Church a sermon with the title 'The Christian Revelation and Scientific Progress'. In it he said nothing which he had not said, or at least implied, in many previous sermons. It was entirely consistent with all the previous cast of his thought. As always, it is hard, if not impossible, adequately to summarize a closely-knit argument. But, in brief, he started from the standpoint that, just as the Copernican and Galilean theories of the heliocentric universe had come to be accepted centuries before, so now the Darwinian theory of evolution as the origin of man was also accepted as truth. He summarized the evolutionary theory in sentences which are all familiar from his previous utterances:

From some fundamental stuff in the universe the electrons arose. From them came matter. From matter life emerged. From life came mind. From mind spiritual consciousness is developing.

The Darwinian theory not only showed that the book of Genesis was not literally history. It also had theological consequences. 'Our forefathers saw that acceptance of it meant the abandonment of the story of Adam; it meant giving up belief in the Fall and in all the theology built upon it by theologians from St Paul onwards.' Thus it did not help just to say that the story was an allegory. Spiritual as well as historical truth was involved. But neither the Old Testament nor necessarily all the New Testament reflected Christ's teaching. 'Christianity does not consist of belief in the scientific value of Genesis or even of belief in the infallibility of St Paul.' But this meant facing up to the implications. 'Can we accept the idea that man and the gorilla have sprung from a common stock and yet hold that man has an immortal soul? I answer emphatically that we can.' Evolution showed that God was working his purpose out and the spiritual consciousness of humanity was the crown of the process.

Science describes the process by which man has come into being. Religion takes man as he is and offers him guidance towards his spiritual destiny . . . Evolution describes facts; the ultimate meaning of those facts Christ's teaching discloses.

At this distance of time it is not easy to understand the furore which this sermon created. The language is striking and even chal-

126

lenging in places. But the basic ideas were far from revolutionary. Indeed, there were people who said that he was tilting at windmills or flogging a dead horse. But if the ideas which he expressed had already been universally accepted, there would not have been the outcry which there was. Some of it of course came from fundamentalists who still believed in the literal inspiration of every word of the Bible as historical truth. But on the whole, although the school represented by William Jennings Bryan was still numerous in America, they were already comparatively few and far between in England. In the reaction to Barnes's sermon, apart from some Roman Catholic commentators, General Bramwell Booth of the Salvation Army was virtually the only prominent person to defend the fundamentalist thesis. Barnes's critics in the main fastened not so much on the question whether evolution was true or not. More important was the corollary. The sentence which, above all, stuck in their throats was that in which he asserted that the theology of the Fall of Man must be abandoned. As they saw it, God had made man innocent; man himself had turned to sin, either by his own inclination or by the agency of the Devil, and had bequeathed sin to all the human race; all men were therefore now born to original sin; man was thus in basic opposition to God; and the Atonement had accordingly been necessary, if man was to be freed from sin and admitted to eternal life. This, grossly oversimplified, was the core of the traditional doctrine, which, as Barnes pointed out, rested on only two passages in the New Testament, both from St Paul's letters: I Corinthians xv, 22 and Romans v, 12 *et seq*. It had led to a variety of theories of the Atonement, mostly mechanistic, such as the idea that Christ needed by his sacrifice of himself to buy back men's souls from the Devil or to appease God's wrath at sinful men. These were in effect theories of Vicarious Atonement, with salvation depending on a supposed action in the past rather than on man's own continuing efforts in the present. The doctrine had also led to a mechanistic belief in the efficacy of the Eucharist as a repetition of Christ's sacrifice and thus a material channel of grace and salvation.

Barnes had not explicitly attacked any of these beliefs. Nor did his critics spell them out in reply. He had been concerned to show that acceptance of the theory of evolution and its implications in no way detracted from Christ's revelation of God and indeed made it easier to accept that 'because of the soul within him, man, as Jesus taught, is meant to be the child of God'. His critics focused on the accusation that a dignitary of the Church was basing his faith in the goodness of God, not on the Book of Genesis or the Epistles of St Paul, but on a scientific hypothesis, incapable of definite proof, elaborated less than a century before.

The spate of letters and articles in the press was such that Barnes decided to try again to explain his position in another sermon at Westminster Abbey the next Sunday, 5 September, with the specific title this time of 'Evolution and the Fall'. In this he made clear that he was anxious to arrest the drift from the churches; that he was convinced that much of this had come about because Christian teaching was linked to incredible stories; and that he had been asked, particularly by younger educated people, to make known that those stories were not essential elements of Christian belief. He reminded his hearers that 'in a sermon published about 1894, Bishop Gore indicated clearly that there was no inherent opposition between Darwin's biological views and the Christian faith'. This critical attitude was another position which he shared with Gore. But he did not rely only on such authority, useful though it was as a debating point. He again, on his own authority, called for open-minded acceptance of 'the new knowledge'. Otherwise 'the closed mind will lead, sooner or later, to the closed church'. He dismissed the idea, which he attributed to the Roman Catholic Modernism condemned by Pius X, that 'a man might accept facts which he knew to be untrue because they had a value for faith'. Truth could not be a compromise. But in any case he saw no value for faith in the story of the Fall. It was an attempt to explain the baffling problem of the origin of sin. But there was no need of such a story to convince people, especially after the war, that sin was real and regeneration needed. Man certainly had animal passions, derived, although Barnes did not actually say so on this occasion, from his evolutionary background. But he also had a Divine Spirit within him. When man sinned, he needed salvation and could find it through Christ, who had through his suffering on the Cross shown the power of the love of God, 'the great guiding principle of the spiritual evolution of humanity'. In other words, man was not naturally in opposition to God; he had the choice between falling into sin or aligning himself with God's purpose for good. As Barnes explained in an article which he wrote a fortnight later for the *Manchester Guardian*, he had found that many people believed that, unless 'the Fall' had occurred, there would have been no sin in the world and thus no

Above
E.W.B.'s mother
Above right
E.W.B.'s father

Going up to Cambridge, 1892

Fellow of Trinity

At the Master's House, The Temple

need for redemption by Christ. The Genesis story was to the effect that there had been a separate creation of perfect man and as a result of that man's 'fall', sin, sex and death had come into being. By this reasoning, sex was essentially sin. But for Barnes, sin was a reality whether there had been a 'fall' or not. Instincts existed in man as a legacy from his evolutionary ancestors. Sex was one of these instincts and, like the rest, could be used for good or ill. Human instincts contained the potential of sin. But sin could be overcome, and only overcome, by man exercising his sense of right and wrong and, in suffering and struggling, making use of the aid of the in-dwelling spirit of God. The example of Christ, living, suffering and risen, and His legacy of the spirit were thus the means of redemption for man. But the triumph of evil in this world was so great and so frequent that the process of man's redemption could only be finally completed in the immortal life of the world to come. As always, then, Barnes was wrestling with the unsolved problem of evil, which he admitted that man could never fully understand. As always, too, he was at pains to convince the critically-minded. This, for example, was one reason why he did not even want to treat the Fall as an allegory, for, as he said,

> Youth in its arrogance tends to regard an allegory as an ecclesiastical synonym for a falsehood which it is inexpedient to deny. Great care must be taken not to offend our younger people by ignoring their demand for absolute straightforwardness.

But in any case he would have rejected the allegorical approach since, as the doctrines of the Fall and redemption were intimately linked, it would not be acceptable for any Christian to regard redemption through Christ as merely allegorical.

Comment was by no means all hostile. The Church papers naturally wrote according to their own or their readers' predilections. *The Times* and the *Daily News* called the first sermon courageous and the *Daily Telegraph* described it as 'a bold and striking declaration of faith in man's reason'. But all three papers recognized in leading articles that Barnes was treading on sore toes. *The Times*, in particular, said that the sermon 'might have led him to the stake not so many generations ago and even today it may bring him into conflict with some sections of clerical opinion'. The *Daily News* started what it called a symposium on the subject. This drew some criticism, some of it oblique like the contribution from William Cecil, Bishop of Exeter, to the effect that the story of the Fall was a helpful parable, but it also showed a wide measure of agreement, even among Anglo-Catholics like Evelyn Underhill.

The two sermons let loose a flood of correspondence. Letters poured in from friends, acquaintances and the public. Barnes's parents both showed some concern for him personally. In one of his rare letters, Starkie Barnes wrote:

> You are quite right in contending for the truth, which is, as you say in religion, vital. My only fear is that you may become worried with the adverse criticisms you are sure to meet and be made ill, as a consequence. I have faith in whatever you may say, as you are a profound thinker and most careful investigator, with the most splendid education and brain-power of the highest order. Who, if not you, is fit for these things? But I do hope you and your dear wife will not be unnecessarily troubled about the 'knocks' you are sure to get through the attempt to root up prejudices that are intertwined with the lives of millions of people and with their ancestors for generations before.

His mother's letter was on similar lines:

> I am afraid you may find the strain of all this controversy very severe. The best advice I can give you is just to deliver your message, leave the results with God, and whenever you can, just get away from it all, and have a romp with John and Toby. You will encounter a lot of opposition, some of it very bitter, but in the end truth will prevail, and right be vindicated . . . The trouble is that there are so many unthinking people, good people too, who accept their fathers' faith, and think any departure from it is very wicked, and one has to deal tenderly and sympathetically with them.

Barnes's own comments are contained in letters to his wife who was staying with her parents at Cambridge:

> August 29th: This is just a scrawl to say that all has gone well. The Lord Mayor, Professors, Secretaries of the Brit Ass &c turned up this morning – & so impressed were the secretaries that they paid me a state visit here at 3 p.m. to ask that the sermon might appear in *Nature*! Fancy *Nature* with a sermon. You said it was short: I preached for 34 minutes. This afternoon's sermon went well – 23 minutes. Now I am slack . . .

August 30th: . . . the pleasure of being told in a *Times* leader that I should have been burnt a few generations ago . . . the two S. Wales local papers tried to summarize the sermon itself with disastrous results.

August 31st: A letter to the Times to answer Gen. B. B. [Bramwell Booth]; an interview with a reporter of the Daily News (they had a leader on the bold & brave Canon today); an article for the Evening Standard tomorrow – such are my activities . . . I'm just done. But a quiet day tomorrow & a letter from my love will put all right.

September 2nd: This letter must be pure brief egotism . . . Yesterday I had a visit from Bruce R[ichmond]. Could I see the Editor of the *Times* today? Yes. He came at 3.45. Would I before mid-October write 4 or 5 articles for the Times – to be starred like the present Tsar articles! – on religion. 'You have complete freedom to state your views. Preach if you like.' There – the clever E. said that he would think about it. What do you say? The Evening Standard sent me £6. 6. & *mirabile dictu* brought 2 favourable letters. N.B. Don't waste that £6. 6. The Weekly Dispatch want an article for Sunday. I said No but perhaps I ought to do it: it w^d. be a sermon. My B.A. sermon is to be cabled to America! 'Will I promise not to give an interview or authorization for its use before it appears?' . . . Both Steed & Bruce R said that the B-B letter in the Times was 'a masterpiece'. I try to keep humble & to remember to preach the Gospel through all this flurry.

September 5th. The sermon is over and I have been to tea with the Charles's. Your letter came too late. It seemed to me that I must discuss the controversy & so I did so – not disappointing a crowded congregation. I hope that I said nothing wrong: you shall judge. Now I will be silent. Don't let this thing make you ill. I know that the newspapers cheapen the message & I have been right to stick to my guns. What you do not realise is that abuse or small errors on my part are forgotten within a week. Modern publicity is distasteful but the truth survives & slowly makes headway. So long as we are happy together & so long as the big things are right the rest does not matter.

September 7th: The deluge instead of getting better gets worse. I have already used £1 in stamps & *all* the single sheets of notepaper. And still they come by every post, mad, bitter, humorous or friendly . . . Why why why does this fever of yours not go? . . . I don't like its persistence. Are you really not worrying about our monkey ancestors?

September 8th: At length the deluge shows signs of stopping. I enclose the cream of today's epistles . . . Much love to kiddies & their mummy. Tell J. B. not to grow up a heretic or they will say hard things of him.

September 9th: The deluge is subsiding . . . The Record is adverse: I am thinking of writing a sort of letter-article for them. The Church Times I will not get or look at: it's sure to be unChristian. The weekly M. G. hits a R. C. correspondent the thwack precisely needed.

September 11th: Hasn't the Times billed us large today? . . . The deluge continues. Lord Kinnaird adverse & Lady Leconfield favourable to put the peerage first. Also the M. G. want a 1000 words by Tuesday aft^n. (a telegram this morning) reviewing the flurry. Knowing your affection for it & Scott I said 'Yes'.

In short, Barnes had in a couple of weeks become a national figure and was rather enjoying it. At least he kept his sense of humour. The relationship between science and religion was henceforth to be regarded as his special subject and he was to be bombarded with requests from newspapers and others to write or speak on it. An early opportunity to do so came at the annual Congress of the Church of England at Southend on 22 October, where he seems from press reports to have attracted a larger audience than usual at those meetings. Here again he drew headlines in the national newspapers by stating, first, that man was not specially created by God but was 'the end of a vast evolutionary process of Divine design' and, secondly, that 'man must be viewed, not as a once innocent being now marred, but as struggling to realise the divinely appointed end of the whole terrestrial process'. These formulations were no doubt designed for specialist churchmen and it must be questionable how far they helped, in this form, to bring even educated younger people back into church. Early in 1921 he went into the question in more detail in a series of five sermons in the Abbey on Evolution and Christian Belief, and evolution remained a constant theme in his preaching and writing. At any rate from now on he was assured of a wide audience for almost anything he cared to say.

Inevitably, therefore, he was now forced to consider more exactly where he stood in the spectrum of churchmanship. He had long recognized that the Church of England contained three schools of thought, the High, the Broad and the Evangelical, and he wanted to see it capable of comprehending all three. While this of itself would incline him to the Broad Church and he was certainly never a fundamentalist, he would probably have called himself for some time past an Evangelical, at least in the literal sense of one who based his reading and his teaching on the Gospels. But he had no hostility to Modernism, except in the form in which it had shown itself in the Roman Catholic Church. Indeed, already in 1914 he had preached at Ripon at the annual conference of the Churchmen's Union, as the Modern Churchmen's Union was then called. But although he took Liberal Churchmanship as his theme, he emphasized that he was not a member of the Union himself. When he preached again to the Union at their conference at Girton College, Cambridge, in 1921, he again affirmed:

> I am an Evangelical; I cannot call myself a Modernist . . . Probably all who have been present would wish to assert that they also are Evangelicals, firmly convinced that the Gospel of Jesus is the religious message of God to man. Yet one or two, in discussing subjects where language cannot adequately express feeling, have seemed to doubt whether the Jesus of history was the unique Person in whom St Paul and St John saw the Only-begotten Son. I weigh, and without prejudice I trust, all that they have said. In the end I feel no hesitation in affirming that Jesus rose from the dead to become the living Christ, one with the Holy Spirit . . . Let us not disguise the fact that there is an element of danger in such public debates as those of the past week . . . I have . . . studied with care reports of the conference which have appeared in certain important newspapers. There has been no intentional misrepresentation; but an unreflective reader might, from some journals, easily get a wrong impression of the balance of opinion among you. It can be confidently affirmed that restatement of the Christian faiths, and not rejection of Christian fundamentals, has been the object – the successful object – of your conference.

This implied reproof was all the more justified because the conference itself led to a furore. Not only the more extreme papers read there but an editorial by Major, summing it up in the *Modern Churchman*, provoked a storm of criticism. Indeed, a London clergyman called C. E. Douglas actually brought a charge of heresy against Major for 'openly teaching doctrine concerning the Resurrection which is contrary to the Christian religion' and 'importing the teaching of a heathen mystic [Buddha] into the Christian religion'. There was a good deal of alarm lest the bishops should condemn the liberal school. Henson, who had warned the Modern Churchmen months before of the risks they ran, was afraid that this would happen. But, luckily for Major and his associates, the Bishop of Oxford, Burge, as required by law, since Major as Principal of Ripon Hall was under his jurisdiction, consulted four expert scholars to see if there was a *prima facie* case. They advised that there was not and the legal charge was dropped. Major himself had rather wanted to fight and had prepared a defence of 25,000 words. But Barnes, who had corresponded sympathetically with him, welcomed the outcome in a sermon at Westminster Abbey on 8 January 1922, and went on to deplore heresy-hunting in general.

During this time, he continued to describe himself as a Liberal Evangelical. When he spoke of the Modernists, he always described them in the third rather than the first person plural. The question of parties in the Church was coming to a head because of the pressure, led by Burge, for the appointment of a Commission to review and determine the doctrine of the Church. Barnes deprecated the idea, because he saw no need to limit the longstanding toleration of the English Church for freedom of belief and also because he realised that the Commission would have a majority of Anglo-Catholics, so that its conclusions would impose a new orthodoxy and increase the conflict within the Church. In the end, a Commission was appointed at the end of 1922, with limited terms of reference, and a rather unrepresentative membership, which Barnes criticized for excluding some of the best theologians in the Church; but as even then it did not report until 1938, when men had other things on their minds beside the doctrine of the Church, no great harm was done.

Meanwhile, however, Barnes was trying to establish the point that the conflict was no longer so much between Catholics and Protestants as between the traditionalist and modernist approaches. Catholics and Protestants alike were to be found on both sides and up to a point he could quote Gore as an example of a modernist Catholic. At the same time, he insisted that Modernism was not a new branch of the Church. It had originally been a term of abuse adopted by the traditionalists, after Modernism had been condemned by Pius X in his decree *Lamentabili* and his encyclical *Pascendi Gregis* of 1907. As late as May 1923, Barnes still described himself as a Liberal Evangelical. But he disliked all labels and would in any case have hesitated to adopt the label of 'Modernist' when he was still criticizing their cocksureness under the gentler name of 'pontifical serenity'.

But increasingly he is to be found defending Modernism, if not Modernists. To him, moreover, Modernism was by no means modern. Its essential approach was to interpret the Bible in the light of the latest knowledge. In this sense it went a long way back. In a course of lectures on 'The Spirit of Modernism' at the Abbey in March 1923, he gave four examples: Origen, who sought to reconcile the Christian faith with Greek philosophy early in the third century; Abelard, who in the eleventh century claimed the right to base faith on reason; Erasmus, who had a passion for learning and the moral temper from which the Reformation arose; and William Sanday, who had only died in 1920 and was taken as a typical example of present-day Modernism, having called for 'the fusion of all secular thinking and all religious thinking in one comprehensive and harmonious whole'. For, to Barnes, the essential principle of contemporary English modernism was that the theologians could not challenge the scientists and scholars on their own ground, while the scientists and scholars could not prescribe spiritual realities. At other times, he would cite the authority of Tertullian, who said that Christ called himself truth, not tradition; and to emphasize his ironical point that 'we are all Modernists now', he called Newman the parent of Catholic Modernism and Hort the father of English Modernism, with Rashdall as its greatest philosopher. To call Hort, whom he so much respected, a Modernist is in itself almost a tacit admission of allegiance to Modernism, even though he remained apprehensive of its excesses. In fact, he still preferred the term 'Modern Churchman' to 'Modernist'.

The three pictures which hung in Barnes's study through the years were portraits of Hort, Wesley and Erasmus. Not only were they models to follow. He certainly felt an affinity with all three. Hort was a Trinity man, who had moved on from a scientific discipline to the study of the Bible and theology. Wesley, whom he described as 'the greatest spiritual leader that the English race has thrown up', had known what it was to arouse acute controversy by his sermons. With Erasmus the parallels are even more striking. Erasmus was a Christian humanist, for whom the classical concept of *humanitas* went hand in hand with the Christian concept of *pietas*; Barnes too saw the fabric of learning and religion as a single weave. The three great motives in Erasmus's life, to reform the Church, to make reason prevail and to see peace on earth, operated strongly in Barnes too. Both saw themselves fighting against obscurantism, superstition and paganism in theology; against ritualism, worldliness and lack of common humanity in the Church; against financial abuses, physical cruelty and sexual licence in society. Both tried to recapture the spirit of the early Church. Both saw education as the key to progress. Both were in a way revolutionaries in their own times. Each was the herald of a Renaissance. One interviewer actually called Barnes 'the Erasmus of our day'.

Another subject which engaged Barnes's attention at this time was the whole new field of experimental psychology and psycho-analysis. He constantly inveighed against the closed mind and in this respect he practised what he preached. Not only was he receptive to new knowledge; he was constantly active in examining it, in meeting any challenge which it presented to existing beliefs and in synthesizing it into his own philosophy and theology. As he once put it, 'theologians must work towards a new *Summa*'. His theology was always a moral theology. He was concerned with the implications of theological study for human conduct. Great as was his concern for truth, he saw truth, beauty and goodness as a single integrated whole. Truth must lead to goodness and both must be seen to be beautiful. These convictions underlay his approach to evolution and the Fall of Man: his denial of false doctrine was not an intellectual exercise but a guide to right action. So too had been his earlier investigation of the claims of spiritualism as evidence of immortality and Christian Science as a sign of the power of mind over matter. So too now was his approach to experimental psychology and psycho-analysis. He realised that new theories of the mind were being put forward which, if accepted, could lead to a deterministic view of human conduct without free will and to a denial of the reality of either sin or spiritual grace. Without referring to Jung's archetypes as such, he also recognized that 'the past is embedded in the mental make-up of us all; old superstitions will spring to life if they get the chance'. The idea of a 'fall' and redemption, for example, seems to be an archetypal hero-myth familiar to the psychologists in their analysis of dreams, as indeed does the theme of a ritual initiation through communion with the god, with its connotations from the mystery-religions. But at the same time Barnes saw that these new theories of the mind could be significant not only for an understanding of Christ's miracles of healing but also for the contemporary possibilities of psychotherapy or faith-healing. In a course of four sermons at Westminster Abbey in June 1921, on 'Some Religious Aspects of Modern Psychology', and in subsequent articles, he set out some of his conclusions. Starting from a definition of modern psychology as the study of unconsciousness, he described in detail the theories of Freud, Jung and others about such things as hypnosis, suppression and repression, complexes and the subconscious 'censor'. He accepted many of these theories as valuable, although he was not prepared to agree with Freud's emphasis on sexual experiences as dominant factors in the sub-conscious. Not only did Barnes think that this emphasis belied the importance of experiences in childhood before the age of puberty; he also condemned as 'nauseous and demoralizing' the exaggerated use made of it by some of Freud's followers. On the contrary, he believed that the unconscious mind was the channel by which man could receive inspiration and make contact with God in a mystical sense. Faith was thus, in the language of the psychologists, a 'suggestion' which implanted itself in the unconscious mind and which could even be 'auto-suggestion' if the individual could attain the properly receptive state. This power of suggestion, coupled with the realisation that mental states could influence some bodily conditions, could well account for Christ's miracles of healing, which Barnes still accepted as fully attested by the Gospels, particularly St Mark's Gospel, and unaffected by any biblical criticism. This was for him essentially a religious process since Christ's spiritual perfection had had a supreme effect on other human beings. But in lesser degree modern man too might by religious experience cure certain bodily disorders. Confession indeed might be good not only for the soul but for the body too. But Barnes was careful not to be carried too far. He rejected any idea that disease was only due to spiritual defect; in effect, he still opposed the teaching of Christian Science. While he admitted that visits to popular shrines or ritual formulae might help cures by the process of suggestion, he denied that God could be localized or compelled to perform mechanical acts. He warned against false asceticism, monastic or otherwise, as an escape from mental troubles. 'Not the obliteration of human instincts which may lead to sin but their control should be our ideal.' Thus he put before his audience a lesson in which he welcomed the new knowledge of the unconscious mind but joined it with a positive belief in good and evil to show how man could, if he chose, receive inspiration from God and, by the exercise of free will, use it to direct his own existence towards perfection.

Two problems of ecclesiastical organization were also prominent in Barnes's mind during these years. The Lambeth Conference of 1920 had looked forward to reunion with the Free Churches and had even authorized Bishops to approve occasional sermons by Nonconformist preachers in Anglican churches. Barnes was keen to take practical steps to that end at once. He would have welcomed an interchange of pulpits with Nonconformists, urging that Westminster Abbey should set the pace by an invitation to Dr Clifford. For the Dean, however, it was a case of *festina lente*. Ryle pointed out that the detailed application of the Lambeth resolution had been left to the different Churches of the Anglican communion and, just because Westminster Abbey was such a focus of attention, it behoved the Chapter to advance with caution, certainly until the Archbishops or the Church Assembly had decided on a policy for the Church of England. Barnes remained impatient and this led to some friction for a time. But when in the autumn of 1921 he preached at the Mayflower Tercentenary Service, he succeeded in having representative Free Churchmen invited, as heirs to the Pilgrim Fathers, to take their places in the Abbey congregation. In fact, the Convocation of Canterbury did not reach an agreed formulation on this problem until 1943 and even then the decisions were largely left with individual bishops.

The other problem was Prayer Book reform. Barnes was anxious to see the liturgy purged of anything which reflected erroneous interpretations of the Bible or which failed to take account of new knowledge, such as the references to the connubial bliss of the Hebrew patriarchs in the Marriage Service or to original sin in the rite of Baptism. After Princess Mary's wedding in 1922, for example, he wrote in the press deploring some of the archaic language to which she had been subjected. At the same time he realised that, if the doors were opened to reform, the Anglo-Catholic majority could well succeed in introducing changes to the Holy Communion, which to his own mind would smack of pagan superstition and would drive the Church back into sacerdotalism and away from its appeal to contemporary thought. He was also, on different grounds, reluctant to see too much tampering with the Tudor language of the Psalms. His pronouncements on Prayer Book reform at this stage were therefore rather ambivalent. But the real struggle was yet to come.

Barnes continued to preach and teach on social as well as ecclesiastical matters. Much of his social teaching still reflected earlier preoccupations: the moral legacy of the war, in the shape of sexual licence, brutality and industrial strife, or the misuse of alcohol, on which he advocated local option, which might lead in different districts either to State ownership of public houses or even to Prohibition on the American model. But he was also concerning himself with new topics, such as prison reform, on which he spoke as a member of the Howard League, betting, a tax on which he opposed because it would imply legalization of gambling, and social misdemeanours like cheating on tax returns or railway fares. Increasingly, too, he was interesting himself in the whole complex of social questions connected with biology and eugenics: over-population, inheritance of defective characteristics, birth-control, divorce of incompatible couples, immigration and racial intermarriage. Many of these more secular subjects he handled mainly in newspaper articles rather than in sermons or addresses. He was now writing regularly in the popular as well as the Church papers and his output was prolific. Not only that; he was also constantly in demand for contributions to books of collected sermons or essays on related topics. While some of these demands could be met by existing texts, many of them called for new work. In 1923, for example, he published, as part of John Drinkwater's *Outline of Literature*, a longish study of 'The Story of the Bible', in which he brought together the results of historical criticism on the nature and compilation of the books of the Old and New Testaments and which attracted favourable reviews. He often used to bemoan his slowness in thinking and writing, but at this stage of his life at any rate he had little justification for such self-reproach.

His own political views were developing meanwhile. Although he had earlier entertained suspicions of the materialistic side of socialism and continued to exercise his mind over the contrast between egalitarian theories and Bolshevist tyranny in Russia, he was now beginning to speak and write of a natural alliance between the principles of socialism and Christianity, as earlier exemplified by Charles Kingsley and Frederick Denison Maurice. By June 1923, for example, he could write: 'By many of the clergy the international and social aspirations of Labour are warmly supported and their motions are not those of "court chaplains to King Demos"'. The reference was to one of Inge's satirical comments. Earlier in the same year he had looked forward in a sermon to the possible advent of a Labour Government, saying, 'When a Labour Government rules us, we need not be alarmed. It will bring neither chaos nor the millennium'. The prospect became reality in January 1924, and again he urged confidence:

I do not believe that the workers will misuse their powers. Political good sense is not limited to one class among us. The aspirations which make up Christian idealism are as strong in the workers and their leaders as in other sections of the community . . . It is folly to imagine that the advent of Labour to power will mean revolution. In all the great nations of the world there is none where the instinct for law and order is more firmly rooted than among ourselves.

He went on to say that people were making a mistake in selling British securities, because a country which had such fundamental unity as the British people possessed could rejoice in its democratic constitution and need not fear the consequence of political change. Stock Exchange tips from the pulpit are rare, but he had made his sympathies plain.

Nor did he neglect international affairs. The success of the League of Nations was still an objective to be ardently pursued. He still praised America's idealism, as in her aid to the Russian people, irrespective of their form of government, or in her policy of reconciliation in China. He looked for similar generosity from the British Government and people, both in their rule of their own empire and in their relations with foreign powers. He remained critical, for example, of what he saw as repression in Egypt and lack of political progress in India. He was, as before, ambivalent about Russia under communism, asserting somewhat prematurely that Bolshevism had failed and accusing Lenin of excessive reliance on force, but maintaining his hope that the future Russia could not fail to be a better place than the old empire of the Tsars. But his criticism was not reserved for communists. As early as 1922 he denounced Mussolini and Italian fascism for trusting in force rather than in liberty. But his bitterest denunciations were reserved for France and above all for her policy towards Germany. He saw her as preserving all the bitterness of wartime emotion in that attitude, particularly in her behaviour in the areas of Germany which she occupied. One aspect of French policy which aroused his sharpest indignation was the use of African troops in the Palatinate and the provision for them of brothels employing German women. This led him into generalizations about French culture as a whole. While he admitted the benefits which England had gained in such fields as art and literature from French influence, and while he singled out for special praise individual Frenchmen, such as Romain Rolland or, rather more faintly, Pascal, he asserted that from France, unlike Germany, we had received nothing of religious value. This he associated with the nature of French Catholicism and the support which it had given to misguided policies, as in the time of Napoleon III and now again after the war. Even Renan, who had broken with French Catholicism and been persecuted by it, was tainted by it in his description of Christ. Barnes's dislike of French Catholicism was typical of a growing aversion for Roman Catholicism as a whole. Not only did he object to what he saw as a magical and pagan sacramentalism derived from the Mediterranean mystery-religions; he also abhorred the frequent association of the Roman Church with authoritarian régimes and the propertied classes. He remained convinced of Acton's dictum about the corruption of power, and he pointed out that, whatever else Christ had taught about economics, He had certainly been hostile to wealth. Speaking of the emergence of Christianity as the official religion of Constantine's empire, he said on one occasion:

> Out of Christianity came the Catholic Church, the powerful heir of the Caesars, sheltering a host of pagan corruptions and moral evasions. With religion, nothing fails like success.

But his attacks on French policy were not based on religious or ecclesiastical prejudices alone. He feared that French policy in Germany, together with the economic collapse there to which it had partly contributed, was sowing the seeds of another war, which would engulf Europe in its ruin, and that, even without that, the economic collapse of Germany could not fail to be contagious for France and other European countries. Thanks largely to the weakness of the churches, Europe had simply failed to make any moral progress since the war. To some extent, of course, his attitude was dictated by his desire for reconciliation with Germany, and he leaned over backwards to do good for Germany and to see good in her. In this spirit, for example, he made an early plea for the return of German missionaries to their former fields of activity. But then, he had always had a deep and justified respect for German education and some aspects of German scholarship. This sometimes led him into strange paths, as when, in a sermon on the Varieties of European Christianity and their Origin, he drew a distinction between the Iberian strain, on the one hand, and, on the other, the Graeco-

141

Teutonic or Aryan strain in European religion. He even went so far as to assert that Anglo-Catholicism in England attracted the element in the British people of Iberian origin and that this could be seen in the physical characteristics of its adherents. But such racialism was rare on his lips; his usual preoccupation was to call on the British people to show both sympathy and generosity to others less fortunately placed than themselves and to remind them that this was their Christian duty. As he put it at the end of one sermon,

> You meet Smith daily in the train. If you talked to him of Christian idealism in international politics, he would laugh at you, regard you as a fool or a bore. So you would suffer for Christ. But your duty, as a Christian, is to convert Smith. That is how Christianity spreads.

Amid all these journeys in the world of ideas, he was also active in the practical affairs of the Abbey. There were many Royal and national occasions during his time there: the Burial of the Unknown Warrior, visits of foreign Heads of State to pay tribute to his grave, the weddings of Princess Mary to Lord Lascelles and the Duke of York to Lady Elizabeth Bowes-Lyon, funerals and memorial services for distinguished citizens, the annual services for the Order of the Bath and the distribution of the Royal Maundy. His interest in the Abbey buildings grew fast and he often lectured on them with slides in and outside London. The lecture remained much in demand and he was still delivering it as late as 1933. This indeed fell within his duties as Treasurer of the Abbey, for in that capacity he was busy with fund-raising for the Dean's Appeal for £250,000, of which £143,000 was raised in the first year. This appeal indeed involved Barnes in a slight passage at arms with the Palace. He had long advocated the use of what was then called the cinematograph as an adjunct to preaching, or even as a substitute for a sermon. Now, on the occasion of Princess Mary's wedding, he wanted to arrange for a film to be taken, not of the service itself but of the bridal party passing the Tomb of the Unknown Warrior on their way out of the Abbey; he saw that such a film could bring a substantial sum to the Abbey funds. But Sir Douglas Dawson replied from the Lord Chamberlain's office:

> With reference to cinematograph within the Abbey, I have already broached the subject, and that of photography, three times to the King. His Majesty is so emphatic as regards both subjects and has such an

objection to either within the interior of a church, that I really dare not raise the point again. It was only with great difficulty I got two photographers allowed, and I feel it would be quite useless to reopen the question of cinematograph.

Tempora mutantur.

One other semi-royal occasion was the Centenary debate at the Cambridge Union in November 1921. The Duke of York attended and spoke, and Barnes, as a tribute either to his former prowess at the Union or to his new-found notoriety, was invited to open the debate. He proposed the motion that 'the reaction from Victorianism is the curse of the age'. This certainly coincided with his own sentiments, but was probably not meant to be taken too seriously. From press reports it seems that he did just this and that his usual lightness of touch deserted him. In any event, the motion was lost by 119 votes to 380.

As Treasurer of the Abbey, Barnes found himself saddled with some unexpected tasks, such as negotiating with Sydney Nicholson, the rather temperamental organist, over the improvement of the musical side of the services. Here his collaboration with Walford Davies at the Temple stood him in good stead. On one occasion he had, rather apprehensively, to persuade Nicholson to allow Albert Schweitzer to play the organ on behalf of his mission at Lambarene. As Barnes described the occasion, he 'began, perhaps unwisely, by urging that Schweitzer was a good modernist, no less than a great missionary. His reply was characteristic: "I know nothing of his modernism, nor of his missionary work, but if he is the man who wrote on Bach he can play on the Abbey organ whenever he likes and as long as he likes." ' In the event, the Abbey was packed out, and thirty years later Schweitzer was to write Barnes a letter beginning '*Je ne vous oublie pas*'.

Luckily he had plenty of physical and nervous energy for this active life. He had long suffered from recurrent attacks of colitis, which gave him a good deal of pain, but with wise medical advice he and his wife were able to keep it under control. She herself, who had been suffering from a mysterious fever at the time of the monkey sermons, was found to have sinus trouble which could only be cured by an operation at the end of 1921; but this was successfully performed by Herbert Tilley, and for the rest of their time in London they both seem to have been in good health. But Barnes's father died in December 1922; he had just given up the last of the committees on which he still sat and both he and Barnes's mother seem to have recognized that his life's work was done and that a long period of inactivity in failing health would be unwelcome. A much bigger change in the family's life was precipitated by the death of the Master of Peterhouse in June 1924. Sir Adolphus had, despite his eighty-six years, remained astonishingly active and continued working and writing virtually to the end. His death meant that Peterhouse Lodge, where the Wards had lived for well-nigh a quarter of a century, had to be relinquished and its contents transferred elsewhere, while a new home had to be found for Lady Ward, who was also eighty-six years old and somewhat of an invalid. They had once bought another house in Cambridge for their retirement and rented it out meanwhile; but it was out of the question for Lady Ward to move into it alone now. Many of the Master's historical books could be and were given to the College, where they form the Ward Library; but hundreds of other books and a good deal of furniture remained.

This would have been a problem on its own. But fate, in the person of the Prime Minister, now intervened with the offer to Barnes of the Bishopric of Birmingham in July 1924. It was Ramsay MacDonald's first episcopal appointment, and he wrote on 18 July:

Dear Canon Barnes

The See of Birmingham is vacant owing to the resignation of Dr Wakefield. It is my duty to submit to His Majesty the name of a successor and, after the most careful consideration, I have come to the conclusion that I cannot better serve the interests of the Church than by offering to you the succession to this important See. On hearing from you that you would be willing to accept this offer I shall be happy to submit your name to the King.

Until His Majesty's approval has been obtained, I have to ask you to treat this offer as conditional.

I am,
Yours very faithfully,
J. RAMSAY MACDONALD

Barnes was not MacDonald's first choice. Prime Ministers are bombarded with suggestions for ecclesiastical appointments and this was inevitably more the case than ever with the first Labour Prime Minister's first bishop. There were said to be five hundred socialist clergy in the Church of England at the time, although it is hard to believe that this was not an overstatement. Many of their claims were canvassed in the newspapers and pressed on MacDonald. The Prime Minister himself had initially sounded Peter Green, Canon of Manchester. But Green, who thought that parish work was and should remain his *métier*, asked not to have a formal offer made to him. Instead, he made some alternative suggestions. Others, including Hewlett Johnson, had particularly urged the claims of F. L. Donaldson, a clergyman, then Canon of Leicester, who had played an active part in London Labour politics and was described as 'one of the only men who can really preach with success to a congregation of the Labour classes'. But, although, or perhaps because, MacDonald had known Donaldson for a long time, this idea did not find favour with him. Yet he does seem to have looked for someone comparatively young, of both academic ability and liberal political outlook, even though his Private Secretary was at much the same time telling one importunate clergyman of socialist views that ecclesiastical preferment was never dependent on political opinions, but only on spiritual gifts. Barnes's name had probably been 'shortlisted' from quite early on. At the beginning of 1924, when MacDonald had offered the Deanery of Carlisle to W. E. Moll, a member of the National Administrative Council of the Labour Party since 1907, Moll had at first hesitated and tentatively suggested that Barnes, whose 'sympathies are all with us', should go to Carlisle, while Moll himself succeeded him at Westminster. In the end Moll accepted Carlisle, although he soon had to give it up again. But his suggestion may well have helped to keep Barnes's name before MacDonald's mind for Birmingham. Moreover, he must also have known of him as a war-time pacifist, prominent in the Union of Democratic Control, like himself. It was also rumoured that MacDonald relied on William Temple's advice on such matters and at this time at any rate Temple might have been inclined to support Barnes's promotion. Another possibility, although there is no evidence for it, is that Parmoor, who was by now Lord President of the Council and always took a close interest in Church affairs and appointments and who had been a like-minded friend of Barnes since Temple days, may have played a part. Whatever its exact genesis, and this certainly seems to have been in Downing Street rather than at Lambeth, the offer was made.

MacDonald's letter was followed the same day by a letter from the

145

Prime Minister's Private Secretary to the effect that the retiring bishop would continue for life to draw a pension of £1250 a year and that the nominal emoluments of £4250 a year would be reduced by that amount while he lived. Wakefield had in fact asked for £1500 a year, but the Prime Minister had demurred at this figure. Barnes, who was at Peterhouse winding up his father-in-law's affairs and cataloguing his huge library, wrote back to the Prime Minister on 21 July asking for 'a few days in which to reach a decision: the important corners of life's high road are not easily turned'. He went on: 'Will you permit me to add that, when I remember the years of the war, I am especially glad that such a proposal should have come from yourself?' This was a reference to MacDonald's stance as a member of the Union of Democratic Control and a pacifist; both men had also been among the few who attended the first party given by the first post-war German Ambassador to the Court of St James's.

Even so, Barnes hesitated to make up his mind. So long did he delay that eventually the Archbishop wired a suggestion that Barnes should see him and talk things over at Lambeth. Davidson's offer seems to have been accepted, and Barnes also consulted Benson and possibly one or two other close friends. But whatever his doubts he must have recognized his destiny. His course had in effect been set when he went to Westminster, and the prospect of Birmingham, the home of his boyhood where his mother and brother were still living, must have had particular attractions. Admittedly, the Birmingham diocese was not going to be a bed of roses, but that may well have been part of the challenge. Above all, he would have still greater authority to deliver his message and expound his teaching. So on 29 July he accepted, although even then he wrote that he was 'in doubt whether I ought to let my name go forward, for I am troubled by many misgivings and I have been happy in the freedom of my present work'. But the die was cast and on 30 July Ramsay MacDonald wrote back to convey the King's approval and to express his own great gratification and his full confidence 'that you will justify the choice that His Majesty has made'. Barnes had become the first English bishop ever to be appointed by a Labour Government.

Davidson foresaw that the move would not be universally popular. Writing on 1 August to Barnes's predecessor at Birmingham in an obvious attempt to avert criticism, he said:

I imagine that there will be some protest, or even outcry, in regard to his nomination, but so far as I am aware there is no real justification for regarding him as a man unsound in the Faith. On the contrary, I think he is a very genuine Christian teacher though of course on liberal lines. When people denounced, a few years ago, a sermon which he preached about evolution, it seemed to me that he was only saying what many of us had been saying for years, though perhaps he worded his contentions or arguments a little differently. The nomination is in no way mine but I have seen no reason to protest against it and I have a very great regard for Barnes himself and I entirely approved of his acceptance of the nomination.

This was hardly an absolute endorsement, and Davidson was washing his hands of any personal responsibility. Nor was it a very wise letter to write to a man who was known to be no longer capable of conducting his own official business and whose resignation the Archbishop had had to extract from him. But such doubts as Davidson may still have had seem to have been put at rest by a letter of 18 August from George Bell, who wrote not only that Barnes's family connections with Birmingham would stand him in good stead but that the English Church Union, which had been trying to organize a campaign against Barnes, had failed, not least because Gore had told them that Barnes 'was not a heretic and would give them fair play'.

Nevertheless, squalls were not to be avoided altogether. The appointment was announced on 1 August. The *Church Times*, which had gained wind of it in advance, had written on an 'astonishing rumour'. It continued:

His modernism is notorious. He is the constant and not too fair critic of the Catholic revival, and he has had no experience whatever of parish work. Birmingham is a great industrial district. Its first Bishop was Dr Gore. It is today the scene of splendid and successful Catholic effort. Is the work of the Lord to be threatened by a Bishop from whom nothing can be expected but criticism and misunderstanding?

When the appointment was announced, the same Anglo-Catholic organ expressed its disappointment in a leading article, which also included the standard complaint about the appointment of bishops by the Prime Minister. 'It would be unreasonable to expect Mr Ramsay MacDonald, who is a Presbyterian, to be in personal touch with Church opinion, but he has friends who might surely have told him something about the condition of affairs in the great Midland city.' The leader disclaimed any intention of starting a heresy-hunt against Barnes and took some comfort from the knowledge 'that he has dissociated himself recently from what he calls the left-wing of the Modernist party and that he absolutely accepts the Creeds'. It ended by promising that 'so long as the Anglo-Catholics in his diocese are fairly treated, they will give him their loyal support'. But in its news columns it quoted some sour comments by Anglo-Catholic and fundamentalist incumbents in that diocese.

The editor had also written in protest to the Prime Minister, who replied on 13 August:

> . . . I did not know that anyone could have objected to the appointment of Dr Barnes to the Bishopric of Birmingham and I have been told that it has been received with great approval.
>
> My only interest is to put men in high position in the Church who really believe in Christianity and who regard it as a spiritual power influencing thought and conduct. If any of the ecclesiastical sections object to my appointment the only way out of the difficulty is for the Church to cut itself off from the patronage of the State. It is really impossible for me to enter into matters for which I have no genius. I am a good Presbyterian and if any of my ancestors knew that I had fallen so far from grace as to take any part in the appointment of Bishops they would turn in their graves! I do my best for the Church, however.

There were equally hostile comments from extreme Protestant quarters. Thus the *English Churchman*:

> He has won a name for himself not by his affirmations, but by his denials, of the great God-given verities of our faith. Such denials seem to be a passport to promotion in these strange days to which we have come. We cannot congratulate the Prime Minister upon his first attempt to fill a Diocesan Bishopric.

But the rest of the national press tended merely to emphasize the sensational nature of the appointment. Typical headlines were: 'New Bishop who refutes Genesis', 'Darwinian Bishop', 'Critic of the Bible', 'Scientific Parson to be Bishop', 'Garden of Eden a myth – new Bishop who does not accept Genesis'; and from Canada, 'New Bishop not orthodox', 'Church of England accepting Evolution, declares new Bishop'.

By no means all comment was hostile, however. The *Westminster Gazette* spoke of:

> . . . a Birmingham man . . . young enough to leave the impress of his liberalmindedness on a city which needs it theologically, socially and politically . . . Dr Barnes will add to the city's few strong-minded public leaders, and the Chamberlain caucus is not likely to swallow him up.

The *Sunday Times* called the appointment 'particularly felicitous'. The *Daily News* remarked that:

> . . . as the Master of the Temple he soon became one of the most noted exponents of the faith in those dark days early in the war . . . A man of wide sympathy and understanding, he is interested deeply not only in national, but also in international and social problems.

From the *Evening News*:

> Canon Barnes will make a notable Bishop of Birmingham . . . Understanding modern thought, he is yet critical enough to weigh it; liberal, he is detached from party allegiances; and he is still young enough to develop as thinker and preacher.

Several newspapers published predictable letters from critics on the Catholic and fundamentalist wings, with more central churchmen rallying to the defence. But, most importantly, Birmingham's own newspapers showed commendable restraint, sticking mainly to the facts and offering a dignified welcome to him and his wife. The Conservative *Birmingham Post* mentioned his sympathy with Labour ideals but quoted opinions as to his modesty, his gracious disposition and his understanding sympathy, while the Liberal *Birmingham Gazette* published an assessment by 'One who knows him', in which he was described as 'a deeply human man with a lovable personality'. One could almost say *quot homines tot sententiae*. With the hindsight of over thirty years, the comments prefigure, often almost word for word, the reaction which awaited Dr Montefiore's appointment to the same See in 1977.

Barnes was consecrated Bishop by the Archbishop of Canterbury in Westminster Abbey on 29 September, the feast of St Michael and All Angels. He was presented to the Archbishop by two old friends, Ryle, Dean of Westminster, and Burge, Bishop of Oxford, and the sermon was preached by Charles, Archdeacon of Westminster. The evening before, the Archbishop had offered, and Barnes accepted, a short private service for his wife and himself in Lambeth Palace Chapel. Even this aroused the misgivings of Haigh, the Archbishop's chaplain, who was afraid that the appointment was already controversial enough and did not want anything out of the ordinary minimum. But Davidson, with his instinct for generous action, overruled his pusillanimous assistant. He even adjusted the time of the consecration itself, so as to make it easier for people from Birmingham to be there.

CHAPTER V

BACK TO BIRMINGHAM
BETWEEN THE WARS
1924-1929

Discipline or Dogma?

Three days after his consecration, on 2 October, the new Bishop was
enthroned in Birmingham Cathedral. The civic and ecclesiastical
dignitaries were present in full force; but so unused were the cathedral
authorities to a married Bishop that they at first shut the doors in
the faces of his wife and two small sons.

Many descriptions of him were published at this turning-point in
his career, and he was certainly a striking figure. At the age of fifty,
he still looked surprisingly young, with his dark hair parted in the
middle above a square, high brow. He stood over six foot tall, and
when he preached would draw himself up in the pulpit and throw his
shoulders back, to deliver his sermons in a measured, rather sing-
song diction, which Benson somewhat unfairly described as sounding
like an old crone. But when he sat or walked in daily life, his shoulders
tended to fall forward in the characteristic 'scholar's stoop' of one
who has spent long hours at his desk. The stoop was to grow more
pronounced with the years, as was the naturally serious cast of his
features. But any sombreness was offset by the sharply penetrating
eyes, on which many who met him remarked, and was throughout
his life relieved by the warm and friendly smile which came so readily
to his lips. It was perhaps this smile, combined with an old-world
courtliness of manner, which made it hard for many people to
recognize the formidable image they had suspiciously constructed
from the newspapers in the man whom they met and actually found

151

themselves liking.

At his enthronement Barnes preached from the text: 'And now, behold, I go bound in the spirit to Jerusalem, not knowing what shall befall me there' (Acts xx, 22). The sermon was generally described as a plea for Christian reunion. He expressed his gratitude for the welcome which he had received from all parties in the Church at Birmingham, including the Anglo-Catholics. In this spirit he called for charity within the Church, despite differences of opinion, and he reaffirmed his hope for reunion with the Free Churches outside it. But he did not shirk the controversial issues, pleading for loyalty to the Articles of the Church and condemning the abuse of liberty by some clergy and the licence to which it sometimes led. In particular, he spoke out against spiritualism, stoical pantheism and pagan sacramentalism, which had entered into Latin Catholicism and pretended that it could create the Bread of Salvation by some magic of ritual and formula. He ended:

> Let us keep to the main tradition of the English Church . . . Strange things are preached in Christ's Name today . . . Our Church, I believe, is needed by the people . . . A hard economic struggle amidst sordid surroundings will produce hopeless apathy or violent discontent unless religion can transform life from within. We bring the Gospel of Christ, not as an anodyne, but as an inspiration. We can by Christ's aid make this England, impoverished by war and disorganized by over-rapid industrial development, a better land, more like the ideal country of our affection and hopes.

The *Church Times* and the *Catholic Times* duly stigmatized the reference to pagan sacramentalism as a declaration of war against the Anglo-Catholics of the diocese. A different point of view was expressed by a man who was arrested for shouting, just outside the cathedral and before the service: 'The man who says we are descended from monkeys is a liar.' The fundamentalists even staged a full-dress protest meeting at Kingsway Hall in London to coincide with the enthronement at Birmingham. But Barnes went on his way. He had many other things to say and to do. He was back in the city of his boyhood, as he said in an early sermon, after an absence of thirty-one years. Birmingham, with a population of a million, was now indisputably the second city of England and the industrial capital of the country. The business of Birmingham was business. But not for nothing had it also been called 'the best-governed city in the world', and its businessmen had made it so. Self-consciously distinct from the social hierarchy of Anglican Tories in the countryside, their leaders had in the nineteenth century almost all been Liberals and Nonconformists, enlisted under the banner of Joseph Chamberlain. With his secession from the Liberal Party over Home Rule and the gradual amalgamation of his Liberal Unionists with the Conservatives, his erstwhile Liberal caucus had become the most powerful Conservative political machine in the country. The Liberals had fallen from the seats of the mighty with an even greater crash in Birmingham than elsewhere. The Labour Party had risen more slowly, partly because industry in the city was still mainly paternalistic in its approach and because there was a general recognition that management and labour must work together in double harness. Thus in 1924, the year of Barnes's return, Labour won its first parliamentary seat at Birmingham, but only one out of twelve. In 1929, when a Labour Government was returned, Labour's share rose to four seats. But in 1931, after the economic crisis, and again in 1935, the Conservatives recaptured all twelve seats and held them until 1945. On the City Council, too, the Conservatives regularly had a large majority and most of its business, with the chairmanship of its main committees, was still conducted by the handful of largely Nonconformist families who had ruled the roost since the middle of the nineteenth century: Kenricks, closely connected with the Chamberlain family, Lloyds, Martineaus, Cadburys, Barrows and Beales. The old names recur again and again in the lists of Lord Mayors and other city functionaries. But the old establishment was careful, unlike its Ulster contemporary, to conciliate the opposition: the first Labour Lord Mayor of Birmingham took office in November 1924, and the Bishop welcomed him at a special service in Birmingham Parish Church.

Yet the city fathers were not just interested in power for power's sake. They worked hard for the prosperity and amenities of their Midland metropolis. Birmingham, as a centre for skilled labour, especially in all kinds of metal trades, had acted as a steel magnet for workpeople, many of them, like the city's water-supply, sucked in from Wales. The First World War had inevitably been a time of great activity and prosperity, but it was followed first by a sharp inflation and then a steep rise in unemployment, in Birmingham and across the country. But Birmingham, with its resources and its skills, and above all its entrepreneurial enthusiasm for exporting, was

153

already by 1924 recovering more quickly than other industrial centres. Inevitably, the price of this recovery was the concentration of family businesses into large industrial empires. This process, which was sowing the seeds of economic and social troubles for the depression a few years later, was exemplified in two of the city's largest employers: Cadbury's and Austin's, both of whom expanded rapidly. But otherwise they typified two opposed approaches to the problem: Cadbury's, with their Bournville model village, were paternalistic almost to a fault, and it was said that you were liable to lose your job and your house if you were seen slipping over the Bournville boundary to a pub in the next suburb, whereas Austin's were accused of impersonal indifference to their workers, who might be laid off seasonally with no certainty of being taken on again in six months' time.

Birmingham's energies found outlets in many other activities apart from industry. Its educational traditions went back with its Grammar School to King Edward VI, and indeed King Edward's could trace its pedigree back to the foundation of the Guild of the Holy Cross in the reign of Richard II. But further education had received ample provision in the nineteenth century, notably with the Midland Institute, opened in 1857, and the Mason College, founded in 1875 by Josiah Mason, whose business, appropriately for a patron of education, was making pens, and transformed in 1900 into Birmingham University. The Art Gallery dated from 1885. The city boasted two large theatres, the Royal and the Alexandra, as well as Barry Jackson's Repertory Theatre of national repute. Two major voluntary hospitals, the General and the Queen's, were supported by several specialist hospitals. Birmingham had no less than two morning, two evening and one Sunday newspaper of its own. Warwickshire had been a first-class cricket county since 1895, and the city's two leading football teams had both emerged from the week-end pursuits of religious congregations, Aston Villa from the Wesleyan Chapel and Birmingham from Holy Trinity Church.

For church and chapel alike were strong in the city. Partly through the sheer growth of population and partly through the rivalry of Anglican and dissenter, the nineteenth century had seen the rise of many new ecclesiastical buildings. By the end of the century it had become clear that Birmingham could no longer be treated just as an outlying province of the Diocese of Worcester. The See of Birmingham had been created in 1905, largely through the efforts of Charles

Gore, who not only contributed £10,000, most of his private fortune, and £800 a year from the Worcester income to its endowment but himself moved from Worcester to give it his own personal impetus as its first Bishop. Joseph Chamberlain, though himself a Nonconformist, had, through his admiration for Gore, given the Bishopric Bill strong support and largely ensured its passage through Parliament. The baroque church of St Philip, designed by Thomas Archer at the start of the eighteenth century, with its contemporary organ by Schwarbrick and its Burne-Jones windows made by William Morris and added late in the nineteenth century, became the pro-Cathedral, in fact the only eighteenth-century baroque cathedral in the Church of England. Gore could not stay long to guide the steps of his brainchild, being translated to Oxford in 1911. He was succeeded by Henry Russell Wakefield, who had been Dean of Norwich for two years but before that, as a London incumbent for many years and a Liberal Mayor of St Marylebone from 1903–5, had played an active part in public affairs and no doubt owed his advancement by Asquith to his political sympathies. His activities included membership of the Royal Commission on the Poor Law and the presidency of the Christian Counter-Communist Crusade. But he had not proved a happy appointment to Birmingham and had himself been restive there. So much so that in 1919 the Prime Minister's advisers had floated the idea that Wakefield might be moved to Truro 'where his genial ways might commend him to the Cornish people' and that Garbett might replace him at Birmingham. Nothing came of this intriguing idea, and in 1923 Wakefield suffered so severe a stroke that his chaplain reported to the Archbishop that he would 'never be capable of another hour's work of a serious kind'. This was the situation which, after prolonged negotiations over his pension, led to his resignation from Birmingham in 1924 and Barnes's appointment as his successor.

The move to Birmingham meant a complete change in the Barnes family's life-style. From a small town-house with a pocket-handkerchief of a garden, hidden away in the precincts of Westminster, they went to live in a spacious dwelling standing in its own fifteen acres of grounds. Bishop's Croft, formerly Harborne House, had been acquired by the diocese only in 1921. The Bishop had lived until then in a red-brick Victorian monstrosity, which Gore called 'the ugliest villa in Western Europe' and which later became the diocesan theological college. Bishop's Croft, on the other hand, dated originally

155

from the eighteenth century, although it had been extended later, and when it became a bishop's house a private chapel was added and consecrated as late as July 1924. Although it stood only three miles from the city centre, it was on the edge of the country and close to the Calthorpe Estate in Edgbaston, where most of Birmingham's more substantial citizens had large houses and gardens and the new University campus was being created. Harborne itself was still a separate village, with a model co-operative housing estate developed by J. S. Nettlefold, another typical Birmingham citizen-industrialist.

The house contained five reception-rooms and some ten main bedrooms. There was garaging for three cars, with two cottages attached. Six indoor servants were needed, with a chauffeur and two gardeners. The boys had their own nurse. For the first time Barnes had a secretary, although she did not live in the house. After the first year at Birmingham, his secretary was Miss N. M. V. Owen, daughter of Bishop Owen of St David's; she gave him devoted service for nearly thirty years and became one of the family's closest friends. In contrast with most episcopal establishments of the day, however, he had no resident chaplain. Indeed, as throughout his married life, he himself read family prayers to the whole household every morning. For the first time, too, he acquired a car, an Austin 12 saloon looking like a square box on wheels. Unlike the present day, the expenses of all this entourage had to be met by the Bishop from his own income, attenuated by his predecessor's pension. The Church Commissioners had not then taken over responsibility for the house and certain other official obligations. The diocesan office three miles away comprised only two rooms and a skeleton staff. All daily correspondence and telephone calls had to be handled by the Bishop and his secretary, while his wife ran the house and garden.

Despite this ample setting, their life was by no means ostentatious. Simplicity was partly imposed on them by their circumstances but much more by their own choice. Twenty-five years later he was to recall:

> When I first came here I wished to give up wearing the traditional episcopal costume which I disliked. I did not know then that I should find it so irritating. But when I mentioned it to my friends I was told that Bishop Gore had expressed a similar desire. He was told that certain Nonconformist leaders would not like it. They subscribed to having a bishop in Birmingham and they meant him to dress like a bishop.

So Barnes adopted the conventional bishop's apron and gaiters of those days and, somewhat surprisingly, took a close interest in his new coat of arms, visiting the College of Arms and deciding to impale the coat of the See of Birmingham with that of 'Barnes of Lancashire'; but, true to his puritan instincts, he refused to wear an episcopal ring, a pectoral cross, purple evening dress or strings in his top hat. Even on holiday, his shirt was always white and his tie plain black. He rarely wore a cope in church and was never seen in a mitre. Moreover, for most of their early years in Birmingham, there was so much poverty and unemployment in the city that he and his wife deliberately avoided anything which could look like conspicuous consumption. In any case, they had little time for anything but work.

Barnes's closest colleagues in the administration of his new diocese were all men older than himself. The Assistant Bishop and Provost of the Cathedral from 1913 to 1937 was Hamilton Baynes, who had been born in 1854 and was Bishop of Natal from 1893 to 1901. As he pointed out in one of his pricklier moments, he had been a Bishop when Barnes was leaving school. Hopton, the Archdeacon of Birmingham since 1915 and a former Moseley scrum-half, had been born in 1861, and Richards, the Archdeacon of Aston since 1920, in 1869. These three, with Ekin, appointed Legal Secretary in 1924, all gave their Bishop loyal support, without always agreeing with him. He found himself less in sympathy with the Chancellor of the diocese, E. W. Hansell, who, although he and Barnes had known each other at the Temple, was an elderly and conservative Anglo-Catholic, who did not relinquish his office until his death at the age of eighty-one in 1937. But the Bishop could appoint his own examining chaplains, and his choice reflects his own background and sympathies: Bethune-Baker, of King Edward's and Cambridge, Cockin of the Student Christian Movement, Luce of Westminster School, Major of Ripon Hall, with two local men, Blofeld, vicar of Edgbaston, who actually ran the examinations, and Stephenson of Acocks Green.

This was a time of manifold activities, as Barnes flung himself into the life of the diocese and the city, as well as the other still independent boroughs within the diocesan boundaries. He was, of course, now and later asked to join countless organizations in and outside the diocese. Unless he had some specific reason not to do so, he normally allowed his name to be used, on the understanding that he could not be expected to play an active part or subscribe money to activities not directly connected with his work. Nor would he join any body with a commercial or party political flavour. During the first three months he is to be found constantly preaching, speaking and writing, starting his confirmations, of which, incidentally, he was later to say that 'in a confirmation address I have never knowingly alluded to controversial questions', instituting a week of prayer and self-denial for the benefit of church funds, dedicating church bells, visiting hospital wards at Christmas, distributing school prizes and attending civic receptions. The subjects which he treated ranged widely: religion and the new knowledge in his first cathedral sermon, mental health and its implications for Christian marriage and population control in an address to doctors on St Luke's Day, the League of Nations and the need to outlaw war on more than one occasion, the new role of women as citizens at the Girl Guides' annual meeting, the moral risks of bad housing at a service for the new Lord Mayor, the need to remove children from cruel parents at a meeting of the NSPCC attended by Neville Chamberlain, the spiritual value of access to the countryside for town dwellers on his first visit to Sutton Coldfield, toleration and Christian reunion to a delegation of Free Churchmen who called on him, and, during the week of prayer and self-denial, the importance of better salaries for the clergy so that they could provide themselves with books and rooms to study and keep their knowledge up to date. But even while he continued to emphasize the importance of education for the intellectual basis of faith, he was careful not to overdo it: 'heaven is not reserved for the highbrows' and 'not every man that says to me "science, science" shall enter into the Kingdom of Heaven' were two of his aphorisms. Nor did he eschew politics, insisting that it was at times necessary to introduce them to the pulpit. He emphasized the parallelism of Labour ideals and Christian faith, he asserted that from the Christian point of view one must favour an advanced social policy, even if one was then accused of indulging in Labour propaganda, he welcomed the Labour Government's efforts to establish friendly relations with Russia, and, in a letter to the press of 31 October 1924, he urged the clergy not to exult over the Labour defeat at the General Election as 'a victory for Christian principles'. It is not surprising that the *Church of England Newspaper* commented within his first month that 'the Bishop of Birmingham is drawing crowds wherever he is announced to speak and is giving of his best'. Nor is it surprising that he was later to say that 'a year after coming to Birmingham I felt like a hoarse crow in a thirsty land'. His wife supported him on most of his public appearances, although her activities were at first restricted by the presence of her invalid mother in the house at Bishop's Croft. But Lady Ward died in December 1924, and Mrs Barnes could now devote herself wholeheartedly to the present and future generations. Naturally enough she was particularly active for women's causes, and one of her first initiatives was to found a Clergy Wives' Club for the diocese.

But the real story of the early years of Barnes's episcopate lies in his struggle with the Anglo-Catholics of the Birmingham diocese. In a newspaper interview on taking up his new office, he had said:

> The really important things that a bishop has to do, so far as I can see, are to maintain such unity as possible in the church life of his diocese; to seek peace and to maintain order at the same time; and more especially, to take the lead in relating the civic life of the diocese to Christian standards.

The maintenance of unity and order was to be no easy task. He had been privately warned that he was succeeding to a sadly disordered and mismanaged diocese. Gore, as a High Churchman, had allowed some ritualist advances but, being also a learned theologian and a strong leader of men, had set certain well-defined limits on them. As Gore had himself said, 'a bishop's chances of doing good lie chiefly in maintaining a high standard of discipline'. But Russell Wakefield had been less interested in theology than in tranquillity and tended in his churchmanship to be all things to all men. Moreover, as his health declined, so did the strength of his hands on the reins. Birmingham was indeed a *damnosa hereditas*.

But the confusion in Birmingham only differed in degree from the turmoil within which the Church of England as a whole was struggling. The Oxford Movement had done its worst only too well. From being a monolithic pillar of the Establishment a century before, the Church had become a chess-board of contending parties and factions. The older evangelicals had gradually seen their pre-eminence decline, and the Liberal Evangelicals tended to fall between the stools of Liberalism and Evangelicalism. In the first quarter of the twentieth century, the self-styled Catholic revival had made rapid strides, and the Anglo-Catholics were beginning to scent victory within their grasp. Untrue to Gore's inspiration, they now put the emphasis on

159

the ritualistic rather than the intellectual or social side of their movement. Ritualism was no doubt assisted by the general flamboyance and extravagance of the Edwardian era. Nor was it unnatural that the convulsions of the war should have tended to drive people either towards complete unbelief or towards the more picturesque manifestations of religion. The educational attainments of the ministry declined, as did its social background. As a result, Broad Churchmen were to be found more and more among the laity, looking with some wonder and no little impatience at the sacerdotal disputes of the clergy.

The Bishops who had to guide their flocks through this turbulent Red Sea were almost as diverse as the Church itself. While many of them were individually men of distinction, some of their more distinguishing characteristics had often become blurred with the passing of the years and the hardening of the arteries. Archbishop Davidson himself had been privy to the secrets of Church and State since the reign of Queen Victoria and, as an ecclesiastical statesman of unrivalled stature, was rightly revered, loved, trusted and respected by all. He had always taken a benevolent interest in Barnes, who responded with a warm affection for him personally. Even Arthur Benson, who had known him since 1882, spoke of Davidson with awe: writing to Barnes in 1916, he spoke of him having 'a mind so much more forceful, definite and cogent than my own . . . I always feel that I am driving, so to speak, in his carriage'. But Davidson was also a cautious man. Writing after another meeting in June 1917, Benson said 'he is naturally anxious-minded – his Scotchiness sometimes comes on like a mist and I can't see through it'. Barnes's own comment, incidentally, on Davidson's 'Scotchiness' was to deplore his habit of giving a tip of only 10/- to the choirboys who carried his train; he thought that Archbishops should tip in pounds. By 1924, Davidson was well on in his seventies; his caution and his evasiveness had increased. His overriding preoccupation was to hold the Church together and he was more concerned with stopping things happening than with making them happen. His brother of York, Cosmo Gordon Lang, soon himself to succeed to the chair of St Augustine, blended his temperamental High Churchmanship with a refinement of tactical adaptability. But he seemed to be concerned primarily with externals, with manner rather than with matter. Of Winnington Ingram, Bishop of London, once the idol of the East End, few praises can be sung as theologian or administrator. The stables of London were

Service for Household Cavalry.
Abbey. April 2. 1919.

Queen Alexandra, E.W.B. & Chapter Clerk
(Mr. Ralph Foster)

Canon of Westminster

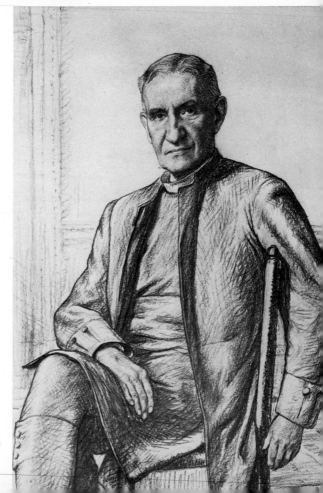

Silver wedding portrait, 1941,
by Francis Dodd RA

Bishop's Croft, Harborne, Birmingham

Church extension in Birmingham, 1929

even more Augean than those of Birmingham. William Temple at Manchester and destined to follow in Lang's footsteps to York and Canterbury, a manipulator of men and a wizard with words, was more interested in his own objectives for social and ecclesiastical progress than in sharpness of doctrine or discipline. As the years went by, his religious thoughts grew increasingly conservative, so that by the end many wondered whether he would not after all have been better employed as politician or philosopher. Even more so was this true of Henson at Durham. Once a champion of reunion with the Free Churches and suspected of heresy over the creeds, he now seemed to have decided to play for safety. His skill at invective was as barbed as ever, but it sometimes led him through loquacity beyond veracity, as when he described the Evangelical opponents of Prayer Book revision as an army of illiterates generaled by octogenarians. Arthur Headlam of Gloucester was an intellectual High Churchman of the Oxford school, whose genuinely constructive contributions to theological learning and to Christian unity were too often obscured by the asperity with which he expressed them. The more extreme Anglo-Catholics were represented on the episcopal bench by a former Colonial bishop in Furse of St Albans and a former monk in Frere of Truro. On the evangelical wing, Pollock at Norwich, as befitted a former headmaster of Wellington, saw the restoration of discipline as the Church's main need, while William Cecil at Exeter, as a Prime Minister's son, was an individualist who could afford to take a fairly detached view of ecclesiastical minutiae. Another robust character was Ernest Pearce at Worcester but, as Lloyd George's ecclesiastical adviser when they were neighbours at Downing Street and the Abbey, his bent was mainly towards organization and administration. Whittingham of St Edmundsbury and Ipswich looked as wise as Socrates and was another evangelical unprepared to compromise with new-fangled extravagances. Another ex-headmaster, David of Liverpool, was making interesting experiments in Anglican-Nonconformist exchanges. *Quot episcopi tot sententiae.* But, while the battle lines were not yet drawn and it was not yet time to stand up and be counted, the omens were not favourable.

Since the Report of the Royal Commission on Ecclesiastical Discipline in 1906, the Church of England had grown increasingly involved in the problem of Prayer Book reform. The Enabling Act of 1920 had conferred the initiative on the new Church Assembly but had left the power of decision in the hands of Parliament. *L'église propose, l'état dispose.* When the crunch came, as come it soon must, it was evident that the main battlefield would lie in eucharistic doctrine and the service of the Holy Communion. With this prospect clearly in view, the Anglo-Catholics had been doing all they could to pre-empt the situation. The Royal Commission had authoritatively declared that various practices, including 'the interpolation of the prayers and ceremonies belonging to the Canon of the Mass', 'reservation of the Sacrament under conditions which lead to its adoration', 'benediction with the Sacrament' and 'hymns, prayers and devotions involving invocation of or confession to the Blessed Virgin Mary or the Saints' were illegal. It concluded that the machinery for discipline had broken down and recommended that these practices 'should be promptly made to cease by the exercise of the authority belonging to the Bishops and, if necessary, by proceedings in the Ecclesiastical Courts'. It further recommended that 'Bishops should be invested with power to refuse the institution or admission of a presentee into a benefice who has not previously satisfied the Bishop of the diocese of his willingness to obey the law' and that a Bishop should have power 'to order the removal of ornaments, objects of decoration, or fittings placed in a church, as to which ornaments, objects or fittings no faculty has been obtained'.

From the time of the Commission's report, the ritualist controversy gathered momentum. Bishop Bell, in his life of Archbishop Davidson, introduces his chapter on the subject by an apt quotation from Edmund Burke, with which he suggests that the issue lay between those who wanted truth to prevail and those who would settle for peace. In this he was right, except that it did not bring out the size of the quietist majority. Throughout the long controversy, the question really turned on the point of permanent reservation of the consecrated elements of the sacrament; that is to say, whether or not all the bread and wine should be consumed at, or at least on the same day as, the service at which it was consecrated or whether some of it could be set aside and kept for other purposes. There was general agreement that consecrated elements could be taken, as early as possible on the same day, to communicate a sick person outside the church building. It was suggested by some that, as an extension of this practice, consecrated elements should be kept indefinitely in the church, in case a sudden need arose for communion of the sick. This would be permanent reservation. But the Anglo-Catholics really wanted such permanent reservation, not only so that the sacrament might be available in emergency for the sick, but also so that they might follow the Roman custom of using it for adoration and benediction with a monstrance. This would of course have established a link with the Roman doctrine of transubstantiation, forbidden by the Articles of the Church of England, since that doctrine provides the theoretical justification for adoration of the 'transubstantiated' elements. Despite the Royal Commission's rulings, the bishops had in 1911 privately agreed that they would tolerate reservation for the communion of the sick, as had in fact been authorized in the 1549 Prayer Book, though not in that of 1662. Even this was now strictly illegal. It had been condemned by both Archbishops Temple and MacLagan in 1900, and the Court of Arches had decided against it in 1907. But in 1911 it seems to have been regarded as a necessary concession to go thus far and no further to meet the demand. Reservation for any other purpose was to remain forbidden. It was perhaps naïve to expect this tactic to work. *L'appétit vient en mangeant.*

There were other points of controversy too, apart from permanent reservation. In 1915 the Lower House of the Convocation of Canterbury had proposed that diversity of vestments should be allowed, namely Roman-type copes and chasubles as well as plain surplices, and that a rearranged prayer of consecration, including a direct blessing of the bread and wine, should be introduced. These would also have been concessions to the Catholic party. But, after Protestant remonstrances, the Upper House of Bishops rejected the proposed new prayer of consecration by 15 votes to 5. In 1916, too, Lord Halifax, the leading Anglo-Catholic layman in the country, had asked the Archbishop if he would turn a blind eye to the use of the 1549 rather than the 1662 service of Holy Communion. By this manoeuvre Halifax claimed that he could prevent the extremists from mouthing parts of the Roman Canon of the Mass under their breath while they were ostensibly celebrating according to the 1662 service. It is by no means certain that all the clergy in question used the Roman Mass as *sotto voce* as Halifax avowed or that the use of the 1549 service would have deterred them from doing so in the future. In any case, the Archbishop wisely declined to be party to such a subterfuge.

On reservation, the Bishops' decision of 1911 in fact failed conspicuously to achieve its purpose of holding the line. The emotions

163

of wartime, seeking new religious outlets, aggravated the pressure. As Bell mildly puts it, 'There were differences and irregularities, especially in the dioceses of London, Chichester and Birmingham.' At Birmingham, Gore had rigidly insisted that reservation should only take place in a secluded chapel, to which there would be no access, so that adoration would be impossible. But in a letter to Davidson of 8 June 1915, Gore complained that this rule had been abandoned by his successor, Wakefield, who was allowing reservation in open church, and that the same thing was happening in the London and Chichester dioceses. Gore hinted that he would no longer feel bound to try to enforce his own rules. It is only fair to add that Gore, though a High Churchman, distinguished the doctrine of the Real Presence, in which of course he firmly believed, from that of transubstantiation. Russell Wakefield took the view that 'not even locked chapels and brick walls would prevent people showing reverence and saying their prayers; he advised the bishops not to attempt to stop them, but to show real determination in the suppression of organized devotions'. It is doubtful, since he had in 1922 been Chairman of the Anglo-Catholic Congress at Birmingham, how determined he really was or showed himself in practice, and certainly towards the end of his episcopate he was too ill to exercise authority. The Bishop of London gave even less evidence of resolution: he frankly admitted his failure to control the situation and made no effective effort to prevent access to the sacrament, even though it was nominally reserved only for the sick. Indeed, it must also be doubtful how sincere Winnington-Ingram himself was: in a letter to Russell Wakefield in 1921, he wrote, 'I am going to try and get my men to give up their Devotions in order to secure permanent reservation all over the country for their less fortunate brethren'. Gore was persuaded in the event to hold his line for the time being. But a memorial signed in 1917 by 1000 Anglo-Catholic clergy, who declared that they would not accept any limitations on reservation, was a sign of the rising tide of revolt, even though the bishops in July of that year again explicitly refused to accept permanent reservation.

The controversy over reservation thus went hand in hand with the question of Prayer Book revision. The Royal Commission on Ecclesiastical Discipline had recommended that the Convocations should 'frame, with a view to their enactment by Parliament, such modifications in the existing law relating to the conduct of Divine

Service and to the ornaments and fittings of churches as may tend to secure the greater elasticity which a reasonable recognition of the comprehensiveness of the Church of England and of its present needs seems to demand'. In other words, the law should be softened in the hope that, once softened, it would then be obeyed. In response, the Convocations had put forward their own proposals for Prayer Book reform. But in 1920 the new Church Assembly decided that it too must be in on the act and appointed a committee to review the Convocations' proposals. In June 1922, this committee reported generally in favour of the proposed changes, except for uttering certain warnings about changes in the Communion service and about reservation. The bishops in October of the same year introduced a draft measure into the Church Assembly, which early in the next year gave it general approval, with three bishops dissenting, Nickson of Bristol, Pollock of Norwich and Pearce of Worcester.

This, then, was the broad position when Barnes joined the episcopal bench. Both over the revision of the Prayer Book and in the administration of their dioceses, the bishops were trying, Canute-like, to stem the tide of the Catholic revival by setting an arbitrary high-water mark and erecting artificial barriers above it. According to their beliefs or their energies, some tried harder than others. The result in Birmingham was that all sorts of ritualist practices were openly conducted, more or less at the whim of the individual incumbents, who were sustained by a ruthless organization in Birmingham itself and by the English Church Union at national level. This often meant that they drew to their churches and on to their Parochial Church Councils sympathizers from all around, so that whole Councils might consist of members not resident in their parishes, while former worshippers who disliked the innovations had to look for acceptable services in the nearest congenial church they could find. The parish system was becoming thoroughly distorted.

Barnes was no doubt satisfied that he was on good legal grounds in opposing reservation and the other practices which the Royal Commission had condemned. He also saw himself as required to fulfil his promise at his consecration 'with all faithful diligence to banish and drive away all erroneous and strange doctrine contrary to God's word and both privately and openly to call upon and encourage others to the same'. But he did not see this just in terms of formal obligations. It was also a struggle for the truth, on which he embarked willingly, determined as he always was to ensure that the

Church's teaching and practice were such as would convince a critical and scientifically-minded generation and, above all, that they should reflect Christ's own teaching, uncontaminated by importations from the mystery-religions or elsewhere. As he said in one interview, 'the language and ideas of the ancient mystery-religions, with a little Christian colour-wash, are set forth as the Catholic Faith' and 'what ought to be the sacrament of Christian unity is in the English Church the centre of its most acute controversies'. As for the Revised Prayer Book, he called it 'an unsuccessful compromise, doctrinally invertebrate'. His policy as a bishop was thus to be based on his thinking and teaching over the previous twenty years.

The first storm was not long in breaking. Barnes's enthronement sermon had put the Anglo-Catholics on their guard. They were ready for the fray. Indeed, they had been ready for some time. In his first sermon at the cathedral on 12 October, the Bishop mainly defended himself against charges that, by casting doubt on the literal truth of the Genesis story of the creation, he was himself disloyal to his consecration promise; but he also took the opportunity to emphasize that the authors of the English Prayer Book had 'sought to make the Church comprehensive, to include all willing to abjure the errors of Rome'. He was doing his best to make clear that there was room in the diocese for all points of view, provided the law was obeyed and the traditions of the Church of England observed. But the Anglo-Catholics, for their part, wanted to force the issue. The *Church Times* was calling the tune. The first bars were sounded in an invitation from G. D. Rosenthal, vicar of St Agatha's, Sparkbrook, for the Bishop to attend a service of thanksgiving for fifty years of Catholic revival. This was an obvious piece of provocation. They cannot have expected him to attend and must have been looking for a field on which to do battle. Clearly Barnes could not ignore the impertinence and he decided to use the occasion to set out his position at length:

I thank you for the courtesy of your letter. It is with regret that I must decline your invitation.

I trust that I judge the Anglo-Catholic movement with the fairness and sympathy with which I would approach all modes of presenting the Christian faith.

I would assure you that I do not undervalue the religious earnestness which is the main element of worth within the movement.

In so far as such earnestness has shown itself in large-hearted sympathy for the poor and oppressed and in enthusiasm for social righteousness, I welcome it cordially.

I recognize, moreover, that people differ so much in temperament that they are attracted by different types of worship. The Church of England has always at its best been inclusive rather than exclusive. Its members ought to be tolerant with regard to minor differences of doctrine and worship which involve no serious departure from the position laid down in the Prayer Book and Articles.

Especially should we show such tolerance at the present time, when thought is both active and progressive and when new knowledge makes necessary some measure of theological restatement.

But it is especially important at such a time to avoid the erroneous teaching tending to superstition which naturally arises during a period of religious unrest and I cannot feel that your movement does this with entire success.

To describe the erroneous teaching given by some of your members, I will not use my own words. I would, in the first place, remind you of some apposite sentences of the Bishop of Gloucester, a High Churchman and one of the most distinguished living theologians. In his recent Visitation Charge we read:

'The doctrine of the Apostolic Succession is taught in a mechanical way. Grace is said to have come down from the Apostles by the golden channel of laying on of hands. And it is implied that, except in that way, the gift of the Holy Spirit is not given . . . We are told that the priest has the power of making the body and blood of Christ. Now all language like this is most harmful. It is bad theology. It suggests a mechanical idea of Sacrament and Divine grace. It puts stumbling blocks in the way of many people. It is saying what the majority of people can't believe and won't believe and ought not to believe.'

In connection with the bad theology of which Dr Headlam writes, some in your movement have introduced the practice of reservation, for purposes other than communicating the sick who are unable to come to church.

I regret to learn that in some churches of this diocese illegal receptacles called tabernacles have been placed. In them the consecrated elements are kept, whereas it is ordered by the rules of our Church that those elements should be at once consumed after the Communion service.

As Bishop I deplore this illegality and still more the false doctrine which lies behind it.

The traditional teaching of the English Church in this matter has recently been lucidly expressed by Canon Storr, whose learning and loyal churchmanship are alike indisputable:

167

'As thinking people we cannot accept the theology which underlies the practice of reservation. Reservation was not heard of until the doctrine of transubstantiation was propounded. It is a direct outcome of the Roman theory . . . The practice of reservation tends to foster superstition. Why stop at adoration of the reserved Sacrament? Why not renew the practice of earlier days and carry it with you as a charm against sickness? We are told it is a help to devotion. I do not deny that it may be for some; but the help is gained at the expense of truth.'

And Canon Storr concludes with the emphatic and true statement:

'A prayer in a barn is as valuable and as potent with God as a prayer before a tabernacle.'

I would not have it appear that in thus condemning certain aspects of the Anglo-Catholic movement I despair of its future. Religious zeal, unless purified by quiet thought, is often extravagant. But tides ebb as rapidly as they flow. I still hope that the leaders of Anglo-Catholicism will abandon the illegalities and false doctrine by which it is harmed and join with other parties in the Church of England to spread the Spirit of Christ.

We need to combine enthusiasm with sound doctrine, and to unite devotion to Christ with a faith which reason can justify. Internal dissensions are a source of grave weakness. They hinder us from preaching the Gospel with united zeal.

None can doubt the urgent need of that combined witness for Christ which, as a Church, we ought to be able to give. Cannot Anglo-Catholicism free itself from error, while continuing to kindle the spirit of devotion by rich and beautiful worship? It would thus make a distinctive contribution to our corporate life and, as Bishop, I could give it sincere approval.

This letter was published on 26 November, and Rosenthal claimed that it reached the press before it reached him. The Bishop had already given his opponents a handle for this type of criticism by his letter to the press on 31 October urging his clergy not to exult over the Conservative victory in the General Election; that letter had already drawn an anonymous reply to the effect that 'the Bishop has lost no time in suggesting that he has no faith in his clergy; otherwise he would have left such matters to their discretion and commonsense'. Rosenthal therefore was able to make his initial reply in the form of a statement to the press:

It is with extreme reluctance that Anglo-Catholics engage in controversy with the Bishop of the diocese in the public press, but his own action makes it inevitable. The occasion of his letter to the press was an invitation addressed to him by me as chairman of the Birmingham Anglo-Catholic Congress Council to be present at a united service of thanksgiving for fifty years of the Catholic revival in Birmingham in connection with the fiftieth anniversary of the death of Dr Oldknow. I pointed out that it had always been our custom to invite the Bishop of the diocese to our united services and meetings and that we desired to extend an equally cordial invitation to himself. And I added that it would be difficult to exaggerate the unifying influence that his presence would have.

This invitation was sent to the Bishop more than a fortnight ago, and it is naturally a matter of extreme surprise to us that his answer should have been communicated to the press before I received it.

The Bishop has thus had a considerable time to think about his reply, which in a note to me he says is a considered statement. It would obviously be unfair to expect us to reply to it in detail on the spur of the moment, especially in view of the fact that any statement we make commits not only ourselves but Anglo-Catholics all over the world. At the moment it must be sufficient to say that we indignantly deny the Bishop's statements that our teaching is erroneous and our practices superstitious. We repudiate his charge that reservation of the Blessed Sacrament is illegal and we do not accept his interpretation of the Prayer Book and Articles. In our view the Bishop's statements on these matters betray a singular lack of informed judgement, and are un-historical, untheological and untrue. And rejecting as we wholeheartedly do the infallibility of the Pope, we are not prepared to substitute for it the infallibility either of Canon Storr or of the Bishop of Gloucester.

May I add that the whole situation is rendered needlessly difficult owing to the fact that the Bishop shows no disposition whatever to consult with his clergy personally, whatever their school of thought. His method of addressing injunctions and rebukes to them through the medium of the public press causes profound resentment not only among the clergy but among the laity as well and is ill-calculated to enhance either his authority or his influence.

This debating reply was not just a personal attack. It was also a declaration of war. Rosenthal followed it up with a press interview in which he accused the Bishop of discourtesy and compared him unfavourably with Gore and Wakefield, but evaded the legal issue by suggesting that, while it would be open to the Bishop to prosecute the Anglo-Catholics for illegal practices, many clergy refused to accept the judgements of secular courts. This was a direct challenge to combat. Needless to say, it let loose a spate of controversy. The Vicar of St Matthew's, Southsea, who had no *locus standi* whatever, referred to Barnes's 'twilight twitterings', described him as 'a poor wretch' and urged that 'his orders should be deliberately disobeyed, his authority flouted and his person ignored'. That was an extreme example of Christian charity. Anglo-Catholic clergy in the Birmingham diocese also published criticisms but on the whole with more restraint. But even so the attacks were sharp enough to draw forth letters in support of Barnes's position not only from the laity but, in the local press, from the Rector of Birmingham and other incumbents and, in *The Times*, from a distinguished group of correspondents, of whom Storr was the draughtsman and Dean Inge the first signatory and who wrote on 18 December:

> The Bishop's cautious and temperate letter was, in effect, an appeal to loyal Anglo-Catholics in his diocese to keep the reins in their own hands and not be dragged along by a disloyal section. The grave danger for the Church at the present moment is that its historic character shall be wholly lost because of the action of certain extremists. We wish to assure the Bishop of our sympathy and support.

A more personal note was struck by an Anglo-Catholic clergyman in the diocese who wrote to the *Church Times* asking that paper to desist from its attacks on Barnes and adding:

> The Bishop is compelling our respect by his force of character, his caution and the fearless statement of his convictions, even when we do not agree with him. He is winning the affection of those who have met him by his sincerity and courtesy. His devotion may not take the form which we employ, but it is none the less intense and spiritual. No one who was present at the Confirmation in this parish last Sunday could fail to be impressed with his deep fervour as he laid his hands upon the head of each candidate separately and prayed for the gift of the Holy Spirit.

The *Church of England Newspaper* commented:

> We congratulate the Bishop of Birmingham upon his outstanding courage and his commendable frankness, combined with a Christian charity which we have learned to expect from Dr Barnes. The *Church Times* last week jibed at the Bishop in its own characteristic fashion, but our contemporary will find that the new Bishop of Birmingham is

not only a great Christian but a man who knows his own mind – a man who will not be cowed by the sneers of the *Church Times* nor deflected from his cause by the worked-up agitation of a group of so-called Anglo-Catholics. But this is not a question merely for the Diocese of Birmingham. It concerns the Church of England as a whole and the Bishop deserves – as we are sure he will get – the prayers and active support of all loyal Churchmen to whatever school of thought they belong.

But Rosenthal and his backers were not to be deterred. On 9 December his considered reply, given with the approval of the English Church Union and the Federation of Catholic Priests, was issued to the press:

After some general remarks, in which, we notice, an implied deprecation of any 'serious departure from the position laid down in the Prayer Book and Articles', you accuse 'some' of our 'members' of 'erroneous teaching tending to superstition' and 'false doctrine'. Such accusations (especially when made by a bishop against the priests of his own diocese) would be universally admitted to be of the most wantonly hurtful and uncharitable kind, unless sustained by serious proof.

Your quotation from the Bishop of Gloucester introduces what appears to constitute the main body of your accusation, namely an attack both upon the ancient and Catholic practice of reserving the Blessed Sacrament and upon the doctrine which underlies Reservation.

We observe that it is not only some particular custom connected with the use of the Reserved Sacrament, but Reservation itself which you condemn; for you pass on from 'the practice of reservation for purposes other than communicating the sick who are unable to come to church' to an appeal to 'the rules of our Church that those elements should be at once consumed after the communion service', and you speak of 'the false doctrine which lies behind'.

But this part of your accusation deprives you of the authority which you claim from the Bishop of Gloucester. For the Bishop of Gloucester, in the same charge as that from which you quote, has sanctioned or has accepted the principle of several methods of reservation.

The quotation from the Bishop of Gloucester in your letter is followed by a quotation from Canon Storr. We have been unable to discover the source of the quotation, and consequently have not been able to examine the context of the sentences which you cite. But, as the quotation stands in your letter, referring to reservation itself, and not merely to some custom in regard to the Reserved Sacrament, it contains a gross historical blunder.

We repudiate the accusations of 'illegality' and 'false doctrine'. We

171

believe that the doctrine underlying the custom of reservation is the true Christian doctrine of the Holy Eucharist, which goes back through the tradition of the centuries to the words of our Lord Himself; and that reservation cannot be treated as illegal in the English Church.

We wish that we could stop here. But, since the question of false doctrine has been raised, we cannot. We trust that we are free from any wish merely to retort. We had hoped to put aside all that gravely disquieted us when we first heard that you were to be our Bishop; to ignore as mere indiscretions what had seemed to us false doctrine of the most deadly kind touching the Holy Trinity, the Incarnation and the Fall.

Your letter has made difficulties for us which it is not easy for us to describe. We shall not cease to pray for you as our Bishop, especially when we stand at the altar in the most solemn moments of our lives. But your letter leaves us unconvinced that you understand our position or that your policy is based on a 'right apprehension of Christian truth'.

We could have wished that any correspondence between you and ourselves of an argumentative character might have been private and that the scandal of public discussion might have been avoided; but since your letter has been sent to the public press, it is necessary for us to follow your example and publish this letter also.

Not much Christian charity in that venomous document. Barnes did not answer it. So far this had been a war of words. But action was soon to come. The first skirmish was bloodless and ended without casualties. In January 1925, C. A. Brown was nominated for the vacant benefice of St Gregory's, Small Heath, an Anglo-Catholic church. Barnes interviewed Brown and a deputation from the parish seeking his appointment. He asked Brown for an assurance that he would not continue 'practices which are not only illegal but also involve a departure from the traditional doctrine and usage of the Church of England as laid down in the Prayer Book and Thirty-nine Articles'. Brown refused to give the assurances and a law-suit was threatened to compel the Bishop to institute him. Barnes thereupon decided to institute him privately in the chapel of Bishop's Croft. By this procedure he could fulfil the task in a minimal way, without associating himself with the new incumbent in a public ceremony. In writing to tell Brown this, he said:

> I shall continue to hope and pray that your views may so change that you are led to conform to the law and doctrine of the Church of England. I feel that, as Bishop, I have done all that I can to persuade you that

172

such conformity is your duty. Some will think me remiss in not seeking to enforce the law. To them I can only reply that I feel compelled to avoid the scandal caused by possible litigation.

I have personally no doubt that within a generation sound theological learning will cause our Church to repudiate the novelties by which you are attracted. But the issue will be settled by the persuasive thought of our best and wisest teachers; and, as Bishop, I would rather wait until their influence asserts itself than try by legal action to preserve sound doctrine. If I took the latter course I might seem to be moved by a personal unfriendliness which, as you know, does not exist.

The institution took place on 4 May. This action no doubt gave the opposition the impression that they had only to threaten litigation for the Bishop to capitulate. In this they were wrong. To some extent Barnes may have hoped, by a conciliatory attitude, to disarm his opponents. But, more importantly, as he had written, he thought that the making and breaking of solemn obligations were matters of conscience which should not be regulated by civil courts. He was also influenced by the knowledge that revision of the Prayer Book was pending and that, while he could confidently forbid practices already rejected by those who were preparing the new Book, it was harder to close the door to anything which the new Book might still admit. As it was possible that it might authorize reservation for the sick only, Barnes was ready meanwhile not to forbid this, provided the consecrated elements were so placed that there was no public access to them. His attitude on this aspect of the controversy was eventually set out in a letter to his clergy in the Diocesan Magazine of 2 October 1925:

> Correspondence in the press has drawn public attention to the fact that a service known as 'Devotions' before the consecrated bread and wine of the Holy Communion is held in certain churches in the Diocese of Birmingham. Three incumbents in the city wrote to the Press on October 7, 1925, to say that such a service was sanctioned by my predecessor at an interview which they had with him on May 25, 1917. They implied that therefore I ought to continue to allow it at the church of St Mark, Washwood Heath. The contention cannot be upheld. More than a year after the interview the then vicar of St Mark's, Washwood Heath, wrote to my predecessor asking leave to have Reservation. My predecessor replied on July 13, 1918: –
>
> I am very sorry that you want to have Reservation, as Saltley has so many churches with it. I can only sanction it if the Sacrament is so

placed that it is not noticeable to the people, and cannot be used for devotional purposes, but I would greatly prefer you not having it except for the sick. I am quite certain that the Church of England does not sanction it for any other use.

The service of Devotions cannot be carried out unless the consecrated bread and wine are publicly placed in what Roman Catholics call a tabernacle, or pyx, in the church. I have enquired of the three incumbents whether they have faculties from the Chancellor for such illegal ornaments. I have also asked them whether a definite form of the service of Devotions was submitted to my predecessor or exists in print. These questions they have so far refused to answer unless I regard their answer as private. I am sure that I am right in holding that questions which affect public worship in the Church of England are a matter of public concern. I will add that the Registrar of the Diocese informs me that no faculties for such illegal receptacles as tabernacles and pyxes have been granted for the churches of any of the three incumbents.

As to the exact outcome of the interview with my predecessor in 1917, it is unnecessary to inquire. The war was then proceeding, there was confusion in every department of national life, and there is no reason to think that the Church in Birmingham escaped the tendency to disorder. But since then progress towards orderly reform in the Church of England has been marked. The Enabling Act has been passed; the Church has now its representative Church Assembly; that Assembly has proceeded far with the work of Prayer Book revision. We know the decision of the House of Clergy and the House of Laity. Neither is prepared to allow public reservation of the consecrated elements of the Holy Communion, or services which imply some doctrine akin to transubstantiation. All that the House of Laity was prepared to agree to is contained in the following motion passed in June last:

'That while this House believes that the great majority of the laity are satisfied with the present service of Holy Communion, the House will nevertheless agree to the insertion by the Bishops in the Prayer Book of one alternative form containing provision for vestments and reservation for the sick only, if, in their opinion, this will promote peace and order in the Church.'

The service of Devotions is illegal, and will continue to be illegal when the Prayer Book is revised. It is based on erroneous and strange doctrine. It is my duty to establish law and order in the diocese. I must therefore ask that illegal services, such as Benediction, Exposition, Devotions, Procession of the Host etc., shall cease, and that no consecrated bread and wine shall be kept in receptacles placed in those parts of our churches to which the public are admitted.

In this directive, as at all times, Barnes was careful not explicitly to allow or approve reservation in any form. But he also took care not to forbid it in so many words, pending a decision on Prayer Book revision and provided the bread and wine were reserved only for the sick and in places to which there could be no public access. But between the affair at St Gregory's, Small Heath, and the time when that directive came to be issued, much had happened.

Throughout this period Barnes had continued to teach, preach and speak on his usual wide range of topics. Increasingly these brought him into conflict with the Anglo-Catholics. The *Church Times* kept up a barrage of criticism. Otherwise many of his utterances were only reported in the local press. But he hit the national headlines, and found himself in conflict with the Anglo-Catholics on a different subject, when in a sermon on 31 May to the Royal Institute of Public Health at Brighton, he deplored the 'reckless child-bearing' which had led to children swarming in overcrowded slums, called for a Christian renunciation of parenthood where necessary and claimed that the community had a right to take measures to prevent the increase of tainted stocks. His renewed experience of the industrial Midlands had already sharpened his interest in the quantity and quality of the population and the need to prevent its decay. But the sermon led to a statement the same evening by the Vicar of Brighton, who had been present and who dissociated himself from the Bishop's views on birth-control as if he had advocated artificial contraception, whereas in fact Barnes had avoided any reference to the actual methods of restricting the population and had indeed implied that only self-control was needed. This sermon also gave a handle to the Duke of Argyll to attack Barnes at the Anglo-Catholic Congress in July, calling him foolish and malicious.

But of course the main cause of conflict and the main source of publicity continued to lie in sacramental theology and eucharistic practice. Thus, on 22 January, addressing a meeting of the Anglican Evangelical Group Movement, he declared that 'Liberal Evangelicalism represents a higher culture than medieval Catholicism' but regretted that

> there are many who prefer a lower culture because they find the higher too exacting . . . Certain superstitions have assumed a dangerous vitality . . . If they conquer our Church . . . either they will also conquer our civilization and another dark age will set in, or our Church will be repudiated by a civilization of which it is unworthy.

175

In passing, he described the belief that a priest could change the substance of a piece of bread by saying words over it as 'intellectually intolerable'. He returned to the charge in a major sermon at Westminster Abbey on 14 June 1925, on Catholicism and Christianity. Taking as his text 'Thou shalt have none other Gods before Me', he said that the present position of the Church caused grave anxiety. The Catholic movement had proceeded apace. The value of the Reformation was belittled and derided by Anglo-Catholics. Doctrines repudiated in the Articles, such as invocation of the Saints, were openly taught. Sacramental practices, such as reservation, not heard of in the Church for 300 years, had been introduced in defiance of the law. These developments had alienated many from the Church. While 'this retrograde Catholic movement' was making headway, as Christianity became Catholicized, religion became contaminated by magic and the spiritual was degraded to the mechanical. The Catholicizing of Christianity was the paganizing of it. The priest was supposed, by virtue of a mechanical succession, to be endowed not merely with authority to act for the congregation but with spiritual powers, so that by correct ritual and words he could endue inanimate matter with spiritual character. This spiritual character could then be transferred to the worshipper who, prepared by priestly absolution, then and then only found salvation, so that the sacraments worked by magic 'or, in more polite phrase, *ex opere operato*'. There was no reason to think that God worked in such a way and no warrant for this belief in the teaching of Christ. Thus there was a fundamental difference of belief in the nature of God.

> We stand at the cross-roads. I cannot foresee the future. But during the last eight months I have seen enough of the situation within our Church to be gravely apprehensive.

He expounded the same theme at the Modern Churchmen's Conference at Oxford in August. While saying that 'no one regrets more than I do that recent developments of Anglo-Catholicism within the English Church have involved us once again in sacramental controversies', he urged his audience to 'abandon all magical views of the Eucharist' and 'insist that the operation of the Sacrament was a psychological process'. Again, at the open meeting of the Bishops to discuss Prayer Book revision on 20 October, he said that he could not vote for changes hostile to the tradition of the Refor-

176

mation. There were clergy who wanted to re-establish the superstitions of the Middle Ages. They desired the cultus of the Reserved Sacrament and that was a recrudescence of fetish worship.

Such statements were widely reported and duly denounced by the *Church Times* as unfair criticism of Anglo-Catholics. But not even the *Church Times* could represent them as unprovoked attacks. *Cet animal est méchant: il se défend.* For, meanwhile, the second wave of the Anglo-Catholic offensive in Birmingham had been launched. Early in 1925 the living of St Mark's, Washwood Heath, had fallen vacant. The Vicar of Saltley, H. D. Neison, who was also rural dean of the area, was patron of the living. After discussing the matter with the Bishop in February, Neison in April nominated H. E. Bennett as the new incumbent. This led to a long controversy and a voluminous correspondence. The parish had been introduced by its previous vicar to extreme Anglo-Catholic practices, including the use of a tabernacle for the reserved sacrament. Neison himself was also an advanced Anglo-Catholic and, at the start of the proceedings at any rate, seems to have been actuated by a desire that these practices should continue. Writing to Bennett on 18 May, Barnes asked for the removal of the tabernacle and an end to reservation. He said that if the law was thus obeyed, he would publicly institute Bennett. If not 'I will not license you either publicly or privately save after an intimation from the patron that if I do not he will take legal action to force me. If he gives such intimation I shall then, to avoid legal action, license you privately in the chapel here'. There may have been some genuine misunderstanding about what passed at the interview in February. But by now the patron obviously thought that the way ahead was clear and that he had only to threaten legal action for the Bishop to capitulate. The threat was duly made in a letter of 4 July and followed up by a solicitor's letter on 30 July to ram the point home. But in a letter of 14 July to Neison, Barnes pointed out that

> if legal proceedings were taken, my action would undoubtedly be upheld; but I have never yet been involved in a law-suit and law-suits between Christian ministers seem to me intolerable . . . I beg of you to consider carefully the whole situation. Is it right or seemly that a Rural Dean should force his Bishop to institute to a Benefice a priest who will not obey the law?

Neison himself seems to have been sincerely anxious to find a compromise solution; but at times he showed impatience and irritation, and at the end of August the press learned from him of the Bishop's refusal to institute. This was followed on 10 September by a long and detailed press statement on Neison's behalf. Meanwhile the churchwardens had entered the act, with a petition purporting to be signed by numerous parishioners, in which they sought an end to the interregnum. At the end of September Barnes sent them a considered reply, making clear his requirements for observance of the law and the doctrinal reasons behind them. He sent a copy of his letter to the press. He had at the same time written to Bennett to urge him to give the desired assurances and to say that he could not believe that the threat of a law-suit was meant seriously. The churchwardens at first sent an argumentative reply, which was also published, and in which they in effect demanded that existing practices should continue, but then withdrew from further correspondence on the grounds that legal proceedings were pending. Bennett, for his part, repeated his refusal to remove the tabernacle or discontinue reservation and demanded institution; he also wrote to the press to accuse the Bishop of prevarication. Barnes on 5 October replied at length to the churchwardens, setting out his requirements in detail. After some further correspondence with Neison, who was evidently growing more worried about his personal position and offering to resign as Rural Dean, the Bishop formulated his requirements even more precisely. They were that the consecrated elements 'must not be kept in any part of the Church to which the public have access' and that the Vicar should give assurances that he would

1. not use the tabernacle in his Church for the reservation of the consecrated elements;
2. not have public services different from those prescribed in the Book of Common Prayer in which the consecrated elements are used;
3. hold public services of morning and evening prayer on Sundays at times convenient for the parish.

Bennett somewhat disingenuously expressed himself ready to accept the three conditions in these words. But this was mere prevarication. For at the same time he insisted on reservation in another place where the public could have access. At this point the Bishop on 18 December formally issued a refusal to license him. In acknowledging it, Neison said that he had advised Bennett to accept reservation in the vestry and regretted his refusal to do so; he offered to discuss another solution for the parish. This changed the whole situation. The patron had dissociated himself from his nominee.

From now on all was comparatively plain sailing. Bennett appealed to the Archbishop of Canterbury, but Davidson, after consulting Barnes, gave him short shrift for insisting on more than either the Bishop or the patron wanted. By February the patron had found another candidate who readily gave the assurances for which the Bishop asked and was duly admitted to his benefice, drawing down upon his head the caustic comments of the *Church Times* for his pliability.

The episode was long-drawn-out but some significant conclusions emerge. First, Barnes had won the second round of the contest, after what had been at best a drawn first round. He had done so without at any time specifically sanctioning reservation in any form, even in the vestry. He had only allowed the inference to be drawn that he would not for the time being try to prevent it there. In refusing to allow it, he based himself on Cripps's *Law Relating to Church and Clergy* (1921 edition), where it is stated that 'the reservation of the sacrament and services connected therewith (e.g. the service of Benediction) are unlawful'. During the controversy he had made mistakes: he had undoubtedly given the impression that he would institute Bennett under certain conditions and had had to change his ground once or twice. He admitted, for example, in a private letter of December 1926, to the Bishop of St Edmundsbury and Ipswich, who had consulted him on similar problems:

I let it be known privately that if the matter were taken before the Courts I would yield under protest. Since then I have come to the conclusion that in this point I adopted a mistaken position. I now state that if in such a case the patron should bring the question before the Courts I will not defend my action neither will I yield: the final result will be that I go to prison for contempt of court.

This was all a new experience for him, he was extremely busy on other affairs and he was working almost entirely on his own, without assistants to draft or devil for him. Moreover, although he often wrote and spoke trenchantly, even harshly, about subjects on which other men were inclined to use more conventional religious language, he did not, unlike his opponents, descend to personal attacks or abusive epithets about them.

179

For the second conclusion to emerge is that, although this was ostensibly a dispute between the Bishop and one of his local clergy, it was in fact a carefully-orchestrated attack at national level by the Anglo-Catholics, who were bent on encompassing the Bishop's destruction or at best making life impossibly uncomfortable for him. As the *Church of England Newspaper* was to remind its readers in February 1929, 'as soon as the nomination of Dr Barnes was announced, an "anti-Barnes" campaign was organized, not in Birmingham, but outside the Diocese. Attempts were made before he arrived in the Diocese to make his position untenable, but the calibre of the man had been overlooked'. Thus the long delay between Neison's interview with the Bishop in February and his nomination of Bennett in April itself suggests that the local plan of campaign was being worked out far behind the front. It is evident from Neison's own letters that he grew to dislike more and more the role of front man which he was under pressure to play. Again, the sophisticated style of the churchwardens' reply to the Bishop of 2 October shows obvious signs of outside briefing. Indeed, when the churchwardens came to see Barnes in January 1926, when the dust had largely settled and they could speak for themselves, they were, according to the Bishop's manuscript note of the interview, quite frank about their dislike of many extreme practices introduced by the previous vicar; the clergy from Small Heath, who had been officiating at Washwood Heath during the interregnum and who almost certainly were dancing to strings pulled in London, had insisted on maintaining these practices against the churchwardens' request. Even at that stage, the orchestration continued: the Archdeacon of Aston, reporting to the Bishop on 6 January after seeing the churchwardens, wrote that 'the Anglo-Catholic caucus is now advising that another man should be nominated for the living. He is to be instructed to keep silence if asked the crucial questions about Reservation etc. so that he cannot be charged with having refused'. Evidence of the national campaign can also be seen in other spoiling attacks by which the Bishop was harassed at intervals. Thus the English Church Union sent a long and elaborately theological protest to the Archbishop of Canterbury against Barnes's Westminster sermon of 14 June, and in his own letter of 21 December to Davidson about the case, the Bishop refers to Bennett 'and those behind him (in particular, Mr Arnold Pinchard)', the Secretary of the Union. Incidentally, the English Church Union's protest and Davidson's mild reply caused Henson to write the Archbishop a letter, of which he sent a copy privately to Barnes and in which he said:

> That the English Church Union should insult an English Bishop is nothing new . . . It was inevitable that the *Church Times* should hail with sycophantic rapture language from your Grace which was sympathetic and almost deferential and which tacitly conceded the Union's impudent claim to be the rightful guardian of Anglican orthodoxy . . . That any man, Bishop, Priest or Layman, should be dealt with as the English Church Union is dealing with the Bishop of Birmingham, violates equity and carries the promise of the gravest mischief.

In his letter to Barnes himself, Henson wrote:

> The action of the ECU is of course tactical: they want to drive a wedge into the alliance of Evangelicals and Liberals by raising a cry of 'the Bible in danger' and to divert attention from their own proceedings . . . If I may take the liberty of a genuine friendship, I would say to you: Do not let the legitimate resentment against very gross unfairness carry you into mere controversy but, for one word of rebuke for Superstition, add two words of advocacy for Religion, that men (the nervous, ill-informed but well-meaning rank and file) may feel that the Interest of the Faith is your concern, and not really that of the Mass-mongers.

Another spoiling attack in the same campaign came in October when three Anglo-Catholic clergy, one of them Rosenthal and one a Canon of the Cathedral, wrote to the press to claim that 'Devotions' had been sanctioned by Russell Wakefield but, when publicly challenged by the Bishop to give chapter and verse, were unable to provide written evidence, although the *Church Times* then extracted from Wakefield, in retirement at Hove, what amounted to an admission that he had felt unable to prevent Devotions in wartime but had forbidden Benediction or Exposition. This was the episode which led directly to Barnes's general directive on the subject. A third attack came in an accusation that Barnes was illegally allowing Free Churchmen to preach in Anglican churches; this led him to produce full guidance on the subject after consulting Henson, who had been at the centre of the fray some years before and who, incidentally, wrote in December: 'I watch with something more than sympathy the good fight you are waging in Birmingham.' A fourth line of attack had been used by a deputation of five Birmingham clergy, including three Canons and

Rosenthal, whom the Archbishop, after obtaining Barnes's agreement, received in July. Davidson dealt with them firmly and fairly and, in particular, while disclaiming any *locus standi* in another bishop's diocese, urged them to accept his directions. One of them in fact took this advice. One more example of the campaign to oust the Bishop from Birmingham came with the death of Dean Ryle of Westminster in August, when a flood of wishful rumours were unloosed to the effect that Barnes would be appointed to succeed him.

The third significant effect was that the controversy did not end at Washwood Heath. Opinion was now aroused throughout the diocese. Even before the business at St Mark's was settled, the Bishop's directive on reservation in the Diocesan Magazine of 21 October led to a remarkable demonstration of support, unsolicited by him. On 5 November 1925, 166 of his clergy signed and presented to the Bishop a declaration of loyalty, of which the operative paragraph read: 'We pledge ourselves anew to give that ready obedience to your lawful directions which we, as loyal members of the Church of England, owe to you as our Bishop.' All clergy in the diocese, 257 in number, had been invited to sign and 214 replied, some of whom declined because they saw no need to repeat the promise of obedience made at their ordination. The signatories included clergy of all points of view, including Anglo-Catholics who rated loyalty above disagreement. To meet them and others, the declaration contained another paragraph: 'Certain of our number, however, in promising obedience, would desire quite candidly to state that they are not in agreement with the reasons of your injunctions as expressed in your Lordship's letter.'

The declaration of clergy loyalty was followed immediately by a similar declaration by 241 lay members of the Diocesan Conference. Of the 394 members, 35 declined the invitation to sign and 118 sent no reply. In acknowledging this declaration, Barnes wrote to G. A. Bryson, the chairman of the Diocesan Board of Finance, who had collected the signatures and who remained until the end of the Second World War a tower of strength in Barnes's support:

> No man could fail to be touched by such a manifestation of friendliness and understanding. I value it especially because it shows that there is in the diocese a strong desire for unity and order . . . I am convinced that there is within our Church a genuine and widespread eagerness to avoid ill-will. We cannot establish truth without public

argument but patient and friendly discussions will in the end lead to unity . . . If clergy and laity in the Diocese of Birmingham repudiate disorder, and are fired by the enthusiasm for truth and righteousness which is now spreading among young men and women, we shall help to make the Church worthy to lead the nation in years to come. Because the memorials which I have received give me hope of such a future, I send thanks which I cannot adequately express.

Meanwhile, however, the Anglo-Catholics had not been idle. The *Church Times* was able to make some play with the fact that only about two-thirds of the possible signatories had in fact signed. But more active opposition was to come. Basing themselves ostensibly on the Bishop's refusal to license clergy who did not accept his directives and on their understanding that diocesan funds were only available to parishes with licensed clergy, fourteen incumbents announced that they would no longer contribute to the Diocesan Board of Finance and would set up a separate board of their own. In substance this was a rather empty gesture, since they received a good deal more from diocesan funds than they put into them, as was made clear by an appeal from the English Church Union for financial support to the parishes in question. The Union claimed, in a letter to *The Times* of 29 December, that 'the Bishop of Birmingham's directions are avowedly part of a campaign against the doctrine of a real objective presence in the Holy Eucharist' and 'the faithful of our diocese ought not to be deprived, by the arbitrary will of a single Bishop, of devotional privileges which are enjoyed without molestation by the faithful of most English dioceses'. Questionable though the last statement was, the Union's support also made clear that this was a concerted act of defiance. It was in fact the famous 'rebellion' in the Birmingham diocese.

Barnes had to decide how to handle the rebels, whom he himself was always careful to call the 'so-called rebels'. Rumours that he intended legal action against them were quickly scotched. Although he never cancelled the licence of an existing curate in a 'rebel' parish, he gradually let it be known that he would not license any new assistant clergy to rebel parishes nor would he accept new incumbents unless they would give him the assurances he sought. The rebel parishes would receive no financial help for assistant clergy, as they had raised their own fund for this purpose; nor would any confirmations be held there or episcopal or other official visits be made to them. In this particular he was, consciously or not, following the line taken by Cosmo Lang, as Archbishop of York, who had written in 1913 to Russell Wakefield to say that he had sometimes provisionally sanctioned reservation for the sick under certain conditions but 'where my directives as to Reservation have not been complied with, I have been so far content to put the church concerned "under the ban", as it is called, that is, I do not visit them, hold confirmations in them or license their assistant clergy'. But Barnes tempered justice with mercy. He did not try to prevent the practices to which he objected while the existing incumbent remained. He was also able to ensure that curates in rebel parishes, misguided though they were, remained entitled to pensions by voluntary, rather than compulsory, contributions to the central funds, and he left it entirely to the discretion of the Committee administering the funds raised by his Church Extension appeal whether they allocated any of them to rebel parishes, as in fact they sometimes did. Nor did he try to break off social as opposed to official relations with disaffected clergy; he consistently invited the rebels to parties at his house, but they equally consistently refused. Deadlock was thus reached.

Luckily, from the point of view of peace and order, no further contest over a change of incumbent in a rebel parish took place for some time. Presumably the Anglo-Catholics were at this stage regrouping their forces, the last round having gone against them. In January 1927, moreover, the Vicar of St Anne's, Duddeston, left, after telling the Bishop that he had already given up some illegal services, and the new incumbent readily gave the required assurances. Barnes, for his part, could afford to wait, although he had to remain constantly on guard that rebel clergy did not slip under the net, as it were, for example by securing the chaplaincy of a sisterhood in someone else's parish. He also determined in future always to obtain in writing the assurances which he sought on obedience, and incidentally advised other sympathetic bishops to do the same. This was to be a long war of attrition, in which some of the rebels came to dislike the situation as much as Barnes did himself, sure that he could not surrender on principle. Some private comments on the situation at the time were made in a letter of 5 August 1926 to Charles Raven, who with characteristic enthusiasm had taken some rebels at their own valuation and offered himself as a bridge-builder:

When I came to it, Birmingham was, bar London, the most lawless

184

and mismanaged diocese in the country. I attempted to obtain a limited amount of law and order and asked that some of the more reprehensible practices should be abandoned. The result was a campaign of abuse and slander ending in a schism of some fourteen churches. It is now realised that the schism was a failure and the extremists are anxious to justify their position. They are told on all hands that what I asked them to do is nothing more than they did in obedience to Gore's directives, that they have broken away from the diocesan system and so forth. These things are obviously true and they are anxious to obtain recognition without if possible obeying the directives which I have issued. If you preach, as you suggest, they will have got the distinguished Evangelical leader Canon Raven to give them such recognition. You will in fact be used as an asset in their propaganda. I suggest that you should say that you will be most willing to preach in their churches as soon as they comply with their Bishop's request to abandon illegal practices based on unsound doctrine.

Meanwhile, the scene of battle had shifted back to another part of the field, the revision of the Prayer Book. The story has been told in full by Bishop Bell. After the draft measure had received the general approval of the Church Assembly in 1923, there had been further discussions on details and numerous representations had been made to the Bishops by various parties in the Church. Briefly, the Evangelicals wanted no change in the Communion service and above all no reservation; the Anglo-Catholics wanted both the changes and reservation, and some of them thought their objective could be achieved by having two alternative forms of Communion service, one more Catholic than the other, for use at discretion. The House of Bishops met in October 1925 to consider the draft and the representations, and unwisely decided to hold their first session in public. The Bishop of Norwich there proposed that the Communion service should be treated as a separate measure, as agreement to other reforms would then be easier to obtain. This was powerfully opposed by the Bishop of Durham, who argued that it meant shirking the main issue of eucharistic indiscipline, and the motion was defeated by 24 votes to 9 (Birmingham, Bradford, Bristol, Exeter, Gloucester, Norwich, St Edmundsbury and Ipswich, Sodor and Man, and Worcester). Barnes spoke and voted in favour of the motion, since he did not want to have to oppose the reforms which he favoured, as in the service of baptism, just because they were lumped together with reservation. His references to the growth of superstition aroused indignant protests from the Bishops of London and St Albans, who claimed that he was calling the whole Eucharist superstitious. St Albans, an extreme Anglo-Catholic, introduced a personal attack by accusing Barnes ironically of 'speaking with all the authority of a distinguished mathematician'. Sensibly, the Bishops decided to hold the rest of their meetings in private.

The meetings and the attendant controversy were to continue for two more years. In his account of the meetings, Bell remarks that 'from the start the Bishops of Norwich, Birmingham and Worcester were seen to be in opposition'. Henson's comment was that he did not envy these three bishops: 'they have invited the barbarians into Italy'. Certainly, a time came when the Bishop of Norwich no longer felt able to attend the meetings and Barnes kept him informed of progress by private letters. By June 1926, the Bishops had approved the idea of an alternative Communion service and taken decisions on three rubrics about reservation: the first allowing it for a particular person's communion on the same day with only one dissentient, the second allowing it for the possible needs of the sick by 19 votes to 11, and the third forbidding it for any other purpose by 25 votes to 6. To a clergyman who wrote to him shortly afterwards deploring the risk of division in the Church, Barnes replied privately:

I have read your letter with great interest and I regret to add almost complete pessimism. The Bishops have chosen their path. A minority of us protest against ecclesiastical reaction; but to it the majority are committed. We are to have an alternative Communion office. Reservation is to be allowed with 'safeguards' which will prove illusory. While Old Testament scholarship is recognized the results of the application of similar methods to the New Testament are tabu. Possibly a generation hence there may be another and healthier stage of Prayer Book revision. At the moment we had better echo the words of Pitt and 'roll up the map'.

But in fact he had by no means given up the struggle. In September 1926, he preached at Westminster Abbey on the 'Necessity for Modernism', a label which he was increasingly accepting for himself. He claimed that

Modernism is not a negative intellectualism . . . Modernists place loyalty to truth . . . above any lesser loyalty to institution or tradition

... Modernists are ... heirs of the Reformation and the Evangelical movement. The gulf between Modernists and the modern Evangelical has practically vanished ... Modernism ... produces the piety mingled with pity and humour which is the natural outcome of a living faith ... Modernism marks the new direction of our religious evolution.

For as he had said earlier in the sermon

Magical sacramentalism, Second Adventism and spiritualism are variants of primitive belief whose day is past ... The alternatives of religious evolution or religious decay lie before us. What is the path of religious evolution? I find it in the words: 'Follow me and leave the dead to bury their dead.'

This passage caused some offence, and the *Church Times* published a long letter from Russell Wakefield, volunteering, 'if a very humble person dare advise a great mathematician', a series of criticisms of the teaching in the sermon. Privately, Barnes stigmatized this intervention as 'an action without precedent in the annals of the English episcopate'; but he asked people to ignore it in view of Wakefield's ill-health. 'My predecessor's criticisms would neither take their present shape nor be made public if he had retained his powers of earlier years.' Unknown to Barnes, Wakefield had in fact more than once approached Davidson behind the scenes in support of the Birmingham Anglo-Catholics and in personal denigration of Barnes; but the Archbishop had given him little encouragement. As so often, while Barnes directed his remarks at facts and ideas, his opponents directed theirs at him.

Another flurry arose in December when some comments of his on false sacramental teaching led a group of Birmingham clergy, representing all points of view and including some 'rebels', to issue a statement denying that they held or taught such doctrines. As the originator of the statement explained in a private letter to the Bishop, it was meant to be helpful to him. But in fact it sounded as if they were criticizing him for crying wolf and thus only gave a new handle to his opponents. He set out his views on familiar lines in his reply, ending:

Cannot you and your co-signatories follow up the disclaimer of your memorandum and unite, on a basis of sound doctrine, to establish law and order in the diocese? The coming of Christmas ought to make us renew our efforts to seek peace through truth.

Peace and truth were always his watchwords. But at present he felt himself surrounded by struggle and falsehood. In accordance with the joint decision of the Bishops, he refused to comment publicly on the Prayer Book problem until the new proposals were themselves made public, as they were on 7 February 1927. He then issued a long statement to explain why he could not 'agree with the majority of the Bishops in commending these proposals in their entirety to the Church'. Paying tribute to the good humour of the discussions, he welcomed most of the changes, notably in the marriage service. Some risks which he saw, as in the permission for extempore prayers which could lead to invocation of the saints, were possibly worth taking. But the alternative Communion office was nearer to the Roman Mass and could give rise to the belief that 'a particular form of words effects a miraculous change in the bread and wine'. But his main objection was to the provision for perpetual reservation and for the Church to make its own rules on the mode of reservation which could open the way to adoration.

The Church of England will thereby seem committed to a belief that spiritual properties can be given to material objects. Economists are familiar with Gresham's Law: where both circulate, bad money drives out good. A similar law operates to produce religious degeneration. Allow superstition its opportunity and in times of religious reaction it will prove stronger than truth.

He saw the contemporary situation as one of emotional disturbance and disorder, and it was a singularly unfortunate time for Prayer Book revision.

So I plead that the nation, as represented by Parliament, should permit the National Church to adopt the practically non-contentious proposals which constitute the great part of those now brought forward. But I would have such matters as the new Consecration Prayer and Perpetual Reservation postponed for a generation. During that time disorder might continue: my experience makes me fear that it will not be ended if all that is now suggested should be allowed. But religious moods and fancies change; and the English people are essentially law-abiding.

This statement earned him a large number of letters, mostly in agreement with his main position but often on minor points which he answered patiently, such as prayers for the dead and for the King, the position of the celebrant at the Holy Table, the use of wafers instead of bread, or the practice of 'intinction' rather than communion in two kinds. Meanwhile, the Bishops continued their work on the recommendations of the Lower Houses of Convocation. Writing to the Bishop of Norwich on 9 March, Barnes said:

> The whole of Saturday morning last was taken up with a discussion of reservation regulations. I was not alone in finding the whole matter very unpleasant. But so far as I can see at the present time, in addition to our two selves only the Bishops of Exeter and Worcester will vote against the book.

This was an accurate forecast. In reply to a letter from Bishop Knox, he wrote:

> I remain astonished that the Evangelical Bishops of the present time should have assented to the new Prayer Book; and I cannot but think that many of them will live to regret that they did not maintain the principles for which Evangelicalism has stood in the history of the last two centuries at least.

The Convocations approved the book at the end of March, not without a public attack on Barnes's attitude to reservation by Canon Long, one of his 'rebel' clergy. The Bishop of Norwich wrote to ask about the attitudes of the Bishops of London and Durham, and Barnes answered:

> I must confess that I personally have no confidence that the Bishop of London will make a steady effort to ensure lawful obedience to the new Prayer Book should it be accepted. He has said nothing to indicate that such will be his policy and unless such assurances come from him in public, we must necessarily assume that the policy of drift will continue in the London Diocese. I imagine that Henson will continue to support the new Prayer Book whatever the attitude of the Bishop of London may be. I had some talk with Henson two months ago and he then led me to understand that he regarded the new Prayer Book as a sort of policy of despair. Some attempt must be made to mend matters: this involved concessions: and we must hope that the concessions would not so radically alter the doctrinal position of the Church of England as to lead to disruption. I hope that I do not misrepresent him: I

189

certainly do not exaggerate when I say that he was filled with gloomy anticipations of the future. I personally see in the proposed rules for Reservation so many loopholes that by an ingenious interpretation of these rules and a little episcopal laxity the whole cultus of transubstantiation can be set going.

Henson's attitude had, indeed, greatly disappointed Barnes. In another private letter about this time, he wrote

Many of us are very sorry at the new attitude of the Bishop of Durham. It has been common talk among his friends for the last two months that he is on his way to join his old opponents and so to stultify his career. The root cause seems to be his fear of Bolshevism and a hope that, by ignoring all differences, the Church of England may be a bulwark against the Communism which he dreads.

And, in yet another letter,

We are passing through the worst period, as I hope, of the post-war reaction and superstition is appallingly rife. Also many are afraid of Communism and think that an Anglo-Catholic Church can possibly avert its oncoming. Within the last month or two, this fear has caused Henson to go over to his old opponents . . . Things will, I believe, slowly get better but we must possess our souls in patience and endure hard knocks.

To do Henson justice, if he lost his courage he never lost his wit. A story is told of the time that one day, meeting at Lambeth, the Bishops were sitting round the fire, when Barnes came in and could find no free chair in the circle. A voice cried out 'Ah, my Lord of Birmingham, come in, sit on the fire and anticipate the judgement of the Universal Church'. That is vintage Henson.

Another story of those days of controversy over magical sacramentalism relates that Barnes went out for a walk in Birmingham and ran into the chaplain of the Roman Catholic convent across the road. Wondering if he should know him, he asked who he was and received the reply, 'The magician at your gate, my Lord'.

More seriously, the question of episcopal authority was the point on which the Home Secretary, Joynson-Hicks, had sought assurances from the Archbishop during February and March but received only vague replies. Similarly, the Archbishop told Storr that the Bishops would act together to secure obedience to the new rules, but he failed to specify how they would do so. Perhaps he either thought that this would be his successor's task or he more profoundly doubted the resolution of the Bishops.

In another private letter later in the year Barnes wrote:

> The Bishops have no immediate settled and agreed policy as regards the maintenance of order . . . they are hoping and praying that disobedience will not be extensive or infectious. There is no indication that they are going to act together or as a body: rather the contrary. Within the last month or two Truro has introduced incense into his Cathedral: the Bishops of London and St Albans have gone out of their way to say that private adoration of the consecrated elements is not forbidden in the new Prayer Book.

At a meeting of the Birmingham Diocesan Conference in June, he again set out his case against the book at length, arguing that it gave two services of Holy Communion, allowed perpetual reservation, did not guard against misuse of prayers for the dead, and opened the way to false doctrine and administrative disorder. Incidentally, he repeated here the argument, which he had used before, that the sacrament was a psychological process and that 'you can no more reserve a psychological process than you can reserve an explosive shell'. But, despite his advocacy, the voting was

Bishop: 1 against
Clergy: 107 for, 47 against, 1 no vote
Laity: 129 for, 99 against, 1 no vote

This local pattern was repeated on the national level. The Church Assembly passed the book in July by large majorities, with the four bishops dissenting, and here again the lay minority was larger than the clerical. This might have been seen as an omen for Parliament, with which the decision now lay. Barnes wrote to a brother bishop: 'I continue to hope that Parliament will once again show that the English laity can save the English Church.' Bishop Talbot and others argued that Parliament should accept meekly the wishes of the Church Assembly, since otherwise the Church would be driven to disestablishment. The Bishop of Norwich wrote to *The Times* dismissing this argument and to Barnes to say 'If I get mangled and mauled in subsequent correspondence, will you have the great kindness to come to the rescue of my feeble body? It would be a pity if I should appear to be an isolated crank'. But Barnes's intervention was not needed. Rather than persuading the Church not to abandon the State, he was at pains both in public and private to persuade the opponents of the book not to leave the Church if it was passed. Preaching at Westminster Abbey in July, he argued that as long as those who held the religion which Jesus taught could worship God 'in spirit and in truth' in their Church, it was their duty to remain in it.

But he was about to come right into the heart of the storm. Since his monkey sermons at Westminster, he had continued to preach on the truth of evolution and its compatibility with Christian belief. In a sermon in February 1925, for example, he claimed the discovery of the Taungs skull in South Africa as proof that 'Darwin had triumphed'; this, incidentally, led Raymond Dart, the skull's finder, to send him an inscribed photograph of it. Now, in September 1927, he reverted to the theme in Westminster Abbey:

Darwin's assertion that man has sprung from the apes has stood the test of more than half a century of critical examination . . . The stories of the creation of Adam and Eve, of their primal innocence and of their fall, have become for us folk-lore . . . Man's special creation was one of the primary assumptions of the Catholic system. In it the Fall explained the origin of sin: and a horrible theory of the propagation of sin, reared on the basis of the Fall by Augustine, was accepted by official Catholic theologians.

Darwin's triumph has destroyed the whole theological scheme . . . Man is not a being who has fallen from an ideal state of perfect innocence; he is an animal slowly gaining spiritual understanding . . . If there be a God behind nature, He can show His creative activity through the process of emergent evolution just as definitely as by special creation.

That He has used evil in His plan is obvious and it puzzles us to reconcile this fact with His goodness and power. But there is no new problem herein. Christ knew that there was much evil in the world which God made, evil for which God must therefore be ultimately responsible. Christ did not offer the delusive explanation which many have thought the Fall provided. But none the less He could affirm that God is the loving father of us all . . . In the belief that God's creation has a purpose we postulate the immortality of the soul.

The modern scientific view of the origin of man's body and mind agrees well with Christ's teaching. But it cannot be reconciled with certain statements of St Paul nor with a belief in the infallibility either of the Bible or the Church . . . Wisdom is God's gift and through wisdom men are blessed . . . Let us walk then as children of light.

Nothing new in this for those familiar with Barnes's thinking. But it let loose a flood of reports, comments and correspondence. The *Morning Post* called it a sensation: 'This sermon will provoke controversies and raise doubts by which the whole structure of revealed religion must be severely tested.' The Archbishop, invited to comment publicly, refused to do so. Gore called it a 'plea that we should be free of obscurantism and this is wholesome counsel'. Others rallied to defence of the Fall and produced their own theories of it, pre-mundane or otherwise. The *Church Times*, true to its habit of personalizing problems, headed its leader 'The over-bold Dr Barnes' and attributed to him the motive of enjoying destructiveness. The British Israelites, for good measure, took up the cudgels for the infallible Bible and described Barnes as pagan.

But this was only the first stage. Two weeks later, on 6 October, at a lunch-hour service in Birmingham Parish Church attended by the Lord Mayor, Barnes deliberately spoke on 'Sacramental Truth and Falsehood'. Although he did not specifically mention the Prayer Book question, it underlay his whole thesis. As he said, 'Today I propose to be controversial . . . I make no apology . . . because the English Church will break in pieces unless unity as to sacramental doctrine can be reached'. After speaking of the value of sacraments in religion as in life as a whole, he went on, again on a familiar theme, but with unusually vigorous language:

> It is fatally easy to pass from the idea that sacraments serve to reveal God to a belief that through them we can mechanically bring God to men, or cause Him to locate Himself in some object or place. Such a belief belongs to the realm of primitive magic . . . The belief that a bronze idol should be worshipped is to us contemptible. But to many an educated Hindu such worship makes an irresistible appeal . . . There are among ourselves today men and women whose sacramental beliefs are not far from those of the cultured Hindu idolator. They pretend that a priest, using the right words and acts, can change a piece of bread so that within it there is the real presence of Christ.
>
> The idea can be disproved by experiment. If there were a *physical* change in the bread chemical analysis would enable us to detect it. All are agreed that this type of change does not take place. Yet if there be a

spiritual change it must surely be possible for man to recognize it by his spiritual perception.

Now I assert . . . that there is no man living who, if a piece of bread were presented to him, could say whether or not it had been consecrated. Personally, I find it hard to attach any meaning to a spiritual change in dead matter, but if it exists there must surely be some living person who can perceive its existence. If there be no such person, belief in such a change is an idle superstition . . .

I am quite prepared to believe in transubstantiation when I can find a person who will come to the chapel of my house and tell me correctly whether a piece of bread which I present to him has undergone the change for which believers in transubstantiation contend . . .

I would be the last to doubt that the Real Presence of Christ can be with men in the service of the Holy Communion. But the whole service is the sacrament . . . Christ gives Himself to His faithful servants: to those who worship Him in spirit and in truth . . . It is a harmful superstition that a Church in which consecrated bread is kept is for that reason more holy . . . The Divine Spirit of Christ is everywhere: He cannot be located in material things . . . Christ dwells not among things that are cold and inert, but with the living Christian struggling, seeking, waiting upon God.

The reaction was immediate, mostly hostile. The Bishop of London said that the sermon had given pain to thousands and the Bishop of Southwark, Garbett, spoke of 'wounding and contemptuous attacks on the beliefs of many of his fellow Churchmen'. Bishop Talbot wrote to *The Times* to call the utterance an outrage and the parallel with the Hindu idolator insulting, and he explicitly linked Barnes's motives with opposition to the new Prayer Book; but Bethune-Baker wrote in reply to emphasize the change in doctrine implied in the new Order for the Communion service and to call it an outrage 'that clergymen of the reformed Church of England should be allowed to speak of "having our Lord" in an aumbry or on the altar'. Of the Church papers, only the *Record* defended Barnes, for reminding people of 'the errors which our Church discarded at the Reformation'.

But there was not time for any official opposition to develop. It was noted that Barnes was to preach at St Paul's on 15 October and there was some speculation whether the Bishop of London would try to forbid him. What happened was even more spectacular. As Barnes took his place in the pulpit, Canon Bullock-Webster, rector of a City church and ironically a distant relative of Barnes's wife, rose, walked forward and, facing the congregation, delivered what he called a Solemn Denunciation and Protest, couched in legalistic language. He denounced the Bishop 'for that by false and heretical teaching in his frequent public utterances he has denied and poured contempt upon the doctrines and sacraments of the Holy Catholic Church' and he called upon the Bishop of London 'to inhibit the said Bishop from preaching or ministering in any church within his jurisdiction' and 'on the Archbishop and Bishops of the Province of Canterbury to try the said Bishop in respect of these alleged heretical and profane utterances and, if he be found guilty, forthwith to depose him and cast him out of the Church of God until such time as he do repent himself and recant his grievous errors'. He ended: 'Now, brethren, lest our ears should be defiled with fresh profanities, I invite all faithful believers here present to join me in leaving this church before the sermon is delivered and to continue our worship elsewhere.' He then left, with those who had accompanied him to the Cathedral, for his own church, where he conducted a 'Mass of Reparation' and read out his protest again.

Barnes had been sent a private warning that something of the kind was afoot since Bullock-Webster was collecting supporters, although as the warning was sent on 13 October it may not have reached him in time. Now he stood silent through this medieval performance and then quietly delivered his sermon, which was once more on the theme of evolution as God's plan for the world. Dean Inge seems at one point to have tried to have the organ drown Bullock-Webster's voice but then perhaps thought that he should be allowed to make an exhibition of himself. When Bullock-Webster sent him a copy of the protest, Inge replied: 'Since you have had the impertinence to write to me in connection with what happened yesterday, I must reply that until I receive from you a full and proper apology for your scandalous and disgraceful behaviour in brawling in the Cathedral, I refuse to have any communication with you whatever.' Brawling was an offence under the Public Worship Regulation Act of 1874. In reply Bullock-Webster, who could certainly have been prosecuted under that Act, refused to apologize unless Inge expressed regret for inviting Barnes to preach. This Inge ignored. The Bishop of London delivered a tepid and half-hearted rebuke to Bullock-Webster, who then to all intents and purposes faded out of history.

But without meaning to do so he had served his purpose. Barnes used to recall afterwards that, in the taxi from St Paul's to catch the train back to Birmingham, he told his wife that this incident would make possible the defeat of the Revised Prayer Book. The method he chose to start this process was to write an open letter to the Archbishop of Canterbury. On a previous occasion, at the height of the conflict over St Mark's, Washwood Heath, he had asked the Archbishop if he might address him such a letter. It had not in the event proved necessary, as the patron gave way at that point. Davidson had then replied, in his own hand:

> Of course I have no sort of objection to your writing me an 'open' letter such as you propose.
>
> You will not, I hope, think me discourteous, or, in the true sense, 'impertinent', if I say to you how strongly I feel that if I were writing what needs putting before these people I should avoid the use of phrases which are not merely irritants but which surely do expose you needlessly to challenge or attack on the part of devout souls nurtured from childhood in deep reverence for sacramental truth. Can we, I wonder, quite dogmatically assert that nothing can 'give spiritual properties to dead matter'? I salute the Cenotaph because of the property which it has by association and dedication acquired of conveying thought to me. The analogy is not exact, but does it not serve to make us cautious of using words like 'magic' when addressing those to whom these things present themselves with a sacred and devout glamour which we must treat without scornfulness. I do not pause to ask as an ignoramus from a master of science whether the bare phrase 'dead matter' quite conclusively covers the ground in regard to things material. Pardon my presumption in saying this, but I do feel the importance of our choice of phrases in which to convey truth without exasperating those whom we want to help thereto.

This exquisitely tactful letter was typical of Davidson's overriding concern for unity and concord. But it had given Barnes the green light for advancing by way of open letter. Bell, in his life of Davidson, prefaces his account of the exchanges which followed with a delightfully apposite quotation from Foxe's *Actes and Monuments*:

> ... Then said the cardinal to them, 'Is this Dr Barnes your man that is accused of heresy?' 'Yea, and please your grace; and we trust ye shall find him reformable, for he is both well learned and wise.' 'What, master doctor,' said the cardinal; 'had ye not a sufficient scope in the Scriptures to teach the people?' ... And Barnes answered, 'I spake

nothing but the truth out of the Scriptures, according to my conscience, and according to the old doctors'. And then did Barnes deliver him six sheets of paper written, to confirm and corroborate his sayings. The cardinal received them smiling on him and saying, 'We perceive then that you intend to stand to your articles and to shew your learning'. 'Yea,' said Barnes, 'that I do intend, by God's grace, with your Lordship's favour.'

Barnes now wrote on 19 October 1927:

Certain reflections upon an interruption to the service in St Paul's Cathedral when I was preaching there last Sunday may well take the form of an open letter to yourself, as the incident has a significance which your Grace will not minimize.

A dozen years ago, I found myself Master of the Temple, and as such minister to that congregation which, with its legal nucleus, is probably the most intellectual in England. Soon I discovered that, while ancient pieties and the stress of war brought men and women to worship in the Temple Church, there were relatively few among them for whom Christian dogma had any vitality. Traditional formulas had withered in the mental environment created by modern knowledge, and had been replaced by a wistful agnosticism. I therefore began to preach sermons in which I set forth clearly my own beliefs and doubts. I found immediate response and shrewd criticism. I was thereby encouraged to read widely. I learned the value of plain speech. If honest conviction is expressed in simple language, and maintained by reasoned argument, the strength of its appeal is great. I still try thus to study and to teach. I neither have, nor seek to have, skill in controversy; so, while I argue forcibly against untrue doctrines, I never criticize individuals who hold them. Most of my teaching is positive – and unreported.

One cause of weakness of the Church has arisen from the apparent determination of religious teachers to ignore scientific discovery. Though all competent biologists accept man's evolution from an ape-like stock, the theological consequences of such belief are still seldom stated. I set myself years ago to expound these consequences and to show why they did not seem to me to upset the main Christian position. On this topic I have preached or spoken scores of times. A sermon which I preached when the British Association met at Cardiff in 1920 travelled round the world and brought me over a thousand letters. I have always admitted that neither evolution nor Copernican astronomy was accepted at the Reformation, when our Prayerbook and Articles received substantially their present form, but the whole theological scheme reared by Augustine on the Fall can be rejected without injury to the main fabric of Christian belief.

The second main reason for the present alienation of educated men and women from the Church of England is growth of erroneous Sacramental doctrines. During and since the War the degeneration of Sacramental belief has proceeded apace, until today late medieval theories, rejected in the bluntest language at the Reformation, are openly taught in Anglican churches. Hitherto those who hold such theories have merely asked for tolerance within our Communion, but at St Paul's last Sunday I was denounced for condemning exactly those Sacramental errors which our Church repudiates. A new era has apparently opened when a Bishop of the Church of England who upholds its traditional Sacramental doctrine is for that reason to be exposed to public attack by those who ignore what is seemly in public worship.

The immediate cause of the outburst appears to be a statement, which I now reaffirm, that the doctrine of Transubstantiation is untrue. As every student of comparative religion knows, it has affinities with the magico-religious beliefs of a lower cultural level than that of our present civilization. I have not hesitated to describe the belief as a superstition, inasmuch as one of our present Articles says that 'it overthroweth the nature of a sacrament, and hath given occasion to many superstitions'. I have pointed out the close parallels between the arguments by which ineffective attempts are made to defend alike transubstantiation and idolatry, and I need not remind your Grace that the final rubric of our present Communion service uses the word 'idolatry'. We have no right to assume the existence of spiritual properties in an inanimate object unless they can be spiritually discerned. Yet there is no man living who possesses the spiritual discernment by which to discriminate between consecrated and unconsecrated bread.

For the last twenty years I have constantly urged in my teaching that our Church formally denies that any change occurs in the bread and wine at consecration. According to medieval theory, matter possesses accidents and substance. The accidents are physical properties, which we can perceive by the senses, and no one has ever suggested that these are changed at consecration. If any change at all takes place it must then be in the substance, but such change of the substance the Church of England declares to be repugnant to the plain words of Scripture. I grieve at the suggestion that we who value traditional Anglican doctrine thereby depreciate the Sacraments. In reply I spoke as follows in the Birmingham address which called forth the recent protest: –

'We understand Sacramental grace in its fullness and power, not by foolishly speaking of bread as if it were God Himself, but when the Heavens open for us and for a moment we see the whole of Creation as the expression of God's purpose and Him Himself in wisdom, might and love, the goal to Whom our striving leads and the end where man's restless spirit has peace.'

In this letter I have endeavoured to set before Your Grace as clearly and decisively as I can the teaching against which objection has been taken. It is not false and heretical. No protest must hinder me as a Bishop, and indeed as a Christian, from upholding religious truth. No man shall drive me to Tennessee or to Rome. It is vital to the welfare of English religion that the officers of the National Church should fear neither to welcome new knowledge nor to maintain all that is sound in ancient doctrine. The standard of education is slowly rising.

I invite Your Grace to consider what steps can be taken to help those of us who are giving of our best to fit the Church to be in the future the spiritual guide of an educated nation.

This letter, of course, calls for no public reply.

The Archbishop's reply of 22 October, which was sent to the press, has been given in full in Bell's life of him. He evidently tried to treat the matter as lightly as he could, deploring the 'unseemly incident' at St Paul's and suggesting that the 'gorilla sermons' had been overrated, both by Barnes in thinking that so many people still clung to old theories and by those who denounced him. No one in England wanted to lead or drive him either to Rome or Tennessee. But there was indignation over his references to Holy Communion. The most careful language possible was needed. Some of Barnes's comments had given real offence and could be interpreted as condemning a much wider range of believers than the Anglo-Catholics, although Davidson did not name them. While deprecating discussion of such matters in the press, he suggested that on further consideration Barnes might want to modify some of his 'negative and destructive statements' and ended by a scriptural plea for meekness and long-suffering.

Bernard Shaw described the Archbishop's letter as 'a heartfelt plea for ambiguity', and a Birmingham barrister composed a limerick:

> There was a Lord Bishop of Birmingham
> Who taught dogmas and truth concerning 'em;
>   But Randall said 'Hence,
>   Go sit on a fence,
> It's the way to earn fees without earning 'em'.

In fact, the many letters which Barnes was receiving at this time showed what a remarkably live issue evolution still was. That is to say, the issue was not belief in the fact of evolution as such, but the implications of it for Christian doctrine. While a few of his correspondents abused him for denying the literal truth of the Bible, many more thanked him for saying something which needed saying and which they had long waited to hear from someone in authority in the Church. Indeed, numbers of these letters came from clergymen, who had either been basing their teaching on evolution with what they saw as boldness or had not had the courage of their convictions from knowledge of the strength of the opposition. On the Archbishop's other point, the vast majority of Barnes's letters came from people who, so far from being wounded by his utterances, had found them of positive help. He took up this point and others in a further open letter to the Archbishop on 27 October, which he himself delivered into Davidson's hands at Lambeth:

I would publicly thank your Grace for your letter in answer to my own.

By your tacit acknowledgement of the truth of the biological doctrine of evolution your Grace removes from Christian ministers of our Church any qualms in proclaiming it. Of course, in my 'gorilla sermons', as you smilingly label them, I have sought to emphasize not so much the doctrine itself as the readjustments of traditional Christian dogma consequent upon its acceptance. Differences of opinion have arisen as to the legitimacy of such action. After your Grace's statement such differences are less likely to occur. I take this opportunity to urge that, in a greater freedom to remodel Christian theology on such a basis, we must preserve rather than disparage the many-sided excellence of the Old Testament. The sombre insight of the Wisdom literature, the inspired internationalism of the Book of Jonah, the spiritual confidence of the Psalms and, above all, the ethical monotheism of the great Hebrew prophets are supremely important in our religious heritage. Because we abandon Jewish cosmogony we must not forget that to understand Christ aright we need to know the spiritual development of His race.

In regard to the Sacramental issue, I note that your Grace repudiates the doctrine of transubstantiation. I have also with satisfaction failed to find any similar repudiation of my own sacramental teaching. Naturally I am sorry that your Grace should have to say that I have given 'real offence' to some members of our Church. Such offence as I have given may to some be aggravated by the knowledge that all my 'controversial' sermons have been most carefully prepared. With grave anxiety I have weighed words and phrases, sought due balance, and tried to advocate truth without giving needless pain. I might plead that some pain is inevitable: truth pierces like a sword: it hurts at times. I need not suggest to your Grace that our Lord may have had this fact in mind when He said: 'I come not to send peace but a sword.'

About 1100 relevant letters have reached me during the past fortnight: less than 40 have been critical or abusive. In these the only serious contention is that any experimental test of sacramental dogmas must be inadequate. Here I cannot agree, and would endeavour to make my reason clearer than it seems to appear.

Medieval method, which still too largely survives in theology, consists in deducing dogmas from the interpretations which particular texts of the Bible have in the past received from a string of scholars or saints. The modern man, influenced by the scientific method of our era, at once seeks to test by experiment any statement which he is asked to accept. This attitude of mind has become commonplace in physics and biology, and is being rapidly extended to psychology. Now the dogma of transubstantiation only differs from that of an objective real presence in the consecrated elements in that the former rests on a now discarded philosophy of matter while the latter has no philosophical basis at all. Both dogmas belong to a domain of religious psychology in which experimental tests can be made. It is surely fair (even if not desirable) to suggest that such tests could be reverently carried out in a suitable place. Moreover, since these tests will show that no man by his spiritual capacity can distinguish consecrated from unconsecrated bread, we can assume that the consecration of material objects causes no spiritual change in them. In short, spiritual grace is given, not to the elements which are its vehicles in the Sacrament of Holy Communion, but to the worshipper who takes, eats and drinks as he comes with faith and prayer and love to Christ.

Your Grace reminds me of Bishop Lightfoot and I would submit that my sacramental teaching does not conflict with his nor with that of his friend and my master Dr Hort. I venture simply to restate it: –

(a) The real presence of Christ can be with his followers in public worship. He is present wherever two or three are gathered in His name.

(b) A special solemnity attaches to the celebration of the Lord's Supper, inasmuch as for most Christians the sense of Christ's presence is then strengthened. For such it is a sacrament, the 'fellowship meal', the communion 'with each other and the Lord'.

(c) There is no *objective* real presence of Christ attached to the bread and wine used in Holy Communion.

Your Grace will not inquire why I thus insist on what I maintain

201

to be alike the true and the traditional sacramental doctrine of the Church. All our serious administrative difficulties as Bishops are due to erroneous sacramental beliefs. From the belief that a consecrated wafer is really (as I recently heard a poor woman say) 'Christ my Saviour' most of the irregularities which have crept into our churches of recent years will naturally follow. Only by continuance of clear teaching can we reach that 'unity of the Spirit in the bond of peace' which your Grace so beautifully commends. To that end I cannot personally regret discussion of such high matters even in the public Press. Surely there can be, among those tasks to which you bid us as Bishops to turn, none larger than to bring the great truths of religion to the mass of men and women now indifferent to all forms of Christian belief. It is our duty to show them the beauty and power of a reasonable faith. We shall never profane the sanctities of our Church if we honestly try by any method open to us to get men to worship Christ in spirit *and in truth.*

The Archbishop's first reply, and he did not send a second, was accorded all the adjectives which it undoubtedly deserved: fatherly, direct, clear, wise, firm, adroit, ironical, statesmanlike. But it was generally seen as a gentle rebuke to Barnes and the rest of the bishops hastened to climb on to the bandwagon against their colleague. Thus the Archbishop of York called him obstinate and spoke of 'methods inappropriate in the sphere of spiritual experience'; Temple of Manchester said that he gave pain needlessly and therefore cruelly and accused him of arguing incompetently; Woods of Winchester spoke of his contemptuous tone and urged him to think again; Henson of Durham described his remarks on the sacrament as a breach of good taste but none the less, with his own experiences no doubt in mind, deprecated a heresy-hunt; the Archbishop of New Zealand suggested that he was contentious and narrow-minded; Gore objected to the abuse, ridicule, obloquy and contempt which he cast on doctrines allowed by the Church; David of Liverpool thought the moment was not wisely chosen for his criticisms; Kempthorne of Lichfield complained that no single bishop could speak authoritatively for the Church of England; Headlam of Gloucester resented the use of crude ideas to criticize the doctrine of transubstantiation; the Bishop of Ely deplored the pain and distress caused to believers; and Russell Wakefield egregiously regretted the burden cast on the aged Archbishop. Of the whole bench of bishops only Pollock of Norwich said that he knew what it was to stand alone, even if he disagreed, while the Bishops of Ripon and Bradford sent a smart rebuke to Bullock-Webster, who had tried to enlist their support. Only Lord Halifax wrote to the *Church Times* to suggest that it was the duty of churchmen to uphold Bullock-Webster's protest, and also privately to the Archbishop asking for Barnes to be 'called over the coals'. The *Church Times* itself wrote of the 'harassed and troubled diocese' of Birmingham, called for Barnes to be disciplined and took the occasion to question the political appointment of bishops, an opinion echoed by the Warden of Keble College in a letter to *The Times*. But, on the whole, reactions as expressed in press correspondence were much more balanced. Criticism focused more on the manner than the matter of Barnes's approach. Thus the *Guardian* spoke of a 'widespread shrinking from the language employed' by him. The *Morning Post*, while praising his lucidity and courage, doubted if his second letter was needed.

Many commentators simply had not bothered to read or understand his remarks and assumed that he was talking of applying physical or chemical tests to the consecrated elements. Thus the Bishop of Winchester suggested that 'You may as well talk of measuring heaven with a footrule'. A correspondent wrote to the Archbishop of Canterbury that 'at present there is nothing to prevent Dr Barnes consecrating a whole loaf and sending it to the Public Analyst', while another critic pointed out that 'before his consecration Dr Barnes, chemically speaking, consisted of water and carbon, a little phosphorus and calcium, the whole worth a few shillings; after consecration, he was chemically the same, and yet he is a bishop'. But others understood more clearly what he was trying to achieve. The *Christian World* complained that no bishops stood by Barnes 'who is left standing alone on the burning deck', and the *Church of England Newspaper* urged that 'Dr Barnes should not be allowed to fight alone' against transubstantiation; 'it is the duty of the Bishops to act unitedly and without delay'. The Regius Professor of Hebrew at Cambridge, in a letter to *The Times*, pointed the same moral for the Prayer Book revision. Similarly, the *Manchester Guardian*, commenting on Davidson's letter, said that peace could be bought at too high a price, and, in the same vein, the *Evening Despatch* held it necessary for churchmen 'to speak out in words that cannot be misunderstood'. The *Daily News* reported that the great majority of letters from its readers supported Barnes. But, as so often, it was left to Dean Inge to make the most pungent and apposite comments. In the *Evening Standard* he wrote that Barnes was not personally insulting High Churchmen but making a stand against doctrines rejected at the Reformation; while, in the *Church of England Newspaper*, he said: 'my chivalrous feelings are revolted when I see archbishops and bishops joining a mob of guttersnipes in pelting one of their own order'.

In short, if the bishops claimed to speak for the 'stern daughter of the voice of God', *vox populi* was way ahead of *vox Dei*, and it was *vox populi* which now mattered for the fate of the revised Prayer Book. As Bell put it, 'the controversy had added to the embarrassment attending the Church's spokesmen in defending the revised Prayer Book in Parliament'. Not to put too fine a point on it, this was just what Barnes had hoped and intended.

His judgement, moreover, was confirmed by his post-bag. By January he was writing to say that he had 'received well over two thousand letters from unknown correspondents. Most of these were extremely cordial, showing warm appreciation of my teachings.' Many came from the clergy, even from bishops, one of whom averred himself 'deeply thankful for your stand against merely mechanical views of the sacrament'. Dean Inge wrote characteristically:

> I hope you won't take Cantuar's letter too seriously. Someone ought to write a monograph on 'The Invertebrate Variety of Homo Sapiens'. But as a Scotch minister said: 'The Almighty is obliged to do many things in his official capacity which he would scorn to do as a private individual.'

Dick Sheppard, equally characteristically, wrote: 'My dear and great Bishop, I long to meet you and sit at your feet.' The Dean of Worcester, Moore Ede, commented: 'Prophets are always stoned, but their words live ... You must expect to be as unpopular as Isaiah, Jeremiah and Wycliff – a goodly company.'

Barnes was delighted to receive by the same post 'one hundred and forty-five letters, including one from an ex-Prime Minister and one from a Nobel Prizeman'. The Prime Minister was Ramsay MacDonald 'who shows real insight and no regret that he appointed so troublesome a bishop'. The Nobel Prizeman was A. V. Hill, who said: 'to many of us the crimes you have committed sound more like platitudes than like blasphemy, though I admire your courage for saying them, knowing what a hornet's nest you stir up by talking a little elementary sense'. Other scientists who wrote in friendly vein were Julian Huxley, William Bragg and Oliver Lodge.

Barnes did his best to reply faithfully, in the full sense of the word, to his correspondents, even when they only wanted to know where to put bones in the family vault. His replies contained such aphorisms as: 'I feel compelled to attribute personality to God.' 'God must be a reasoning Being, for he must transcend all objects of His creation, man included.' 'Between God and that which He has created there is a decisive separation.' 'The mere fact of sin is sufficient to cause the necessity for redemption; there is no need to have in addition some theory as to the origin of sin.' 'Inasmuch as moral understanding is bound up with immortality, it is not to be expected that we should be able to point to the precise steps at which survival value first appeared in man and so gave him the potentiality of eternal life.' 'Evolution places us in a dilemma, where we must either reject it and incur the scorn of educated men everywhere or reject the historicity of certain of the early Genesis narratives.' 'It is now customary to think of personality as including intellect and soul; in place of St Paul's threefold division of man, there is now a twofold division of body and personality.' 'St Paul associated with the Eucharist words and even ideas derived from the mystery-religions.' 'Between matter informed by life and therefore presumably by mind and matter which does not belong to an organism, there is a vast qualitative difference; it is quite true that, according to Einsteinian physics, matter is a form of energy, but there is all the difference between a living person and a corpse: the former is capable of response to the presence of God; the matter in the latter has no such capacity.' The wife of an ex-Lord Chancellor must have been surprised to be told:

There is no room in the evolutionary scheme for the Garden of Eden. Slowly with the dawn of human rationality there came knowledge of good and evil; but at first such knowledge was horribly imperfect. Only gradually has man risen to his present, civilized level and it seems as if it will be long before he grows 'unto the measure of the stature of the fullness of Christ'.

To some credulous souls, who claimed to be able to detect the Real Presence, he was naughtier and caused his secretary to write:

Is he to understand that you claim to possess the ability to distinguish between consecrated and unconsecrated bread and that you are able, if say twenty pieces of bread are placed before you, to state which have

205

been consecrated and which not? If so, you are the person whom the Bishop has been trying to find; and if you can experimentally establish your contention, he will be prepared to believe in transubstantiation.

The challenge was never taken up.

He gave practical advice too, urging his doubting admirers to stay in the Church and emphasising that doctrinal matters could not be settled in courts of law, at least while the ecclesiastical courts stayed unreformed. Or again, when he wrote 'I still hope for a religious revival as the upset of the war dies away; if we can get that before the Church of England is disendowed, it may have another century of valuable life and service to the nation'. Or yet again, 'such an incident as the outburst at St Paul's will do good if it awakens fresh interest in the arguments by which transubstantiation and allied doctrines were driven from the field in the sixteenth and seventeenth centuries'.

For, if his ultimate objective remained the purification of the teaching of the Church of England, the *causa proxima* was still the defeat of the revised Prayer Book. To this end, too, in the middle of all this other activity, he published in November 1927, his first book, entitled *Should Such a Faith Offend?* He was constantly asked over these years to provide material for publication and had occasionally contributed to volumes of essays or addresses. But now he decided that the attacks on him, based as they seemed to be on a misunderstanding of his teaching and a belief that it was wholly destructive, merited a more substantial and positive reply. He therefore yielded to a long-standing request from Hodder & Stoughton for a volume from his pen alone. In fact, it was a reprint of sermons delivered from 1920 to October 1927, prepared for the press by Bezzant, Vice-Principal of Ripon Hall, with a preface written by Barnes for the occasion and a dedication to 'that best and most severe of critics – my wife'. It even included the sermon preached on the occasion of Bullock-Webster's brawl and, to the publisher's credit, came out within a month of that edifying episode. It was published at 7s 6d and by April 1928, 12,000 copies had been printed. Although it went out of print shortly before the Second World War, Barnes continued to receive letters about it until 1950.

In a letter of thanks for a copy, Bethune-Baker quoted a correspondent in the Birmingham legal and business world as saying: 'Decidedly hard things are said of the Archbishop's attitude and it is unanimously considered that the Bishop of Birmingham was leading on the 3rd round, meaning his 2nd letter to the Archbishop of Canterbury . . . The average man has a real aversion towards the Anglo-Catholic.'

Davidson's own letter of thanks for his copy of the book is therefore all the more interesting:

> I am exceedingly thankful that you have published it. It gives obvious and conspicuous endorsement to what I have been, for months past, reiterating to critical friends as to your power of Christian teaching of a forceful and definite kind. No one can again talk the nonsense about 'episcopal unbelief' which I have been trying to controvert wherever I heard it.
>
> You will realise that what I said in a recently published letter which you evoked from me did not in the least imply any imputation of that foolish and wrong sort. I am full of admiration of very many of your sermons and addresses in the volume and feel sure that it will do a great deal of good.

The sermons and addresses covered ground familiar to those who knew Barnes's teaching. In the preface he said, among other things:

> It will surprise certain readers that, in practically every sermon and address here printed, the positive faith which I affirm occupies more space than the repudiation of false or obsolete beliefs.
>
> Some of my friends, and among them men for whose work I have a warm regard, maintain that a Bishop should neither criticize nor condemn beliefs which may be lawfully held within the English Church. A Bishop, they say, ought to be an impartial administrator, not a partisan . . . It is surely an intolerable proposition that a Bishop should be silent on all questions whereon differences of opinion may exist more or less legitimately within the Church. To impose such constraint on him would often be to hinder him from speaking on vital issues and would make him a mere register of well-established opinions . . . Shades of Athanasius, of Augustine, of Cranmer, of Tait, not by such dexterous silences did you take your places among men memorable in the history of the Church . . . I remember how once at Cambridge an undergraduate was asked his opinion of an episcopal sermon in the College Chapel. 'Inoffensive chatter' was the boy's trenchant reply . . .
>
> Much in the present volume expresses my conviction that the main fabric of Christian belief is unharmed by acceptance of the biological doctrine of man's descent from an ape-like stock . . . I fear that, as usual, the pendulum will swing too far and that there will be a tendency

to disparage the spiritual excellence of the Hebrew scriptures. We need to emphasize that Christianity cannot be severed from its Judaic background without being harmed . . .

It was only when I became a Bishop that I fully realised how vast a departure from the traditional Anglican position had taken place . . . All the serious administrative difficulties of Anglican Bishops today are due to newly-introduced practices which have no sense or meaning unless some erroneous doctrine akin to transubstantiation is held . . . Only by argument, patient, clear and cogent, can error be banished and truth affirmed. In the interests of law and order within the Church of England it is the duty of its Bishops to define its sacramental position . . . The root principle of idolatry is belief in a Deity localized in material objects through the invocation of a priest . . . Some to whom the science of experimental psychology is strange have imagined that I proposed to apply a chemical test to the consecrated elements! Needless to say, I made no such childish suggestion . . . We must assert that Christ's judgement after death will be a moral judgement. No sacramental mechanism can alter it. We do not need to be fortified against the love of God and no rites of the Church can fortify us against his justice. A wafer by itself has no more value than a penny placed in the hand of a dying man to pay his fare to the grim ferryman who shall take him safely across the Styx.

But, to redress the balance of this renewed criticism, he re-emphasized his belief in toleration:

To the political creed which I learned from Acton I am still loyal. As a liberal I abhor persecution and am prepared to trust, and get others to trust, not in force, but in the slow efficiency of argument, the persuasive power of reason. Yet, if I wrote anything new at the present juncture, there are some who might read into the most general principles allusions to particular incidents of current controversy.

So he ended his preface by a long quotation from his sermon on Toleration in Westminster Abbey as long ago as St Bartholomew's Day, 1913.

The reviews were on predictable lines, mostly reflecting the known positions of the papers for which they were written. The general tenor was for critics to recognize the quality of the matter but to deprecate some aspects of the manner. The references to idolatry and to experimental tests stuck in several throats, and even Dean Inge commented that the tone sometimes seemed 'a little too unsympathetic for a Bishop'. This led G. K. Chesterton to have some fun at the expense of allies falling out, but to call a plague on both their houses, because 'the Dean is a pagan Roman of the Senate House; the Bishop is a pagan Teuton of the swamps and fens'. But there were frequent tributes in the reviews to the range of Barnes's knowledge, reading and interests, and even the *Church Times* recognized the positive aspects of his faith. The more percipient reviewers saw the significance of the book for Prayer Book revision.

For controversy continued and the crisis was at hand. As far as Barnes himself was concerned, Bullock-Webster had been trying to enlist support *ex post facto* for his protest and had sent a circular 'fly-sheet' to the Bishops individually seeking their endorsement. When, after being rebuked by Burroughs of Ripon and Perowne of Bradford, he returned to the charge, they issued an even more magisterial rebuttal, which unluckily would have gone over the heads of most laymen. *The Times* refused to print their letter, and Barnes wrote to Burroughs:

> I am sorry that the Times suppressed your letter, but it has steadily suppressed the greater number of important letters sent to it in defence of the traditional Anglican sacramental position. I am in a position to realise alike their number and importance because their authors have written to me somewhat indignant at the treatment they have received.

Catholic influence on *The Times* was a constant theme of his complaints. It is perhaps relevant that Douglas Woodruff was one of its leader-writers for several years from 1927. The Modern Churchmen's Union also rallied to Barnes's support with an open letter endorsing much of his position; but support from that quarter was preaching by the converted and did not add much to his strength. A more embarrassing problem arose when Russell Wakefield chose this moment to propose himself to open a sale of work at St Agatha's, Sparkbrook, Rosenthal's church. Barnes, overwhelmed with correspondence, wrote back: 'I hope that you will not associate yourself with the activities of any of the so-called "rebel" Churches of the Diocese. Forgive a brief reply to your letter.' Wakefield lost his temper and wrote, 'I am sorry that your letter should be so curt, though judging from your recent one to the Archbishop of Canterbury your longer communications do not err on the side of courtesy'. He immediately regretted it and sent an apology, but the harm was done: he had also written unguardedly to Rosenthal, who was able to make capital out of it morally and financially, inviting a prominent fundamentalist to take Wakefield's place and claiming that Barnes's action had swollen the bazaar's receipts. 'No comment' from Bishop's Croft.

Now the House of Commons debate on the Prayer Book was fast approaching. Barnes was invited at short notice to address Labour MPs before it, but could not leave Birmingham. Indeed, at his Diocesan Conference the day before the debate opened, he repeated his view that he regarded the possibility of the book's acceptance with profound misgiving. 'Chaos is . . . likely if it becomes law . . . By passing the measure, Parliament will, in my judgement, give such an implicit approval to erroneous doctrines as will perpetuate discord within the Church, and leave us unprepared to profit by the next religious revival in England.' Although he had done all he could, he clearly no longer felt the same confidence as he had immediately after Bullock-Webster's outburst.

It is therefore not surprising that, when on 15 December the House rejected the book by 238 votes to 205, he let out a paean of public praise:

The representatives of the English people have saved the doctrine of the English Church. The Commons have shown that they will not surrender the religious heritage which comes to us from the Reformation. I am profoundly thankful. If I may use the language of the engineer, we have passed the peak of the danger-curve as by a miracle. Now the way is open for constructive reform which shall preserve the traditional character of the Church of England. I urge that the majority of the Bishops should show magnanimity and take such action that all the non-contentious proposals for Prayer Book Revision speedily become law. There is not the slightest doubt that Parliament would accept the whole of the Revised Prayer Book if the proposals for Reservation and for an altered service of Holy Communion were abandoned. Simultaneously, there must be a reform of Church law and Church courts. When a man breaks the solemn oaths and promises which he has made at institution to a living, it ought to be possible to deprive him of that living. At present all that a Bishop can do is to make such a man a martyr by getting him sent to prison. Indignation with the present lawlessness in the Church is widespread. But I believe that many Bishops would maintain law and order if they were given the necessary powers. Such powers should be carefully guarded: I am no advocate of episcopal tyranny: nothing must be done to make it possible for an unwise Bishop to bully law-abiding clergy whose views he may dislike. The debates in Parliament have shewn conclusively that interest in religion and in the welfare of the National Church is deep and strong. If the Church will take the right steps to set its house in order, it can plainly count on the steady goodwill of the Country and its representatives.

His troubles were by no means over. But the crisis was past.

Thus ended, if not an *annus mirabilis*, certainly a memorable year of intense activity on Barnes's part. But his energies in the three long years since he came back to Birmingham had by no means been absorbed by the struggle with the Anglo-Catholics and their doctrines. There were all the routine obligations of the diocese, intensified by the fact that he was still learning his way around it and its inhabitants. Not only did he constantly visit his own churches: he continued to pay marked attention to close relations with the Free Churches. In this context he gave warm support to invitations to women as well as male ministers of those Churches to preach in pulpits of his diocese, within the terms of the Lambeth Conference resolution of 1920. This was in full accord with his long-standing advocacy of women's education. But his major effort in church administration at this time was his appeal in November 1926, for £30,000 for church extension in Birmingham's new housing areas. The city itself, where, as Barnes used to remind people, there had only been three churches in 1815, was now well supplied with them. One of those three was the cathedral, for whose renovation funds were also successfully raised at this time. But the object of the new appeal was not to build churches as such but rather church halls, which could be used both for worship and for other parish activities. The Anglo-Catholics had complained that he should from the start have given this task priority over 'persecution' of them and even now they criticized the sum he sought as too small. But £16,000 of it was raised in the first week, Barnes having secured a letter of commendation from Austen Chamberlain, the Foreign Secretary and Birmingham's most prominent national figure. A year later more than £24,000 had been found, and the fund eventually reached over £28,000. Barnes and his wife contributed £500 to the opening subscription list.

Now that he had achieved national notoriety, the press were on the look-out for sensational quotations and he did not disappoint them. Thus in his Galton Lecture of February 1926, he is to be found, albeit tentatively, advocating sterilization of the feeble-minded. In

October of that year he aired the possibility that the alleged stigmata of St Francis of Assisi had merely been sores due to the saint scratching rather than washing himself. This aroused some protests and he explained to his correspondents that Christ 'did not extol verminous asceticism as an ideal and He preached unselfishness rather than poverty. In both these matters St Francis was wrong'. In October 1925, so far from preaching poverty, Barnes had actually come out in favour of capitalism, saying that it was not an invention of the devil and deploring 'the dead hand of bureaucratic control in a socialist state'. The press gleefully recalled that he had been appointed by a Labour Government and there was a cartoon of a shattered Ramsay MacDonald being reproached by a bomb-carrying Bolshevik. No less a person than Oswald Mosley, then a Labour candidate in Birmingham, wrote to the papers to ask if Barnes distrusted the Labour Party's social policy. Barnes in reply disclaimed any such intention, asserted that 'my political sympathies, which I am debarred from expressing in public, remain unchanged', and declared that the Labour Party, by repudiating Communism, had shown that it agreed that 'it would be madness to destroy our present system until we have some tried and obviously better machinery to put in its place'. Mosley drily commented that he would enrol himself 'as a warm admirer of the Bishop's great work in relating Christian thought to modern science'. In a private letter at the time, the Bishop wrote:

I do not think that I have ever varied in my economic outlook. What seems to me wrong with our commercial system is not an uneconomical device called capitalism but the unChristian spirit of those who engage in industry and commerce. I do not see what alternative there is to capitalism; it would certainly continue to exist in the socialist state. Naturally I am in favour of the socialization of monopolies. But I doubt whether we should not erect barriers to social progress if the state were to check individual, commercial initiative by taking to itself the complete control of industry.

During this time Barnes remained deeply apprehensive of Russia, where he saw anarchy as having produced terrible misery, although, while he agreed with action to promote religious liberty there, he insisted that this must be done consistently with friendly relations between the two countries. But in international matters as a whole he remained determinedly progressive, continuing to preach peace through the League of Nations, denouncing competition in armaments, rejecting militarist Fascism in Italy and advocating missionary work in China, on which he accused Lord Inchcape of deplorable ignorance in attacking the work of the missions at the annual general meeting of P & O. In domestic affairs too he remained active in liberal causes, notably over the long-drawn-out coal dispute before and after the General Strike of May 1926, joining a delegation of the Churches to the Prime Minister and taking the lead among Birmingham churchpeople in calling for a reorganization of the industry to avert industrial conflict. Betting, drunkenness, bad housing and the lack of film censorship were other social evils to which he repeatedly drew attention. In his moral teaching generally he continued to avoid absolutism. Thus he preached temperance rather than total abstention; he found dancing acceptable even in parish halls, if it was decently conducted; and he refused to condemn Sunday golf, provided no caddies were employed, even though he was much stricter in his own Sabbatarian habits and, for example, never had a Sunday newspaper in his house. On gambling he was even able to claim first-hand experience of watching the deplorable effects on the addicts at Monte Carlo; and indeed his *carte d'entrée* to the *Salle des Jeux* still survives. Similarly, he took a liberal line on moral issues of ecclesiastical controversy: he advocated cremation, on grounds of hygiene and land-use and because it was accepted by those who believed in the resurrection, he advised clergy to remarry the innocent party to a divorce in church and, although he could not say so in public, he privately approved marriage with a dead wife's sister. In his references to birth control, he did not publicly advocate the use of contraceptives but said nothing to indicate opposition to it; his private advice was 'that parents do well to consult their medical adviser and to use such of the resources of medical science as he advises'. He refused, for much the same reasons, to join in any condemnation of vivisection, which he considered a scientific necessity, if humanely conducted, as he believed it normally to be, and, somewhat surprisingly, at this time of his life he opposed abolition of the death penalty.

He was of course much in demand for sermons in a scientific context. Thus he preached for the national celebrations of the bicentenary of Newton's death and the centenary of Lister's birth. His ecclesiastical colleagues, too, even those who disagreed strongly with his theology, would often turn to him for advice on science or

213

mathematics: on a natural explanation for the Flood, on the lowest common denominator of Christian unity, or on the astronomical arguments for a fixed Easter. Other academic recognition which came his way was the award of honorary degrees of Doctor of Divinity at Aberdeen in 1925 and Edinburgh in 1927 and of Doctor of Laws at Glasgow in 1926. It is interesting that only the universities of Presbyterian Scotland accorded him this honour; none of the English universities followed suit, until Birmingham did so in 1953 to mark his resignation, when it was too late to matter. In 1925 too he was invited to give the Gifford Lectures at Aberdeen; although in the event he could not start to deliver them until 1928, he was already in 1926 and 1927, amid all his other preoccupations, heavily involved in their preparation.

But neither the Prayer Book controversy nor the struggle with the Anglo-Catholics was at an end. The Prayer Book dispute was to prove the shorter. Immediately after the book's rejection by Parliament, the bishops sat down in private to prepare a revised draft. When their proposals were published, Barnes issued a statement on 20 January 1928, describing them as 'gravely inadequate'.

Little has been done to remove objectionable features or to lessen the misgivings expressed in Parliament. In fact, the recent private debates of the House of Bishops have increased my own serious concern and I feel it my duty to indicate to my fellow-Churchmen why, after what has passed, I cannot accept the new proposals.

He justified thus lifting the veil as follows:

From the beginning I have pleaded against the secrecy which has surrounded the Bishops' deliberations. We ought, I contend, to have taken the country into our confidence and to have allowed reporters to be present at all our important debates. I could not persuade my colleagues to agree to this policy. But I have repeatedly maintained, and sub silentio it has been conceded, that I was present at our discussions not by invitation but by right of my position as a diocesan Bishop; and, in consequence, I was at liberty to describe what had passed if I so wished. My first duty as a Bishop is to the Church and Nation, and that duty must override the wishes of my colleagues if the two seem to conflict. Nevertheless in what follows I omit certain facts that have caused me anxiety or regret because I do not wish, in challenging a general policy, to refer to individuals.

He then went on to suggest that the Bishops should have included 'a simple statement of our doctrine of the Holy Communion', even if this took some months to prepare, rather than relying on the so-called Black Rubric of 1662 to prevent adoration and then introducing 'over-hasty' legislation. He criticized the decision not to forbid continuous reservation and the proposed rules to govern it, which would not prevent abuses. The possible abuses he described in detail and suggested that a bishop's directions could easily be by-passed. The only argument for continuous reservation was that some clergy insisted that they must receive Communion fasting; but the bishops had refused to include a reaffirmation that non-fasting Communion was a sin. On discipline, he added that the bishops had rejected a proposal whereby clergy should only receive their stipend from the Ecclesiastical Commissioners if their bishop certified that they were obeying the law. Finally, he declared:

The Commons almost of necessity must reject the present proposals. The Episcopal majority may then say that, if they cannot have continuous reservation and the like, they must ask for disestablishment. The reply I conceive would be a measure, stern and far-reaching, by which no endowments of the Church of England were available for Catholic propaganda. I should regret such an outcome for, in the sort of dispute to which we seem to be drifting, the Church of England, which I love, would be ruined.

The *Morning Post* supported his arguments, concluding that 'a disestablished Church would, in our opinion, be a disaster for the whole nation; and an openly divided Church lose the spiritual power and authority very necessary at this time. In that sort of dispute, as the Bishop of Birmingham says, the Church of England would be ruined'. *The Times*, reflecting Barnes's view that Catholic influence was dominant there at this time, was more concerned with manner than matter:

There will be no response to the encyclical against 'secrecy' which is promulgated this morning by the Bishop of Birmingham. Men of affairs all recognize that a series of public debates would have been impracticable and perfectly futile – except indeed for purposes of self-advertisement, which none of the other Bishops seems to have desired – and that this public revelation of some of their differences, if it cannot be called a positive breach of confidence, is yet an offence against the ordinary decencies of public life.

The other bishops too were understandably critical. Thus Garbett of Southwark wrote to *The Times* to challenge Barnes's account and to justify the proposals on Reservation because 'to attempt now to forbid continual reservation would be very difficult; it would mean the narrowing of the comprehensiveness of the Church of England; it would cause grief and perplexity to a number of men who have been obedient to authority and who believe conscientiously that reservation is required for the performance of their pastoral duties'. In short, administrative expediency and private feelings were to take precedence over law and truth. David of Liverpool also accused Barnes of misrepresentation, while Burroughs of Ripon, who seems to have blown hot and cold through the whole business, wrote to *The Times* to complain of Barnes's lack of sympathy for his colleagues and to justify his own vote for the majority, while at the same time pleading for a statement that fasting Communion was not expected. It is only fair to remember that many of the Bishops were dragged reluctantly along the road to reservation, even if in the end they agreed to it. The Archbishop of Canterbury had himself said in the House of Lords on 12 December:

> When I began to sit on the Committees dealing with this matter, I was in hope that we should not find it necessary to sanction Reservation at all. It seemed to me that the danger of superstition loomed rather large and that the need had not been adequately proved, and I felt rather doubtful whether I could ever whole-heartedly join in recommending it. I was convinced otherwise simply by sheer strength of evidence.

God is on the side of the big battalions? Others, like Henson, were obsessed by the relations of the Church with the State, holding that the Church must be free to take its own spiritual decisions and perhaps forgetting that most Churchmen were not bishops but laity who were effectively represented in the House of Commons. Another factor was that this dispute coincided with the end of the Malines conversations about Roman Catholic/Anglican reunion. When the report of the conversations was issued in January 1928, Barnes had commented that Cranmer, Latimer and others had been burned because they denied Papal supremacy and transubstantiation. Those

216

dogmas would not be accepted now. 'We . . . are not prepared to admit the Roman Church to our communion until the Vatican reforms more than its theology.' But when the Pope also disowned the Malines talks and forbade their continuance, the paradoxical reaction of many English High Churchmen seems to have been to show that they could be just as Catholic as the Pope without re-union with Rome. The only exceptions were the extreme Romanizers, who continued to hold that even the new Book did not go far enough for them.

At the Church Assembly in February, the battle-lines were un-altered, and there were the usual large majorities for the new Book, except that the Bishop of St Edmundsbury now joined the minority. In May a public meeting was held at Birmingham to consider the new Book and Parliament. Here Barnes revealed the draft statement on the Communion which had been considered but rejected by the bishops:

> Lest the provisions made in this Alternative Order for the Communion of the Sick should be misconstrued, it is hereby declared that there is intended thereby no use of the Holy Sacrament other than that which our Saviour Himself commended. Moreover, while His Presence in the Lord's Supper is ever to be most reverently and thankfully acknowledged, it is likewise to be remembered that, as we are taught in the Holy Scriptures, He dwelleth by faith in the hearts of His people; that where two or three are gathered together in His Name there is He in the midst of them; and that He Himself hath said: 'Lo, I am with you alway, even unto the end of the world.'

For himself, Barnes added: 'I say bluntly that if the new Book is passed, all hope of unity within the Church will be at an end.' But, lest he should seem merely negative, he again urged that the Church should submit to Parliament non-contentious proposals for Prayer Book reform, omitting the changes on the Communion and on reservation which had led to the previous rejection. He followed the same line at the Diocesan Conference in June, shortly before the Parliamentary debate, and took the occasion to express his warm regard for Davidson, who was known to be on the point of retirement. In the event, Barnes's prediction was fulfilled and the House of Commons on 15 June duly rejected the new Book. As a former Labour Minister had privately prophesied to him, the majority was even larger than before, 266 votes to 220. But this time he was careful not to crow in public. Writing in reply to private letters of congratulation, he said:

> Non-controversial revision of the Prayer Book is much to be desired. It may, however, be deemed wiser by those Bishops who now desire such a revision not to urge it until a certain feeling of soreness consequent on the recent vote of the Commons has passed away.

To a closer friend he wrote:

> The result is gratifying in that it shows clearly that the people of England will not have Roman superstitions. But it also reveals the serious weakness of the Church for more than half of those who spoke on behalf of the Measure indicated that they were not Church people in any effective way. The most serious factor in the present situation is the poor quality of candidates for the ministry. In a generation the leaders of the Church will only too probably be ignorant and self-assertive. If, however, we can in the near future get through a non-controversial revision, we may meet bad weather with a fair measure of success. I wish that I could be more hopeful.

Writing to Storr, he struck the administrative note:

> We may now take it as an axiom of practical politics that the Church of England can only get transubstantiation and the practices which lead up to it at the price of stern disendowment. Such disendowment would in Birmingham cause us to close two-thirds of our Churches: elsewhere its effects might not be so serious immediately but in a generation the Church would be a relatively insignificant Anglo-Catholic sect.

Soreness there certainly was, and Henson, and those who thought like him, certainly wanted to assert themselves against the State. The bishops now began furiously to think what their line should be in the new situation. This thought-process was to take place under the guidance of a new Archbishop. Davidson's retirement in 1928 set off a chain reaction of ecclesiastical appointments, although the general post was not as sweeping as the Prime Minister would have liked. Inge, who later made a brief reference to the matter in his published diary, told Barnes at the time that the government's full plan was: Lang to Canterbury, Ingram to Hereford, Linton-Smith to

Chelmsford, Warman to York, and Temple to London. But Ingram refused to be shifted from London, having been told by the extreme Anglo-Catholic Prebendary Mackay that 'if he yielded to the government's pressure his would be the worst martyrdom since the Reformation'. So to Henson's chagrin, Temple went to York instead of London, while Warman succeeded him at Manchester; and the only move which actually took place from the government's first series was Lang's translation to Canterbury. Unlike Davidson, who, despite their public exchanges, had in private always treated Barnes with fatherly gentleness and for whom Barnes in return had great affection and respect, he held Lang in little admiration. In those days of aprons and gaiters, he used to speak scornfully of the way Lang went around Lambeth in a purple cassock, 'as if he was another cardinal, instead of the head of the Church of England', and he took malicious glee in handing Lang copies of *Nature*, 'which would not otherwise have found its way into Lambeth Palace'. More serious were their differences of churchmanship. Davidson at heart had been a Broad Churchman, whereas, as Barnes wrote to a close friend early in 1930, 'What becomes the more clear the more I see of Lang is that he is an almost fanatical Anglo-Catholic, and I have little doubt that it was his pressure which made Davidson propose to concede reservation'.

Despite the differences friendly relations were maintained on the surface. But that the differences were never far below the surface even in early days, and they grew wider later, is shown by a letter from Lang in his own hand in October 1927:

> Today's Times has opened upon you a full bombardment of archiepiscopal artillery – the great gun Lambeth and the little gun from York. I don't want to meet you, as I hope I shall this week, without having sent you a personal letter to tell you how much I hated having to refer to you in this way in public. But there was a pressure of time and expectation up here that I should speak which made it difficult to be silent. I wonder if you realise how your method of conducting your controversy about the doctrine of the Sacrament pains not only multitudes of loyal churchpeople but also many like me who would wish to be your friends. Such pain might be necessary if the cause of truth demanded it. But what pains is not your desire to reach truth in this matter, but your tone and spirit and unfair exaggeration. Why in attacking the crude literalism of the doctrine of transubstantiation, which the Church of England forbids, should you seem to attack a very

different conception of the nature of the presence of Christ in and through the Sacrament which the Church of England at the very least permits? We want to turn men from these crudities: but we shall not succeed by alienating all those who repudiate these crudities. Forgive me if I say very bluntly that you seem to be in danger of becoming *obsessed* in this matter and of pursuing your campaign in the spirit of a vendetta. It is really hindering the contribution you have to make to the thought of the Church . . . I wanted before seeing you to let you know how really distasteful and distressing it is to me to see you spoiling your opportunities and needlessly increasing the difficulties of the Church and to put this personal and friendly plea before you.

Here again expediency prevails and, as so often with Barnes's critics, the argumentation is directed *ad hominem* rather than *ad rem*. But Lang's was a complicated character which has been exhaustively analysed by his biographer.

The result of episcopal soreness was that by the end of September the majority of the bishops had tentatively decided to allow the use of the 1928 Prayer Book, subject first to consultation by individual bishops with specially convened Diocesan Synods and then to an affirmative vote by Convocation. Pollock wired from Norwich: 'Please are you dissociating yourself from Bishops' statement or approving.' Barnes must have consulted Pearce of Worcester, who wrote the same day:

I have just wired to Norwich: – 'Barnes and I think you should state the disagreement of us four if Exon is willing.' I expect he is in communication with Exon. My sister suggests that the phrase 'the Bishops generally' is intended to hint at some dissent. If so, it is a poor attempt at hinting.

Perhaps William Cecil demurred at quadripartite action. In any case, Barnes was left to make his own statement on 7 October. In it he said that he had hoped not to criticize publicly, but as his correspondents were assuming that he agreed with the majority of the bishops, he had to break silence. The Bishops must not be lawbreakers. If they flouted Parliament, their moral authority for restraining lawlessness would be at an end. 'The situation will in fact be as though judges of the High Court sanctioned theft up to ten pounds and visited the stealing of larger sums with severe censure.' Synods would have no legal status and he would not call a synod at

Birmingham. Even if Convocation approved use of the 1928 book, it would be illegal without the Crown's consent and a formal quarrel would be opened with the State. This would lead to disestablishment and disendowment. But even that would be better than encouraging the clergy to break the law.

In private letters he expressed his misgivings even more strongly:

> When one is part of a system, one must not jolt the framework more violently than is absolutely necessary . . . The Bishops in our meetings showed themselves singularly unable to realise what would be the attitude of the country as a whole to administrative action which is illegal. Few among them are gifted with the insight of statesmen and too often they live in an atmosphere of petty adulation . . . Since my pronouncement on Monday, I have had a letter from the Archbishop of Canterbury asking what I propose to do. To him I have urged again the importance of seeking from Parliament approval of the non-controversial portions of the rejected Prayer Book. I have also pointed out that the action of the episcopate is bound to lead to a general quarrel with the House of Commons which will end not merely in disestablishment but in the drastic disendowment of the Church of England. Hints reach me that both Lang and Temple are disturbed by the atmosphere which the pronouncement of a fortnight ago has created, but I do not know how far such hints have a solid basis in fact. At the moment the situation is such that these two men alone have the power to change the avowed policy of the Bishops; the fact that this policy was said three times over to be provisional may indicate that a way of retreat has been deliberately left open.

A little later, to the same correspondent, who had published an article on the subject, he wrote: 'Even the blindest bishop ought to perceive that the recent policy of the majority of my brethren is indefensible . . . but it is increasingly plain that Lang is the key to the situation. On the hidden working of his mind the whole future of the Church of England depends – and I am apprehensive.' For, as he wrote elsewhere, Lang's 'lack of sympathy with liberal theology is notorious'.

In the event, neither his hopes nor his worst fears were realised. The Church was neither disestablished nor disendowed. But the proposals were not withdrawn, although the progress of the synods revealed plenty of doubts about their wisdom. Barnes adhered to his decision not to hold a synod and when the Archbishop's chaplain wrote to ask the result of consultations in his diocese, he replied:

'I have not consulted the clergy or laity of the Birmingham diocese in the matter of the Prayer Book: I assume that all will obey the law.'

Relations with his brethren were not growing easier. In a sermon at Westminster Abbey in June 1929, he commented, almost in passing, that 'in their Prayer Book proposals the Bishops made what are now generally seen to have been in effect concessions to religious barbarism'. His main theme was the need for the Reformed Churches to unite in a spiritual religion based on the simplicity of the teaching of Jesus. Again almost in passing, he remarked that 'the vast majority of living Churchmen who have felt the influence of scientific method find miracle no aid to faith'. He ended with a stricture on the standard of candidates for holy orders:

> Many of those who now come forward are inadequate alike in mental capacity and morale. Some wish social advancement; they should be rejected. Others have the lamentable confidence which the seminary produces. Too many . . . cloak ignorance and inefficiency beneath an extravagant sacerdotalism . . . We cannot be content until more of the best of our young men enter the ministry of our Church.

Ten days later at Church Assembly this brought down on his head an accusation by Henson that he had spoken contemptuously of subsidized candidates and that in future the clergy would have to be largely recruited from the 'artisan class' and the intellectual standards adjusted. Furse of St Albans also seized the occasion to complain of the 'scandalous behaviour' of Birmingham, Exeter and Norwich for contributing so little to central Church funds and offering no apology for their failure. The choice of targets was obviously inspired by voting differences over the Prayer Book, and Barnes retorted that in the south of England the Church was mainly the Church of the well-to-do, whereas in Durham and Birmingham it was the Church of the poor, while in Birmingham itself most wealth was in the hands of Nonconformists and the churchpeople were mostly artisans. A right and left, which even Henson could not forbear to cheer in his diary.

But the crunch was to come at Convocation in July, where the resolution to allow bishops and parishes in agreement to use the 1928 book was to be debated. Barnes consulted the Archbishop, who asked him to act as he thought best, and then put forward an amendment, for which he sought the support of some bishops who might be sympathetic:

> For the prevention of misunderstanding it is hereby affirmed that nothing in these resolutions purports to change the law and doctrine of the Church of England as contained in the Prayer Book of 1662 or to imply censure on those Bishops who in conformity with such law feel conscientiously bound to refuse to permit alike the practice of reservation and the use of an alternative service of Holy Communion.

During the debate Furse obviously decided that attack on the minority was the best means of defence for the majority's proposals. After a sideswipe at Exeter, he waded in without warning against Barnes's Westminster sermon, quoting parts of it, protesting against wounding language and complaining that Barnes claimed a freedom of belief which he did not allow to others. When Barnes asked him to quote more fully, the Archbishop of Canterbury twice intervened to say that the Bishop of Birmingham had other opportunities to make his views public and used such vehement language that he should not be surprised if others drew attention to its implications. Later, in summing up, Lang reverted to the subject, saying that he received daily protests against Barnes's language and appealing to him not to use 'provocative language which cannot advance his cause and does a great deal to disturb the whole life and movement of the Church of England'. Barnes, in a personal statement, replied:

> I recognize that there are many within the Church who do not agree with the views which I maintain but I think it of primary importance to put forward in language as clear cut as it can be made, the doctrinal truths which I am convinced belong to the Anglican Church. I stand, of course, in some sense as a prominent member of what is known as the Modernist movement. That movement is loyal to the Church, but it also seeks to be loyal to the truth. A couple of years ago protests against my teaching culminated in a regrettable incident in St Paul's Cathedral. This led me to put out this teaching in a book, of which no fewer than 10,000 copies were sold within a few months. That book brought me from all over the world letters of a most enthusiastic character. For one letter of disapproval I received, there were a dozen thanking me for bringing out these views in this sort of way.

There was some public and much private comment, some of it even from bishops who had voted the other way, on Lang's obvious partiality, but Barnes tried in a press interview and in his replies to private letters to play down any personal animosity. In fairness, the Archbishop also caused his chaplain to tell people that he was not attacking Barnes or his views but only the words in which he sometimes expressed them. But *The Times* as usual was hostile:

> It may well be that the theological views of the Bishop of Birmingham are very widely held. Certainly they are not so uncommon or so original as his language sometimes suggests. In his case the difficulty seems to be not so much one of doctrine as of manners; and the lack of courtesy with which he permits himself to speak of the cherished religious convictions of others would quickly bring him into the same difficulty in any other responsible position.

A member of the Lower House suggested that Barnes should be made Dean of Gibraltar, presumably because there were monkeys on the Rock there. But Lord Birkenhead, commenting on Furse in another context, called him 'an extremely foolish bishop, who was a contemporary of mine at Oxford, and who was made a fellow of his college for his muscular rather than his mental qualities'. Furse was 6′ 6″ tall and Barnes used privately to speak of him as the embodiment of the Church militant.

On the main issue Barnes withdrew his amendment and voted against the resolution, which was none the less carried by 23 votes to 4 and in the Lower House, after slight amendment, by 96 to 54. There was a similar result at York. So, despite all Barnes's efforts, bishops were authorized to be guided by the Prayer Book of 1662, subject to the deviations in the 1928 book and no others, provided they had the assent of the Parochial Church Councils concerned. Here ended the great Prayer Book controversy of the 1920s.

Barnes, who had received hundreds of letters of sympathy and support, confined himself to a public statement which he told his friends was intended to preclude any further personal argument. He did not want to appear to be attacking either Lang or Furse and he did not want others to do so for him. On the substance, he began:

> Modernists who give me friendly support may expect a statement in view of the debates in Convocation last week. Of episcopal policy little need be said. The majority of my colleagues have resolved upon action which has not the sanction of law. The future will decide whether such action can succeed. I doubt it.

He went on to urge the need for unity to be based on sound doctrine, particularly sacramental doctrine. The principles at stake were so vital that it was impossible to avoid giving offence. 'We may try as we may, but if our teaching is clear and decisive those whose views it condemns will be hurt.' 'While we must teach clearly, we can and must completely avoid all personal attack.' Modernists were in a minority but their views must prevail if the Church was to become again the Church of the English people. We must serve God by searching out the meaning of the life of Jesus. But we must unite faith in Christ with enthusiasm for social welfare, as in the wide-ranging humanity of Jesus. This meant working for international peace, better housing, less unemployment, more education. With these rather anticlimactic phrases he sought to defuse the passionate resentment of his supporters. It is of incidental interest that he is now openly calling himself a Modernist. But he refused to join any organization using that name. As he put it:

> Liberalism in religious thought is not to be confined within the limits of an organization. We can, working as individuals, create the attitude of spirit which we wish to spread among the community.

Prayer Book revision and Birmingham diocesan administration were still opposite sides of the same coin. To turn the coin again, the battle in Birmingham was still joined, although for much of this time its noise was comparatively muted.

In April 1928, the Roman Catholics staged at Birmingham, with 1500 participants, a Mass of Reparation 'for Bishop Barnes's attacks on the Real Presence'. In 1929, too, Father Woodlock, SJ, came specially to the city to deliver a series of lectures obviously directed at Barnes and his teaching, causing Rendel Harris to write to Barnes to congratulate him 'on having drawn the fire of the Jesuits. That is much more satisfactory than Anglo-Catholic gunnery'. But, in fact, his dispute was not with the Roman Catholics, much though they disliked each other's doctrines. Indeed, relations were quite amicable and Barnes was very willing to appear on the same platform as the Catholic Archbishop of Birmingham to plead for after-care of schoolchildren. Again, when a Catholic priest used some particularly offensive language in Birmingham about Barnes and Inge, the national President of the Catholic Council wrote Barnes a handsome letter of apology and received a cordial reply. There was no legal problem involved for the Church of England in Roman Catholic doctrine, and Barnes, for example, always maintained that, whatever Rome might say of Anglican Orders, the Church of England for its part accepted the validity of Catholic orders and Catholic confirmation and there was no need for a Catholic convert to be baptised again on returning to the Church of England. He was less tolerant of the political activities of the Roman Church: in 1927 he refused to attend a League of Nations Unions meeting where a Catholic priest was to be on the platform, on the ground that Mussolini was the most dangerous opponent in Europe of the League's ideals and that Rome's policy towards him was at best ambiguous.

The real conflict was with the Anglo-Catholics within the Church of England, for whom, incidentally, most Roman Catholics held no brief. In Birmingham, Rosenthal kept up small-arms fire, telling the Anglo-Catholic reunion at the Town Hall in May 1928, somewhat illogically, that they were rebels not against constituted authority but against bureaucratic tyranny. Bigger guns were brought to bear at the Church Congress at Cheltenham in September of that year, when Lord Halifax, at the head of a battalion of 724 clergy, formally protested against invitations to Barnes and Major. Gore gave him some general supporting fire in a sermon, though with no names mentioned. But Headlam, as chairman of the Congress, easily repelled the assault, and Barnes and Major both duly addressed the gathering, Barnes's contribution being a learned discourse on 'The Uniformity of Nature and the Freedom of Man', which attracted attention not only for its philosophical range but also for his refusal to push his argument to dogmatic conclusions.

Another rebel church came into line with a change of incumbency at All Saints', Small Heath, in January 1929. But a more prolonged engagement began in March, when the Vicar of Stirchley died. This was one of the most extreme rebel parishes. Two successive vicars had changed its ways to advanced ritualist practices and in the process alienated many of the former congregation. Now in June 1929, Lyle, the curate left in charge, refused to give the Bishop the assurances for which he had asked, either to cease reservation or to remove illegal ornaments. On the ornaments, after a delay while he said he had sought legal advice, he used the specious plea that as some of them had been put there by faculty they could only be legally removed by another faculty. This legalism showed that strategy was again being dictated from headquarters. Events for a time then moved quickly. The Bishop warned Lyle that, if he persisted in his refusal, his licence would be revoked. Lyle saw Barnes and chose to resign his curacy on 25 July. The churchwardens, who at an interview with the Bishop in May had agreed to remove the ornaments, now went back on this undertaking and, on behalf of the Parochial Church Council, intervened on behalf of Lyle and of reservation. Barnes replied on standard lines, except that this time he suggested that 'those of your Council who desire Roman Catholic uses based upon the erroneous doctrine of transubstantiation should join the Roman Church'. Meanwhile, the Protestant faction in the parish were actively pressing the Bishop to stand firm and, with his agreement, the living had been offered to E. H. Parslew, who had accepted and promised the required obedience. But Barnes did not want to institute him until the illegal ornaments had been removed, for fear that he would seem to have condoned their use. At this point the Parochial Church Council appealed to the Archbishop of Canterbury, who on 27 July, incidentally only ten days after the scene in Convocation, asked Barnes for his comments. The Bishop formally advised Lang that he could only reply that he had no status to intervene. But at the same time he sent the Archbishop a revealing private letter:

> The only official reply which I can make to your letter I send herewith. Privately, I could say much. The case of Stirchley is a singularly bad example of that clerical insubordination which has done much harm locally to the Church and to the cause of religion.
>
> The late vicar was ten years at Stirchley. In spite of indignant, and sometimes pathetic, protests from his parishioners, he replaced moderate Anglicanism by so-called Catholic usages. I tried to get some *rapprochement* with him but in vain. When, some three years ago, we raised £28,000 for Church Extension in the Diocese, one of the first two Church Halls built from the money was in his parish. He insisted that the services in the Hall should be 'Catholic' and they are a dreadful failure, so much so that people complain that our Church Extension money has been wasted. At Stirchley Church itself the congregation is eclectic: I am told that relatively few are parishioners. Wakefield *may* have given permission for reservation: if he did, he kept no copy of his permission in the files which I now have. It is certain, however, that no consequent petition for a faculty for an aumbry or tabernacle went forward. At another 'rebel' church, St Anne, Duddeston, which I restored to order, there was an exactly similar state of affairs. The new incumbent, when

he went there some years ago, ceased to reserve and has never found any need of the practice. He sent this information to *The Times* some three weeks ago, but his letter was not published. I have now obtained order in several 'rebel' churches: as I will not take legal action, I have to act when benefices become vacant. At such times I interview church-wardens and Parochial Church Councillors. I find almost invariably that, though they may like ornate ritual, their doctrine is that of the Reformation and as a rule they agree to my requirements without regret. The letters of expostulation and so forth which appear in the Press are usually written in the ECU office or by local leaders of the 'rebel' clergy.

When the Rural Dean heard of the document which you are now considering, he rang up Mr Weston [secretary of the Parochial Church Council] and asked who wrote it. He was told 'Canon Long and Mr Rosenthal'. He asked what they expected to get by it from yourself. The answer, with a laugh, was 'Sympathy'. He enquired whether they thought they would get reservation. Another laugh and 'No'. Such a story I can well believe, for on May 12 I had the two churchwardens to tea and discussed the whole position with them. I told them that the tabernacle, the image and the holy water stoups must go, but that I would agree to the appointment of a convinced Anglo-Catholic (so Percy Herbert described him) who could be trusted to be loyal to my requirements, which included the giving-up of reservation. Parslew, the man in question, has not had reservation at his last charge in Blackpool. The churchwardens assented to my proposals and a peaceful concordat was made. It was broken, however, when the ECU sub-sequently put pressure on the late curate and on the Parochial Church Council. If I broke an engagement in that sort of way, you can imagine how my perfidy would be spread abroad.

The tabernacle, image and stoups have no rightful place in the church. They have been put there without any faculty. The two former are not fixtures. They can, and should, be carried away. The plea that the service of Devotions has been confined to weeknights reminds me of the man who, when accused of ill-treating his mother-in-law, urged that he had never hit her on Sundays.

When I came to Birmingham it was, after Wakefield's misrule, the most disorderly diocese in England, London excepted. It is getting better. There are now only some twelve 'rebel' parishes and of several in the original rebellion the incumbents have come to me privately to say that if they could get preferment elsewhere, they would be loyal in new surroundings. Unfortunately no other Bishop cares to take Birmingham rebels.

I shall continue to refuse to institute incumbents, unless they give me before institution a pledge in writing in the following form which includes, of course, the disuse of reservation:

> In asking you to institute me to the benefice of − − − − − −, I write to say at your request that I am willing in public worship to obey the regulations of the Prayer Book (or alternatively of any revised Prayer Book which may become lawful) and that I will not depart from the law as therein set forth, unless I have it from you in writing that you will raise no objection to action such as I may desire to take. I will also urge the Parochial Church Council to contribute the assessment made by the Diocesan Board of Finance.
>
> With that pledge I can win through. Some say that I have no legal right to demand it. I reply that I shall not contest a legal action. One way of proceeding by law would lead to my incarceration for contempt in Winson Green Gaol. Another way, as I am told, would lead to the institution of a potentially rebel clergyman by Your Grace. Either would be a curious and interesting outcome of an attempt to preserve the purity of the faith of the Church of England.

The Archbishop duly told the parish that he could not intervene and sent Barnes a friendly reply. When Barnes in thanking him mentioned his 'deluge of letters', Lang wrote in his own hand, 'Let the deluge of letters drown itself and take a good holiday'. But this was too optimistic; the Chancellor of the Diocese had intervened to complain:

> I have read in the *Church Times* of the 5th instant what doubtless is a correct copy of certain correspondence which has passed between your Lordship and the Revd. R. V. Lyle then and still Curate of Stirchley and the Parochial Church Council. From this it would appear that on the death of the Vicar you ordered the removal from the Church of certain articles or ornaments and stated that you would require other changes. Such an order to whomsoever addressed constitutes a serious invasion of the functions and jurisdiction assigned to the Consistory Court of the Diocese and by his patent to the Chancellor as judge thereof. Articles of a substantial and permanent nature e.g. a statue (the Court does not concern itself with trivial matters such as hassocks) can only be rightly removed if and when an order for removal made in a properly constituted suit by the judge of the Court has been obtained and not on the mere motion of anyone else. As judge of the Diocesan Court with all due respect to your high office I feel bound to make a protest against this usurpation of jurisdiction and to express the earnest hope that now that the matter has been brought to your attention you may see fit to refrain from like action in the future.

Barnes, who was already in touch with the National Church League over the legal aspects of his problems, sought advice through them and replied to Hansell on the basis of a draft prepared by Sir Thomas Inskip, who was honorary treasurer of the League and had been a doughty opponent of the Revised Prayer Book in Parliament:

> I beg to acknowledge the receipt of your letter of the 10th of July in which you refer to certain communications which passed between a clergyman then holding my licence and myself.
>
> I am well aware that it would not be right for me to interfere with your jurisdiction, and in the event of an application being made to you for the grant of a faculty, either for erecting or removing an ornament of the church, I should not presume publicly to intervene. I feel bound however to remind you that I have duties to perform which are entirely outside the functions and jurisdiction assigned to the Consistory Court of the Diocese; and if you will allow me to say so, I must use my own judgement as to the occasions on which I shall direct my clergy in regard to the observance of the law.
>
> If in the case in question a faculty is required for the removal of certain articles or ornaments which, in my judgement, have been placed in the church without due authority, no doubt an application will be made by the persons concerned in due course. I presume that you would not question my right to direct any of my clergy that it is their duty to apply for a faculty in certain cases. So far as the case of Stirchley is concerned I do not propose to relinquish my right to enjoin one of my clergy to remove articles which I am informed have been placed in the church without any authority whatsoever.
>
> As you have thought fit to complain to me of what you describe as the usurpation of your jurisdiction, I hope I may be allowed to say that I think that it would have been better for the Judge of the Consistory Court of the Diocese to refrain from taking an active part in the movement of certain clergy in the Diocese to resist my episcopal authority. Your contribution to the fund which was raised in connection with the so-called group of 'rebel' churches to which Stirchley belonged was an unfortunate episode which could not fail to diminish the respect which all churchmen would desire to pay to the Chancellor of the Diocese.

Hansell, who was in fact a Vice-Chairman of the Council of the English Church Union, reacted with a rather lame and disingenuous defence:

> In 1925 I sent a small subscription to a public fund raised for the financial assistance of several Parishes in your Diocese. You now for

the first time complain of my doing so and say that Stirchley happens to be one of those Parishes of which fact I was previously unaware. The fund was raised because rightly or wrongly it was widely felt that the Church work in those places was in danger of being unduly hindered and I believe was supported by numerous subscribers.

Although Barnes probably won that contest on points, it did not help him to have the illegal ornaments removed, as a faculty for their removal still had to be sought from Hansell as Chancellor. Meanwhile, Parslew's institution was held up. The sequestrators managed early in August to empty the tabernacle and take possession of its key, with the agreement of the churchwardens and no open protest at the church. But the other ornaments remained. Through the National Church League and the Church Association, opinion was marshalled in favour of their removal and in November the Parochial Church Council unanimously resolved to seek a faculty accordingly. But a former member of the Council was found, presumably by the English Church Union, to oppose the petition and early in January 1930, Hansell not surprisingly gave judgement in his favour on a technicality. Inskip gave his opinion that Hansell was wrong and that an appeal would succeed. But it was then learned that an appeal would not be opposed: presumably the English Church Union thought they had gone far enough in legalistic antics and in any case they now had a hotter iron in the fire at St Aidan's, Small Heath. Barnes thereupon decided to institute Parslew on the understanding that the new vicar would then apply for a faculty and remove the ornaments. The institution took place in February, when Barnes explained the background to the congregation and welcomed them back into the fold. He made clear that his objections were only to illegal practices:

In matters which it is possible to regard as non-essential I take the typically English view that a *via media* is worth following . . . I have little patience with those who tell us that the alternatives by which we are confronted are literal subservience to the Prayer Book or complete anarchy. There remains the golden mean which can be discovered by English common-sense.

To complete the story, Hansell issued the faculty in July and the ornaments were removed by October.

All the main correspondence over Stirchley had been published and

Barnes had not helped his case by calling a statue of the Virgin Mary and Infant Jesus 'a female figure with a child, before which candles burn'. This was grist to his opponents' mill, and even his friends remonstrated with him. To one of them, he admitted that perhaps it

> was not a happy phrase. It occurred in a quasi-legal demand and its point was inasmuch as the image was placed in the church without a faculty it must be removed whatever it purported to represent. If I had described it as 'the Virgin and Child' and then had been told that it was really 'St Catherine and a bambino' the further plea would have been put forward that as I had not correctly described the object which I wished to be removed I could not later enlarge my demands to have it taken away. But these are the casuistries of illegality.

Two happier skirmishes also occurred at this time. Barnes's dislike of commerce in advowsons had long been made known. The English Church Union had early in 1929 taken great pride and pleasure in buying the advowson of Solihull Parish in the Birmingham Diocese. In the summer of that year, when the vicar of Boldmere resigned and the patron, Edward Ansell of Ansell's Aston Ales, died shortly afterwards, it looked as if the advowson would again be bought from his estate by a group who would support a 'rebel' nominee. Barnes therefore stirred himself to raise £800, plus legal expenses, from a group of friends, to buy the advowson in the autumn and transfer it to the Diocesan Trustees, who thus could and did ensure the appointment of a loyal clergyman. Barnes contributed £100 himself.

The other engagement was initiated by Canon C. E. Douglas, the London incumbent who had earlier tried to prosecute Major for heresy. At the end of October, he put down a motion in Church Assembly calling on Convocation to 'inquire into the cause and extent of the troubles in the Birmingham Diocese with a view to proper synodical action for their appeasement'. This he apparently did on his own initiative, and later claimed that he was merely concerned with the dispute between Bishop and Chancellor. However that may have been, reaction was swift. The Diocesan Board of Finance, which met the day after the news broke, issued a protest, echoed by others in the diocese, and even Canon Long found it expedient to point out that the move was not backed by the Anglo-Catholic party, who had no wish to be investigated by the Church Assembly. Douglas rapidly withdrew his motion.

Lang and others could assert that over these years Barnes seemed obsessed by sacramental doctrine. If so, they can only have had a blinkered view of his interests and utterances during the first half-dozen years of his episcopate. His own vision ranged wider. He and most of his contemporaries still saw themselves living in a post-war era. The recovery which they expected, for which some of them had confidently hoped, had not occurred. All around were confusion and uncertainty. The drift to the cities had accentuated the stresses and strains of contemporary life and posed new moral and social problems. Without the prospect of prosperity around the corner, industrial relations had assumed a new hardness. Man's inhumanity to man was growing everywhere more apparent. This was as true abroad as at home. Just as the class struggle grew more tense, so did the arms race. The old familiar demons of European rivalry were once more raising their ugly heads, often capped by even uglier ideologies. True, there were those who could plunge into ecclesiastical conflict, oblivious of political alarums and excursions without. But Barnes was not of their number, even if his opponents were. With Donne he could say, 'I am involved in mankind', or, with Terence, '*homo sum, nihil humani alienum a me puto*'. He saw the post-war era as a time of turmoil, comparable with the corruption at the end of the Roman Empire or with the disillusion after the Black Death in fourteenth-century Europe. The hungry sheep not only looked up and were not fed: they had also lost their way. They needed sustenance and guidance from their shepherds. In social and economic terms, this meant that there must be a dole for the unemployed, must be a new deal for the miners, must be garden cities in place of slums. But during the General Strike of 1926, while he publicly expressed sympathy for the miners, he declared that the strike would do no good; force would be met by force and this could lead to class tyranny. The government and the miners should open fresh negotiations and 'past friction be forgotten in a new spirit of goodwill'. In political terms, while he preached 'a wise conservatism' in the English tradition, he foresaw the return of Labour to power in 1929 and its general acceptability, whatever an earlier generation would have thought. For internationally, too, he saw the British national temper and the political system which reflected it as infinitely preferable to either communism or fascism, of which he was an early critic, and he remained anxious whenever possible, as when a delegation of German pastors visited Birmingham in June 1928, to stretch out the hand of friendship to former enemies. These pre-occupations only served to strengthen his growing interest in population problems. The population of Europe had trebled in the nineteenth century and the consequent pressure had been a strong factor leading to the First World War. The quality of the population had suffered at the same time and as early as 1929 he was calling for a restriction on the immigration of 'people of lower culture', among whom he included the Irish and brought down on his head the wrath of Father Martindale, SJ, who sprang to Irish Catholics' defence. For, even if he did not make the link specific, Barnes certainly associated an unrestricted birthrate and a consequent cultural decline with the influence of Catholicism.

These were practical problems which politicians sought to solve within the art of the possible. Barnes saw the added need to hold out the hope of the desirable. He retained his keen interest in education, which for him should not be directed at worldly success but at the formation of character. Above all, he dwelt often on the need for the best men to enter the service of the Church, so that an educated clergy could respond to the needs of an increasingly educated community. For this purpose he appealed for private subscriptions to found a Faculty of Theology at Birmingham University.

The preparation of his Gifford Lectures provided a fresh spur to drive all these wide-ranging interests into a consistent philosophy, towards which he had for years been working. Increasingly, he was conscious of the apparent dualisms in the universe: the alleged dualisms of mind and body, space and time, past and future, nature and the supernatural, the spiritual and the mechanical. Within these great divides were the lesser divisions of Church and State, of capital and labour, of Britain and her neighbours. He was not content to accept these dualisms. His mind was constantly bent on the search for a single coherent explanation and for him as a Christian it could not be a solution in terms of this world alone. Into his scheme of things he had to integrate his conclusions from the study of evolution: he was constantly concerned with its implications for the future of man, both as an individual and a race. Thus he repeatedly asserted his certainty of human immortality. He speculated on the possibility of life on other planets. He wondered, if man was only an episode in evolution, what higher forces of life might develop. To the extent that modern science obstructed the evolutionary elimination of the unfit, he emphasized the need for man to exercise eugenic choices.

Often he came back to the insoluble problem of evil in a divinely-ordered evolutionary system. These were the themes of his sermons and as those sermons were now prominently reported they were also the themes of many newspaper headlines throughout the English-speaking world and even beyond it. So much so that his private letters at this time were full of complaints that his footsteps were so dogged by reporters that he could now only visit unimportant or inconspicuous churches to deliver commonplace addresses. At least, that made a good excuse for refusing unwelcome engagements; his remarks were rarely commonplace.

But in practice he was driven on, as before, by the search for truth and the need to proclaim it. Religion in those days was news and he could be sure of an audience, even if to some extent this was a *succès de scandale*. Like Tennyson's Ulysses, his purpose held 'to strive, to seek, to find and not to yield'. Or, as Emerson wrote,

> God offers to every mind its choice between truth and repose. Take which you please – you can never have both. Between these, as a pendulum, man oscillates. He in whom the love of repose predominates will accept the first creed, the first philosophy, the first political party he meets . . . He gets rest, commodity and reputation; he shuts the door of truth. He in whom the love of truth predominates will keep himself aloof from all moorings and afloat . . . He submits to the inconveniences of suspense and imperfect opinion, but he is a candidate for truth, as the other is not, and respects the highest law of his being.

For Barnes the choice between truth and repose was clear. If he was obsessed at all, he was obsessed with truth.

CHAPTER VI

BIRMINGHAM
BETWEEN THE WARS

The Thirties, Part I, 1929–1931
Rump of the Rebellion

In retrospect, the 1920s look like post-war years while the 1930s have a pre-war air. As the twenties grow into the thirties, a clear shift can now be seen from relief and hope to disappointment and apprehension. Economic crisis and political dictatorship cast ever deeper shadows across the scene. But this distinction between the two decades was not immediately apparent to those who lived from one to the next. Certainly there was no such sharp firebreak in the concerns of the Birmingham diocese. Before the problem of Stirchley was settled, the affair of St Aidan's, Small Heath, had begun.

No satisfactory account of the St Aidan's affair has been published. Of the great contemporaries in the Church, Archbishop Lang played a prominent part in the affair, but his biographer dismisses it in a single superficial paragraph. Temple was not directly involved and his biography only contains oblique references to the doctrinal points at issue and nothing on the events themselves. Headlam did intervene, but his biographer is also silent on the subject. The same is true of Bell, whose intervention was concerned more with the need for compromise, as exhibited by his early policies in his own diocese, than with the intellectual substance of the dispute. Gore, who would have had strong views on the substance, was by now almost at the end of his life and took no part in the affair; nor is there any reference to it in the official life of him. Henson too, although his three-volume autobiography is liberally sprinkled with characteristically candid

236

comments on Barnes's actions and ideas, as he saw them, is silent on St Aidan's as such. But by this time, after the Prayer Book débâcle, Henson's objectivity was diluted by his obsessive desire for disestablishment as a universal panacea for all ecclesiastical ills. Inge's *Diary of a Dean* contains two brief comments, but there is nothing in his biography. Apart from a partial and *ex parte* account in Vidler's *Scenes from a Clerical Life*, and even he had the grace to admit in a footnote to a later revised and more generous estimate of Barnes, the minor Anglo-Catholic clergy involved have not blossomed into biographies or autobiographies. Malcolm Muggeridge, as a friend of Vidler, took up his literary cudgels from the Anglo-Catholic corner in his autobiography, with some personal remarks which only go to show that a little knowledge is a dangerous thing. Barnes himself published nothing retrospective, for indeed he never had time to do so. So the cupboard of history is bare. But it all caused a great stir at the time and perhaps marked the end of an era in the life of the Church.

Without any doubt the Anglo-Catholics, with the English Church Union in the van, had for some time been spoiling for a showdown. From the course of events since 1925, if not indeed from 1924, it can be inferred that they did not merely want to vindicate their own dogmas and rituals: they were determined, if they could not force Barnes out of his diocese, to humiliate him as sharply as they could. They could perhaps claim a draw in their favour at St Gregory's, Small Heath, where Barnes later admitted that he had made a mistake in yielding. But they had lost at St Mark's, Washwood Heath, where the threat of a lawsuit proved a broken reed, and again at Stirchley, where the cards were stacked against them, as by lapse of time they lost the right of presentation and could therefore only take the question of ornaments to the Chancellor's Court. They had scored an unconverted try at Solihull, but had been outwitted at Boldmere. No doubt their wounds were smarting. Metaphors of conflict and even of warfare are not inappropriate to the spirit in which they directed their attention to the Bishop himself rather than to his views, even though the religious question turned on some of the most sacred points of Christian theology.

Small Heath in the mid-nineteenth century merited its name. By the end of the century it had become engulfed in the industrial heart of the city. To minister to the inflowing population, St Aidan's Mission had in 1891 been carved out of the parish of All Saints. It was, and remained, a perpetual curacy, rather than a parish on its own. Although at the time of St Aidan's foundation the diocese was largely in the grip of what Barnes was to describe as 'black fundamentalism', St Aidan's itself had from the start been designed as a spearhead of the Catholic revival. High Mass had been introduced in 1896, and there had been continuous reservation since 1912, significantly the year after Gore was succeeded by Russell Wakefield. The recent tradition had been one of celibate clergy, living together in a clergy house. They were the clergy who had provided the strategic reserve to keep the flag flying at St Mark's, Washwood Heath, nearby, during the 1925–7 interregnum there. But in 1929 the curate-in-charge, Barlee, resigned on grounds of ill-health, thus creating the next vacancy in a 'rebel' church.

Early in October Barnes heard in a private letter from someone who had attended a meeting of the English Church Union that that body planned to nominate a clergyman, with no black mark against him in the past, who would refuse to give an assurance not to have reservation. If the Bishop then refused to license him, the ECU would prosecute and indeed it had already raised enough funds to meet the cost of such an action. The trustees, who held the right to present to the benefice and who were plotting this edifying recourse to law, included one of Barnes's fellow-bishops, Frere of Truro, and one of his own cathedral canons, C. N. Long. Frere, a former monk, had been appointed to the episcopal bench in 1923, at Davidson's insistence, expressly as a representative of the Anglo-Catholic school of thought, and he fulfilled his terms of reference to the letter. Long had from the start been one of the Birmingham 'rebels' and had himself earlier for some years served as curate in charge of St Aidan's.

On 3 November the trustees wrote to the Bishop to say that they had offered the living to G. D. Simmonds of Tyne Dock and that he had accepted. Barnes promptly wrote to Henson, as the diocesan concerned, to ask if Simmonds could be safely received, and to Simmonds himself to ask for assurances that he would abide by the Prayer Book, not practise reservation and contribute to diocesan funds. The Bishop of Durham, with his tongue rather obviously in his cheek, gave Simmonds a clean bill:

I am sincerely sorry to lose him. He is . . . an Anglo-Catholic, but this, I think, ought not to trouble you. St Mary's, Tyne Dock, is carried on moderately and, so far as I know, without extravagances. I should be surprised if you do not share my good opinion of Simmonds and hope very much indeed that he will share my good opinion of you.

Simmonds, for his part, after asking for time to consult the trustees, duly refused to go beyond 'the prescribed declarations' and 'the oaths required by law'. Barnes had meanwhile consulted Guy Johnson, General Secretary of the National Church League, who had helped him over Stirchley, telling him:

> What I wish is that the English Church Union should be compelled to go to the civil courts so that ultimately I may be sent to prison for contempt of court. I propose to offer no legal defence and to give all possible publicity to my case throughout the proceedings. By such action the courts will either rule that I can ask for an assurance or the law will be changed.

Johnson showed some amused interest in the prospect of the Bishop going to gaol but thought the opposition would be too astute to let it happen. Meanwhile he advised against including the reference to diocesan funds, and on 26 November Barnes wrote again to Simmonds asking for an assurance without that reference. This too Simmonds refused on 3 December. Through Ekin, his Legal Secretary, Barnes then told the trustees that he refused to institute. He took care not to base himself on the Benefices Act, 1898, which allowed certain other grounds for refusing to institute, but made clear that the refual was based on Simmonds's own refusal to give the required assurances. Indeed, he followed closely the wording used by Bishop Knox in the proceedings which gave rise to the case of Gore-Booth v. Bishop of Manchester, 1920. In that case, Lord Coleridge had held that it was not unreasonable in law to ask a prospective incumbent if he proposed to regard his oaths and declarations as binding; for it to be urged that a presentee was willing to make the statutory declarations, although he did not intend to keep them, was, in Coleridge's view, to trifle with common sense. It was on these grounds that Barnes's Legal Secretary advised him that he would win the case if he fought it. This was in fact to become a key question as the affair proceeded.

On 17 December the trustees' solicitors wrote to say that they had been instructed to issue a writ against the Bishop. It was a writ of *quare impedit*, calling on the Bishop to show cause for his refusal to institute. This brought matters into the open. So on 23 December Barnes issued to the press the following statement, which was accompanied by copies of his correspondence with Simmonds:

An issue of fundamental importance with regard to order in the Church has arisen in connection with the benefice of St Aidan's, Small Heath.

In November 1925 I published a letter to the Clergy of the Diocese in which I asked *inter alia* that in public worship unauthorized services such as Benediction, Exposition, Devotions, Procession of the Host etc., should cease. Such services, as I have often pointed out, imply erroneous doctrine akin to Transubstantiation. They encourage false sacramental teaching which I as Bishop am pledged to banish and drive away. When my letter was written I did not, pending the final form and ultimate fate of the Prayer Book proposals, actually forbid the practice of reservation, suitably safeguarded. Nevertheless my request to the clergy was disobeyed by rather more than a dozen incumbents in Birmingham, who moreover banded themselves together to induce their people not to subscribe to Diocesan funds.

Against these so-called 'rebel' Vicars I could successfully have taken legal action; but in the existing state of the law the incumbents would ultimately have elected to go to prison for ignoring an order of the High Court of Justice which I could have obtained. Now when I was made Bishop I resolved that I would not try to restore discipline in the Diocese by legal action. Before being instituted to a benefice every clergyman solemnly promises to use in public worship the form of the Prayer Book and none other, except so far as shall be ordered by lawful authority. He also swears the oath of Canonical Obedience that he will obey the Bishop in all things lawful and honest. I say that a clergyman has no right to set aside such solemn obligations: if he does so it is a grave moral fault which I will not try to correct by processes of law.

But naturally when any 'rebel' parish has fallen vacant I have refused to institute as its next Vicar any man presented to me unless I have an adequate assurance that he regards his promise and oath as binding. Hitherto I have always received such an assurance. But at St Aidan's the Trustees (Dr J. Notley, Canon C. N. Long, the Rev. J. J. Agar-Ellis, Mr S. R. Shore and the Bishop of Truro) propose to go to law to challenge my right to make such a demand.

If they succeed any Diocesan Bishop will in future have to institute a clergyman presented to him although that clergyman may intend to introduce the whole Roman sacramental system. The hope of restoring Order in the Church will be at an end.

Our service of institution in Birmingham is most solemn and moving.

In it at the end the Bishop prays to God that He will give the newly-instituted minister 'grace truly to perform the solemn vows and promises by him made'. Now I will not turn such a prayer into a mockery: no Court of the realm could make me do it. If, however, I defended the proposed action I might appear to allow that the Court had such power of compulsion. Hence, though I am assured that if I defended the suit I should win, I will not enter a defence. The issue is moral and spiritual, not legal. With all respect to the High Court, the order which the Trustees seek is not one which I could obey, were it issued.

I am told that when the action has been begun I may make no statement to the Press. Hence I now publish the relevant correspondence and ask that those who believe in the power of prayer will pray that God will guide the course of events which we must leave in His hands.

Interviewed by the press, Simmonds himself commented that it would be a test case, as other bishops did not make such demands, and Rosenthal characteristically claimed that, while Barnes sought to enforce the law against the Anglo-Catholics, he was refusing to obey it himself. The newspapers themselves were chary of comment, lest the case be held to be *sub judice*, although there were some deprecating remarks about Frere invoking the secular arm against a brother bishop. On this particular point, when a correspondent later drew his attention to Romanizing practices at Truro, Barnes replied:

There is a good tradition in the Church of England that one diocesan Bishop shall not interfere in the diocese of another . . . But though . . . Dr Frere broke the convention of non-interference, I must not follow his bad example.

Even so, the Bishop of Truro was not saved from the attentions of ecclesiastical lawyers of the Protestant persuasion and was led to protest to the Archbishop of Canterbury against them.

Barnes meanwhile had been taking legal advice. He first consulted Inskip, who had helped him over Stirchley and who now agreed that he was legally justified, on the strength of Gore-Booth v. Bishop of Manchester, in asking for the assurances. He also agreed with Barnes's decision not to appear in court. Shortly thereafter, however, Barnes received a private letter out of the blue from Sir Lewis Dibdin, the Dean of the Arches and Vicar-General of the Province of Canterbury. Dibdin was thus a highly experienced ecclesiastical lawyer, who, with the preamble 'You seem to me to want a knowledgeable friend and for more than one reason I do not think your Chancellor would be a good adviser in this case', expressed the firm view that the Bishop was not legally entitled to ask for the assurances and would therefore lose the case if he did not appear and could not cross-examine Simmonds. Dibdin incidentally cast some doubt on Inskip's knowledge of ecclesiastical law, even though he had been a junior counsel in Gore-Booth v. Manchester, and maintained that to rely on Coleridge's dictum would be to rest on a broken reed, since Coleridge had misdirected himself by entering into ecclesiastical matters over which he had no jurisdiction. Dibdin for his part advised that Simmonds should be asked what he had done in the past and, if this showed that he had voluntarily adopted illegal practices, the Bishop could legitimately refuse to institute. But by now the writ had been issued and served, and it was too late to ask Simmonds any more questions. In fact, Dibdin's intervention was less friendly than appeared on the surface. For he was at the same time in touch with the Archbishop of Canterbury, to whom he wrote on 28 December, enclosing a copy of his letter to Barnes:

> It seemed to me that the Bishop of Birmingham was taking a line in his letters which would lead to his defeat (for which I care nothing) but which would also allow the Anglo-Catholics to say that their views were permissible in the Church of England, although the result of the *quare impedit* would mean nothing of the sort.

It is doubtful whether Lang would have been equally disturbed by this justification of the Anglo-Catholic cause. But he continued to consult Dibdin throughout the affair.

Barnes's decision not to appear in court caused some distress to his friends. Both Inge and Major wrote to urge him to defend the case. Inge thought he could show that Frere and Co. could be made to admit that, when a man said he would obey his Bishop 'in all things lawful and honest', 'lawful' for them did not mean 'sanctioned by the law of the land'. Major, as an Erastian, feared that Barnes would be seen as unconstitutional in ignoring the courts. Others were afraid that he would seem to be admitting his guilt by not offering a defence. Barnes took the consistent view in reply that this was a moral and spiritual issue, on which Truro's action was widely regarded as unseemly, and he himself would do better not to make himself a party to it; moreover, if he defended the case, he would have to obey the decision of the court. In another letter he quoted a fellow-bishop as saying to him that 'if the court decides in my favour, we can gradually restore order in the English Church but, if the decision is adverse, complete chaos must result'. Barnes was also privately in touch with H. T. A. Dashwood, who was not only a personal friend but also Legal Secretary to the Archbishop of Canterbury and therefore anxious to help both diocesan and metropolitan. As ever, all the lawyers disagreed: Inskip doubted if the Bishop would ever be committed for contempt; Dibdin thought the writ, if disobeyed, would go over his head to the Archbishop; while Dashwood held that the patrons could not do this but would either have to drop the writ altogether or proceed for contempt.

Perhaps Dashwood was already in touch with the Archbishop. At any rate on 4 February 1930, Lang asked to see Barnes and a date was made for 12 February. It transpired that the trustees had approached Lang. This was why the case had not come to court. The Archbishop now suggested on their behalf that Barnes should withdraw his request for assurances from Simmonds and that instead the patrons themselves should offer a general understanding that Simmonds would not use illegal services connected with the reserved sacrament. Through Johnson, Barnes consulted Inskip, who confirmed his own view that the proposed understanding was far too vague. The essential point was that reservation itself was illegal. On 17 February Barnes gave his answer to the Archbishop:

Since you kindly asked me to stay at Lambeth last Wednesday night I have carefully considered the suggestion which I then learned that the Trustees of St Aidan's had asked your Grace to put before me. In view of the great administrative importance of the whole matter and your own feeling that the suggestion might ultimately be made public I have also consulted friends whose opinions I value.

To avoid the possibility of misunderstanding I will first state what, as I apprehend, is the suggestion of the Trustees. They are willing to let me have some sort of assurance that they present Mr Simmonds with the knowledge that, if he is permitted to reserve the consecrated elements at St Aidan's, he will accept my directions as to the manner of reservation and that he will not have, in connection therewith, illegal services such as Adoration, Benediction and so forth.

Now this suggestion is equivalent in effect to a claim on the part of the patrons that they, and not the Bishop, may determine whether the practice of reservation shall be allowed at St Aidan's. But, as I need

243

not remind your Grace, it was the proposal to make reservation legal which wrecked the Prayer Book proposals of 1927 and 1928. I have heard it urged that the Church sanctioned reservation by allowing those proposals to go forward: but your Grace will agree that definite sanction can only be given by means of a new Canon and that no such Canon has been passed. Moreover, even by the proposals of 1928 the Bishop before issuing a licence for reservation was to be satisfied that need for it existed. It is true that an appeal against his decision would have been possible to the Archbishop and Bishops of the Province. But the proposals were rejected. Subsequently by a majority the Bishops in the Upper House of Convocation resolved

'that the Bishops in the exercise of that legal or administrative discretion which belongs to each in his own Diocese will be guided by the proposals set forth in the Book of 1928'.

But – I quote your Grace's own words – 'that discretion remains with the Bishop in each Diocese. It is for him to decide in any particular case how far he may think it right to follow the guidance of these proposals'.

I am therefore with much regret unable to accept the suggestion of the Patronage Trustees of St Aidan's. But those whom I have consulted and I myself appreciate your Grace's anxiety as to what may be the ultimate outcome of the action of the Trustees. I will go so far therefore as to say that I will not press for direct assurances from Mr Simmonds provided that the Trustees will extend their offer and inform me in writing that they have some understanding with, or assurance from, Mr Simmonds that he recognizes that I, as Bishop, have authority to require obedience to the provisions of the Prayer Book and that he will give such obedience as I may ask for, and that, in particular, I have a right to refuse to permit the practice of reservation at St Aidan's and that he will obey the direction as to the discontinuance of reservation that I shall give.

I am aware that neither such an understanding obtained by the Patronage Trustees nor a direct assurance from Mr Simmonds would give me pledges not covered by the Declaration of Assent and Oath of Canonical Obedience. But either would constitute 'a gentleman's agreement' which a man of honour would not repudiate. As your Grace knows, I will not try to restrain ecclesiastical disorder by process of law. The repudiation by a clergyman of most solemn pledges is a moral and spiritual issue which I am not prepared to bring before the lay Courts.

Lang, who had been trying to find a way out which would not

publicly involve himself, replied briefly that he could do no more and that the exchange should remain confidential. Clearly, he did not relish publication of Barnes's letter. But somewhat disingenuously he did send a copy of it to the Bishop of Truro. Commenting on this episode a dozen years later to Hunkin, the new Bishop of Truro, who had consulted him on a similar case, Barnes wrote:

> Before the trial in the High Court I had a long interview with the Archbishop in which (this is private) he – as I thought most indefensibly – offered on behalf of the patrons that their presentee would obey all my instructions with regard to reservation provided I would permit the practice. I refused this offer, although His Grace made it plain that he would institute the man over my head. I asked him how many times he was prepared to take similar action, and realised by his annoyance that it was unlikely that he would do it twice. Since then nobody has dared to put him in the position where he would have to do it. If you adopt my position, you can feel quite certain that His Grace will not institute a man over your head, however much he would like to take such action.

At this point the trustees changed tack again and applied to have the writ transferred from the King's Bench to the Chancery Division. Barnes's Legal Secretary thought that this was because it would be easier to enforce a Chancery judgement without committing the Bishop to gaol, while Dashwood opined that they were afraid of the case coming before Charles J. or Macnaghten J., did not want to proceed in the Court of Arches, where Dibdin had already given a judgement unfavourable to their case, and were satisfied to have Mr Justice Bennett in Chancery.

On the last point they were probably right. For, after an adjournment for their counsel to clarify just what he wanted, the Judge on 2 April issued an order to the Bishop to license Simmonds and to pay the costs of the action. Barnes had at the last minute decided to allow Colonel Errington to hold a watching brief for him, and on Errington's advice the Court was not told of the correspondence which had passed between the Bishop and Simmonds. So the Judge did not know of Simmonds's refusal to obey orders, and in the circumstances his decision was virtually inevitable. But even so it did not satisfy the trustees. They knew that they were back to square one: they could only press Barnes himself to do as he was told by the Court, and he had no intention of doing so, even though Inskip had privately advised him to obey the Court and at the same time to repeat his request to the trustees for a promise of co-operation. That Barnes was right to refuse immediately became clear. On 4 April the trustees offered a new compromise: he should accept the present state of affairs at the rebel churches if in future they fully identified themselves with the work and finance of the diocese. The case could then be dropped. Needless to say, Barnes refused this deal, writing on 8 April to reiterate that 'reservation at St Aidan's must cease'. He tried to soften the tone of his answer by adding: 'You will, I trust, believe that in the stand which I feel compelled to make I am animated solely by a desire to preserve the purity of the faith of the Church of England.' On the same day Lang again intervened to ask if Barnes wanted to reconsider his attitude and, if so, to discuss the affair with him again. Barnes replied to the effect that he must stand pat and need not trouble Lang with another interview. To Inskip and Johnson he wrote that the trustees seemed to be in a false position, as he understood that they could only obtain a writ of attachment against himself or his possessions and could not apparently claim damages or an order of the Court to the Archbishop. He realised that the Archbishop could, of his own accord, make a visitation to the Birmingham diocese, suspend Barnes meanwhile and admit Simmonds in the course of these proceedings; but he doubted if that would appeal to Lang.

In fact, Lang had during this stage kept in private touch with Truro, who, as soon as the result of the court hearing was known, had tried to extract from the Archbishop a promise that he would if necessary intervene. But Lang was too canny a Scot for that. Although he showed his sympathies by telling Frere that his last conversation with Barnes 'leaves hardly any hope that he is prepared to listen to counsels of moderation or reconsideration', he also told him, after consulting Dibdin, that, since the trustees had adopted the procedure of *quare impedit* rather than *duplex querela*, when the Archbishop could have been joined in the suit, he himself as Archbishop had no *locus standi* and could not accept a court order requiring him to institute the presentee. 'In the event of the Bishop declining to act upon the order made by the Court against him, what remedy you would have against him beyond applying for his commitment is not for me to say. Your legal advisers must give you advice on that matter.' This was not music to the trustees' ears, and Frere replied with a long, legalistic letter, quoting sixteenth-century precedents and urging Lang to act *proprio motu*. Dibdin advised him to do no such thing: he had no power to meddle with the Bishop's administration of his diocese. Truro was 'trying to bluff'. What would he say if his own diocese was involved? In any case, his sixteenth-century precedents were bad. It was his own fault for choosing a legal rather than a spiritual remedy and then going about it the wrong way. Lang was evidently not happy with this and saw Dibdin on 30 April, after which he recorded that it was not for the Archbishop to pull the trustees' chestnuts out of the fire but that he gathered from Dibdin that in his opinion

the Bishop of Birmingham had exceeded his legal rights in refusing to institute Mr Simmonds without examination and with an attempt to extort promises not required by law. If therefore the question came before the Court of Arches I expect that the Judge would intimate to me that the Clerk ought to be instituted and that it would then be for me either to institute or to depute the Vicar-General to institute after I had myself examined the Clerk.

This seems to be as much Lang's opinion as Dibdin's, and suggests that the Archbishop was already arming himself with justifications for his preferred course of action.

Meanwhile, the case being no longer *sub judice*, Barnes had on 14 April issued a statement to the press to define his position:

I think that at the present time I ought to explain, for the sake of many who are puzzled by legal arguments and proceedings, what has led up to the recent action brought against me in the Chancery Division of the High Court by the Patronage Trustees of St Aidan's, Birmingham.

When I became Bishop of Birmingham in 1924 I knew that the most serious of the problems before me was how to end ecclesiastical disorder in the Diocese. The erroneous sacramental teaching of the Roman Church was so thoroughly accepted by a small but vocal section of the clergy that I was actually rebuked for referring to the errors of Latin Sacramentalism in my Enthronement Address. The disunion within the Church weakened its moral authority in Birmingham: the prevalence of false sacramental teaching alienated thoughtful and educated people. Obviously sound Anglican teaching was needed; and, gradually, illegal services copied from Roman Catholicism had to be made to cease.

To provide sound teaching was easy, in part because the strength of the liberal and Evangelical movements in the Church at large has grown steadily during recent years. To get a general obedience to the

Prayer Book was a harder matter.

I went slowly. I did not, even after a year's delay, ask that the practice of reservation should cease altogether, because it was not then known how far reservation 'for the sick only' might be sanctioned by the Church and Parliament. But in November 1925 I demanded that *public* reservation of the consecrated elements of Holy Communion should cease and that also such Roman usages as Benediction, Adoration and Procession of the Host should be brought to an end. Most of the clergy shewed friendly loyalty; but some fifteen Churches refused my request and formed the so-called 'rebel' group. What was I to do with them? The incumbents concerned were undoubtedly acting illegally, in defiance of the solemn Declaration of Assent which each had taken before being admitted to his living. Each had sworn canonical obedience to his Bishop, in all things lawful and honest, and was consequently false to his oath. Of course, I could have taken legal action against each. At the cost in every case of possibly £1000 I could have had the incumbent removed from his living. In the struggle his lawyers might, and probably would, have so arranged matters that he went to prison for contempt of Court. Such proceedings, to say the least, would have been unedifying. But, apart from lesser considerations, I could not bring myself to quell religious disorder and enforce moral obligations by 'going to law'. So I resolved both to give no countenance to the so-called 'rebel' Churches and also to refuse to institute new vicars, when vacancies occurred, unless I had an understanding from the men presented to me that they regarded their Declaration and Oaths as binding obligations.

There was always the possibility that some patron, eager to perpetuate disorder, would tell his nominee to refuse to give such an understanding: and that the patron would then bring an action against me. I resolved that I would not defend such an action if it should be brought: the issue would really be moral and spiritual. As Bishop I ought to be able to preserve sound doctrine and to get order without fighting legal actions. If I cannot, Parliament must ultimately intervene: and, if I suffer for my principles, Parliament will not be indifferent.

I confess that I did not expect that a responsible body of Anglo-Catholic patronage trustees, including a Diocesan Bishop, would abandon the old High Church doctrine of the spiritual independence of the Church and appeal to the lay Courts. Such action aims, in fact, at forcing me to allow reservation at St Aidan's, although Parliament, by a vote popular within and without the Church, refused to legalize reservation both in 1927 and again in 1928.

In answer to overtures which have reached me I have said that reservation at St Aidan's must cease. If the Patronage Trustees or their

Presentee are willing to assure me that reservation shall cease, I will proceed to institute at once. Failing such an understanding, whatever the consequence, I must continue to refuse institution.

In this event undoubtedly the Trustees can go again to the Chancery Division of the High Court. If their appeal caused me to be sent to prison I should without complaint thus serve the cause of Reformed religion.

I wish it to be understood that, in refusing to permit reservation at St Aidan's, I am not only respecting the decision of Parliament but I am also protesting against the error that a spiritual presence can be attached to, or inhere in, inert matter. This error runs through primitive religion and is common in lower forms of faith. The Church of England repudiated all ideas of this kind at the Reformation. The present difficulties of Bishops, elsewhere than at Birmingham, have made it clear that, if reservation be conceded as an administrative convenience, doctrines akin to transubstantiation will be taught, and devotions to a spiritual presence assumed to be associated with the consecrated elements will be arranged. My earnest desire is to prevent the lodgement of such doctrines and practices within the English Church, lest the faith we profess becomes contaminated. It is essential to our continued well-being as a Church that we should preserve a faith worthy to hold the intellectual, no less than the moral, respect of the English people.

Apart from some desultory efforts by the trustees' solicitors *pour la forme* to seek Barnes's compliance with the court order and to pay the costs, as he also refused to do, a long pause now ensued. The trustees were evidently scratching their heads to see how they could make a dignified exit. Nothing more was heard from them on the substance of the case until November.

One embarrassment meanwhile was that Lang was due to attend the twenty-fifth anniversary celebrations of the Birmingham diocese in June. Dashwood wrote on 25 April to ask if this could be postponed in case Lang was asked to do something about St Aidan's, and Barnes replied:

I must not presume to give his Grace advice but I do not think that he will be wise to intervene publicly in this dispute save under the appearance of compulsion from the Courts. If out of sympathy to Frere and his co-trustees he puts into St Aidan's a man determined to have reservation contrary to the instructions of myself, as Bishop, and takes such action under the suspensory power supposed to lie in a visitation, the days of the Establishment are most certainly numbered. What, of

249

course, he ought to do is to tell Frere and the rest that they are in an impossible position and that so long as reservation is illegal they must recognize that I have a right to forbid it. The 25th anniversary celebrations take place at the beginning of June. To postpone them, as you suggest, would cause the whole diocese to assume that his Grace intends to intervene in the St Aidan's dispute on the side of the trustees. If necessity arises, the celebrations must, of course, be abandoned; but I do not like assuming the worst until it happens.

In the event, the Archbishop wrote, with every protestation of distress, on 27 May to say that his doctors insisted, with the Lambeth Conference ahead, that he cancel all his engagements for June and that this was being announced next day. He had been seriously ill in 1929 and was to be so again in 1931; his biographer attributes the trouble in 1930 to a 'growling' duodenal ulcer, and there seems no reason to think it a diplomatic illness brought on by St Aidan's. But it left Barnes precious little time to find a substitute for 3 June. In fact, the Archbishop of York nobly stepped into the breach and the celebrations passed off well, coinciding as they did with an interdenominational Crusade to increase Christian influence in the City.

While all was temporarily quiet on the St Aidan's front, another minor skirmish on the field of the 'rebellion' took place in the autumn of 1930. Brown, the vicar of St Gregory's, Small Heath, whom Barnes had instituted under threat of legal action in 1925 and regretted it ever since, asked for permission to engage a curate called Pike. The Bishop replied to the effect that he refused to license curates to 'rebel' churches. He also saw Pike to explain his position directly. When Brown indicated that he intended to go ahead none the less, Barnes said to Pike that in that case he would 'have no alternative but to appeal to the Archbishop of Canterbury, as head of the Church of England, publicly to rebuke you and to ask you to depart'. He can hardly in practice have expected Lang to do any such thing and, as he explained in a private letter, he realised that the Archbishop had no official *locus standi* but hoped that he might use his moral influence. Despite this, Brown took Pike on without licence, although it appears from his letters, which varied from extreme truculence to wistful gentleness, that he was by no means happy about it. The Archbishop, not surprisingly, did nothing.

Lest it be thought that they were yielding the field, the English Church Union at this stage sent a circular letter to all the bishops putting on record their determination to support patrons against any attempt to extract non-statutory assurances. Barnes replied publicly, reiterating his own determination to stick to his guns.

Behind the scenes, however, the trustees of St Aidan's had been busy and had now dug up some precedents showing that the Court could direct the Archbishop to admit an incumbent over the diocesan bishop's head. This was, in fact, what Dibdin had expected from the start, but Barnes had, perhaps unluckily, not been in touch with him for nearly a year now. Possibly Dibdin himself had felt that, with the case in the courts, he personally, as Vicar-General of Canterbury, could no longer be involved. More probably, he had found himself in an equivocal position giving advice to both Barnes and the Archbishop. In any case, he now complained that Lang had not consulted him lately and had allowed Dashwood to make various mistakes. But Dashwood had been doing his best for the Archbishop. For example, now that the Archbishop was made a party to the suit, Barnes had readily agreed to Dashwood's request that he release Errington to advise Lang, especially as Dashwood indicated that the Archbishop would only want to be told to 'institute some suitable person presented by the Patronage Trustees'. As Barnes put it in a letter on 11 December:

The Archbishop declared that, if the order to himself was that he must institute a particular person, he could not entertain it. I gather that his Grace felt that to obey such an order would be to allow that the constitution of the Church was Erastian. Obviously, if the Court told the Archbishop to admit a clergyman who intended to be a 'rebel', he would be in an unfortunate position.

He was too optimistic. The case was heard on 16 December before Mr Justice Maugham, who gave judgement in February directing a writ 'to be issued to the Archbishop, ordering him to institute a fit and proper person to the vacant benefice'. Walter Monckton represented Lang in court and secured the desired result for him. But Lang was again ill and out of the country, so that nothing could happen immediately. Barnes wrote to the Archbishop's chaplain to explain that in these circumstances he had refrained from public comment. The only other intervention came from the Bishop of London, who with misguided helpfulness offered to find Simmonds a London living. This was not at all what the trustees wanted; their pound of flesh was a Birmingham benefice.

But in May Lang was back, and Dashwood wrote to say that the trustees had presented Simmonds and it was now the Archbishop's duty to examine him. Barnes at once replied, reserving the right to publish his letter. After rehearsing the background again, he continued:

I presume that His Grace in examining Mr Simmonds will ascertain whether he not only proposes to take but will also keep the Oath of Canonical Obedience to me as Bishop of the Diocese. If Mr Simmonds will undertake to obey such lawful directions as I may give with regard to public worship, I will gladly welcome him to the fellowship of the diocese. But I would point out that the regrettable delay and litigation of the last eighteen months have been due to the fact that Mr Simmonds refused to give any such assurance.

In addition to asking for the discontinuance of the illegal practice of reservation I should ask for the cessation of other irregularities, the existence of two of which I would bring to the notice of His Grace though I fear they may distress him. In April 1930 the following appeared in the St Aidan's *Monthly Magazine* under the heading 'The Altar of Repose':

'It has been suggested that we should explain what this is. It is the place in Church (in our case, the Lady Chapel), where the Blessed Sacrament is taken after Mass on Maundy Thursday and where it remains until the Mass of the Pre-sanctified on Good Friday. During this time the altar of repose is made as beautiful as human devotion can make it. Candles are kept burning, and it is surrounded with the choicest flowers, and what is still more important, the faithful are encouraged to come and spend some time during Maundy Thursday in prayer before our Lord in the Blessed Sacrament. It is obvious that this is a most fitting day for this devotion,' etc.

His Grace will observe in this regrettable paragraph that we have teaching which can only be described as false sacramentalism. It is assumed that the priest has by formula and ritual act caused our Lord Jesus Christ to dwell within the consecrated elements of Holy Communion. The teaching and language are alike Roman Catholic.

Recently public attention has been called in the local press to the fact that there is at St Aidan's an image of the Virgin Mary in front of which there are framed the following verses:

'Blessed Lady when I pray
To our Lord who loves you so,
Will you tell me what to say,
You're His Mother so you know.

Then when I have done my best,
Will you pray to Him for me?
And just tell Him all the rest,
I could not say properly.'

His Grace will, I trust, agree that the literary style and the theology of
these verses are alike deplorable.

I would finally urge upon His Grace that the errors and puerilities
to which I have drawn attention do very great harm to the Church in
Birmingham. They cause intelligent people to be contemptuous of us
and are thus a grave hindrance as we try to preach the Gospel of Christ.

But Lang had now determined on his course. He had had to make
up his mind to act, however little he wanted to occupy the front of
the stage. Certainly, he had no intention of making a visitation of
one of the dioceses in his province, suspending its bishop and
exercising his *jus metropolitanum*, as had on occasion been done by
Archbishops Cranmer, Parker, Grindal, Whitgift and Sancroft.
Monckton and Errington had, in January 1931, advised him not to
acquiesce in an order to institute Simmonds but only 'a fit and
proper person': he should not be seen to be acting with the plaintiffs.
But in March Henson had volunteered praises of Simmonds: 'he has
been ill-served and in a sense victimized by the oppugnant bigotries
of Birmingham, episcopal and patronal'. Moreover, even Dashwood
advised in May that it was the past of the clerk which mattered: only
if he had already committed an offence against ecclesiastical law,
could he be asked for more than the Oath of Canonical Obedience.
Thereupon the Archbishop on 13 May again saw Dibdin, who,
according to Lang's record, 'considered that Reservation was not a
matter of spiritual learning but a ceremony or practice and that, as
the evidence showed that he had never adopted this practice, it
would not be right for me to ask whether, if admitted now, he
would or would not do something which he had not hitherto done.
Sir Lewis said that in his judgement (unless he was much mistaken
about Mr Simmonds) I should be obliged to admit him'. Again Lang
seems to be bolstering his case for doing what he already wanted to
do. But in any case his mind was now made up. He actually put

Simmonds up for the night before the examination and in the interview itself seems to have shown him every friendliness. According to Lang's own record, after satisfying himself as to Simmonds's beliefs and past practices,

> I then explained to him that what followed would be a personal conversation between me as his Father in God and himself in view of the difficulties in which we were both placed. I asked him to consider whether, even if I found him to be a fit person and were ready to admit him, he might not, in view of these difficulties, having won for himself and the Patrons the main point, withdraw his acceptance of the Benefice. He promised to give this matter consideration. I urged him to do his utmost to meet the request of the Bishop so far as he conscientiously could. Continuous Reservation has been practised at St Aidan's with the consent of previous Bishops for many years, but I asked him to think whether Reservation such as he had been accustomed to might not suffice even at St Aidan's and whether he might not make, and get his congregation to make, an act of sacrifice, for the sake of restoring fellowship with his Bishop.

Whether Lang really expected Simmonds to respond to either request or not, he had not made it more likely by indicating that he intended to admit him in any case and by showing his own acceptance of a degree of reservation. In any event, within ten days Simmonds refused to withdraw and even persuaded Lang to make some drafting changes in his record. Lang also wrote to Frere about Simmonds, saying 'I liked what I saw of him and I think he has behaved with great self-restraint during a very trying time'. In short, Lang had played straight into the trustees' hands. He conveyed the result to Barnes in two letters of 30 May, one public and the other private. The public and formal letter read:

> As you are aware, in consequence of your non-appearance in the action of Notley (and others) versus yourself, a Writ was issued to me by the Chancery Division of the High Court of Justice dated 11th March 1931 requiring me as your Metropolitan to admit a fit person to the Benefice of St Aidan's, Birmingham. I have felt bound to accept this Writ and to act upon it; and it is now my duty to inform you as to what I have done and purpose to do in accordance therewith.
>
> The Patrons of the Benefice have presented to me the Rev. G. D. Simmonds, Assistant Curate of the parish of St Mary, Tyne Dock, in the Diocese of Durham, requesting me to admit him to the cure. It

therefore became my duty to decide whether Mr Simmonds was a fit person to be admitted.

I have examined Mr Simmonds. I was entirely satisfied as to his age, Orders, and moral character; and I received warm testimony from the Bishop of Durham as to his character and services to his present curacy where he has served since his Ordination. As to his spiritual learning and soundness in the Faith, he has satisfied me in answer to my questions that he sincerely holds the Catholic Faith as it is held in the Church of England; and in particular that as regards the Holy Communion he does not hold and will not teach the people that any adoration 'ought to be done unto the sacramental Bread and Wine' or 'unto any corporal presence of Christ's natural Flesh and Blood'.

I also examined Mr Simmonds as to ceremonies and practices in the Church where he is at present officiating and specially as to Reservation of the elements of the Sacrament of Holy Communion. He informed me that in that Church there has been and is no continuous reservation, and consequently no Services have been or are held in connection with the reserved sacrament. He would of course be liable, subject to the Bishop's veto, to suits promoted in the Spiritual Courts for any ceremonies or practices as to which on the ground of their alleged illegality he might hereafter be accused. But it would not be in accordance with precedent and would be manifestly unjust that he should be questioned as to ceremonies or practices which he has not used or adopted.

No doubt a clergyman can be refused admission to a cure if in the past he has so acted that were he admitted to the cure he could be prosecuted in respect of his past acts. But the principle involved in such cases is quite different from that in which I have to act. I am simply asked to certify whether now Mr Simmonds is a fit person to be admitted. In these circumstances, I am obliged to find that Mr Simmonds is a fit person for the cure to which he has been presented; and, subject to the month's notice required by the Benefices Act 1898, section 2(2), I propose to admit him thereto accordingly.

I shall then certify to the High Court of Justice as to the manner in which I have executed the Writ issued to me. You will I am sure believe me when I say that it is very distressing and indeed painful to me to be thus obliged to intervene in the administration of your Diocese. But I must not allow personal feelings to affect what seems to me to be my duty.

The private letter, though ostensibly couched in terms of distress, was in fact more of a complaint:

The enclosed letter will tell you the decision to which I have come in this most difficult matter. As the letter is formal and as it deals with a question of public interest and a situation which has already been unduly prolonged I am sending it at once to the Press. But in first sending it to you I must accompany it with this personal and private letter. I cannot tell you how distressed I am on every personal ground that I feel obliged to act in the manner set forth in the enclosed letter.

You are of course aware of all that has happened and particularly of the Writ addressed to me by the Chancery Division of the High Court of Justice requiring me to admit a fit person to the Cure of St Aidan's. This was the consequence of your own action. When you refused to admit Mr Simmonds to the Benefice your decision led to an action in the High Court of Justice. You declined to appear at the hearing of the case and the decision of the Court was against you. In accordance with your intentions already announced you ignored the order of the Court. The Patrons of the Benefice were naturally unable to acquiesce in this position and applied to the Chancery Division of the High Court for a remedy. I understand that the Court was convinced that a remedy must be found but that it was unwilling to provide a remedy by merely issuing an Order of Attachment (I think that is the correct phrase) to you with all the painful consequences which such an Order might have involved. And indeed this would have been in every way a barren remedy. The Court therefore availed itself of certain precedents according to which the Archbishop had been called upon to act in the case of the default of a Bishop of his Province. As the Writ left it entirely to my discretion to decide as to the fitness of any person presented to me by the Patrons and as it seemed to be the only way of avoiding a situation which had become intolerable, I felt bound to accept this Writ and to be willing to act upon it.

The Patrons duly presented to me for admission the Rev. G. D. Simmonds. It then became my duty to decide whether he was in my judgement a fit person. I examined him at Lambeth. In this examination I was bound to keep within the limits which the law enjoins and which indeed justice to the clergy of the Church of England requires. I need not point out to you, though it is often forgotten, that there is a very great difference between the questions which a Bishop acting as Patron of a Benefice is entitled to ask of any clergyman whom he thinks of appointing to that Benefice and the questions which acting simply as Bishop he is entitled to ask when other Patrons present a clergyman to him for admission. With regard to such questions, the Bishop is carefully restricted in his action by law and precedent. Accordingly in my examination of Mr Simmonds I was obliged to keep within the limits so imposed. As I have shortly stated in the enclosed letter I found that he held no opinions which were in my judgement inconsistent with the teaching and formularies of the Church of England, particularly as

Confronting the Archbishop of Canterbury, 1947

Confirmation

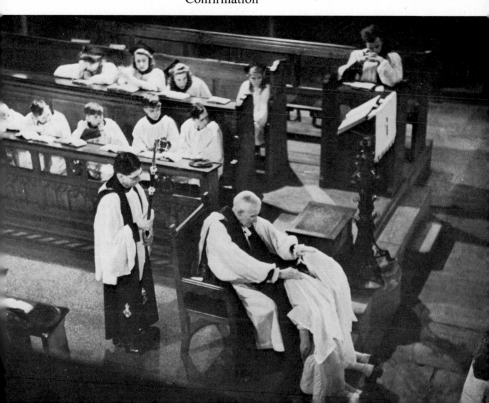

Birmingham Cathedral

regards the subject of the doctrine of Holy Communion. I examined him also as to ceremonies and practices used in the Church in which he has served since he was ordained. I found there was nothing in this respect which could prevent me from regarding him as a fit person for admission or could legally justify me in requiring from him a statement of his intentions in taking the Oath of Canonical Obedience or promises or undertakings as to what he would or would not do in the future in regard to circumstances which had not arisen. Thus I am obliged to conclude that I cannot refuse to admit him to the Benefice, and in accordance with the injunction laid upon me I propose in due course to admit him.

But I must emphasize in writing to you now personally what I have said at the end of the enclosed letter as to the distress and pain which it gives me to admit to a Cure in your Diocese a clergyman whom you yourself declined to admit. I can only say that I did not ask for this Writ. It was imposed upon me, only I could not for the reasons given contest it or refuse to obey it. As I have said before it seemed to me the only solution of a situation which had arisen largely through your own course of action and which could not without real scandal to the Church continue. Nevertheless the action I am bound to take distresses me I think more than any action I have ever taken in my public life. I heartily wish I could have avoided it. But I can only do what seems to me to be right.

I may add that after my examination of Mr Simmonds was concluded I tried to impress upon him the duty of doing his utmost to put and keep himself in fellowship with his Bishop. In spite of all that has happened I am sure that you on your part will do all you can to make this relationship possible.

The Archbishop had, in effect, while doing what he could to fix the responsibility elsewhere, committed himself to support the Anglo-Catholic trustees. Barnes had expected this *dénouement* ever since his interview with Lang before the case came to court. Indeed, in view of that interview, it is hard to acquit the Archbishop of insincerity at the very least. So Barnes replied at once on 1 June, publishing his letter immediately so that it might appear at the same time as the Archbishop's to him and explaining this privately to Lambeth:

I beg to thank Your Grace for your letter of May 30 in which you inform me that you intend to admit the Reverend G. D. Simmonds to the benefice of St Aidan, Small Heath. I am pleased to hear that you have examined him and that, so far as your examination has gone, he has satisfied you as to the soundness of his sacramental doctrine. But Your Grace is aware that the ultimate question between myself and the Patronage Trustees of St Aidan's is as to whether the illegal practice of reservation shall continue at the Church. I therefore beg to enquire whether Your Grace ascertained that Mr Simmonds accepts the fact that 'the Sacrament of the Lord's Supper was not by Christ's ordinance reserved, carried about, lifted up, or worshipped'; and whether, in accordance with this fact, he will obey the rubric of our Prayer Book which says that if any consecrated bread or wine shall remain after the Communion the priest with such others as he may call to him shall, 'immediately after the Blessing, reverently eat and drink the same'.

I notice that Your Grace says that it would not be in accordance with precedent and would be 'manifestly unjust' that Mr Simmonds should be questioned as to ceremonies and practices which he has not used or adopted. I submit that the existing situation is unparalleled and that Your Grace is, in fact, making a precedent; and I would inquire why it is 'manifestly unjust' to ask a man presented to a Church, where grave irregularities take place contrary to the law of the land and the Bishop's express directions, whether he will cause such grave irregularities to cease. Let me suggest a possible parallel. Suppose – as is not incredible in this age of confusion – that a clergyman with the goodwill of his Patronage Trustees should cease to recite the Creeds in public worship. On his retirement the Bishop would naturally be anxious to know whether the man presented as his successor would continue the same practice. I gather that Your Grace is of opinion that you could rightly ask such a man as to his doctrinal beliefs but that it would be 'manifestly unjust', if he had recited the Creeds in public worship in the past, to enquire whether he intended in his new benefice to restore the lawful order of public worship.

Your Grace reminds me that after Mr Simmonds has been presented he will be liable to suits promoted in the Spiritual Courts on the ground that he continues illegal ceremonies or practices. This suggestion of further litigation troubles me greatly. The recent litigation with regard to St Aidan's has been a scandal which has done grave harm to the Church; and I have not been a party to it. That Your Grace should contemplate that further litigation may result from Your Grace's present action implies that our Church is in a state of disorder from which disruption is likely to result. As Your Grace knows, I personally will not try to restrain ecclesiastical disorder by process of law. Mr Simmonds, when instituted by Your Grace, will have to make the Declaration of Assent and to take the Oath of Canonical Obedience to me as Bishop of Birmingham. Should he repudiate the solemn pledges which he thus gives, such repudiation would be a moral and spiritual lapse which I could not bring myself to lay before either a Civil or a Spiritual Court.

Such communications as have reached me directly or indirectly from the Trustees during the past eighteen months I have been asked to regard as confidential. A request of such a nature on a matter of public importance cannot rightly be made. But, inasmuch as in this matter I am most anxious to avoid all personal issues, I will merely repeat that the issue of reservation has throughout been fundamental. Had I been willing in February 1930 to allow Mr Simmonds to practise reservation at St Aidan's under the conditions laid down in the abortive Prayer Book of 1928, I should have been exposed to no further litigation. But the suggestion that reservation should be made legal caused Parliament to reject the Prayer Book Proposals of 1927 and 1928. I have heard it urged that the Church sanctioned reservation by allowing those proposals to go forward: but Your Grace will agree that definite sanction can only be given by means of a new Canon and that no such Canon has been passed. Moreover, even by the Proposals of 1928, the Bishop before issuing a licence for reservation was to be satisfied that need for it existed. It is true that an appeal against his decision would have been possible to the Archbishop and Bishops of the Province. But the Proposals were rejected. Subsequently by a majority the Bishops in the Upper House of Convocation resolved

'that the Bishops in the exercise of that legal or administrative discretion which belongs to each in his own diocese will be guided by the proposals set forth in the Book of 1928'.

But – I quote Your Grace's own words – 'that discretion remains with the Bishop in each Diocese. It is for him to decide in any particular case how far he may think it right to follow the guidance of these proposals'.

The St Aidan's Patronage Trustees have in effect claimed to decide that reservation shall be continued at St Aidan's Church contrary to the will of Parliament. I must with respect point out that, unless by a more complete examination Your Grace assures yourself that Mr Simmonds will not adopt reservation at St Aidan's, your present action will make it possible for the decision of Parliament to be over-ruled in any instance where the Bishop is not willing to bring a legal action against a clergyman whom Your Grace may admit.

Nevertheless, fortified by advice from Temple that 'it was most improper of the Bishop of Birmingham to make a public reply to your letter', the Archbishop went ahead and licensed Simmonds privately at Lambeth Palace on 7 July, although he omitted to write to tell Barnes so until 11 July, when he said:

> I took the highest possible legal advice as to the limits imposed by law
> and custom upon a Bishop in instituting a clerk prescribed to him by
> the proper Patrons and I was obliged to keep within these limits. In
> observing them, I found no reason to question Mr Simmonds's fitness
> and accordingly I was obliged to admit him. I have had some talk with
> him and have pressed upon him the duty of meeting your wishes as far
> as he conscientiously can. I hope that you will take an early opportunity
> on his return from his holiday to see him and have a friendly and
> fatherly talk with him. I know how much my action has been mis-
> understood but I have deliberately refrained from entering into any
> public correspondence about it.

But Barnes had read the newspapers and had written direct to
Simmonds on 8 July:

> I see in this morning's newspapers that you were yesterday licensed by
> the Archbishop of Canterbury to the benefice of St Aidan, Small Heath,
> in this diocese. I understand that you made and took the usual declar-
> ations and oaths. Thus by the Declaration of Assent you solemnly
> stated:
>
> > 'I assent to the Thirty-nine Articles of Religion, and to the Book of
> > Common Prayer, and of the Ordering of Bishops, Priests, and
> > Deacons. I believe the Doctrine of the Church of England, as therein
> > set forth, to be agreeable to the Word of God; and in Public Prayers
> > and Administration of the Sacraments I will use the form in the said
> > Book prescribed and none other, except so far as shall be ordered by
> > lawful authority.'
>
> You also, as I understand, took the Oath of Canonical Obedience in
> the form:
>
> > 'I do swear that I will pay true and Canonical obedience to the Lord
> > Bishop of Birmingham and his successors in all things lawful and
> > honest. So help me God.'
>
> That you should have felt able to give these pledges encourages me to
> hope that you are coming to this diocese in a spirit of loyal co-operation.
> I should have liked to have had an interview with you this week to
> discuss the situation at St Aidan's Church which has caused me much
> distress. I understand, however, from the public press that you intend to
> be absent on holiday during the next month. I must, therefore, postpone
> the interview until your return. But as your Bishop I ask that you will
> at once give orders that the illegal practice of reservation at St Aidan's

is to cease forthwith. There have been in the recent past at St Aidan's other irregularities and puerilities, some of which I set out in a letter to the Legal Secretary of the Archbishop of Canterbury written on May 14, 1931: I trust that when we have an opportunity of talking matters over you will see your way also to bring these to an end as they do harm to the reputation of our Church among thoughtful citizens of Birmingham. But for the present I merely ask that reservation shall cease and, in view of the importance of the matter, I trust that I may at once receive a reply from yourself stating that you have obeyed my instructions. Such a reply I should desire to publish together with this letter.

To the Archbishop he replied privately:

I would thank Your Grace for the tone of your letter of July 11 and would assure you that I appreciate the difficulty of Your Grace's position. As soon as I saw that Your Grace had instituted Mr Simmonds, I wrote reminding him of his pledges and asking him to bring reservation at St Aidan's to an end forthwith. I explained that I was informed by the newspapers that he had gone away on holiday, and that otherwise I would have invited him to see me at Bishop's Croft. To my letter I have as yet had no reply. When this reply comes I may find myself under the painful necessity of public reference to Your Grace's action. I hope not. But it seems to me that I must not duplicate in a private letter arguments against Your Grace's public policy. But I doubt whether Your Grace can have realised either the strength or the quality of the feeling which has been excited by your decision. In such expressions of it as have reached me I find little disposition to treat seriously the religious belief involved: the belief that a priest can cause a spiritual presence to be associated with a piece of bread seems generally regarded by educated men as something they need no longer consider. But that Your Grace should have allowed a clergyman to make a Declaration and to take an Oath when he had declined to say whether he would keep to the pledges thus made has aroused surprise combined with what I can only describe as moral contempt. It has suddenly appeared that the standards of ecclesiastical procedure are lower than those of the community. Unless Your Grace can do something to free the Church from this apparent acquiescence in a low moral standard, the best elements in the community will be ranged against us. I trust that Your Grace will forgive me for writing plainly, and that you will pardon any public criticism of Your Grace's action that I may feel obliged to make. I will, as always, try to avoid anything that may seem to be personal and to be studiously respectful.

As expected, Simmonds in a short reply refused to abandon reservation, and Barnes thereupon wrote a further public letter on 15 July to Lang:

When I learned that Your Grace had licensed the Reverend G. D· Simmonds to the benefice of St Aidan, Small Heath, in my Diocese, I at once wrote to him. Naturally I am most anxious that St Aidan's shall no longer be one of the so-called 'rebel' parishes of the Diocese and I hoped that, as Your Grace had found him a 'fit person' to be licensed, he would obey my directions as Bishop. I enclose copies of my letter and of his reply. On the tone of the reply I will not comment. But Your Grace will notice that, instead of forthwith acting in accordance with the pledges which he solemnly gave as a condition of institution, Mr Simmonds will consult unnamed persons 'who have a right to be consulted'. No such persons exist, as Your Grace knows full well. Naturally the reply makes me most anxious and, therefore, I write as strongly as I can to beg Your Grace, while there still seems a possibility of obedience, to urge Mr Simmonds to be loyal to his promises.

Your Grace cannot be ignorant that grave harm to the Church will be caused by his refusal. From a torrent of letters, and from expressions of personal sympathy which meet me wherever I go, I have learned two things. First, the ecclesiastical procedure adopted by Your Grace which allows a man to make pledges, although there may even be an expectation that he will not keep them, arouses grave moral disquiet. Secondly, the religious teaching behind the Birmingham 'rebellion' is set aside as absurd. That a spiritual presence is to be found in the consecrated elements of Holy Communion is regarded as a superstition, properly rejected at the Reformation. When the Prayer Book controversy was upon us the House of Laity agreed to accept 'reservation for the sick only'. Parliament, as I think wisely, rejected the proposals because of a fear that continuous reservation would open the way to erroneous belief in a miraculous change in the consecrated elements and to forms of worship based upon it. At St Aidan's, as Your Grace was informed last month, 'Devotions' occur weekly. I learn that the curtains of the Tabernacle are drawn back and, with Roman forms of prayer, priests, acolytes and congregation bow in adoration before the consecrated elements. Such a type of worship proves that Parliament was wiser than a majority of the Bishops; and I ask that the law as affirmed by Parliament should be obeyed.

Your Grace, we have a hard task in Birmingham. We are struggling, in a great city of a million people which has added 600,000 to its population during the last half-century, to proclaim spiritual truth as revealed by Christ and to spread social righteousness. The clergy, with the exception of the so-called 'rebels' in thirteen parishes, are loyal friends with whom I am proud to work. Among them there is probably a higher percentage of men of exceptional quality than in any diocese in England. The Church now takes to a gratifying extent a position of moral leadership in our community and has won intellectual respect. But such a position cannot be retained if we are to be associated with untrue sub-Christian beliefs or with the repudiation of pledges most solemnly undertaken.

Much public attention has naturally been given to the St Aidan's case, and that Churchpeople may know both how and why I am doing all I can to obtain respect for law and sound doctrine I propose to give publicity to this letter.

The Archbishop replied privately and tartly on 18 July, promising a public reply, 'but as I have not your aptitude for letters to the Press and am very much pressed by engagements I fear that a day or two must elapse before I can send such a reply as I think to be necessary'. He also deprecated public exchanges of letters either between Archbishop and Bishop or Bishop and clergy. When his public reply came on 21 July, it read:

I had hoped that as between you and me the matter of St Aidan's, Birmingham, had now been concluded. But there are some statements in your letter of July 15th which you sent to the Press on which I am compelled to make some comments.

You say that 'the ecclesiastical procedure adopted' by me 'which allows a man to make pledges although there may even be an expectation that he will not keep them, arouses grave moral disquiet'. These words which imply that I have personally and on my own initiative adopted a particular procedure show a complete misunderstanding of the facts. As this misunderstanding seems to be shared by many others I think it well to set forth as briefly as possible the real facts of the situation. When the patrons of St Aidan's presented a clerk to you for admission to the benefice you did not examine him as to his fitness but required him in writing to make certain promises. Believing that in so doing you had exceeded your legal rights he declined to make these promises. You then refused to admit him. When called to vindicate your action in the Courts of the Realm you declined to appear, and in your absence an order was issued directing you to admit the clerk. This you refused to do and thus you deliberately placed yourself in contempt of the law. It would have been permissible for the patrons to apply for a Writ of Attachment against you which might have involved imprisonment. The patrons were rightly anxious to avoid such a possibility. Accordingly, following certain established precedents, they

263

applied to the High Court and obtained a Writ addressed to me as Metropolitan directing me in your default to admit a fit person to the benefice. I accepted the Writ. It seemed the only way of ending a situation which by your own action had become intolerable. The patrons then presented to me the clerk whom you had refused to admit. I examined him and for the reasons stated in my letter to you of May 30th I satisfied myself that he was a fit person. In accordance therefore with the Writ addressed to me I have admitted him to the benefice; and there my responsibility ceases.

It has to be remembered that a Bishop when acting as himself the patron is entitled like any other person to require from anyone whom he thinks of appointing to a benefice such conditions or promises as he thinks fit. But when another patron presents a clerk, the Bishop in deciding whether or not to admit him is restrained by certain well-known and well-defined principles of law. In examining the clerk presented to me for admission to St Aidan's I was careful to observe these limitations, and I was assured by the best possible legal advice that it would not be in accordance with them to attempt to obtain from him the pledges or promises which you desired. There was no proof that he had already committed any breach of his vows – on the contrary I had high testimony from his Bishop as to his character and loyalty – and I would not have been legally justified in requiring proof that he would not do so in the future. If the law in this respect ought to be changed it must be done either by a decision in the Courts, which you might have sought and refused to seek, or by legislation. So far as I am concerned I have simply adhered to the law. Thus to imply that I have adopted some new ecclesiastical procedure is to ignore the real facts of the case.

May I add that it seems difficult to reconcile your determination to compel some of your clergy to obey decisions of the Courts of Law with your own refusal in matters affecting your own action to acknowledge the obligations of such decisions?

There is one other point in your letter to which I feel bound to refer. You say that you have learned from letters and expressions of personal sympathy that to believe 'that a spiritual presence is to be found in the consecrated elements of Holy Communion is regarded as a superstition properly rejected at the Reformation'. Apparently you endorse that opinion. All I would say is that such words seem scarcely consistent with the words of Article XXVIII that the Body of Christ is given, taken, and eaten, in the Supper after an heavenly and spiritual manner, or with the words of the Catechism that the Body and Blood of Christ are verily and indeed taken and received by the faithful in the Lord's Supper. I cannot but ask, is it charitable, is it just, to brand as mere superstition a belief, whatever you yourself may think about it, which is held by multitudes of your fellow Churchmen, and which is consistent with the formularies of the Church?

I have written this letter with the greatest reluctance, for it is most distasteful to me – it is not I think in itself seemly – that I should be involved in a public discussion with one of my brother Bishops in the Province of Canterbury.

Barnes himself thought it necessary to send a further public letter on 22 July:

With the first part of your letter I will not at present deal. Your Grace was directed by the High Court of Chancery to admit to St Aidan's a fit and proper person presented by the patrons. I do not yet know whether Mr Simmonds will prove himself a fit and proper person by being loyal to the solemn pledges which he gave in Lambeth Palace Chapel. I renew my appeal to Your Grace to urge him not to bring moral discredit upon the Church by any repudiation of those pledges. In the meantime I await his action before reviewing a situation which, from the standpoint of episcopal administration, is of much gravity.

But grave though the situation created by Your Grace's action is as regards discipline in the Church, its gravity does not compare with the statement as to doctrine with which Your Grace's letter ends. I do not exaggerate when I say that that statement seems to me the most seriously disquieting of any made by an Archbishop of Canterbury since the Reformation. It is true that Your Grace does not commit yourself to belief in a spiritual presence in the consecrated elements of Holy Communion. But you state that such a belief is held by 'multitudes' of our fellow Churchmen, you claim that it is consistent with the formularies of the Church, and you ask whether it is charitable or just to brand it as a superstition.

Your Grace, the assertion that a priest by the act of consecration can cause Christ to come to dwell within the bread and wine of Holy Communion is the so-called 'miracle of the mass'. It was a crucial issue at the Reformation and is the source of most of our present irregularities in public worship. It was formulated by the Roman Church as transubstantation which, by Article XXVIII of our own Church's doctrine, 'is repugnant to the plain words of Scripture, overthroweth the nature of a sacrament and hath given rise to many superstitions'. Men were not burned at the Reformation because they doubted whether the philosophy of transubstantiation was adequate but because, under the influence of the enlightenment of the Renaissance, they denied the alleged fact which the philosophy attempted to explain.

Your Grace must forgive me if, in view of the immense gravity of the issue which you have raised, I write very plainly. The belief that a Christian priest can by consecration cause the presence of Christ to dwell within the consecrated elements is exactly analogous to the belief held by the Hindu that his priest can by consecration cause the god to dwell within its image. The cultured Hindu protests that he does not worship the image but the god within. If the fact be granted the worship can be justified. Similarly in Birmingham the poor woman who wrote to me that I had banished Jesus from her Church, because I had forbidden reservation there, was justified if there be truth in the belief which Your Grace will not term a superstition.

But, Your Grace, the belief that a spiritual presence can be made to inhere in a piece of bread by consecration is false. It is a cardinal principle of modern science – and the term includes religious psychology – that assertions must be justified by experience. Religious or spiritual assertions must be justified by religious or spiritual experience. It is true that the Hindu can point to a glow of religious exaltation on the face of those who worship the idol. But if an unconsecrated idol were surreptitiously substituted for that which had been consecrated no worshipper could tell the difference. Similarly there is among all living men no-one who by any spiritual perception can tell whether a certain piece of bread has been consecrated. The spiritual presence alleged to exist in consecrated bread no-one can detect, however delicate his spiritual perception may be: and to say that something exists though no-one can detect its existence receives curt incredulity today from thinking men and women.

The true Anglican doctrine of Holy Communion is surely that the bread and wine are, to speak metaphorically, vehicles or channels of spiritual grace. Through their use Christ comes to the devout worshipper. We know that this fact is true because we have experienced it. Similarly the beauty that is in God has been revealed to us in a sunset; and often Christ is brought to the soul through the ever-living pages of the Gospels.

The doctrinal implications of Your Grace's statement are immeasurably serious. I submit that Your Grace cannot find adequate authority for the doctrine which you desire me to tolerate, either in our Articles or in any explanatory statement of an Archbishop of Canterbury since the Reformation. If I were a parish priest, and believed that Jesus was in the consecrated bread, I too should desire a tabernacle in my Church, though loyalty to my institution vows would restrain me. I also should wish to have 'adoration' and 'devotions' and all the illegal forms of worship which your great predecessor undertook to try to bring to an end if reservation, as allowed by the revised Prayer Book of 1927, were accepted by Parliament.

I beg Your Grace to withdraw the dangerous implications of your statement. The Church of England must again repudiate the belief which that statement seems to countenance or the people of England will not heed us when we proclaim the Gospel for they will deem us disloyal to truth.

This letter produced a strong reaction from Temple, who wrote to Lang: 'His arrogance is something overwhelming. The assumption that "thinking men" is a proper description of those who agree with himself underlies everything he writes.' Temple went on to enclose his father's Charge of 1898 as Archbishop of Canterbury, in which he held that, while the Church of England did not explicitly teach the Real Presence in the elements after their consecration and before their reception, this was not excluded by the Articles or the Prayer Book, and the Privy Council in the Bennett case had refused to condemn it; it amounted to consubstantiation and was not unlawful in the Church of England. Barnes was familiar with Temple's views and was indeed apprehensive at this time that the Archbishop of York would exert his influence to 'secure a declaration on the Real Presence as extreme as anything allowed by the Bennett judgement'. But Lang had no more stomach for niceties of this kind. He had by now decided that discretion was the better part of valour and refused to enter into any more public exchanges about the doctrine of the Holy Communion. To Barnes he added:

As I am writing to you privately I will content myself with saying that the whole conception of the relations of spirit and matter which seems always to underlie your reiterated utterances on this deep subject seems to me to belong to a past age both of science and philosophy, and in this respect I am bound to say that I wish you were a better Modernist.

To this Barnes sent only a private soft answer, although he also persuaded the *Record* to publish an article, in which he summed up his sacramental position. After asserting that public discussion was desirable, he went on:

Many think that the nature of our spiritual experience in the Holy Communion is not suited to discussions in the secular press: and I personally shrink from any public mention of so intimate a matter. But I believe that we are wrong to be thus reticent. Did we write more frankly of what we experienced, others would more easily appreciate the reality of our faith and errors in doctrine would be more clearly recognized. I will therefore write briefly of the sort of experience at Holy Communion which at times, as I suppose, comes to us all and of the conclusions which can rightly be drawn from it. But I am merely sending what I write to some of our Church papers.

Let me first insist that we must argue, as do men of science, from experience, individual and collective. The time has passed for spiritual assertions which have no basis in spiritual experience. The modern man of science does not consult a series of dead pundits. He experiments, observes and deduces conclusions from a careful examination of his own experience and that of others. We also must be scientific. Unfortunately, there is among certain religious apologists a curious inability to realise that there are many branches of science and that the methods of experimental psychology are not those of chemistry.

As regards my own argument in the open letter to the Archbishop it was gravely stated, in the apology for sacramental superstition to which I have referred, that 'it is sheer stupidity to suppose that a spiritual presence can be discovered by chemical analysis'. No one has asserted this fact more strongly than myself. But that the statement should be made in connection with my psychological argument against the existence of a spiritual presence in a consecrated material object shews the mentality of a child. I will give a close parallel. A doctor recently suggested to his wife that an elder daughter, who was shewing symptoms of nervous disorder, might advantageously be psychoanalysed. A small son, over-hearing the conversation, went to the garage and fetched a spanner for the purpose. The boy confused the science of experimental psychology with that different branch of science which deals with machines. Some of our religious apologists similarly confuse the scientific examination of religious experience with chemical analysis.

What now is our experience in Holy Communion? I, of course, can only speak at first hand of my own reaction. It is that at times, but by no means invariably or regularly, I have when I take part in the Service a peculiarly vivid sense of nearness to Christ, a heightened feeling that through Him the innermost nature of the Universe is revealed. All the inspiration that normally comes from a reflection upon His life and death is suddenly intensified. Such an experience cannot be separated sharply from spiritual illumination which comes through other channels. Moreover I personally do not get it more often if I go to Holy Communion more often: that is why I will never lay down a rule of participation in the Sacrament more stringent than the bare three times a year ordered by our Church. I know that my own experience is shared by others, alike in my own and in the Free Churches. We describe such experience as the Real Presence of Christ in the Sacramental Worship of Holy Communion.

Catholic apologists often argue that our conviction that we thus experience the Presence of Christ is no more scientifically verifiable than the belief that He inheres in, or is associated with, bread and wine as a result of consecration. I say, on the contrary, that the two beliefs differ fundamentally. The belief that Christ can come to the soul through sacramental worship is a reasonable deduction from a religious experience which is as real to many, perhaps most, Churchmen as any experience in life. Of course, in using such a term as the Real Presence to describe the experience, we are implicitly giving an explanation which may be mistaken. I can only urge that my faith is reasonable: I know of no reason for regarding Christ's presence as an illusion. On the other hand, the belief that Christ inheres in the consecrated elements rests on no basis of human experience whatsoever. There is no person, out of the 2000 million human beings now living, who can by spiritual insight, or by some other form of perception, discover whether bread has been duly consecrated. Yet there must be some fact of observation on which to build argument. If the Catholic apologist could produce but one person capable of so ascertaining the presence or absence of Christ that he could tell whether a wafer had or had not been consecrated, I would at once acknowledge my conversion to his faith. Similarly if the Hindu idolater could produce one person capable of so perceiving the presence of the god that without other knowledge he could state that the idol had been consecrated, I would be converted to his faith. But all that I know of the Universe makes me confident that such conversions will not occur. Assertions of spiritual presences in material objects belong to a past phase of religious fancy which humanity is outgrowing. I believe that, as man develops, he will enter into new depths of communion with God. But God is not to be found in articles of food from which He can be assimilated when these are eaten. Neither does God dwell in idols. He reveals Himself, it may be *through* material channels, directly to the soul of man; and, I would add, in such direct revelation there is peace and great joy.

For a time the trustees' lawyers tried to extract the costs of the action from the Bishop, who persisted in his refusal to pay. It no doubt gave the English Church Union satisfaction to notify him in October 1931 that they had themselves paid them.

Thus ended, after two long years, the affair of St Aidan's, Small Heath. The whole affair turned on two questions, the first legal and the second theological. The two questions are, of course, intertwined, but can to some extent be kept separate. The legal question concerned the assurances which the Bishop could properly require of a presentee to a benefice before agreeing to admit him. The Benefices Act of 1898 had provided machinery whereby the Bishop could deal with an existing incumbent for the inadequate discharge of his ecclesiastical duties and the incumbent could be deprived of his living under the Church Discipline Act of 1840. The Public Worship Regulation Act of 1874, designed expressly to check ritualism, provided for recalcitrant clergy to be sent to prison and four of them had in fact been imprisoned between 1877 and 1882. But this had not proved popular and there was a general disinclination among all parties in the Church to make use of the Ecclesiastical Courts, especially as those courts suffered from many other inadequacies. Indeed, the Royal Commission on Ecclesiastical Discipline had commented in 1906, in paragraph 381 of its report, that 'the present structure of the ecclesiastical judicature, taken as a whole, is in our view one chief cause of the growth of ritual irregularities in the Church of England'. The Commission made a further relevant observation, in paragraph 392 of its report:

It has been urged before us that the Bishops might do much to stop illegal practices by refusing to institute to a benefice a presentee whose antecedents render it practically certain that he will, if instituted, disobey the law. There are only a few instances in which any Bishops appear to have felt themselves justified in adopting this course. We recognize that a difficulty exists in the state of the law. At present we understand that a Bishop has no general right to require an undertaking from a presentee that he will obey the law in any particular; although, if a clerk has in a former sphere of duty rendered himself by his conduct liable to prosecution, the Bishop has a right to refuse him institution, and, as a condition of not exercising his right, may require the clerk to give an undertaking to obey the law. We think that, if the Bishop's power in this respect were rendered clearer and larger, the refusal to institute should be steadily maintained in all cases of grave irregularity; and we have made a recommendation with that view.

The Royal Commission's sympathies clearly lay with the line which Barnes later adopted, and even their statement of the law is qualified by the phrase 'we understand that'. But their view of the legal position is evidently that on which Lang relied in limiting his examination of Simmonds as he did, even though he was careful not to spell out his 'well-known and well-defined' legal grounds. Indeed, on the strength of his letter, the Archbishop can hardly be acquitted of casuistry. He had also argued that it was open to the Bishop to prosecute if, after admission, the incumbent violated his oath. On this general point, Barnes had received conflicting legal advice. Inskip had written in December 1929, that 'your correspondence with Mr Simmonds does not refer to the question of his past practice but in the circumstances of this case I think your enquiry and your request to Mr Simmonds afford ample justification in point of law for your refusal to institute him'. But Inskip was relying on Gore-Booth v. Bishop of Manchester, 1920, and Dibdin shortly afterwards advised Barnes to write again to Simmonds to say that he was refusing institution 'because, in a former sphere, he has done these things for which if he did them in the living to which he seeks institution he might be deprived' and to ask if he had done them under compulsion. Barnes then replied that Simmonds had 'as far as I can ascertain, been carefully chosen as a man whose past is blameless but whose sympathies are such that he may safely be counted upon to continue the traditional irregularities at St Aidan's'. Dibdin nevertheless maintained that Barnes could examine Simmonds and that his intentions 'would certainly come out and you could act upon it'. Errington, too, in an opinion given in November 1931, when all was over, took the view that 'St Aidan's Birmingham failed primarily because Simmonds was not examined'. It certainly seems that, if only from his own point of view, Barnes would have done better to see Simmonds; and this, incidentally, might also have given a more human image to his position. But he was concerned from the start with the public presentation of a problem affecting the whole Church. It is true, too, that when Lang examined him, Simmonds established his past innocence to the Archbishop's satisfaction, for what that was worth, although from information reaching Barnes from the Church Association at the time it is by no means certain that the activities of his former parish had been as blameless as Simmonds asserted. It must also be doubted how strongly Lang pressed Simmonds, or wanted to press him, even about his past. In short, the Archbishop's action was legal, but it was not the only permissible legal action open to him: he could, if he had wished, have insisted on the trustees presenting another nominee.

271

Certainly on arrival at St Aidan's Simmonds continued the extreme Anglo-Catholic practices which had been in use there, not only practising reservation in a tabernacle in open church but also holding services involving the consecrated elements. This led Dashwood in November 1931, to urge Barnes to prosecute Simmonds as he was fully entitled to do. Dashwood added:

> I know you have had in the past strong views against taking any legal action but as you are out to do a public duty it is necessary to act in a way the public will understand. *No one* understands, nor I think appreciates, why when necessary you have not defended or taken legal proceedings.

But Barnes was not to be persuaded. He would not go to law on moral and spiritual matters. Perhaps this is the difference between the lawyer and the clergyman; perhaps, after the Prayer Book, he was too confident that time and public opinion would be on his side, whereas, even twenty-five years after his death, the Church of England had still not achieved legislation which would enable Bishops to ask prospective incumbents about their future intentions. Simmonds, incidentally, kept in private touch with the Archbishop after his arrival at St Aidan's and received sympathetic and encouraging replies to his letters. He obviously felt himself to be in a strong position.

Barnes had also been overconfident that the trustees would have to proceed against him only, so that he could block them, and that there would be no way of circumventing him via the Archbishop. But here again the legal precedents were against him, and Dibdin had warned him early on that this recourse might be open to the trustees. In 1868, Archbishop Longley had instituted Marshall after a refusal by the Bishop of Exeter, and in 1875, Archbishop Tait had instituted Walsh when the Bishop of Lincoln had refused. These cases were admittedly based on objections to simony, but the famous Gorham case, when Archbishop Sumner instituted over the head of Bishop Philpotts of Exeter, was more parallel to St Aidan's as it involved a straight doctrinal question of Gorham's views on baptismal regeneration. In each of the three cases, the courts had issued a writ to the Archbishop.

The theological question at issue in the St Aidan's affair was the doctrine of the Real Presence of Christ at the Holy Communion.

This too had a long legal history, mainly affecting the ritualistic practices to which versions of the doctrine gave rise. But Barnes was determined to fight the battle not just in the legal area, but on the underlying scientific and philosophical ground too. Because he did not defend the case, the legal aspects of the matter were not considered in court. In the arguments surrounding the affair, his opponents variously cited the cases of Archdeacon Denison (1856), Sheppard v. Bennett (1872) and Read v. Bishop King of Lincoln (1892), in all of which the Anglo-Catholic respondent could on the face of it be claimed to have won the case for his doctrines and practices. But in point of fact Denison only escaped because the appeal was time-barred by a statute of limitations, and Bennett's words were held to be 'perilously near a violation of the law' and he was only acquitted because the court, having regard to the penal nature of the proceedings, gave him the benefit of 'any reasonable doubt' and 'thought his words capable of a construction which did not call for judicial condemnation'. As for Bishop King, the prosecution was in form concerned with ritual practices, and in his judgement Archbishop Benson laid down stringent conditions for their use. None the less, the plain fact was that reservation was illegal. On this there were plenty of authorities: the Thirty-Nine Articles, the 1662 Prayer Book, the Archbishops' decision of 1900, the Court's ruling of 1907, and Parliament's rejection of the Revised Prayer Book. By the same token, transubstantiation was certainly not accepted by the Church of England. It followed *a fortiori* that all acts of adoration to the consecrated elements were also illegal; on this point the leading cases were probably Martin v. Mackonochie, which Barnes cited in letters at the time, and Westerton v. Liddell. Here the Bishop was on strong ground, and even Lang, who was so careful to justify himself at every stage, found himself drawn on to the slippery slope of selective quotation. He tried to dodge the theological issue behind the legal hedge, but could not avoid it altogether. In seeking to defend a view of the Real Presence different from Barnes's, he argued in his letter of 21 July 1931, that, according to Article XXVIII of the Church, 'the Body of Christ is given, taken, and eaten, in the Supper, after an heavenly and spiritual manner'. But he omitted the key word, for the Article reads: 'only after an heavenly and spiritual manner', as many of his readers at once pointed out.

For this point was at the root of the argument over the Real Presence. In effect, three versions of the doctrine came under discussion in the controversy. First, there was the Roman dogma of transubstantiation, by which the very substance of the elements was changed at consecration from bread and wine to body and blood. It was on this dogma that many Anglo-Catholics in practice justified adoration and so on, even though, if pressed, and knowing it to be illegal, they usually denied that they held it. The second version of the doctrine was that the elements, after consecration, were changed, not in their substance but in their essence, to become vehicles of spiritual grace and thus to achieve a sanctity of their own. This version could, of course, give rise to a wide variety of interpretations. Luther, for example, had advocated consubstantiation, which Archbishop Frederick Temple had declared legitimate in the Church of England. According to the particular interpretation accorded to it, the doctrine could or could not be held to justify acts of veneration towards the elements themselves, rather than to the grace flowing through them. All this was highly metaphysical; but, whatever the subjective interpretation of the doctrine, it did not alter the hard legal fact that reservation and adoration of the elements were illegal in the Church of England. Thirdly, then, came Barnes's own defence of the doctrine, set out most succinctly in his article of 7 August 1931, in the *Record*, that the service of Holy Communion itself was the Sacrament and that the Real Presence existed in the experience which that service brought to the communicant, even though it might be conveyed through a material vehicle. On this he was accused of being a 'receptionist', of saying that the presence only existed in the belief of the communicant. But this he denied, even though it could have been justified by Article XXVI, which proclaims that the effect of the Sacrament is not hindered by the unworthiness of the Ministers. To him, Communion was both a personal and a collective experience, and in that experience, and not in any objective or localized manifestation, lay the Real Presence of Christ.

Nor did he associate the Presence of Christ exclusively with the sacrament of Holy Communion. To a correspondent who described a personal experience he wrote:

The sudden sense of peace and joy and of a Presence who is pure love is the essence of conversion. It is the outcome of spiritual dissatisfaction, of yearning and striving. You can read of such experience, unassociated with any sacramental belief, in the biographies of evangelical leaders. Religious Englishmen, like Lord Tennyson and John Addington

Symonds, who would probably have hesitated to subscribe to the creeds of the Church, described and valued such experience in their own lives . . . God reveals himself directly and through innumerable channels, to the human soul.

But even this did not devalue the importance which he attached to Holy Communion.

He may not have been very skilful at conveying his inmost thoughts, particularly at emphasizing their positive aspects, and his language and his analogies were not always of the happiest. It was not perhaps very wise, for example, to play into his opponents' hands by saying that 'to me scientific discovery is truly sacramental'. Even though he scrupulously abstained from personal attacks on other people themselves, his strictures on their ideas often aroused unnecessary antagonism. The references to magic, paganism, barbarism, puerility and Hindu idolatry, in particular, stuck in sore throats. Nor did his description of vestments as 'ecclesiastical millinery' endear him to his opponents. He was convinced that controversy could not be avoided and that the issue of magical or spiritual sacramentalism must be faced. He was probably wrong in holding that truth must always be proclaimed, even if it hurt. More selective proclamations would have produced fewer screams at the wounds. But it does not necessarily follow that, as his detractors often declared, he did not understand the doctrine of the Real Presence. This was the brush-off superficially administered by Lang's biographer; Headlam for his part accused Barnes of confusing material and spiritual experience and of ascribing to the Church 'a crude mechanical theory which is never held or taught'; Inge too regretted that Barnes mixed up 'the question of ecclesiastical discipline with doctrinal controversies about the Eucharist, which, to speak frankly, he does not understand very well' and later asserted that Barnes did not realise 'how easily a Catholic could answer him'. Lang and Headlam were, of course, High Churchmen; but Inge was President of the Modern Churchmen's Union and his failure to give support was distressing to Barnes, who wrote to a friend: 'I have been a little puzzled by one or two *obiter dicta* of his recently; but, without repudiating his whole past, he cannot accept the notion of a divine presence in the consecrated elements.' Many books have been written about the doctrine of the Real Presence, and many subtle variations of it are possible. Those who attacked Barnes for not understanding it sometimes merely meant that their own interpretation was different. Sometimes they had simply not read what he said. For example, he was often attacked for saying that consecration made no physical or chemical change in the elements, whereas he always insisted that he was discussing perceptible spiritual changes. Similarly, those who accused him of confusing the Real Presence with transubstantiation failed to see that he was attacking not the doctrine of the Real Presence as such but those practices which implied a belief in transubstantiation.

He was always at pains to make clear that, apart from reservation, which was illegal, his target was not ritual irregularity as such, but only any ritual practice which implied false doctrine. Thus he did not insist on the use of the 1662 Prayer Book and none other. Without authorizing departures from it, either in a Catholic or Modernist direction, since they were strictly illegal, he was prepared to tolerate them when they were harmless. He took no exception if as much consecrated bread and wine were left on the Holy Table, though not in a pyx or aumbry, as would be needed for the communion of the sick during the morning; this he regarded as 'extended communion'. Despite his support for lay activity in the church, however, he showed no sympathy for any idea that a layman might in emergency administer the reserved sacrament. He realised the dangers of infection from a single cup, and while he came to dislike 'intinction' as 'messy', he thought that the use of individual cups was preferable, even if not authorized in the Prayer Book, and he would have been ready to accept communion in one kind, despite its Romish associations.

In this context a broadsheet was issued, with his concurrence, by one of his friends and supporters a year or two later. With references omitted, it read:

What the Bishop actually said:
Read these words of Dr Barnes, the present Bishop of Birmingham, and compare them with what is reported of him: –

I. If there were a *physical* change in the bread, chemical analysis would enable us to detect it. All are agreed that this type of change does not take place. Yet if there be a *spiritual* change, it must surely be possible for a man to recognize it by his spiritual perception.

II. We can apply scientific tests to inanimate matter and demonstrate that the spiritual properties supposed to be inherent in it have no existence apart from the rites and ceremonies to which it has been subjected.

Note: These tests, of course, would be psychological, not physical or chemical. We must test 'holy matter' by the reaction of a human being and not by a galvanometer or chemical reagent.

III. They (i.e. the Reformers) unfortunately had neither the methods nor the language of modern experimental religious psychology. We today say smoothly that, if the alleged spiritual change has taken place, there must be someone by whom it can be spiritually perceived.

Barnes had agreed to the broadsheet, even though he was not himself prepared to answer specific criticisms in detail. He preferred to repeat and develop his own teaching and to avoid direct personal conflicts with individuals. He always maintained that he was not a controversialist and did not reply to criticisms. He often quoted the maxim 'Never complain, never explain'.

More important, perhaps, in historical terms, than the detailed substance, or essence, of the controversy are the reactions to it and its after-effects. It aroused intense interest at the time, in the national press as well as the Church newspapers. There was, it is true, a greater interest then than later in matters ecclesiastical and this had been recently awoken by the Prayer Book controversy. No doubt too the public imagination was titillated by the prospect of a Bishop going to prison, and Barnes was not above exploiting this, even though it was probably never really on the cards. In the sixteenth and seventeenth centuries, when bishops had been imprisoned, or deprived of their offices, the *causa proxima* was political, even if the *ultima ratio* was theological. *Praemunire* was never likely to be invoked against either Lang or Barnes.

Some comment was, of course, consistently hostile, and un-necessarily personal, notably from *The Times* and *Church Times*. Thus, *The Times* in truly avuncular style, summed up the story on 6 August 1931:

There will be an improvement, no doubt, when, without necessarily changing his views, Dr Barnes changes his method of expressing them . . . There may be many opinions among his clergy from which he will love to differ. There should be none from which he cannot differ in love.

In other words, auntie says that small boys should be seen and not heard. But, although the more ebullient Anglo-Catholics were inclined to accuse Barnes of lacking a sense of humour, they expressed shocked surprise at his flippancy when in May 1930 he attended a Wesleyan Methodist gathering and started his speech by saying:

> You all read the newspapers and must know that I really am a bold, bad bishop. As I understand, books – though I do not read them – are written to prove this fact and I believe there is even talk of putting me into prison . . . In fact, I continue to protest, as a true child of the Reformation, against magical, mechanical conceptions of God's action. And that is really why I am a bold man. I expect most of you agree about magic, but then there are monkeys. I am not sure that you are all quite sound there. Perhaps, therefore, I had better not develop that theme. Some people are sensitive about their poor relations. But that is a weakness and you should not condemn those who do not share it. Merely let me give you a word of advice founded on painful experience. It is probably unlikely that many among you, even the youngest, will become Anglican bishops, but if you should reach that distinction – or fate – then I suggest that you be silent with regard to magic or monkeys. Happiness and peace may then be your lot.

But deeper than these considerations lay a national sense of justice and fair play. Barnes's post-bag, which was enormous at each crisis of the affair, from clergy and laity alike, testified not only to the widespread distrust, which he himself shared, of foreign importations, in the shape of Romish practices, but also to the strong feeling that he had been left to champion his cause alone, even by those who in their hearts agreed with him, and that the Archbishop had let him down. The last sentiment was most concisely expressed in a postcard which read: 'Canterbury ought to be unfrocked, the contemptible apostate.' The evidence certainly suggests that Lang, who was in fairly close touch with the trustees throughout, was not unhappy to support their cause where he could do so without damage to his own public position. As Barnes put it in a letter to Wickham Steed in July 1931:

> The situation is grave. That the Archbishop should have publicly indicated his sympathy with doctrine which is at the basis of all our most serious disorder in public worship is almost certain to lead to grave trouble. I do not believe that in the long run sacramental superstition can maintain itself; but the Church of England may be destroyed in the doctrinal conflicts which, so far as one can see, are now inevitable.

In private letters to closer friends, Barnes was even more outspoken:

> Even those who are critical make no attempt to defend the absurd superstition of a spiritual presence in the consecrated elements. How an educated man like the Archbishop can openly advocate toleration of such an idea passes my comprehension.

or again:

> I think that he realises that it is not easy for an Archbishop of Canterbury to give a formal defence of the root principle of idolatry; but the odd thing is that he appears to believe in it.

Temperamentally, Lang and Barnes were poles apart, even though they were both men of the world and preserved the outward courtesies.

Moreover, in later years, Lang continued to show sympathy for the Birmingham Anglo-Catholics. Thus in March 1934 he saw Rosenthal at Rosenthal's request, stipulating that this meeting behind the Bishop's back must be kept strictly confidential, and acceded to a suggestion that he should consider appointing a Birmingham rebel curate to a benefice in his own gift. His first attempt to do so fell through, because the nominee resigned. But, as Lang then told Rosenthal, 'I had hoped this would be regarded as a token of my sympathy with some of the clergy in Birmingham whose difficulties I so fully appreciate'. When on Rosenthal's death in 1938 it was reported to Lang that Barnes had visited St Agatha's to have illegal ornaments removed, he made no effort to check the facts but replied:

> I expected that the Bishop would make reprisals after the death of the good Rosenthal and it is pitiful at the present time to think of his way of doing things and his threat to take legal proceedings . . . But I cannot control the Bishop and I do not think there is anything I can fitly say in public without being so general as to be pointless or so pointed as to invite a retort from the Bishop.

To another correspondent he wrote that 'past experience shows that writing to him never leads to anything but a long vindication of his own conduct'. So Barnes could hope for little support from his metropolitan.

Not all the other bishops are equally to blame. Whittingham, for example, rallied to Barnes's defence in the columns of *The Times* of

28 July 1931, when Strong of Oxford had attacked him over the Real Presence. Both Whittingham and Burroughs of Ripon at this time also took courage, as their private letters showed, from Barnes's example to resist disloyal nominees, but they were luckier than Barnes in that both nominees withdrew at the first whiff of grapeshot; perhaps they did not have the same promises of support from the English Church Union, whose prime target was the Bishop of Birmingham. But other bishops only confined themselves to private encouragement. Some, like Henson, who entered the lists publicly, were concerned to ride their own hobby-horses, in his case to use the affair as an argument for disestablishment on the grounds that, if Barnes refused to use or accept the law, there was no justification for the establishment. It was certainly ironical, to say the least, that the Bishop who was insisting on obedience to the law in his diocese refused to obey the courts himself, while those who resisted the supremacy of the State over the Church were ready to have recourse to the organs of the State to enforce their wishes. But most of the bishops looked at the affair with the eyes of administrators. True, they had lived through the Prayer Book battle and wanted time to heal its wounds. George Bell, even though he wrote of Barnes as 'an eccentric bishop', was a true man of peace and could argue for peace and quiet rather than controversy. This, towards the end of the affair, was also the plea of the ecclesiastical press, even the *Church of England Newspaper*, which had otherwise given Barnes loyal support. Bell's own early experiences in his diocese of Chichester, as recorded by his biographer, must have shown him the dangers and difficulties of giving an inch, for the sake of peace, when an ell was promptly demanded, if not taken.

Barnes, however, was not concerned with these arguments of expediency, but with the pursuit of the truth as he saw it. As he caused his secretary to put it to one correspondent:

> You think it better to believe that God can and will act magically than not to believe in a God at all. The question as to whether a false God is better than no God does not interest the Bishop: he desires religious truth.

Other churchmen, like Gallio, cared for none of these things. They might have used to Barnes the words which George Eliot causes Savonarola to put in the mouth of his critics; 'Come now, Frate, leave your prophesyings; it is enough to teach virtue.' Administration of their dioceses would be easier if sleeping dogs were let lie and not encouraged to howl in churches, let alone in courts. But, as when Lang claimed in a public letter that he had no control over services in the dioceses of Durham or Birmingham, this was an abdication of responsibility. He was not the only ecclesiastical politician who realised where lay not only his own sympathies but also those of the Anglo-Catholic majority in the Church. Appeasement was soon to become a national, as well as an ecclesiastical, policy.

But even the contemporary political ambience cannot be ignored. There is some quite independent evidence of correlation between periods of economic insecurity and declining interest in ecclesiastical affairs. Be that as it may, the St Aidan's affair began, for the public, a month after the collapse of the New York Stock Exchange on 28 October 1929; it ended in the same month as the economic crisis which led in Britain to the formation of the National Government and the retreat from the gold standard. Despite the interest which St Aidan's aroused, the media, as they were not yet called, had other things to think about as well.

Against this background, not all Barnes's calculations were right. He was wrong in thinking that Parliament would intervene with legislation to support his stance. While Parliament had rejected the Church's initiative over the Prayer Book, it recognized that the initiative did lie with the Church. He was also wrong in asserting that the success of the action against him would destroy the Church and lead to its disestablishment and disendowment. Although he said that he 'would rather see the Church of England disendowed than catholicized', he did not in the event have to face either contingency. Nor indeed would he have welcomed disestablishment. He had always seen the Church of England as a national institution, with the Anglican tradition reflecting the English temper. The establishment worked both ways for good: the State by its patronage maintained the quality of the Church, for in his view Crown appointments were almost always more distinguished than local nominees, while the Church, as the conscience of the country, preserved Christian standards in national policies. In any case, Henson's campaign for disestablishment, sparked off by the rejection of the Prayer Book and the return of Labour to power, struck most of his colleagues as more romantic than practical. No one seriously expected an early descent of godless Communism on the British scene.

Moreover, even without the financial motives, neither Lang nor Temple, for very different reasons, was the man to want to challenge the State or to break the links with it. It was far easier for them to set up, as a lightning-conductor, an Archbishops' Commission on Church and State, to which incidentally Barnes refused to give oral evidence, on the grounds that no change was needed in relations between the two institutions and it had been a mistake even to appoint the Commission, although he did supply written material on the state of discipline and the traffic in advowsons in his diocese.

Nor were his worst fears of catholicization of the Church fulfilled. Indeed, he could with truth write in 1930 that 'already the triumphant Anglo-Catholicism of 1925 is a thing of the past'. True, the 'rebels' remained rebellious. But the majority of his clergy showed in August 1931 that they took a different view, by offering another spontaneous and public expression of support, in which they emphasized Barnes's tolerance of views different from his own, always provided that the law was obeyed on reservation. This remained the barrier. When a well-meaning Evangelical incumbent tried at the 1932 Diocesan Conference to effect a new *rapprochement*, Barnes replied that no one welcomed this initiative more than he did, but the law must be obeyed.

That this underlying difference remained is clear from the one tailpiece to the St Aidan's affair. In 1937 the vicar of St Jude's, Birmingham, of his own volition told the Bishop that he intended in future to cease to be a 'rebel' and accept the Bishop's wishes. Barnes welcomed this, on the understanding that reservation could only continue within the limits of the rejected Prayer Book while the present incumbent remained and must cease altogether on a change of incumbency. This was agreed. In 1941 the vicar of St Jude's was appointed to a living in the Carlisle diocese. Barnes suggested to the Crown as patron that the prospects of post-war reconstruction should not be prejudiced by the immediate appointment of a new vicar, who would thus have a vested interest, and that there should only be a curate-in-charge for the rest of the war. Various names were discussed in correspondence between the Bishop and 10 Downing Street. Eventually in December a candidate was put forward. But after seeing Barnes he refused to give the usual required assurances. This led to voluminous correspondence, in the course of which Barnes pointed out that there were now only four 'rebel' churches and that since St Aidan's he had never failed to obtain the assurances he wanted, partly perhaps because Lang had not wanted again to be put in a position of impeding his suffragan in his endeavour to secure obedience to the law. Barnes also asserted that the legal issue about the assurances which could be sought had never been finally decided: Cecil at Exeter and Whittingham at St Edmundsbury had both tried to arrange test cases to decide the Bishop's right but without success. Meanwhile, the affair dragged on, the nominee withdrew, the Crown tried to appoint another man, who also refused to give the assurances, and eventually in April 1943, Barnes appealed direct to the Prime Minister. He told the Archbishop of Canterbury the whole story, and Temple in reply made an interesting comment:

1. I have always sympathized with your wish that Bishops should be able to make this kind of enquiry as a condition of institution.
2. I have also recognized that we are, in fact, not empowered by the law to do so, and I think it most dangerous to start making unauthorized enquiries as a condition of institution, because the practice may be followed in such extremely different ways.

Temple added that he was probably biased by his father's refusal in 1869 to give extra assurances as a condition of his appointment as Bishop of Exeter and hinted that the practice could rebound on liberal churchmen.

Not surprisingly, Winston Churchill refused to be drawn in personally and asked Stafford Cripps to sort the turbulent priests out for him. Cripps saw Barnes, as well as Ernest Canning, the prominent Birmingham industrialist, who played a most helpful part in this as in other diocesan matters. As a result it was fairly soon agreed that the Diocesan Advisory Committee, with the Bishop at its head and assisted by a Crown representative, should choose a temporary diocesan chaplain to take charge of the parish during the war. He was to be acceptable to the congregation and to give the Bishop the necessary assurances. On this basis a new appointment was made in December 1943. The last round had been a long slogging-match. But the Bishop won it.

On the main issue, Barnes's consistent optimism was more justified in the result than his occasional pessimism. Indeed, his warnings of the dangers of catholicization may at times have sprung more from tactics than conviction. He was known to say that 'enthusiasts are short-term optimists'. While he may sometimes have been pessimistic about immediate prospects, and by 1938 was expressing his weariness of sacramental controversy, a long-term optimism lay at the heart of almost all his thoughts and utterances. Even at the height of the St Aidan's affair, he could write that 'opinion is slowly but quite definitely swinging round from Roman error to Anglican sanity' and 'gradually we shall reach a new regard to the great Anglican tradition'.

To this tradition, although the Anglo-Catholics had in his view done it great harm, he recognized that High Churchmen had made a substantial contribution, not least in their advocacy of social reform, but also in the beauty and dignity of ceremonial. He retained his confidence in the capacity of Englishmen to find a *via media* or golden mean. Or, as he put it himself, 'the English Church is as illogical and, at its best, as sensible, as the average Englishman'. Since the time of the disputes in which he was a protagonist, that confidence has largely been justified. The Church has absorbed ideas from different sources, and its doctrine and ritual have settled down on a median line, even if that line is perhaps rather higher than Barnes himself would have drawn it. The 'new knowledge' has become widely accepted and High Churchmanship has lost its emotional aggressiveness. Indeed, in so far as the Anglo-Catholic movement was itself a counter-attack against 'black fundamentalism' or Laodicean Latitudinarianism, so the extreme vanguard of the counter-attack found itself without new objectives and, with the disappearance of some of its more extravagant champions, its momentum was spent. In the end, an armistice was tacitly accepted on broadly-agreed positions, and for many years the name of Anglo-Catholic almost ceased to be heard in the land.

Moreover, soon after the St Aidan's affair, the thirties were to be engulfed by the rising tides of unemployment at home and fascism abroad. Thereafter, new problems increasingly engaged the attention of Christians, as of Barnes himself: war and reconstruction, race and colour, atheism and oecumenism, violence and permissiveness. It was not until the 1960s that doctrinal doubts would again force themselves to the surface and then they would not be about magic and monkeys, so much as metaphysics and mythology.

Henson, who had of recent years been one of Barnes's sharpest critics, was to write in 1943:

it would not be fair either to my friend Bishop Barnes or myself to let the extracts from my journal stand . . . without adding that . . . I think that his episcopal administration in Birmingham has gone far to disallow the apprehensions and misunderstandings which shadowed its beginnings and has, when fairly judged, made apparent the exceptionally difficult conditions under which he has had to fulfil his duty. Nor can I doubt that he has rendered important service to the cause of theological liberty in the Church of England and thereby to the supreme interest of true religion in the nation.

As for the Birmingham diocese, by 1947 there were only two 'rebel' incumbents left. One resigned due to ill-health in 1948, and then there was one. He resigned in March 1953, and the so-called 'rebellion' finally ended in the closing weeks of Barnes's episcopate.

CHAPTER VII

BIRMINGHAM BETWEEN THE WARS

The Thirties, Part II, 1930–1934
Authority and Authorship

Unlike some of his brother bishops, Barnes never had to trouble himself with the risk that he might be called upon to be an archbishop. It is hard to think of Lang as anything but an archbishop. William Temple was born to the purple. Garbett moved smoothly up the hierarchical ladder. Henson in 1929 confided to his diary his ambitions for York. Bell was warned from his earliest days as a bishop not to disqualify himself for the primacy, which many expected to come to him in 1944, if not before. Barnes was never remotely *papabile*, if in his case the adjective is not a contradiction in terms. Even if he had ever wanted promotion, it must have been clear to him and everyone else from the start that it would never be offered. Only Charles Raven, with typical enthusiasm, told an audience of Modern Churchmen in 1929 that 'if there had been a free election for the Archbishop of Canterbury the Bishop of Birmingham would have got in first with nobody else in the field'. But even Raven must have realised that this was not practical politics, if indeed he believed what he was saying. Barnes himself knew that his future lay in Birmingham. When he was asked in 1932 by a wishful member of the Chester diocese if he would exchange Birmingham for Chester, he answered 'at the present time my work lies here and it is of very great importance'. His decision would have been the same, even if he had known that the vacant see would be filled by Geoffrey Fisher and prove a stepping-stone for him to Canterbury.

When Arthur Balfour died in 1930, a newspaper floated Barnes's name as a possible Chancellor of Cambridge University; but the Conservative interest put forward Stanley Baldwin, then leader of the party, and no one else stood an earthly chance. The only consolation prize was that, when in the same year *Punch* chose a World Rugger XV, the front row of the scrum consisted of Philip Snowden, Herbert Hoover and E. W. Barnes. The half-backs were G. B. Shaw and D. Ll. George, and the three-quarters C. Lindbergh, A. Menjou, M. Chevalier and W. Churchill. According to *Punch*, Barnes would be useful in the loose. On the other hand, J. A. Kensit, the redoubtable leader of the Protestant Truth Society, asked a meeting why the Bishop of Birmingham was like the Boat Race and gave the answer: 'Because the Oxford movement went well until it came to Barnes'.

But if preferment was out of the question, he had become the recognized leader of a party in the Church. This depended on no formal position. For a long time he did not even belong to the Modern Churchmen's Union, of which Inge was president for many years. Barnes regarded Modernism as the leaven of the whole loaf, not a slice of the cake. It was 'not a creed but an attitude of mind'. As he said, 'Modernist Christianity is not to be classified among the religions of authority; it is a religion of the spirit'. But authority, or what the Romans would have called *auctoritas*, dwelt in him none the less. He was even asked if he would care to form and lead a Modernist Order of the Holy Spirit, on the model of the Jesuits, but replied that 'Modernists need to emphasize to the full the present activity of the Holy Spirit among us . . . but I fear that I am not the person to try and found a religious order, and I have some doubt as to whether such an order would not within half-a-century of its founding become reactionary'. But, unstructured though his leadership was, all sorts and conditions of followers turned to him for help, advice and information. He suffered this epistolary bombardment gladly and, while he always tried to keep the rallies short, he usually managed to include one scoring shot in his return of service.

For he set himself high standards. He never signed an article which he had not written himself. As is clear from internal evidence alone, all letters purporting to come from his secretary were in fact dictated by him in the third person singular; this of itself tended to underline his reputation for being impersonal, even though the impression was usually dissipated at close quarters. To his friends, indeed, he tried hard to be as informal as he could. Thus, when the

Bishop of Truro wrote to him as 'Dear Bishop', he answered, 'Dear Hunkin. Please let us drop formalities, forgetting that we are bishops and remembering that we were once Cambridge dons. I increasingly loathe the episcopal halo.' His sermons and addresses were always meticulously adapted to local circumstances, incorporating carefully researched references to the history, geography, economics or even geology of the parish or suburb where he happened to be speaking. For he would have been miserable if he could not read, mark, learn and inwardly digest. In a rare moment of self-revelation, at the re-opening of the Cathedral after its restoration in 1929 he said:

In Westminster Abbey five years ago today I was consecrated Bishop of Birmingham. I hesitated long before accepting the office. A friend who could speak with intimate knowledge wrote that 'in the circumstances of this evil time, the position of an English Bishop is the least enviable of all the positions open to men'. I was never a pessimist and I find the present time exhilarating rather than evil. But my own instincts and inclinations were, and still are, for the study rather than the pulpit, for quiet meditation and not for administration. It is horrible to turn from the urbane wisdom of thinkers and dreamers and to find oneself entangled in public controversy. I felt when I came to Birmingham that I should be driven from that realm of intellectual adventure which is open to any man who has leisure to think and access to books. Fortunately, my fears have not been wholly realised: I can make some spare time for study and thought.

In the same spirit, he could write to his old Cambridge coach in 1932: 'I find increasingly that as a relief from ecclesiastical routine it is a pleasure to turn to mathematics.' The Gifford Lectures were thus both an added burden and a precious safety-valve. He could tell his audience at Newton's bicentenary that 'the mathematician, like the poet, is born, not made'. But his own taste in poetry stayed with the favourites of his youth; he had little time to study the *avant-garde* and confessed at this time to finding his relaxation in Edgar Wallace and P. G. Wodehouse. They never stopped him sleeping, unlike Dean Inge who, staying at Bishop's Croft, was given a who-dun-it to take to bed; asked next morning at breakfast if he had slept well, 'No, but I finished it'. This was typical of Inge, who liked to say 'I rhyme with sting, but not with cringe', and who could write in a private letter 'how stupid of the old Christians to depict hell as having a warm climate and no music; it makes me long to be there'.

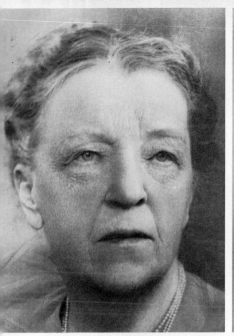

Above
Happy warrior
Above left
'That best and
most severe of
critics – my wife'

Three generations,
1949

Overleaf
Student to the end

Barnes's taste in art paralleled his taste in verse. He remained a Victorian. He believed in the moral purity of artists such as Burne-Jones or William Morris. This is not surprising: more than one critic has noted the evangelical element in pre-Raphaelite art. Asked to advocate a revival of religious art, he replied: 'I personally am satisfied by such representations as those of Holman Hunt; and if Epstein represents the moderns, I do not desire more of them.' At another time he declared that 'some modern portraits to me suggest the licentious mental deficient'. His judgements were more ethical than aesthetic, even though he always spoke scathingly of a candidate for a Trinity fellowship who failed to distinguish Manet from Monet. Nor, unlike his wife, who had once been a talented amateur actress, did he take much interest in the theatre. This was not from moral principle. He was proud of having seen Pavlova dance in younger days, as indeed he was of having seen Spofforth, the demon bowler, in action, and would go to school plays at King Edward's or occasional special performances, such as Sybil Thorndike's St Joan, at the Birmingham Repertory Theatre, out of public spirit; and his wife persuaded him to see Noël Coward's *Cavalcade*. But otherwise he preferred real life to make-believe. His only other literary pastime seems to have been composing limericks in the duller moments of public meetings. When a missionary speaker pronounced Antigua as three syllables, Barnes rapidly rose as chairman to announce:

> There was a nice girl of Antigua,
> Who said 'My repasts are too meagre';
> So she ate this and that,
> Things rich, sweet and fat,
> And entirely destroyed her slim figure.

For he was quite ready to deflate himself. Giving the Lloyd-Roberts Memorial Lecture at Manchester in 1930 he began:

At the outset I would apologize for the ponderous title of this lecture. In self-excuse I can urge that I suggested as an alternative possibility 'God and the Gene'. But, when Bishops speak in monosyllables, their ideas may excite alarm. Words of four or five syllables are impressive and comfortable. So I am discussing 'Heredity and Predestination'.

It was a pity that others could not take him as lightly as he often took himself. For he continued to arouse venomous personal attacks. In the *Sunday Express* in October 1932, for example, he was described as 'an intolerant agnostic or sceptic, who expects religion to lick the boots of science' and 'a sour don with a narrow academic training and no parochial experience' and accused of taking 'his salary without shame, although he is defiantly disloyal to the Church which pays it'. Admittedly, scurrilous attacks of this kind probably rebounded on the marksman rather than the target; and, incidentally, as Barnes told a friend privately, his official income had suffered heavily at that time from being invested in railway stocks. On another occasion, when a correspondent complained that the nation paid him to preach the religion of Enoch and Moses, he replied that 'the nation expects me to preach Christianity, not Judaism; my salary is paid not by the nation but from a fund raised by the late Bishop Gore, who, like most educated men, accepted evolution'. A more sympathetic, if still critical, portrait of him at this stage is given in Henson's diary:

> He is a striking figure, the very model of a 'heresiarch'. He might have been Huss in front of the fathers of Constance, or Luther at the Diet of Worms. Tall, pallid with much study, with stooping shoulders, and a voice at once challenging and melancholy, he commands attention as well by his manner and aspect as by his opinions, which are almost certainly oppugnant to the general mind. He is a good man, but clearly a fanatic and, in a more disciplined age, could not possibly have avoided the stake.

Perhaps the tribute which he would most have relished in difficult days came from a headmaster, who asked him: 'Is it any consolation to have lived before one's time?' For, while he would not have resented comparisons with the giants of the past, such as Huss and Luther, still less with Wesley or Erasmus, he much preferred to peer into the future. There was a constant conflict between his respect for the heritage of the past and his search for new forms in the future, between his religious Erastianism and his political internationalism. At all stages of his life, he tended to dramatize the current religious situation as a state of tension out of which something better might be born: it was always a period of turmoil or unrest, decay or degeneration, or, very rarely, and then usually in the future, of revival. Whether the actual state of affairs justified his descriptions or not, this divine discontent undoubtedly helped his restless spirit in the search for new solutions.

Preoccupied as he was in practice with eucharistic doctrine and sacramental controversy, this was not ground of his own choosing. These were but the communication trenches. Through them he was trying to find his way towards victory on a much wider front. This wider front 'involved the enquiry whether the Church could give its priests miraculous spiritual powers which others could not acquire or possess'. This he could not accept, for 'those principles of reason to which science is pledged will continue to be outraged so long as it is pretended that by the blessing of a priest oil receives holy properties, or that through baptism an infant mechanically escapes God's condemnation, or that the bones of saints have spiritual value, or that disease is healed by visits to sacred shrines'. 'I cannot, by blessing oil, cause God to give to it therapeutic or spiritual properties. I cannot turn water into Holy Water for the sanctification of the faithful.' For such reasons he refused to support what was called 'spiritual healing'. Could incurable diseases be cured by spiritual means? 'I am myself satisfied that we in the English Church shall continue on traditional lines to use prayer in cases of sickness. A return to "Holy Unction" I view with grave misgivings.' Still less could a blessing confer spiritual value on motor cars. 'You are just as likely to have an accident in a motor car which has been blessed as in one that has not been the object of any such ceremony.' 'Do you think that because it is blessed it conveys people more safely or makes them more courteous in driving?' 'It is sound Anglican doctrine that divine grace is conveyed to persons and not to things.'

But again these were only examples of underlying religious truth. This went back to the Reformation, for 'by asserting the priesthood of all believers, the Reformers cut at the root of the pretension that the priest had any special supernatural powers'. Again and again he reiterated the legacy of the Reformation. No doubt he romanticized the Reformers, who were not always activated by the highest motives, for example in their spoliation of the monasteries. But Barnes was concerned with their doctrinal views. 'The Reformers were instinctively asserting the fact of God's direct communication of Himself to the human soul.' They had set the Church on the right path. 'Erasmus at the Reformation, the Cambridge Platonists of the seventeenth century, the much-abused Latitudinarians of the age of the Enlightenment and the Victorian Broad Churchmen were the spiritual forefathers of the Modernists of today.' Not that he underrated some of the precursors of the Reformation: for him the three men who had shown the purest theological insight since the New Testament were Roger Bacon, Wycliff and Abelard. Bacon had said 'authority may compel belief, but cannot enlighten understanding' and 'the end of all true philosophy is to arrive at a knowledge of the creator through knowledge of the created world'; Wycliff had questioned the theory of transubstantiation; and Abelard had given the best explanation of the Atonement. In the same spirit Barnes would have welcomed at this time a celebration of the quater-centenary of the Reformation, if its advocates could have agreed on the right date to celebrate; but he strongly deprecated any cele-bration of the centenary of the Oxford Movement, of which he said that it was 'reactionary on its inception and its influence has led to a lamentable increase of sacramental superstition in our Church'.

Men like Froude, Pusey and Newman harmed English religion . . . The more Newman is ignored the better. He had no message by which we should desire to remember him.

But for him the problem went back further and deeper than the human controversies of the past three or four centuries. What mattered was the authority of Christ Himself.

He had a spiritual flair which we can link to our latest knowledge and find in the combination a harmony that satisfies. Apply such a test to others, St Paul, Augustine, Luther, and all fail in varying degrees.

Doubts about St Paul were recurrent in Barnes's teaching, despite great admiration; thus he contrasted Jesus the lover of the country with Paul the apostle of the town and regarded Jesus as a natural artist in words as against the tortured language of Paul. But on the great religious issues, it followed that 'the spiritual authority of Jesus must be spiritually discerned; it cannot be substantiated by proof that He had exceptional powers to control nature or to heal disease'. So, while he did not at this time directly question the miracles of the Incarnation, Barnes was increasingly concerned to suggest that argument about them was beside the main point. For there could be no dualism between the natural and the supernatural. 'God works through nature which is the expression of His purpose.' 'The theory of a supernatural realm existing in opposition to a realm of nature is indefensible. It dishonours God. The whole realm of nature is His.' 'The spiritual and the natural belong alike to God's realm; they form a unity; the laws of the spirit do not contradict the laws of nature.' He set out his views at length in a Cambridge University sermon in October, 1934:

> Breaches of the so-called laws of nature do not occur . . . Those of us who believe in God do so because we think we find a unity of purpose and place in the Universe . . . Our minds are akin to the Mind of the Creator . . . I myself have no doubt that God reveals Himself to those who wait upon Him . . . Thus I accept what one may call 'psychological miracles'. Mind-states exist that reveal the active presence of God. But adequate evidence for the existence of material miracles . . . is not forthcoming. We may grant that God can work such miracles; the evidence that He does so is lacking.

From this philosophic background and from this interpretation of the Divine nature, he also interpreted human nature. For he argued that human and divine were not mutually exclusive terms; our minds were reproductions of the Divine mind; and every human soul revealed God to some extent, the more perfectly to the extent that that soul was free from evil. For Barnes, this was the point at which scientific knowledge and moral philosophy interlocked. 'The Modernist today is trying to reconcile two great forces: scientific humanism and moral religion.'

To Barnes the right type of moral religion was what he repeatedly described as 'ethical theism'. 'My own philosophy is essentially that of James Ward and Hastings Rashdall. Both accepted ethical theism no less than the modern scientific outlook.' Unlike the dogmas of Rome or the tenets of fundamentalism, ethical theism did not purport to deal in certainties.

> Our attempt to reach absolutes continues to fail and in consequence we live in a world of relativities. I believe however that such knowledge as we have attained in the moral sphere points toward reality; and thus I would base the search for ultimate reality on ethics rather than on physics or biology.

This was not asking 'religion to lick the boots of science'. Nor was it the doctrinaire arrogance of which he was sometimes accused. Indeed, he retained the humility of intellectual doubt. Speaking of the human personality, he said 'Mind and body are not separate entities; they are two aspects of a single unity whose nature we do not at present understand'. This led him on, as so often, to the two great recurring problems of ethical theism: freewill and immortality. In both his faith was unshaken. The existence of evil, hard as it was to understand, proved the existence of freewill. This was a matter of personal experience. 'One of my Cambridge friends years ago put the matter briefly and bluntly when he said: I may be a fool but I am not an automaton.' Immortality too was an ethical question. The struggle for righteousness against the reality of sin could not be resolved in this world alone. Man must achieve immortality by overcoming evil. Not all men could do so. 'We cannot affirm that man is a part of God lest thereby we allow that a Borgia or a Rasputin is divine.' But again the problem should not be seen in dualistic terms; where St Paul spoke of the resurrection of the flesh, we should think in terms of the survival of the whole personality. As he said in a private letter: 'What matters is not the resurrection of the body but life everlasting; as we ignore the one and cling to the other, we, I am sure, get to the essence of Christ's teaching.' Incidentally, when asked if he could believe in the survival after death of the higher animals, he refused a definite answer, declaring himself an agnostic on the subject. Nor for that matter was he prepared to answer the question whether Peking man had an immortal soul. But of course he recognized that with these formulations he was coming into conflict with the literal interpretation of the creeds, which he saw as a greater obstacle to acceptance of the Church's teaching than the Thirty-Nine Articles.

In 1933, he wrote a commendatory foreword to *The Gospel of Modernism* by R. D. Richardson, one of the leading Modernist clergy of the diocese, who in the book cast doubt on the literal truth of the Virgin Birth and the empty tomb. This led to a challenge to the Bishop at his Diocesan Conference in the summer of 1934 on his own acceptance of the creeds. In his reply, Barnes made no bones about his views; he asserted the need to believe in the doctrines of the creeds, in the Incarnation and in 'the ever-living Christ who guides his Church', rather than in the formulation of individual clauses, which were reflections of knowledge at the time when they were written. He emphasized, too, that there was no mention of the Virgin Birth in the writings either of St Paul or St John. Shortly thereafter, at Richardson's institution as Vicar of Harborne, Barnes returned to the theme, holding that the Declaration of Assent did not imply literal belief in all the clauses of all three creeds. 'The great

Victorian half-forgotten heads of the Church knew that the creeds could not be regarded as infallible.' Few people now accepted the damnatory clauses of the Athanasian Creed; even Archbishop Tait had said that nobody took them in their plain and literal meaning. The Nicene Creed showed the differences between Eastern and Western Christianity. 'To an Orthodox Patriarch the Pope is an unbaptised heretic.' So, too, was an Anglican bishop.

> Behind both the Apostles' and Nicene Creeds lies the three-storey, pre-Copernican picture of heaven, earth and hell, which no one now believes. The resurrection of the body means the resurrection of this present flesh of ours, a belief which modern chemistry has destroyed . . . The creeds are of value not because they are verbally infallible, but because they were intended to present certain fundamental beliefs as to God, Christ, the Holy Spirit and the Church. These we still accept: they are the cement which gives us unity.

Beyond this he was not going to venture on to doctrinal quicksands. As he wrote at another time:

> I am afraid that my Trinitarian theology is functional rather than metaphysical. Of the works of Christ and of the operation of the Holy Spirit we can have knowledge or expression on which to base argument. But metaphysical distinctions between the three Persons of the Trinity seem to me so precarious that I prefer not to work with such categories.

But his Christology remained central and certain as ever: 'to say that Jesus was God *tout court* is to fall into heresy. He was both God and man. You make His manhood illusory if you claim that He was omnipotent and omniscient'. Just as he maintained that the Divine and human natures were linked in all men, so he saw Christ as the perfect human revelation of the Divine nature. His true humanity affirmed His true Divinity. Accordingly, Barnes sharply distinguished himself from both Unitarian and Manichee. Indeed he came into trouble with his Unitarian friends in 1934 for asserting that their theology was based on eighteenth-century deism, which had been replaced by 'a theism which stresses the immanence of God' and on which was based the doctrine of the Incarnation. They claimed in reply to assert both the immanence and the transcendence of God, but without explaining how they related these doctrines to the nature of Christ, with which Barnes was immediately concerned.

These random samples from his addresses and his correspondence in these years show the range of questions over which people sought pronouncements from him. The experience of his early years at Birmingham had increased his suspicions not only of Catholicism, but of fundamentalism too. So he wrote to a like-minded clergyman: 'Anglo-Catholics and Evangelicals are uniting under the fear of Humanism and regard the Modernist as a traitor within the gates.' He now speaks openly of non-Christian elements in Catholicism. He insists that, in mixed Roman/Anglican marriages, the Catholic partner should change allegiance for the sake of the children. He declares that he himself could never contemplate marrying a Roman Catholic or having children of that faith. Much as he also mistrusted fundamentalism, he kept an open mind, bringing an expert to Birmingham to lecture the clergy on Karl Barth's 'thought (if it can be so termed)'. For, in another context, he privately described Barthian theology as 'the outcome of an anti-intellectual reaction'; and of another German ecclesiastic of the same school, he wrote in a personal letter that 'Providence which allowed Brunner to pose as a theologian also fortunately enabled man to invent the wastepaper-basket'. He also at this time took a surprisingly favourable view of the Oxford Group Movement, which he seems to have seen in its early days as a manifestation of ethical theism, sought by direct experience of God; perhaps he even hoped at first that it might be something like a new Wesleyan movement. 'I believe that the Groups seek to serve and find the Lord.' His judgement may have been swayed by people whom he respected and who had joined the Movement. But he declined invitations to Buchmanite house-parties. On reunion with the Free Churches, he held firm, insisting that the Communion in Anglican Churches should be open to all Christians, conducting an interdenominational Christian Crusade in Birmingham which led to the formation of the Christian Social Council, and inaugurating the practice of a regular interchange of pulpits on Armistice Day. He did not just loose off theological aphorisms as exercises in theorizing; they bore fruit in his administrative practice.

Religion and science remained opposite sides of the same intellectual coin for him. They could not be kept in separate compartments. Exaggerating Barnes's views, Bernard Shaw wrote in 1932: 'the Bishop of Birmingham has just warned his flock that the scientific party is drawing nearer to Christ than the church congregations. I, who am a sort of unofficial Bishop of Everywhere, have repeatedly warned the scientists that the Quakers are fundamentally more scientific than the official biologists' and, with similar over-statement, he referred to 'the Bishop of Birmingham's observation that scientific atheism moves towards Christ whilst official Christianity pulls savagely in the opposite direction'. Barnes might have agreed with the second leg of the last paradox; but his object was not to distinguish between religion and science, but to unite them. Certainly, he was as well qualified to do so as any contemporary in the Church of England. At the centenary meeting of the British Association for the Advancement of Science in 1931, he not only preached the sermon but took part in a seminar on the evolution of the universe, at which other participants included Jeans, Eddington, Lodge, Lemaître, de Sitter, Millikan and Smuts. His treatment of these questions, there and in other addresses, attracted headlines chiefly because of his belief that elsewhere in the universe there must exist other highly developed forms of life. This might not be on the nearer planets. 'If life existed on Mars, it was probably parched and struggling; on Venus we might expect it to be luxuriant and lethargic. In neither case should we expect that it would have reached the level of humanity.' But

> it is quite possible that animal types which would appear to us strange and unpleasing carry the highest types of intelligence in distant worlds . . . If intelligent life exists and is progressive elsewhere in the Universe, then there is no reason why contact with it should not ultimately be made . . . Where light can travel, wireless can travel also. Doubtless we are at present incapable of creating or receiving wireless waves that can cross the depths of space. But need such inability endure for ever?

This sounded like science fiction and as such was grist to the newspapers' mill, although the Bishop had in fact been told by so reputable a scientist as Marconi that he too had looked for such messages. But Barnes saw it as a manifestation of the uniformity of God's action in the universe. The origin of life was a mystery; but if, under God's plan, life could emerge from the lifeless on earth, then 'when on any other planet conditions become ready for the existence of life, life will appear'. This was not sheer metaphysical speculation, but a reasoned deduction from his studies of the laws governing the phenomena of the natural world. He presented it against the background of a discussion of mathematical cosmology with the leading arithmeticians and physicists of his day. No other Anglican Bishop of that time, or perhaps since that time, could have held his own in such international scientific company. Ironically, from Barnes's point of view, there have in recent times been more scientists of world repute among Catholic priests: Mendel with his peas at Brno, Lemaître who invented the big bang theory of the universe, Breuil opening the cupboards of pre-history, Teilhard de Chardin and his idiosyncratic biology, or De Vaux the archaeologist of Palestine. To some extent this may be due to the influence of the learned religious orders within the Roman Church. More probably, these Catholics have been able to keep religion and science in separate compartments, authoritarian and speculative respectively; this Barnes could never do.

But while he kept abreast of current researches into the origin and nature of the universe, his scientific interests were turning more and more to problems of eugenics. This was of course a natural offshoot from his interest in evolution. 'Man's descent from an ape-like stock' is an almost inevitable King Charles's head in his pronouncements of those days. So much so indeed that he was sent a cutting from an Egyptian newspaper showing a naked youth proudly exhibiting a tail at the end of his spine. He was also delighted when a correspondent accused him of having, to prove his point, taken a monkey with him into the pulpit, just as he was interested to be told that he had experimented on producing a frog by radiation in order to prove the immaculate conception of Christ. But, more prosaically, his interest was also nourished by his observation of the Birmingham slums. He saw not only the poverty and the overcrowding but also the way in which those who had the ability and the desire to better themselves moved away to small houses in the suburbs, so that it was the poorest and the weakest members of the population who remained to breed large families at the city centre. Only too often these families showed evidence of the inheritability both of mental defect and of moral delinquency. The only answer which he could see to this problem, the only way to limit the population's size and improve its quality, lay in birth-control. He came under constant private pressure from all sorts and conditions of men and women, including Bertrand Russell and Marie Stopes, to speak out in favour of contraception. To them all he made clear that, as a member of an organization, he must be careful not to give unnecessary offence to his fellow-members; it was better for him to draw attention to the problem than to support particular methods for its solution. But he did publicly deplore the refusal of the Birmingham city fathers to allow contraceptive advice to be given in health clinics, just as, for rather wider reasons, he attacked the refusal of the Birmingham hospitals to admit women doctors who could also have given family guidance. At this stage he was mainly concerned with weeding out bad stocks from the population. On this, indeed, he took a strong and positive line.

> Surely, such things as feeble-mindedness and congenital diseases of speech and sight are evils. Surely, it is a religious duty to prevent such evils from being handed on to future generations. If, in the troubled years that lie ahead, England is to save herself by her exertions, and the world by her example, she must be racially sound. We cannot indefinitely carry the burden of a social-problem class, riddled with mental defect and comprising one-tenth of the community.

This, incidentally, drew another comment from Bernard Shaw, to the effect that if Barnes had his way, Shaw himself would never have existed. But, although Barnes could share the vision of William Pitt, unlike Aldous Huxley in *Brave New World* a year or two later, he had not reached the stage of positive genetic engineering. Nor did he then accept abortion, taking the traditional view that the foetus was a living entity from the moment of conception. Similarly, at this time he refused to express any public opinion on euthanasia, holding that population-control was the overriding problem on which to concentrate. He was not going to be found attacking life from both ends at once.

On the contrary, officiating at what he thought was a private and unreported wedding, of an architect to an accountant, both of whom he saw as belonging to valuable elements in the community, he told them that a deliberately childless marriage was a hopeless marriage and recalled advice which he had given before, that unless there was an average of nearly four children to a marriage, the fall in the birth-rate would continue and the population diminish. This may have surprised the young couple, but it also intrigued the newspapers. So much so that the *Manchester Guardian* used the headline 'Bishop Condemns Birth Control' and drew a pained letter from Barnes:

> All my friends who read the Manchester Guardian will today be shaking their heads and saying: 'Alas, poor man, he is getting old and reaction

is coming upon him'. So please will you allow me space to say that I would as soon condemn the use of soap as the practice of birth control?

He was not just concerned with population as a social problem. Nationally he thought that Britain's position was declining as she was compelled to support a population larger than she could afford; and, in international affairs, countries with uncontrolled populations, often under Catholic influence, would menace peace by the expansionist policies they would be tempted to adopt. In the same vein he deplored the risk that countries might adopt dangerous courses to overcome unemployment. For the dangers of war and the need for disarmament came readily to his attention, even if at this stage of history they were not prominent in the public mind. In 1930 he preached on the need for the Naval Conference to succeed and, as a member of the National Council for the Prevention of War, joined in a letter to the Prime Minister on the same subject. Speaking in Convocation the same year, he denounced competition in armaments which 'must ultimately lead to the destruction of peace, for if you prepare for war, you will get war'. The next year he was specifically calling on his clergy to preach sermons on disarmament, with the forthcoming Geneva Conference in view. Early in 1932 a Disarmament Sunday was observed throughout the Birmingham Diocese. In several addresses at that time he dwelt on the economic burden of armaments and their futility as a means of keeping the peace, and also on the impossibility of solving problems by war, which would destroy civilization. 'If we have another international war like the last, we may as well put up the shutters and let in the Bolsheviks.' But he was not just arguing from expediency; his pacifism was growing more absolute:

I know of no war in our recent annals from which we would not have done well to keep free. I distrust all preparations for war and I will not associate myself with any military organizations . . . The dedication of a war memorial may easily be made an occasion for glorifying, or at least, for excusing war.

What is more, he was drawing political conclusions. 'Nationalism has been a curse to Europe during the last hundred years . . . We ought to have a confederation – the United States of Europe.' This in February 1932. It is not surprising therefore that in June of that year he took the lead in denouncing the British Government's insistence on retaining a capacity for aerial bombing, even if it was only justified as a deterrent for police purposes or the tactics of surprise. As he saw it, bombing raids could not fail to kill or maim women and children and were morally indefensible. 'He is a bad Englishman who says: "I support my government right or wrong." ' Nor is it surprising that in the spring of 1933, soon after the Nazis had come to power in Germany, he was publicly deploring their treatment of the Jews and helping to organize a united Christian meeting of protest in Birmingham, at which he was careful to express understanding and sympathy for the German people as a whole against the background of the Versailles Treaty.

He soon went further in his apprehensions for the future. Speaking in November 1933, he said that Russia was suffering under a gigantic experiment, Eastern Europe was in financial and economic chaos, France was out-at-elbows and nervous, in Italy there was no true freedom, while Germany was suffering from political hysteria on a scale unequalled in known history. In January 1934, he declared, speaking of the last war,

> Germany probably lost more and suffered more than any other nation. As a result, she has at length succumbed to a despotism which has surprised the world by its crudity and its cruelty . . . During the last year in Germany leading men of science and her leaders, some of her very best, have been exiled or imprisoned. Einstein is exiled and his personal possessions have been meanly confiscated . . . But events in Germany during the past year would not be so profoundly disturbing were it not for their apparent menace to international peace . . . The next war, should it come, will virtually eliminate Christian ethics . . . The nations of the earth are now so closely interdependent that a policy of isolation will be most difficult to maintain . . . The only hope for the future is that the leading nations of the world shall, in their own interests, unite to preserve peace, peace through international righteousness.

In another speech the same month, he foresaw that if Europe continued in a suicidal policy of international war, other races and peoples would lead the development of mankind. This would not be based on Christian ethics. There might be a unity possible between Buddhist ethics and the Christian tradition. But the Japanese were showing 'the fierce nationalism which made the continent of Europe almost unendurable'. This was a challenge to Europe.

In February, in lighter vein after dinner with the Architectural

Association, he expressed the view that Birmingham University, copied as it was from medieval Siena, did not give one the feeling of palaces that stand along the Grand Canal. 'I feel that if indeed Western European civilization is to be destroyed by the aeroplane, possibly as the poison gas is rolling up to the heights of Harborne, there may come a telephone message to say that bombs have completely destroyed the University, and I shall reflect in my dying moments that even destruction has its compensations.'

By June, however, he was back in more sombre mood. By now, too, he was dissociating himself more sharply from British official policy. Preaching to the National Peace Congress, he spoke of his wish for universal disarmament.

> But if all attempts to secure such disarmament fail, I would have my own country disarm, and for its safety trust to a policy of international righteousness, so generous as to seem quixotic. Such a programme . . . might end in disaster. But any alternative policy . . . will lead ultimately to large-scale war.

He went on to advocate the return of her colonies to Germany, self-government for India, the submission of all disputes to an international arbitration tribunal and the abandonment of military or economic sanctions by the League of Nations, whose authority must be moral. This thorough-going pacifism brought down on his head attacks by Geoffrey Lloyd, then the Prime Minister's PPS, who described him as gambling with British liberty and British safety and, in the House of Lords, by Londonderry, Secretary for Air, who insisted that the Government must provide adequately for the air defence of the country. But Barnes was not to be deterred. In September 1934, he took the occasion of a lecture on the Old Testament not only to attack anti-Semitism, which was used to disparage the Jews' greatest contribution to human civilization, but also to recall the Hebrew prophet's advice to trust in the Lord 'when once again the nations are beginning to pile up armaments in fear of one another'. Again, in November, arguing that there was no adequate defence against aeroplanes, he suggested that the Government should 'take a great risk and refuse to create or maintain an air force'.

The main point at issue at the time was the need, as the Government saw it, to keep bomber aircraft for police purposes against tribal raiders on the North-West frontier of India. This was in effect a policy of punitive reprisals and the Government spokesman claimed that warning was always given, to avoid unnecessary loss of innocent lives. Barnes pertinently asked how warning could effectively be given from an aircraft flying at 3000 feet, but, in reply to correspondents who wrote to point out the brutality of the tribesmen and the need to punish them, his main point was the Christian objection to retaliation as such: 'I have yet to learn that Christ taught: "Ye have heard that it hath been said, Love your enemies, do good to them that hate you, but I say unto you, an eye for an eye, a tooth for a tooth, aeroplane bombs for swords, poison gas for rifle bullets." ' His own remedy was that the British should drive roads through the area and then use them to bring elements of civilization to the tribes. In the same vein, he enlarged on the theme, also much discussed at the time, of the iniquity of private manufacture of armaments and of armament salesmen in close alliance with 'warmongers'. 'In the next war, as in the last, Englishmen will be killed by English-made munitions.'

This was not the only subject on which Barnes found himself at odds with the Government. When they introduced the Incitement to Disaffection Bill in October 1934, he described it as foolishly provocative and dangerous to freedom. He had tried privately to find out if secret attempts had been made to seduce the armed forces; he could hear of none but only

> that some members of the Cabinet, obsessed by the spectre of Communism, having had an attack of nerves, have forced their unhappy colleagues to sponsor this wholly unnecessary measure. Such nervousness might be excused in an elderly spinster given to credulity and a reactionary newspaper. It is unworthy of statesmen.

He went on to argue that the Bill made active pacifism in time of war a criminal offence. This brought him into conflict with the Attorney-General, none other than his old ally Inskip, who published a letter to an unnamed correspondent and, in trying to allay criticism, suggested that Barnes should look at the Bill more carefully, as it did not abate by one jot the freedom of speech already enjoyed. Inskip also wrote a friendly private letter to Barnes at the same time, trying to reassure him. Unluckily his letter did not arrive until the Bishop had made his public rejoinder. Barnes sent Inskip a conciliatory reply and their good personal relations were unaffected.

Publicly, Barnes thereupon propounded an imaginary case in which he denounced as unChristian air bombing of tribesmen on the North-West frontier of India and said that Christian men should not act under such orders. Since his words could reach members of the Royal Air Force who might then refuse to take part in the bombing, he would be committing an offence under one section of the Act and, if his wife had in her possession a marked copy of the newspaper containing his statement, she would be guilty under another section and they could each be fined £200 and given two years' imprisonment. Nye Bevan took up these remarks in the debate on the Bill, and Inskip replied that if Bevan had 20,000 copies of Barnes's remarks, with evidence that he intended to give them to members of the forces, he would be subject to the Bill. But he declined to say that possession of leaflets and writing a letter to the press would be an offence; there must be overt acts showing an intention to subvert the persons to whom leaflets were sent. There the matter was left, and Barnes's position was never put to the test. Once again there seemed to be no great desire to send him to gaol.

Religion, science and peace, then, were his main interests during these years, and to each he gave a highly personal flavour. They were not exhaustive. He maintained, for example, his interest in education, working in particular to ensure religious teaching in state schools rather than to protect Church schools from state interference. He continued to champion women's causes, doing all he could to encourage the ministry of women and advising the girls of Wycombe Abbey not to end up as old frumps, painted frivolities or tired drudges. He took an active interest in missionary work and remained deeply concerned with the cause of Indian freedom. But when Gandhi came to Birmingham in 1932, he found their interview strangely unsatisfactory, not only because he had to sit on the floor, but because of the Indian leader's negative and unconstructive approach; Barnes had hoped for something better than Hindu nihilism. None the less, in later years he was to describe Gandhi as the greatest man he ever met and to couple him with Sun Yat Sen and Lenin as men who had shaped the future.

Nor did he eschew domestic political controversy. With unemployment rising fast, he took an active interest in the plight of the workless, joining in public demands for an allowance to them of more than 2/- for each child and for the school leaving-age to be raised to fifteen. He strongly supported the provision of free night shelter for the destitute, visiting the Birmingham Shelter and writing to the Home Secretary when a vagrant who could have been sent there was imprisoned instead and promptly died in gaol. More directly, at a town-planners' dinner, at which Neville Chamberlain was the chief guest, he challenged the ethos of the Conservative Party. Over town planning, there had been apathy, dislike of new ideas, regard for vested interests, suspicions that planning was socialistic or communistic.

> I have no politics; therefore I can speak impartially. This apathy has shown itself most in the rank and file of the Conservative Party. The leaders of the party, of course, have ideas . . . But when you meet with suspicions of novelty you must take care to conceal your own desire for rapid change . . . How is it that Mr Baldwin tries to lead his followers by always talking, not in the vein of fertile idealism that is within him, but of the black pigs of Worcestershire ? . . . In the New Testament there is a valuable text: 'Make friends with the mammon of unrighteousness'. I suggest that you should make friends with the young intellectuals of the Labour Party.

He went on to advocate taking over land for community needs without excessive compensation and, as an example of new ideas being accepted, cited free meals for schoolchildren.

> Not long ago . . . that proposal was regarded as socialistic, quite impossible. Yet it was only a week ago that I saw a photograph of one of Mr Chamberlain's Ministerial colleagues sipping mid-morning milk with school-children carefully washed and brushed for the occasion.

This was over thirty years before another Conservative Minister was described as 'milk-snatcher'.

Barnes did not always have to swim against the stream. Much of his teaching had been endorsed by the Lambeth Conference of 1930, the first which he attended. It reaffirmed the wish for Christian reunion, with particular reference to the South Indian scheme. It declared that war was incompatible with Christ's teaching and no war should be countenanced unless the dispute had first been submitted to arbitration. It gave guarded approval to contraception, in the only resolution where the Bishops found it necessary to quote the majority, 193 votes to 67, by which it had been passed. Barnes had been a member of the committee concerned with marriage, sex, race, peace and war, but had not attended any of its meetings. He chose to concentrate on the committee on the Christian doctrine of God, where, under the congenial chairmanship of a kindred spirit in Archbishop D'Arcy of Armagh, he must have been well satisfied. Indeed, with D'Arcy and the Bishops of Oxford and Carlisle, he seems to have been mainly responsible for the drafting of its report. The resultant resolution contained a number of statements valuable to his position: 'In view of the enlarged knowledge gained in modern times of God's ordering of the world and the clearer apprehension of the creative process by which He prepared the way for the coming of Jesus Christ, there is urgent need in the face of many erroneous conceptions for a fresh presentation.' 'It is no part of the purpose of the Scriptures to give information on those themes which are the proper subject matter of scientific enquiry.' 'We recognize in the modern discoveries of science . . . veritable gifts of God.' 'We especially desire to impress upon the younger clergy that the Church requires the service of men who will devote themselves to the study of theology in all its branches. The Church needs learning, as well as spiritual power and practical ability, in its clergy.' 'Christian theology should be studied and taught in Universities in contact with philosophy, science and criticism and to that end Faculties of Theology should be established in Universities wherever possible.'

Indeed the Conference was not only profitable but enjoyable. He took pleasure in contacts with his brethren from overseas, as when he wrote that 'yesterday the Bishop of Tennessee informed us that the Ascension was a proof of the existence of a fourth dimension.' No wonder he had told Davidson that he did not want to be driven to that diocese.

It was no doubt partly out of affection for D'Arcy of Armagh that in 1932 Barnes paid his only ecclesiastical visit overseas. He went to Northern Ireland to take part in the celebrations of St Patrick's arrival there 1500 years before. It is surprising to find him preaching the virtues of a saint with such marked Catholic connections, but he praised him both as man of learning and missionary of the faith. In return the Dean of Sligo bombarded him with literature designed to show that St Patrick had lived not in the fifth, but the second century AD.

In February 1933 Barnes gained further authority, or at least a further platform was added unto him, when he entered the House of

Lords. His supporters were his old allies of the Prayer Book front, Pollock of Norwich and Cecil of Exeter. It was a further pleasure that the Lord Chancellor, before whom he subscribed the roll, was his old friend Sankey, who had earlier halted his procession into the House to greet Barnes's wife and sons. When he joined the House, Barnes said that the only vote he would happily give there would be for its abolition. But in fact he was to find it useful on more than one occasion, and in wartime he became quite reconciled to it as the only place in London where he could have cream in his coffee.

In all his activities throughout these years his wife gave him the strongest support. She ran house and garden with smooth efficiency. Although they rarely entertained purely for pleasure, the demands of official entertainment were heavy and Mrs Barnes expected high standards of service. The Bishop knew that he could always invite someone to a meal or to stay the night and the machine would respond without hesitation. There was a constant flow of guests through the house. Each year they gave two or three garden-parties for the clergy and other Diocesan colleagues, to which, incidentally, the 'rebels' were asked without discrimination. Three times a year the Bishop held an ordination, normally at the cathedral; but the candidates for ordination spent the three preceding days in retreat at Bishop's Croft, under the guidance of an examining chaplain or other specially invited clergyman, whose wife usually came too. Here again Mrs Barnes helped to relieve what might have been the tension of some difficult days. The meetings of the retreat took place in the chapel, except that each candidate had to preach a sermon in the Parish Church across the road, empty but for the Bishop sitting in criticism in the back pew. Many ordinands seem to have found the ordeal alarming. But they slept in the house and ate with the family. On Sunday morning they all appeared at the breakfast-table in brand-new clerical collars, to which no overt reference was ever made, and after the ordination service each of them brought his parents or two other members of his family to luncheon.

But, apart from thus running what amounted to an hotel, Mrs Barnes accompanied her husband on virtually all his public engagements, meeting the womenfolk of the city and diocese. He submitted his manuscripts to her scrutiny, and she fully earned his description of her as the 'most severe of critics'. Her criticism was perhaps more of manner than of matter, for on substance she was totally loyal to him, and in her frequent public speeches she produced ideas more or less indistinguishable from his own, though expressed in less trenchant language. She herself spoke mainly on moral and social questions from a strongly religious standpoint, though without venturing into the higher realms of theology. She was an outspoken advocate of both pacifism and birth-control and, like her husband, vigorously opposed the doctrine of original sin. A local paper indeed described her as 'the most accomplished woman speaker in Birmingham' and went on to record 'Small, but packs tremendous vitality into little compass. Dresses quietly, with a decidedly original taste in hats'.

But she was by no means a carbon copy of him. She had a mind and plenty of activities of her own. Thus she continued to preside over the Clergy Wives' Club which she had founded, inviting a regular flow of speakers to address it. Her loyalties to Manchester University and to Royal Holloway College took her often to functions at both of them. Like her father before her, she was a Governor of Wycombe Abbey. She was in frequent demand to give prizes or lay foundation-stones in her own right. But her main independent activity lay in the National Council of Women; she was active in its Birmingham branch, of which she served as President, and was soon elected to the national executive and eventually to a national vice-presidency. This involved her in regular meetings in London, where she usually stayed at the English Speaking Union, and brought her into touch with a wider circle of friends. As Barnes himself generally went to the Athenaeum or the Oxford and Cambridge Club, they tended to go their own ways in London, if their visits coincided, and to compare notes on their return to Birmingham. He too in those early years as a Bishop liked to meet such people as he could in London, and to take cross-bearings on subjects which might otherwise look rather onesided from a Midlands slant. He preferred to sleep at the Athenaeum but, as he rightly described that club as a place of high thinking and plain living, to eat at the Oxford and Cambridge, where in those faroff days the waiters were expected to know to which university you belonged and to give you a plate with a dark or light blue rim accordingly. *Eheu fugaces.*

The great event for them both in 1933 was the publication of Barnes's Gifford Lectures under the title of *Scientific Theory and Religion*. They had been delivered as long ago as 1927–9 at Aberdeen, where the large but mostly uncomprehending audience had gone into

308

ripples of laughter as Barnes inscribed ever longer mathematical formulae across two or three widths of blackboard. He and his wife had been most hospitably entertained by the Principal and Lady Adam Smith, of whom they made firm friends. George Adam Smith was a biblical scholar after Barnes's own heart, and there was, too, his close family link with J. J. Thomson, Barnes's old friend and colleague, by now Master of Trinity. Since delivering the lectures, Barnes had devoted virtually all his spare time to preparing them for publication and would, for example, come down to dinner with some such remark as that, having spent all day in calculation, he had reached the conclusion that space had a negative curvature. In this he seems to have been more conscientious than some other Gifford Lecturers, several of whose books appeared in quicker time and shorter compass. For he not only added to the lectures material which time had not allowed him to deliver: he also did his best to keep abreast of more recent knowledge in the fields which they covered, so that he might deliver an up-to-date and comprehensive survey to his publishers. Despite pleas from Hodder & Stoughton to publish for him again, his academic loyalties led him to offer a scholarly work of this kind to the Cambridge University Press, who accepted it and arranged with Macmillan for the simultaneous issue of an American edition. A book of this kind, nearly seven hundred pages long and full of mathematics, could hardly be a best-seller. There was at first talk of an abridged, popular version, but this never materialized, perhaps because of later illness. However, 1100 copies were in fact sold in the first three years, and it did not go out of print until after the Second World War.

The subtitle of the book, Barnes's major published work, was 'The World Described by Science and its Spiritual Interpretation'. His declared objective was to 'take the world as revealed by natural science and consider its spiritual interpretation with the absence of bias shown by men of science in their special investigations'. As he said in his foreword to the lectures, his aim was to give them

> an inner coherence. I trust that they express the attitude of the modern man of science who, as he hopefully makes theories, is aware of the limitations of his knowledge and also, in part because of his loyalty to truth, bears in mind the reality and the claims of the spiritual world.

This broad approach had indeed been enjoined by the founder of the lectures. By the terms of the Gifford bequest, their purpose was 'promoting, advancing, teaching and diffusing the study of Natural Theology in the widest sense of that term', and Lord Gifford had expressly prescribed: 'I wish the lecturers to treat their subject as a strictly natural science, the greatest of all possible sciences, indeed in one sense, the only science, that of Infinite Being, without reference to or reliance upon any supposed special exceptional or so-called miraculous revelation. I wish it considered just as astronomy or chemistry is.' Barnes was therefore precluded, even had he wanted to do so, from simply making religious assertions, based on his own authority or that of the Bible or the Church. He was fully entitled, indeed almost required, by the terms of reference, to start from first principles and proceed from them to his own conclusions. As he put it in a letter to Oliver Lodge, 'the mathematics is at times stodgy, but I was anxious to bring out clearly that from a comparatively few assumptions the various theories of space and general relativity could alike be developed.'

The argument of such a book cannot be summarized. It was certainly a remarkable synthesis of knowledge, as the scope of the index alone testifies, and the reviewers naturally accorded it such epithets as 'noble', 'massive' and 'monumental'. For *The Times Literary Supplement*, 'this work has something of the solidity and majesty of St Peter's Dome, and pilgrims through the enchanting realm of science, whose staff is the tensor calculus, their scallop-shell the higher algebra, will in years to come stand in admiration before it'. The *British Weekly* declared it 'a book which is essentially one for today, yet whose positive contribution will form the stock in trade of many theological tomorrows'. The *Guardian* opined that 'even those who most violently disagree with Dr Barnes's theology will scarce forbear to cheer that an Anglican bishop should have produced what is probably the best outline of science in the English language'. Even so, there were the expected criticisms from the Catholic, fundamentalist and nationalist press. But the serious and especially the scientific reviewers, though naturally taking issue with specific points, were generally favourable. Barnes himself was particularly pleased with the notices by Eddington and E. A. Milne in the *Cambridge Review* and *Oxford Magazine* respectively; Inge in the *Church of England Newspaper* and J. S. Haldane in *The Listener* were also markedly friendly.

As befitted his own academic discipline, Barnes approached his task through mathematics. But, as he said in his introductory lecture,

'knowledge is measurement' and mathematics is the science of number. Alternatively, in words attributed to Robert Boyle, 'mathematics is the alphabet in which God wrote the world'. In the thirteenth century, Roger Bacon said with truth 'he who knows not mathematics cannot know any other sciences; what is more, he cannot discover his own ignorance or find its proper remedies'.

Some idea of the scope of the book can be derived from the twenty lecture-titles into which it is divided. After an introductory lecture, they read: Matter, Space, Riemann's General Theory of Space, Space-Time: the Special Theory of Relativity, General Relativity, the Electrical Theory of Matter, Heat and Light, Quantum Theory and Röntgen Rays, the Solar System, the Galactic Universe and Great Nebulae, the Origin of Life and the Geological Record, the Evolution of Plants and Sex, the Evolution of Animals and Mendelism, the Machinery of Evolution, Man's Origin and Past, Scientific Theory and the Real World, God and our Belief in His Existence, Religious Experience, Immortality. Thus they move from general definitions fairly rapidly into mathematical physics and cosmology, thence to biology and onwards into philosophy and theology. Or, as Barnes himself put it more succinctly in his introduction: 'this course of lectures falls naturally into four divisions: Space and Time, Matter and Stars, Life and Evolution, Man and Mind.'

To those familiar with his thinking, this sequence of ideas should occasion no surprise. But they were supported by a wealth of detail, much of it in algebraic or geometrical form, which few could expect to follow. What is perhaps surprising at first sight, as there were not wanting critics to point out, is the relative weight given to 'scientific theory' at the expense of 'religion'. The more captious of these indeed asserted that they could see little direct connection between the two parts of the book. This Barnes himself would have vigorously contested, and with justice. Not only does he continually assert the interpenetration of the natural and spiritual realms; the spiritual interpretation of scientific knowledge is not confined to the closing chapters but interwoven into the web of the argument. For, as he says at one point: 'If by an examination of fundamentals we are led to realise the extent to which both religion and science rest on faith and are a reasonable interpretation of experience, we may hope that the hostility between them which has been too frequent in the past may change to that sympathetic understanding which ought to exist between the different loyalties of the human spirit.'

Indeed, this note of humble enquiry, this refusal to assert logical certainties, runs right through the book. 'In science, we are never free from possible errors of perception.' 'An element of agnosticism, or willingness to say "I don't know", is necessary in the attitude of every honest thinker.' 'These questions leave some of us the more bewildered the more we think of them.' 'The world of scientific description is . . . an imperfect picture. Only as we recognize the reason for its imperfection do we understand why we cannot derive from it that sense of the presence and power of the Spirit which religion finds in the world.' Barnes repeatedly reminds his readers that scientific conclusions can only constitute 'a series of ever closer approximations to the truth'. This is the student of asymptotic functions speaking. 'We do not discover causes; we only observe sequences.' Thus he often calls in aid the Heisenberg uncertainty-relations as justifying the limitations of scientific knowledge. But the ultimate apprehension of religious truth must be by other means, though aided by reason and not contradicting its results. This is not the approach of the dogmatic rationalist, fighting his aggressive battles under the banner of invincible science, with the device *Gesta Dei per mathematicos,* whom his critics often portrayed.

In this spirit Barnes proceeds to consider the origin and nature, first, of the whole Universe, then of life within it, and then progressively of man as a speaking, thinking and moralizing animal. His categories are often original. Just as he analyses the differences between Euclidean, Lobatchewskyan and Riemannian space and comes down tentatively in favour of Riemann, so he surveys man's progress through what he calls the Reindeer, Metal and Electrical Ages and concludes that man is only a stage in evolution and, if the Universe is conceived as a unity, life must exist elsewhere within it. For a constant theme of the book is the need to resolve apparent dualisms into underlying unities. Just as space and time constitute a single continuum, for example, so are body and spirit joined in one personality. In modern terms, he is always seeking to dissolve 'either-or' into 'both-and'.

Barnes finally defines his philosophical position as 'moderate realism' and his theological stance as 'ethical theism'. By moderate realism he means that 'a physical world exists independent of any human mind' and 'it is possible to separate out objects from the subject-object relation of our experience'. But, as he formulated it succinctly in a letter a year or two later, 'the picture of the world which you take as objective truth is a mental construct depending for its correspondence to fact upon the adequacy of our senses and our reasoning powers; for us, therefore, mind and not matter is fundamental'. Further, he insists that objects 'have a real and independent existence because they exist in the Mind of God'. Thus the world presented to us in experience has a reality derived from God. But God is not the only reality. The existence of evil and of freewill shows that 'the world has a certain measure of independence given to it by God'. Here then is the link between 'moderate realism' and 'ethical theism'. The world as seen by science requires a creative Mind. Moreover, this creative Mind must still be active in the world it has created. Some men have seen God as winding up the world and leaving it to run down by entropy. Others see Him as intervening to produce changes which science cannot explain. But 'the God of the trigger is as little satisfying as the God of the gaps'. Although causation is obscure, and while the laws which the physicists discover may be mainly statistical, they disclose the operation of Divine will. Moreover, God works through the minds of men. In this sense the transcendence of theism is necessary rather than the pantheism of immanence or the deism of the absentee landlord. But the transcendent God cannot be proved by the conventional arguments, ontological, cosmological or teleological. The only valid proof of the existence of God is the moral argument. Thus theism must be ethical. Beauty, goodness and truth exist as absolute values and attributes of God. As human nature, though imperfectly, reflects the Divine nature, man as a moral animal can have direct experience of God. But as evil and freewill also exist, there are inevitably also in this world sin and suffering, which can only be overcome if this world is not the end but if personal immortality is also a reality. This incidentally means that we must accept some puzzling facts, hard though they are to comprehend. Thus evolution is non-moral and moves down as well as up, even though the ultimate purpose of creation is progress towards the good. Just as a failure in evolution is destroyed, so will a man who fails to triumph over sin or suffering have to pay for his failure. For God is sternness as well as love. Thus there seems to be a time-element in immortality, at least in its early stages. But it is difficult to say that God is in time; perhaps the idea that time is in Him comes nearer to the truth.

313

Such are but the barest bones of a body of argument which is sustained over hundreds of pages with rigorous logic and a high level of abstract thought. No skeleton can do justice to the face or the figure. The book must be read to be judged. The style is sometimes heavy, but almost always clear. It is shot through with humorous asides and homely analogies. Thus, of the reality of the feelings of different individuals rather than the content of those feelings, 'any doubts which this statement may cause can be set at rest by reflection upon the difference between toothache in oneself and knowledge of exactly similar toothache in another'. Or, on the difference between conscience and instinct, 'from speech and from the associated development of writing such things as Gifford Lectures have resulted; no one will pretend that such lectures, good or bad, could be intelligible to our anthropoid cousins'. Or, on various aspects of evolution, 'the existence and cause of appendicitis are singularly difficult of explanation by those who contend that man was specially and directly created by God'. 'A vestigial organ in man is the group of muscles which once served to enable some ancestor to move his ears; some among us can still use some of these muscles and many a boy, by reason of such prowess, has won the respect of his schoolfellows.' 'When I was a boy I learned, as part of a widely believed folklore, that a pig when it tries to swim cuts its own throat; I have heard this belief used to vindicate the truth of the story of the Gadarene swine. It appears, however, that in a distant past era a mammal, not wholly unlike a pig, did learn to swim and became a whale.' Again, Haeckel's law that ontogeny recapitulates phylogeny is interpreted as the embryo 'climbing up its own ancestral tree'. Long before the days of Robert Ardrey, Barnes was doing his best to popularize evolution. Incidentally, his researches into the subject led him into some strange byways. Thus he was fascinated to find that the wife of an Archbishop of Canterbury had inherited webbed toes. He found too that an unfortunate woman living near his home suffered from an hereditary disease which usually only afflicted sheep, so that their legs stiffened and at any loud noise, instead of their legs collapsing beneath them, they could only fall over sideways; but he would not let his sons go and startle the poor woman concerned, to see how she fell.

The heroes of the whole story are Newton, Darwin and Einstein in the scientific chapters, Hort and Rashdall in the theological. Riemann and Planck also feature as *jeunes premiers*; as Barnes was to say in

1937, 'it is the quantum theory even more than relativity which differentiates the science of the twentieth century from that of the nineteenth'. Of the other seminal thinkers who created the modern world, it is strange that there is no mention of Marx, Wittgenstein or Freud, nor, among lesser lights, of Whitehead or Pavlov. But Barnes always regarded Freud with aversion; though revolutionary on public morality, he was completely conventional in private morals and, when he praised something as wholesome or denounced it as disgusting, it was usually with a sexual connotation. He never had much affinity for Whitehead's thought and may have seen Wittgenstein and Pavlov as unrepresentative of solid reality in philosophy and science. Marx perhaps he saw belonging neither to scientific theory nor religion, but to politics. Nor could he be expected to foresee Leakey's discoveries in Tanganyika or Steinheim man's appearance in 1933 in Europe. He was not alone in accepting the validity of Piltdown man, although he perhaps exaggerated its significance for western Europe's place at the peak of the evolutionary process. Nor could he anticipate the advance of linguistic philosophy, even in the genetic form given to it by Chomsky. He did not foresee space travel in the near future; nor would he have wanted to look forward to the nuclear bomb or the permissive society. Indeed the forecasts in his concluding pages are both too optimistic and too pessimistic at once. He expected Christian morality to extend its sway over men's minds and hearts and, as late as 1933, made no allowance for the early possibility of another war. This may well have been wishful thinking. Of scientific knowledge, on the other hand, he foretold a period of quiescence and absorption after the rapid advances of the previous century. In fact the pace was to quicken and Barnes would have been among the first to welcome man's mastery of new fields of science, if not the uses to which they were sometimes put. Even so, he was confident enough to write in 1949 that, in the sixteen years since the book's publication, 'there has been much scientific progress. I doubt, however, whether the fundamentals of our understanding of the universe have changed as markedly as in the previous half century, and I do not think that such changes as have taken place have altered the religious bases of our understanding'.

Other faults can of course be found. A serious objection advanced by some critics was that, although he distinguished himself from Bishop Berkeley, his definition of his self-styled 'moderate realism' seemed to show little difference from Berkeley's idealism. But this is

315

perhaps at worst a matter of terminology. There are one or two howlers, as when he describes heat waves as shorter than those of light; but slips of the pen or tongue are venial sins in 657 pages of text. There are some sweeping, sometimes naïve, generalizations, often irrelevant to his theme, as when he asserts in passing that 'modern research has established that the Philistines were more cultured than their Israelite enemies'. On the other hand, he gives full recognition to the fact that only Judaism and Christianity have achieved ethical theism. But at the same time he shows less understanding for oriental religions, condemning Hindu idolatry and dismissing Buddhism with the statement that 'popular Buddhism in China is recognized as degenerate by all who have studied its origin'. There is often evidence of what one reviewer called 'eclectic reading', but this is hardly surprising in an author with so many other commitments. For the same reason, perhaps, too many quotations are not ascribed to their sources. His *obiter dicta* are sometimes subjective, without much evidence adduced for them. The assertion that life must exist on other planets is a typical case in point. But as in his sermons the *obiter dicta* are often what give the lectures their special flavour. The personality of the lecturer cuts through. Admittedly, there is little poetry in him and he can be heavy-handed, as when he tacks some remarks on the Virgin Birth on to a discussion of parthenogenesis in insects. One reviewer complained that 'his style lacks the quality of persuasiveness; he likes to ram things down our throats'. This may be true of subjects where his prejudices break through, as in his familiar criticisms of Catholic doctrine or of organized religion in general. 'Churches die of respectability just as they become a nuisance through superstition.' But here again the style is the man. The aphorism is a throw-away line and the allegation of unpersuasiveness cannot be applied to the carefully channelled flow of the main argument.

It is more valid to describe him as subjective when, for example, he dismisses a claim to spiritual experience before a real presence in the consecrated elements, while asserting the validity of his own religious awareness. But the passage in which he does so is striking enough to merit quotation in full:

Four or five times in life, the first time when I was a boy some fourteen years old and the last time at the age of thirty-three, I have felt, enjoyed and wondered at a sudden exaltation which seemed to carry with it an

316

understanding of the innermost nature of things. So vivid has been the experience that I could today go to the exact spot in the street of the Oxfordshire village where the flash of revelation first came. Always such experience has occurred in sunshine and out-of-doors, never in church. Always it has been unexpected. Always I have been alone. There has never been ill-health as an exciting cause. On the last occasion, which still remains vivid, I sat down in the early afternoon on a piece of bare turf in a foam-covered river near the sea. I remember that I was going to bathe from a stretch of shingle to which the few people who stayed in the village seldom went. Suddenly the noise of the insects was hushed. Time seemed to stop. A sense of infinite power and peace came upon me. I can best liken the combination of timelessness with amazing fullness of existence to the feeling one gets in watching the rim of a great silent flywheel or the unmoving surface of a deep, strongly flowing river. Nothing happened; yet existence was completely full. All was clear. I was in a world where the confusion and waste and loss inseparable from time had vanished. At the heart of the world there was power and peace and eternal life. How long this blank trance, so full and so empty, lasted I cannot say. Probably a very short time indeed. It passed, leaving me neither tired in body nor mentally irritable. The memory remains. And it is because an inexplicable quality of supreme significance attaches to it that it remains precious.

This passage casts an unexpected light on a man commonly regarded as what was later called a desiccated calculating-machine. Much the same can be said of Housman's famous Leslie Stephen lecture on the Name and Nature of Poetry, delivered a few years later: the same attachment to daily life, the same reaction to country things, the same sudden elevation of spirit, even though Housman tried to play it down by linking it with a pint of beer or the cut of a razor. In Barnes's case, was it wishful thinking? Or self-deception? If so, it cannot have been deliberate. Whatever objective reality can be attached to his feeling, it obviously meant a great deal to Barnes himself. Was its introduction into the lectures self-dramatization, for the effect on his audience? This would be too much out of character, too far removed from the cool precision of his usual scientific analysis. He seems to have felt a compelling need to communicate his experience to others.

In another passage he makes no personal claim or confession. But it is hard not to recognize the standard against which he measured himself:

The great religious teacher is one in whom religious emotion is not only strong but also pure; and who, to preserve its purity, is quick to test by the dry light of reason the knowledge which such emotion seems to give him. When in such a one moral earnestness is joined to spiritual enthusiasm we ought to recognize a true prophet of God.

In human terms, Barnes was not a modest man: he knew his own powers and he was conscious of his worldly achievements. But, confronted with the eternal problems of scientific theory and religion, he was essentially a humble man. For here he was wrestling not against flesh and blood, but against principalities, against powers, against the rulers of the darkness of the world, against spiritual wickedness in high places. Prophecy is no doubt a gift, but teaching was a duty. He would not have relished the terminology of canonization, but, while he may sometimes have seen himself as *avocatus diaboli*, he always acted as *servus Dei*.

So in this spirit he wrote the last page of his long book:

I now end a piece of work which for more than six years has absorbed my vacations and occupied all my leisure hours. The task has been singularly enjoyable: in itself and also because by its means I have escaped from the pettiness and insincerities of ecclesiastical disorder to learn of the men now living, who are making discoveries as significant as any in human history. I have, in truth, been rarely fortunate in having had to try to understand the intellectual splendour of our own great era of scientific achievement. As I have followed the rapidly changing growth of knowledge I have felt that I too shared the excitement of research and the joy of discovery. Moreover, I too have realised how vast is our ignorance of the world in which we find ourselves and to which we belong. Can it be, I am compelled to ask, that with such a feeling of ignorance I shall pass to a realm where knowledge is not, because consciousness has ceased? Must we allow that the desire to understand God's works and ways, which is one of the strongest and purest of human passions, is a vain and hopeless by-product of man's search for material comfort? Do we but rise for a moment above the waters of unconsciousness and, after a brief glance around, sink again to eternal oblivion? If such is indeed our fate, then surely the mystery of human life is unfathomable; unreason must sit enthroned above meaningless change.

Now I, for one, cannot believe that within a few years my attempt to understand the universe will have ceased. So, as I come to the end of these lectures, I turn to whatever awaits me with hope and courage. The world is full of surprises and perplexities: but it is not a chaos. There

318

is order within it. Reason and beauty and much goodness have gone to its making. I am, like each of yourselves, one of its children. Our high thoughts and hopes and desires belong to the life of the Spirit manifested within it. Behind the world, controlling Nature, is the Creative Spirit to Whom we are somehow akin. That Spirit is not a cold foe working through blind and pitiless forces; but is the source of our aspirations, friendly to our search for knowledge, the kindly guardian of our destinies. Therefore I am certain that our search will not end with death: labour and struggle will not be in vain. At the last we shall know even as we are known.

Gibbon's reflections when he finished his great history have often been quoted and naturally come into our thoughts as now we go our separate ways. 'A sober melancholy was spread over my mind, by the idea that I had taken an everlasting leave of an old and agreeable companion, and that whatsoever might be the future date of my history, the life of the historian might be short and precarious'. We, I feel, end any piece of work to which we put our hands with a confidence which Gibbon did not possess. To no companion of earth's short journey need we give an everlasting farewell. What we begin here we shall finish hereafter, if indeed it be worth the finishing. The fact that life is short and precarious matters little, inasmuch as those who have travelled with us here shall be our companions beyond the grave, if we and they alike seek the City of God.

CHAPTER VIII

BIRMINGHAM
BETWEEN THE WARS

The Thirties, Part III, 1934–1939
Alarms and Excursions

Barnes often said, and how right he was, that the Birmingham diocese was no bed of roses. But nor, for all that, was it a bed of nails. To change the metaphor, it could not be described in the 1930s as all kicks and no ha'pence. Kicks there were a'plenty, from Anglo-Catholic forwards and archiepiscopal goalkeepers. The ha'pence too were squeezed by the Depression. But, with controversy muted for the moment and the Gifford Lectures off his mind, he could range rather wider afield.

Holidays had always been precious to him. He could recharge his batteries from the power-house of history and the springs of natural beauty. While they lived in London and the Wards were still at Peterhouse, Barnes and his wife had usually spent their holidays in East Anglia, familiar to them both from Cambridge days and within reach of her parents. In April 1925, they had been able, for the first time since the war, to revisit Italy, which they had both known and enjoyed before their marriage. Partly to celebrate his own progress and partly to console his wife for the death of both her parents within a year, they sailed with the two boys on the SS *Ranpura* of the P & O from Tilbury to Marseilles and then on by train to stay at Bordighera, Siena and Pisa, among other haunts of bachelor days.

Thereafter, for seven lean years, every holiday had to be devoted to preparing his Giffords or polishing them for publication. From

Birmingham in the early years they used to take houses in the Cots-
wolds, revisiting the background of Barnes's mother's family and his
own boyhood. But more and more they began to be drawn to
Devonshire. This county too Barnes had known as a young man. He
liked to recall how he had fulfilled the ritual of negotiating the
Dartmoor quagmires on foot, jumping from tussock to tussock to
post a letter to himself in the swamp-infested pillar-box of Princeton,
thence to be retrieved by the next intrepid boghopper. But now the
attraction was the South Devon coast, and above all the sea. Barnes
had not swum since his marriage, and his wife never learned to do so.
Now, from 1928 onwards, he had his sons for company in the water.
While he pondered his problems, the waves could seep through space-
time, mollify mind and matter and even refresh recollections of rebels.
He enjoyed it so much that he was soon advocating a lido at Birmingham.

For a decade or so they rented houses, but more and more they
wanted a house of their own. They searched the area round Honiton
and Axminster; but it was not until 1938 that they bought the Long
House at Seaton, a low white rough-cast building perched on top
of the cliff but within walking distance of shops and beach. Strangely
enough, this was the first and last house which either Barnes or his
wife ever owned. Otherwise their life together was confined in the
strait-jacket of official houses. Seaton itself, not to put too fine a
point on it, was an ugly little seaside resort, which filled up with
holiday-makers in summer but otherwise presented a bare and bleak
front to the winds and waters of the Channel. But the Long House
turned its back resolutely on town and trippers. Its windows gave on
the sea, and for Barnes it was a constant delight to look out across
the chalk and sandstone cliffs and to listen to the recurrent murmur
of the waves a hundred feet below.

Nor was nature the only interest. He steeped himself in the
geography, geology and history of the area. The great Duke of
Marlborough had been born five miles away, in a little farmhouse at
Musbury. On Farway Common, where he could watch the buzzards
hovering above the bracken, Granville-Barker's plays had been
written. In Seaton itself his neighbour was St John Ervine, a staunch
modernist Ulsterman who had written the life of General Booth of
the Salvation Army. So Barnes did not lack for intellectual stimulus
when he wanted it, while on Sundays he could and did, as an un-
noticed member of the congregation, attend one or other village

church in the valley sheltered from the sea-coast, where the services had remained unchanged since the Reformation and the architecture for longer centuries still.

By now not only had he started to swim again. When nearly sixty, he had learned to drive a car. With his usual application he found this a totally absorbing pursuit, even though he learned on an ancient rattletrap with a most alarming wheel-wobble. Many a curate, coming to luncheon at Bishop's Croft and expecting to discuss his religious duties or doubts, was disconcerted to find himself being cross-examined first about the type of car he owned and then as to what went on under its bonnet. To their 1924 Austin 12 the Barneses soon added, as a gift from an old friend, a Renault built in 1908. This museum-piece had the advantage that from its high back seat the passengers could see over the hedges, even in the deepest Devon lanes, but also the drawback that, if out after dark, they had to dismount and light the acetylene headlamps with a box of matches. The Renault did yeoman service into a hoary old age, until in the 1930s it was replaced by a Rolls-Royce, slightly less antique but even so of a vintage when the radiator slats were horizontal rather than vertical. The gearboxes of both these venerable cars kept even the most accomplished double-declutcher on his mettle.

Now, with the Giffords out of the way, the Barneses felt too that they could travel abroad again, for their own pleasure and the boys' edification. Thus already in 1931 they had gone to Rome as a family for Easter, with the boys under strict instructions never to eat salad, for fear of typhoid, and never to be heard mentioning the name of Mussolini, for fear of unwelcome attentions from the *carabinieri*. In 1933 they ventured further afield, taking a cruise with the Hellenic Travellers' Club for some more assiduous sight-seeing. By dint of preaching and lecturing aboard, Barnes was given a free passage, with reduced fares for his wife and family; it was hardly surprising that the Hellenic Travellers were usually in the red. That summer too they took the car abroad for the first time, touring Normandy and Brittany ostensibly for the sake of the boys' French. So, in the spring of 1934, they could leave their elder son with a French family, while the rest of them drove through France and Italy, to Naples and back.

But now, whether it was the effect of seeing Naples or not, Barnes's life was sharply interrupted by illness at the end of 1934. He had been expending his energies recklessly for years and now an infection had lodged behind his nose, whence it could only be removed by an operation. The operation succeeded in its immediate purpose; but he was away from work for the best part of six months and was left with emphysema and shortness of breath for the rest of his life. Indeed, this was to put him out of action again for most of the next winter and, although he still had nearly twenty years of active life ahead of him, his health was never quite the same again. At the age of sixty he was forced to realise that he could no longer be the happy warrior of his youth and that he should husband his resources when he could. But, despite doctor's orders, he spared himself little. He continued to fulfil a heavy programme, his mental powers were as strong as ever and he still had unquenched zest for the causes in which he believed. Given the enforced limitations, it remains astonishing how much he could still draw from life and give to it.

To recuperate from his illness, he went with his wife in the spring of 1935 to the Middle East, for the first time visiting the Holy Land. Mrs Barnes suppressed the photograph of herself on a camel in Egypt. The next year they drove up the Rhine and in the spring of 1937 across France for another Greek cruise. On this occasion he not only lectured on board ship, but also on shore, to the Anglo-Hellenic Society at Athens. The Hellenic Travellers' Club had its usual complement of distinguished members, including some notable liberal friends such as Gilbert Murray and F. W. Hirst, and their conversations off the isles of Greece bore fruit in some vigorous protests against the dictatorship of General Metaxas, including a contribution to the *Manchester Guardian* by a young lawyer called Elwyn Jones. In the same summer Barnes and his wife took ship to the Baltic, visiting Danzig and eating hot-dogs at the open-air opera in Zoppot, while 1938 saw them driving along the Loire and down into south-west France. So, despite illnesses, wars and rumours of wars, there was still plenty of *joie de vivre* and plenty of opportunity to see some of the trouble-spots of those harassed years. Incidentally, too, the experiences and observations of his travels were put to good use in his comments on public affairs. Nor were his interests always highbrow. He much enjoyed singing, with verve but no tune, a music-hall ditty of his youth, of which the refrain ran, ' 'Ow they missed 'im when 'e'd gawn, 'ow they missed 'im when 'e'd gawn, 'ow they missed 'im when 'e'd gawn . . . and the teapot, and the alarm-clock, and the silver spoons, and the front-door knocker . . .' and so on according to one's inventive capacity. To this his wife would usually reply with a spirited rendering of 'the waiter bellowed down the hall: we don't serve bread with one fish-ball'.

This, then, was a close-knit family group. Barnes relied greatly on his wife for the infrastructure of his life and she stood up imperturbably to his occasional impatiences. He also took a constant and active interest in his sons' progress. Having never been to a boarding-school himself, he would have preferred them too to stay at home and attend day-schools. He made no secret of his view that the grammar schools ruled England and that the products of Public Schools lacked intellectual interests and social sympathies. But he accepted the difficulties of applying these strictures to his own family, especially with the busy life which he and his wife were leading, and both boys went as boarders to the Dragon School at Oxford and from there one to Winchester and the other to Westminster. He would never have admitted to any pride in their achievements, and his only comment on his elder son's scholarship at Winchester was that no doubt he would come home talking a language of 'notions' which the family would not be able to understand. But by constant admonition, as well as by organizing their foreign travel, he pushed their education forward. Whatever his political creed, he was an élitist with regard to education and constantly urged on them both the need to found their careers on first-class degrees. 'What degree did he get?' was often his first question about any man. He was particularly pleased to have his younger son in the familiar surroundings of Westminster, especially when he became Captain of the School in Coronation year and his parents went to hear him recite the prologue to the Latin Play before the King and Queen. Barnes was of course even more pleased that both boys went on to Trinity and even put on his doctor's scarlet gown to watch his elder son take his degree in 1939.

During these years too he could regularly visit his mother, who lived on at Birmingham into a serene old age until her death in 1938. He also kept in touch with his brother Stanley and gave him loyal support, notably in his creation of the Queen Elizabeth Hospitals Centre at Edgbaston, then the last word in hospital building. But Stanley, as the leading physician in Birmingham and Dean of the Medical School of the University, had his own busy life to lead and his own circle of friends and interests, particularly as a keen and successful fly-fisherman. So, although they shared some interests, such as Stock Exchange investment and the study of hereditary disease, they could not see a great deal of each other and their views, especially on politics, diverged too far for them to be really intimate. When Barnes was in London, he usually dined with his other brother, Sidney, but as neither of them wore his heart on his sleeve and as they too probably disagreed on most matters of belief, their talk was mainly confined to neutral, worldly topics.

This tendency to concentrate his personal relationships on a restricted family circle was reinforced by the nature of his life at Birmingham. It was not easy to make close personal friends: the clergy were professionally deferential and he had little time to fore-gather socially with laymen. In any case, the business of Birmingham was still business, and most of the businessmen, when they had finished making money during the day, preferred to put their feet up in carpet-slippers rather than dress for dinner. Nor was Barnes himself ever a night-bird; he told the chairman of one organization, 'You must not expect me to attend many of your meetings if you put them at 8 p.m., since by that time I am ready for dinner and bed'. There were some kindred spirits, such as Charles Grant Robertson, Vice-Chancellor of the University, who could be counted on as stimulating company for an evening. But there were few people who could challenge Barnes on his own subjects. His old Cambridge friends, who could and would have done so, were fast disappearing. They had mostly been older than himself. Arthur Benson, one of the few who used to offer candid criticism, solicited or not, had died as long ago as 1925. R. V. Laurence went in 1934, and he and Barnes had seen little of each other for some years before that. Figgis too was long since dead and Foakes Jackson exiled across the Atlantic. In any event, Barnes was now hardly ever in Cambridge; and in London, where he went mostly on business, while several of his brother-bishops were his intellectual equals, few of them could be called friends and he would not have relished an excess of ecclesiastical conversation.

All these circumstances were conducive to an increasing loneliness of spirit. He had fewer opportunities to test and refine his ideas in the crucible of other equally strong intellects. He had always been a loner and had plenty of confidence in his own judgement. But now perhaps, as his thoughts increasingly fed on themselves, his reasoning tended to lead him to more extreme conclusions. Increasingly, too, as the 1930s wore on, he seems to have developed an opposition mentality. He realised that he was often in a minority and bound to remain so, often a voice crying in the wilderness, even if, like Cassandra's, it was usually the voice of true prophecy. He could no longer hope to convert the Church establishment to his way of thinking. To those who are naturally in opposition, it becomes more important to be right than to be popular. As Gore's biographer says of him, 'to have found himself in a majority might well have caused him both discomfort and misgiving'. So too with Barnes. But, even if his conclusions were often extreme, that is not to say that they were by any means always wrong. More and more he seems to have felt a desire to challenge the conventional wisdom, or at least, the conventional ecclesiastical wisdom. What he said was always news, and this gave him plenty of welcome opportunities to provoke thought in his hearers. The trouble was that often he provoked hostility too. But even then he was not necessarily wrong.

Yet if Barnes struck discords among the band of bishops, he was not always out of tune with public opinion. It was not for nothing that in 1938 *The Spectator* could say that he had the ear of the lay public more than any of his colleagues. Popular interest was growing, for example, in the reform of the marriage and divorce laws. The Church was naturally under pressure to make its position clear. So in 1931 Convocation had appointed a Joint Committee on Marriage, with the particular task of applying the conclusions of the 1930 Lambeth Conference. Barnes was appointed to the Committee and, within it, to the Sub-Committee on Nullity, Divorce and related subjects. He made it his special task to ensure that the Committee was provided with expert advice on the eugenic aspects, as they affected not only the merits of a marriage before it took place but also the grounds on which it might eventually be dissolved. He was also determined that the legal advice given to the Committee should not represent only one school of churchmanship. To this end he kept in touch with recognized liberal authorities, including Buckmaster, the President, and Geikie-Cobb, the Chairman, of the Marriage Law Reform League, and other experts such as Claud Mullins, the metropolitan magistrate, and Herbert Gray, the Nonconformist minister. When the Joint Committee reported to Convocation in 1935, the majority of its members recognized that it would be impossible to oppose all or any extension of the grounds for divorce and wrong to exclude divorced persons without exception from Holy Communion; but basing themselves on the indissolubility of Christian marriage, they insisted that the Church could not overtly endorse the remarriage of anyone who had been divorced. Barnes, alone among the Bishops, and supported by only two non-episcopal members of the Committee, advocated the minority view that only the guilty party to a divorce should be refused a second marriage in church. Then, and throughout the controversy, he argued that divorce with the right of remarriage must at times be allowed. Divorce was an unhappy necessity. He would do nothing to make it easier without good cause. In particular, like all other bishops, he would not agree to the ordination of a divorced man. But if the State allowed divorce, the Church could not absolutely oppose it, however unsatisfactory the Church thought it. Moreover, the State should certainly enlarge the grounds for divorce. For example, the inheritability of mental defect posed for him the question whether a marriage in which one partner was found to be feeble-minded or suffering from venereal disease, and to have concealed the fact, ought to be allowed to last. Indeed, such cases might call for sterilization as well as divorce. But he took his stand on wider ethical principles too. Certainly, divorcees should not be excommunicated; here he fully endorsed the view that it would be wrong 'to fence the altar'. As he put it in 1937,

Does it harm me if I know that a man who has done wrong in the past goes to Communion with me? I am not so perfect that I can condemn others. Admission to Communion is a confession of need of moral help, not a certificate of moral excellence.

This he applied to the guilty as well as the innocent party to a divorce. As to remarriage after divorce, he did not agree that it was necessarily unchristian. Of course, a lifelong union was the ideal. But Christ was a prophet, not a lawgiver. He had set principles; His followers must apply them as best they could. There had been divorces among the early Christians, and after the Reformation the Church had accepted divorce for adultery and had not imposed an absolute ban on re-marriage. In any case, he maintained that on these matters the Gospel of St Matthew more correctly recorded the teaching of Jesus than the Gospel of St Mark; indeed, he was convinced that teaching other than Christ's might well have been ascribed to Him even by Mark writing thirty-five years after the crucifixion. Barnes could not therefore accept that someone who had, through no fault of his or her own, had to bring to an end an intolerable marriage, should be debarred from again finding happiness in marriage. While he continued to advise against the remarriage in church of people guilty of adultery, and while he recognized that collusion could lead to doubts about guilt, he thought it lacking in social understanding on the Church's part to deny a church marriage to the innocent party, particularly when poor people were involved. Such absence of charity could only encourage irregular unions. He could not, in his official capacity, insist on the right of divorced people to remarriage in church, while the Church of England remained formally opposed. If officially consulted he could only indicate that, after a civil cere-mony, the couple could come to church, with a few relations or friends, to have their marriage quietly blessed. But in practice he made clear that the remarriage of divorced persons was a matter for the discretion of individual clergy; he allowed marriage licences to be issued for innocent parties to divorce suits, once their decree absolute was served; and he was even prepared in private to give the name of a clergyman known to be ready to perform such marriages.

These discussions came to a head with the presentation to Parliament of A. P. Herbert's Marriage Bill, of which Herbert himself has told the story in his book *Holy Deadlock*. Lang, seeing himself in a cleft stick as churchman and statesman, refused either to support or oppose the bill and would have liked his brother bishops to follow his example. This, in fact, was the line he took in the House of Lords in June 1937. But Barnes, while admitting privately that the Arch-bishop's speech was 'a dexterous way out of a difficult situation' was not to be muzzled into temporizing. Indeed, he would no doubt have applied to this occasion the aphorism which he attributed to Canon Streeter: 'The fact that the ark rested on Mount Ararat is no reason why the leaders of the Church of England should always sit on the fence.' He himself made a strong speech in favour of the bill, after receiving advice from A.P.H. himself, refusing to adopt Lang's view of it as a concession to human frailty, but commending it positively as a measure 'in accordance with the spirit of Christ'. He only regretted that the provision for conciliation of married couples had been dropped. *En passant*, he took the opportunity to urge the appointment of some women divorce judges, just as he was ready to advocate the consecration of women as bishops. At the Committee stage, too, he again differed from Lang in arguing the case for insanity as a ground for divorce. It was not surprising that Low produced a cartoon with Colonel Blimp declaring: 'Gad, sir, A. P.

Herbert is right. The Archbishop of Canterbury ought to be pad-
locked to the Bishop of Birmingham for five years, just to see how
he'd like it.' In *Punch*, Bernard Partridge depicted Barnes and Henson
giving the infant bill a fatherly helping hand up the steps of the
Non-Ideal Home Exhibition with the admonition to 'come along
and be a little ray of sunshine in there'. When the bill passed into
law, Barnes described it as 'a valuable piece of social legislation' and
joined in the tributes to A. P. Herbert as 'the man who with signal
ability sponsored it through Parliament'. Herbert responded that
'without the support in the Church of such courageous prelates as
yourself, I do not think that we should have done what we did'. On

Episcopal Aid

Bishops of Durham and Birmingham 'Now come along and be a little ray
of sunshine in there.'

this occasion, for once, Barnes was on the side of the big battalions.

But he acted on his own in a sequel to this drama. First, he had new instructions printed in his Diocesan Kalendar to make clear that, although the clergy could not be compelled to marry a divorced person, they were at liberty to marry innocent parties, including those who had obtained a divorce on the grounds of the other spouse's insanity. Licences would not be issued for the marriage in church of guilty parties, but even they could have their marriage blessed in church if the clergyman concerned was satisfied that their motives were truly religious and provided the service was a small, family affair, not a social occasion. He brought these new instructions deliberately to the notice of the press and the Archbishop, without adverse reaction. But, secondly, he went further than this. He had long held that it was wrong for the Church to forbid marriage to a 'deceased wife's sister' when the State had allowed it since 1907, and he had urged revision of the tables of affinity in the Prayer Book on this and other grounds. But he had felt legally bound to accept the Church's position and tell his clergy not to solemnize such marriages. He was therefore delighted when, in 1939, the new Chancellor of the Diocese was able to give him fresh advice that marriage to a deceased wife's sister could rightly take place in church. This was based on the ground that the Canon Law of the Church was only valid if it did not conflict with the law of the land; since the law of the land now allowed marriage with a deceased wife's sister, the prohibition by Canon Law was no longer valid. Barnes therefore issued a public statement to apprise his clergy of the Chancellor's interpretation of the law. Not surprisingly, perhaps, the *Church Times* objected and Lang promptly intervened once more. The Archbishop wrote to complain that the tables of affinity were being considered by a special committee with a view to action by the Lambeth Conference of 1940; he asked if Barnes would withdraw his statement to the newspapers and treat the matter as something for his own diocese only. But when Barnes explained that his advice to his clergy was simply permissive, the Archbishop did not press the point, and one of the first bride-grooms to profit from this relaxation was the Provost of Birmingham Cathedral. Barnes himself officiated at the wedding.

Strongly as he felt on both morals and peace, he could treat both subjects in lighter vein if he wanted to put his views across. Thus in 1937, when he invited St John Ervine to address the Diocesan Conference on Christianity and the New Morality, he intervened in the discussion to deplore the way in which the death of men in war upset the balance of numbers between the sexes and thus encouraged immorality:

> To avoid sex immorality you must get rid of such wars as impair the balance of the sexes. From the point of view of sexual morality in the future, the aeroplane is valuable in that it destroys men and women in equal numbers. It is possible, too, now that the old lady has learned to drive a motor-car, that it will be found that she can be put in the trenches instead of the young man. When word comes by wireless that the enemy is going over the top, the old lady in the trenches, with her hot-water bottle and air-cushion, will advance, adjust her spectacles to the periscope and, at the appropriate moment, touch a button that will fire a battery of machine-guns in her charge. The enemy will be repulsed. If we have a development of that kind, the war may not lead to disorderly sex morality.

He hastened to add that he was not advocating even that kind of war.

Barnes also played an individualistic part in the events preceding the abdication of King Edward VIII in 1936. Perhaps unwittingly he helped to light the fuse which led to it. In a sermon at the Chapel Royal on 1 November, he expressed the personal view that the Coronation Service proper would be better separated from the celebration of the Holy Communion which had previously been an integral part of the ceremony. This would, he thought, give the Coronation a wider national appeal and, incidentally, allow leaders of the Free Churches, including those without sacraments, to take part in it. He particularly mentioned General Evangeline Booth of the Salvation Army, with the Army's concern for the condition of the poor, and reminded his hearers of the signs of the King's own apparent interest in social welfare. This at once produced from Lang a long letter which he described as a 'friendly expostulation'. With his customary self-pity he complained that, while Barnes could speak 'with more freedom than responsibility', he himself could not. He wished that Barnes had consulted him first; but, although he was 'inundated by requests' to comment, he could not make any public reply. He had told the Free Churches that they could not take part in the Coronation and had promised them a letter for publication. Now Barnes's proposals had complicated the situation and there might be an agitation. Already General Booth had written to the Archbishop, who did not think the Free Churches or Church of

Scotland would favour her inclusion. He added 'very confidentially':

> Your sermon may embarrass my relations with the King himself. His temperament predisposes him to be restive about these religious obligations, and if your suggestions were to reach him they might, for all I know, disturb the present most satisfactory relations which I have had with him with regard to the Coronation.

In the light of other published accounts of relations between the two men, this last remark was perhaps less than frank. Barnes replied that the genesis of his sermon was an approach by one of his clergy, who said that he and others disliked any appearance of compulsion over reception of the Sacrament. 'There is, it appears, a widespread belief that the King does not normally make the Holy Communion a part of his religious life. If the belief is founded in fact, the compulsion is, or so it was put to me, "intolerable".' He went on to say that he had found Free Churchmen eager to take part in the Coronation. If they did so, this should make easier the negotiations for reunion. There were obvious reasons why it would be difficult for them to take part in the service of Holy Communion. That was why he concluded that the Coronation should be put in a new setting. He had made clear that he was speaking for himself alone; but he believed his views were widely shared and enclosed a couple of newspaper cuttings as evidence. He urged that the Archbishop could 'ignore my intervention as intrusive and irrelevant, and, should the King approve, state that the Coronation would be independent of the service of Holy Communion'. 'The nation is supremely interested in the Coronation. To free it from any suspicion of religious exclusiveness or of religious unreality would, I am convinced, do much good.'

Although Barnes did not say so to the Archbishop, he had already received a letter from the Moderator of the Free Church Council warmly thanking him for his sermon. Lang, for his part, refused to be mollified or to argue the matter. He also refused to 'take the responsibility for altering what has been an essential feature of the Rite for centuries'.

> I need scarcely add very privately that the King's personal position with regard to this matter is one that gives me great concern. But he has in this respect as you well know a constitutional position not merely as an individual but as the representative of the nation. My responsibilities

in connection with this whole matter are very grave. Though I thank you for your letter I must admit that your sermon has not made these responsibilities easier to bear.

This hardly agrees with Lang's earlier reference to his satisfactory relations with the King. But there, as far as Barnes was concerned, the matter rested. Then on 1 December came the famous speech by Bishop Blunt of Bradford to his diocesan conference, in which he reasserted the link between the Coronation and the Communion Service, emphasized the need for a recall of the nation to religion and seized the opportunity to complain of the King's lack of interest in the religious side of his office. This was the key which unlocked the flood gates of publicity, brought the King's private life into the public domain and led directly to the events culminating in the abdication. The Bishop of Bradford was described as Blunt by name and blunt by nature. He was later to assert that his speech had been composed six weeks earlier and in ignorance of the rumours about the King's personal affairs. On the face of it, this can hardly be true. The speech was manifestly a riposte to Barnes, a continuation of the sacramental controversy between the Bishop of Birmingham and his brethren. In the second paragraph, after speaking of the Coronation as 'a solemn sacramental rite, linked up as an integral part in a service of Holy Communion', Blunt continued:

> The Bishop of Birmingham has indeed suggested that this connection might be severed. Such an action might well suit those who regard all sacramental ordinances as effete superstition. It would certainly minister to a derogatory view of the Holy Communion Service.

He then developed his argument. But Barnes's sermon had only been preached a month, and not six weeks, before Blunt's speech. If Blunt did not know about Mrs Simpson six weeks before he spoke, he must have known by 17 November when Lang held a meeting to acquaint the bishops with the situation and consider whether circumstances were ideal for the issue of the planned Recall to Religion. The Bishop of Bradford's sensibilities must have been very blunt if he still did not realise the import of his words. Lang's biographer denies that the Archbishop instigated Blunt's speech or was privy to it. As far as the personal comment on the King is concerned, this may be true. But in view of Lang's exchange with

Barnes earlier in November, it is at least likely that the Archbishop may have prompted Blunt to reply to Barnes's proposals. It is significant that another Archbishop eleven years later was to put up the same Bishop of Bradford to conduct an argument with the same Bishop of Birmingham. If so, Blunt may perhaps have exceeded his instructions on this occasion.

Whatever others may have hoped or contrived, Barnes was certainly not put up to say what he did. Nor did he have any intention of publicly criticizing the King or trying to promote his abdication. His concern was simply with the religious aspect. Indeed, on 4 December he strongly endorsed the Archbishop's appeal that there should be no reference to the crisis in Sunday sermons and urged the diocese to offer special prayers for the King and his ministers. Although he did not condone the moral side and came to accept that abdication was the only solution, his sympathy for the King, whose social interests he had, like others, probably overestimated, remained strong. When the abdication came, he described it as 'high tragedy' and said that for the former King personally 'there is much sympathy, for an Englishman is not a Pharisee, nor is he a harsh judge'. This compares with the notorious broadcast in which Lang censoriously condemned the King and his friends. In the true Greek sense, tragedy it certainly was. But Blunt appeared more as a figure of comedy. Lang's chorus too was widely criticized and the storm of protest which his broadcast aroused may well have contributed to his cautious attitude over marriage and divorce in the debates on the Herbert bill the next year.

Despite the tragedy of the abdication, Barnes greatly enjoyed the next year's Coronation, for which, for the first time in his life, he bought himself a purple cassock. So much so, in fact, that shortly afterwards, to his wife's astonishment, he put himself down for a levee, where he would wear the purple cassock again. He even went so far as to ask Lang to present him, although the Archbishop excused himself as he was presiding over Church Assembly at the time.

A happier story concerns the renewed appeal for church extension in new housing areas of the Birmingham diocese which the Bishop launched early in 1935. The 1920s and 1930s had seen a great expansion of the city, in terms of geography if not of population. Between 1921 and 1938 over 94,000 houses were built in Birmingham, of which nearly 83,000 were in the outer suburbs. By 1935, therefore, 300,000 people were living in these areas, with few churches to serve them, and the appeal was therefore aimed at the ambitious target of 100,000 guineas or, for those no longer familiar with that currency, £105,000. Over two years were to pass before the target was achieved; but achieved it was in October 1937, thanks largely to determined leadership by Barnes himself, indefatigable work by J. C. Lucas, an incumbent who was transferred from his parish to be a Canon and full-time secretary of the appeal, and vigorous support from a body of laymen headed by Ernest Canning, who most appropriately became Lord Mayor just as the appeal succeeded. Barnes had long thought that Birmingham was over-centralized and growing in a disorderly way and that it would be better to develop it systematically as a mother-city with daughter-towns grouped around her. To some extent this was happening as the population moved out from the centre to peripheral districts. This, together with the growth of education and emancipation of the young, obviously called for new approaches by the Church. If the younger inhabitants of the new areas, in particular, were not to become totally secularized, the services of the Church must be brought to them and in modern forms which they could accept. They could no longer be expected to travel long distances to attend old-fashioned ceremonies in traditional buildings. This was the broad philosophy which underlay Barnes's determination to make a success of the appeal. The Church in Birmingham was for him the Church of the poor and must remain so; her resources must be devoted to their service and welfare. His personal enthusiasm for this cause, dogged though he was by illness at the time, soon became known to city and diocese. He organized a series of public meetings, bringing distinguished speakers from outside to second his efforts. Even Lang put controversy aside and made a generous speech to a large meeting in the spring of 1936. Barnes and his wife contributed £1000 at the outset and £500 more in April 1937, when the last £10,000 seemed to be hanging fire and a final heave was needed. Generous gifts came from individuals outside the diocese and, indeed, outside the Church. Lord Nuffield subscribed £5000, and Barnes was particularly touched one day to find on the doormat a yellow envelope containing a cheque for £1000 pushed through the letter-box by a Quaker Cadbury. Meanwhile the clergy were made to realise that their efforts should be concentrated on the appeal and that the dead, for example, should be commemorated by gifts to the new areas, not by the beautification of old churches. One incumbent has recorded how he unwisely asked the

Bishop to come and dedicate an oak screen in memory of the last vicar, only to receive the reply: 'Certainly not. At a time when the Diocese is straining every nerve to build new churches, you have been raising money for a sheer luxury, the oak screen. It is scandalous'. But soon afterwards the same incumbent received a telephone call: 'For a long time we have been trying to get you on the telephone but you have always been engaged. I can only surmise that you have been busy ringing up your brethren warning them of the danger of putting luxuries into their churches'; the purpose of the call was to appoint him Rural Dean. By such methods success was assured, and Barnes had the satisfaction of inaugurating several of the new buildings erected through the appeal. In fact fifteen new churches were erected in Birmingham between 1928 and 1939, all but one of them over three miles from the city centre. True to his principles, they were not to be neo-Gothic edifices dedicated to saints, but multi-purpose church halls called after favourite sons of the Birmingham Church, such as Bishop Westcott, Archbishop Benson and Charles Gore. Nor must they slavishly follow conventional forms of worship. While Barnes was always careful to make clear that he could not authorize departures from the Book of Common Prayer, he asserted at the same time: 'I do not feel called upon publicly to protest against such departures from the authorized liturgy as involve no change of doctrine and would be practically certain to receive the sanction of Parliament.' In other words of his, he saw no need to insist on formularies which would be 'mumbo-jumbo to the average Church worker in an industrial parish'.

Now too, for the first time since his arrival at Birmingham, changes had to come about in the diocesan general staff. Barnes had been singularly lucky in having as his closest associates men who, despite differing views, were not only loyal to him personally but ready to soldier on indefinitely. But some of them were now old men. In 1937, Hamilton Baynes, aged eighty-three and a bishop for forty-four years, resigned as Provost of the Cathedral. Having once taken a first in Greats and possessed of an old-world courtesy of manner, he had filled his office with quiet distinction. To succeed him, Barnes appointed J. H. Richards, hitherto Archdeacon of Aston and already sixty-eight years old. Richards was a capable administrator who had also served Barnes loyally; the other Archdeacon, Hopton of Birmingham, was in some ways a stronger personality, but at seventy-six years of age could not expect further preferment. To the vacant Archdeaconry Barnes would have liked to appoint his former diocesan secretary, S. D. Morris, if Morris, who was an exceptionally able administrator, would give up his work for the Peace Pledge Union. Other pacifists urged that he should be allowed to plough both furrows in double harness, but Barnes realised from the start that this could not be defended. Later events were to prove how right he was. Instead he picked as Archdeacon of Aston Harry McGowan, one of the most effective incumbents in the diocese, later to be Bishop of Wakefield. As Hamilton Baynes had been able to act not only as Provost but also as Assistant Bishop, Barnes appointed J. H. Linton, who had been Rector of Handsworth since 1935, to succeed him in the second capacity. Linton had been a notably successful Bishop in Persia for sixteen years and, though badly hampered by deafness, had impressed Barnes with his evangelistic flair.

At all times, Barnes was determined to find the best man for the job, irrespective of his exact type of churchmanship. Anglo-Catholics were by no means excluded, provided they were loyal to their vows and to the Prayer Book. Archdeacon Hopton, for example, was a strong High Churchman, but his relations with the Bishop were always excellent. The appointment of Lucas, another Anglo-Catholic, to run the Church Extension appeal was also a case in point. Later too there were examples of men appointed or approached even less in sympathy with the Bishop's viewpoint, but welcome none the less for their capacity and character. Barnes always pretended to dislike administration; but, whether this was true or not, he applied himself to it with consistent efficiency. He held fast to certain principles. He always used to say that the only disqualification for a job was to ask for it; and he spoke scathingly of a certain Canon of St Paul's whose footsteps, whenever a bishopric was vacant, could be recognized in Downing Street. Barnes refused to ordain or accept in the diocese any candidate without a university degree. He recognized that the clergy must increasingly be recruited from a wider social background, which he often described by the painful phrase 'the lower middle classes', but was not willing to relax the educational qualification. Even so, he often had difficulty in finding men who could afford to take the jobs offered to them. These were days when £50 a year of so-called 'private means' could make all the difference for a clergyman between poverty and survival; there were no minimum salaries and no equalization of stipends. For conditions in Birmingham, too, he also had to reject men whom he thought too old and reluctantly he had to refuse to employ blind clergy. There came a time as well when he decided that, while he had nothing against Welshmen in principle, the diocese already seemed to have its full quota of them. His wife used to tell the story of a garden-party when, the guests having been invited alphabetically, she kept up with twelve Joneses shaking hands in succession. Ecclesiastically, however, this was better than the Bishop's secretary finding herself introducing Mr Lomas to Mr Hymas. Eucharistic differences were not always so easily bridged.

Barnes's standards were high, and he could sometimes seem intolerant. Partly, this was due to sheer pressure of work and, when his curtness in letters gave offence, as it often did, he could be quick and generous to make amends, even apologizing to an argumentative 'rebel' who had scored a valid point. He was less patient with sententious bores, of whom there were not a few, who were inclined to preach at him on general moral principles, no doubt with the best of intentions. While he treated his intellectual equals with a certain wary respect, however sharp their disagreements, he did at times with others expose himself to accusations of a lack of human sympathy. Even some of his fellow-bishops resented what they saw as his 'superior' attitude and a tendency to lecture them as if they were all scientific ignoramuses. These were times when much more was put in writing than would be the case today, and Barnes's epistolary style was formal even for those days. The telephone has its drawbacks; but it is easier to forget than the written word. *Littera scripta manet.* Both Barnes and his correspondents were often strangely quick to take offence. Great as the provocation to him frequently was, he would sometimes have done better to sleep on it. His motto was 'Do it now', which he interpreted as meaning 'answer by return'; but he was not always wise to act on it. Even so, when he thought a man honest and sincere, whatever his churchmanship, he would go to great pains to help him in his career. Despite the 'rebels' ' deliberate estrangement from him, he kept himself informed of their personal circumstances and was quick to show active sympathy in cases of ill-health or bereavement. For example, he greatly valued his right to nominate to some country livings in other dioceses, where *otium cum dignitate* could be offered to the tired incumbents of Birmingham slum parishes. His judgement was not infallible: sometimes his swans proved to be geese, if not actually black sheep. But when so many were disloyal, he can hardly be blamed for doing his best to reward loyalty where he saw it. He was naturally distressed that there seemed to be such a strong prejudice against modernists; in 1937, he quoted the dictum that 'when a modernist's name is suggested for important office in the Church, the reply comes: "if he is below the age of fifty-five, his views are dangerous; if he is above that age, he is too old to be a successful administrator".' He was no dog in the manger and was quite ready to see his own stars rise in other firmaments. Guy Rogers, for example, the Rector of Birmingham, who was a tower of strength in city and diocese and who saw eye to eye with his Bishop on many matters social and ecclesiastical, could with Barnes's approval have become either Dean or colonial Archbishop, and was indeed more than once considered for an English diocese, but preferred to stay in Birmingham. The *Church Times* and others liked to depict the unhappy state of affairs in the Birmingham diocese; but they spoke for a small and recalcitrant minority. From most of his clergy, as well as from lay churchpeople, Barnes commanded undoubted respect and no little affection. After twelve years of man-management, he was probably justified in 1936 in claiming that 'it is well-known that both socially and intellectually the Church in Birmingham can successfully challenge comparison with work done by Church teachers and leaders in any other part of the country'.

One other important change took place at this time. Hansell, Chancellor of the Diocese and long a spiky thorn in Barnes's modernist flesh, died in 1937. He had clung to office, exercising partial jurisdiction and refusing to resign ten years earlier, as his legal colleagues expected, when he was appointed a Master in the Supreme Court. Now Barnes was free to appoint a Chancellor of his own choice and, what was more, to ensure that the new Chancellor would work in harmony with his Bishop's wishes. No longer, for example, would licences be automatically refused for the remarriage of divorced persons in church; nor would faculties be granted for pyxes and aumbries where reservation could be made easy. On this aspect and on the selection of a man, Barnes once more had valuable help from Dashwood. He himself would have liked his old friend Francis Newbolt, but Newbolt's health was failing fast. Stafford Cripps also declined, on the surprising ground that he had no degree. On Dashwood's advice, seconded by Errington, Barnes then approached William Cleveland-Stevens, an Old Westminster of Lincoln's Inn, who readily accepted and gave him strong and devoted support for the rest of his episcopate.

Church extension was only one of the ways in which he saw the life and growth of the diocese as indissolubly linked with the development of the city. He kept up excellent relations with the civic authorities of all parties and was in constant demand at city or business functions, sometimes *ex officio* to give grace or blessing, but often as an after-dinner speaker in his personal capacity. Postprandial oratory is usually ephemeral. But one example can perhaps be quoted, at an accountants' dinner:

> I have no right to be here tonight. I am a mathematician. I try also to be a theologian but my claims are impugned by some of my critics. All my life I have suffered from the mathematician's traditional inability to do arithmetic. I have never mastered that ingenious process called book-keeping by double entry . . . Of course the income-tax authorities do their best to spread the art of amateur accountancy among the general population. Once a year I am bathed in honest perspiration as I endeavour to avoid six months' imprisonment and treble the duty chargeable: I believe that constitutes the penalty. My labours completed, I send the result to a professional accountant, who tells me that my income for last year is partly what I received the year before last and partly something else. He also tells me that my wife's income is mine, a proposition I should not venture to put to her in that crude form. Then the income-tax people do the sum differently, but always to my disadvantage, and finally I pay the price of civilization . . . I sometimes wonder what Dr Einstein would make of an income-tax return.

And so on. Incidentally, he often had to appear at one of the many royal visits to Birmingham and used to say that royal personages always made a bee-line for him; they knew who he must be, because he was wearing gaiters.

His enquiring and free-ranging mind still led him during these years to express idiosyncratic views on many subjects. In Church affairs, while sacramental differences aroused less public controversy, the main difference between Barnes and those who disagreed with him continued to be that they were primarily ecclesiastical politicians, who set the collective interest of the Church, obedience to established authority and respect for other people's feelings above the need, as Barnes saw it, to proclaim the truth irrespective of the consequences. These were two different sets of values and led to complaints from other bishops that he was forcing the pace and encouraging a party spirit within the Church. But he was going strongly for the high ground when many of his colleagues and contemporaries were casting fearful glances down the backstairs of the Church of England. Too many of them instinctively set out to blur distinctions in order to facilitate administration or, to put the best face on it, to preserve unity. Where others tried to invent compromises, Barnes's mathematical mind drove him to define alternatives, although he was always seeking unity on the proper intellectual basis. He would say that 'when an unpalatable truth is put before a religious partisan, he shuts his eyes and closes his ears'. On his critics, he commented 'if you have no defence, abuse the plaintiffs' attorney' and he warned that one 'should always verify statements by ecclesiastics on subjects of controversy'.

Even so, he reserved many of his more progressive or provocative statements for private correspondence, as when he expressed his readiness to receive Communion from Free Church ministers or asserted that there was nothing incompatible between Christianity and freemasonry. But his public statements were often advanced enough. He continued openly to advocate cremation when it was still anathema to religious conservatives: he justified it on grounds of both land use and public health, and affirmed that it was accepted by those who believed in the resurrection, although he advised that the ashes should be buried in a church or churchyard and not just scattered to the winds. On eugenic questions, too, he was growing more outspoken. He not only spoke positively of the chances of breeding new types of human beings. He made clear in private that he now thought there were cases where the termination of pregnancy was justifiable and he stated publicly in an Oxford University Sermon that it was wrong 'to keep alive individuals whom doctors know to be doomed from birth to a sub-human existence'. This last pronouncement, which was of course more concerned with euthanasia than abortion, not surprisingly evoked another of Lang's requests for an explanation. Barnes took the opportunity in reply to point to the gulf which he feared was widening between Church and people on problems of population, and euthanasia in particular, largely because of the silence of the Church's leaders. He appealed in effect for leadership from the Archbishop, who however declined further combat and brought the correspondence to a hasty close.

For this was a time when many were preoccupied by the problem of relations between the individual and the community. Such thoughts were sharpened by the growing conflict between democracy and totalitarianism. Barnes had consistently worked for a positive attitude towards Soviet Russia. This went back to his relations with Ramsay MacDonald and his support for that Prime Minister's decision to resume diplomatic relations with the new Russia. In 1937, he was the only Bishop to support the National Congress for Peace and Friendship with the USSR and, while deploring Soviet atheism, he drew attention to the lessons which the industrial West could learn from social progress in Russia. But at the same time he made clear his view that Russia, too, could learn from the West, for example, how to achieve freedom, especially religious freedom, without anarchy. At a time when many English intellectuals were falling over each other to unite with the Russians in a populist heaven, Barnes was no collectivist. Society was of course important; but the individual was in the end more important still. Nor was he a Marxist determinist. The spirit had not come to reside in the machine. He believed in the power of mind over matter. He believed that man was the maker of events and not their product. In scientific terms, he believed in establishing the eugenic and hygienic environment in which the heir to the right heredity could flourish. In a way he believed that there is a spirit of the age and that man reacts to the needs of his situation. But man should not just be trying to reflect the Zeitgeist; he should be reshaping it in his own image, in fact re-forming it. The need for reform is the historical necessity for the individual. Mutations make the man for the moment.

These were not, and would not have been, Barnes's own words. But beliefs of this kind coloured not only his approach to the international situation but his domestic political statements too. He begged Christians to stand aloof from unhealthy material enjoyment. Although he refused to join in a campaign against nude statues in the Birmingham streets, he remained a stern sexual moralist and condemned the spread of what he called 'semi-popular, semi-scientific' sex books. Already he was advocating industrial co-partnership and declaring that business should not challenge the principle of redistributive taxation. Now indeed he was convinced of the need for strong trade unions; this was a far cry from his earlier fears of 'syndicalism' and of the dangers of workingmen being advised to withhold their labour for politico-economic purposes. Even in 1937, he openly expressed the view that, while electricity and transport should be nationalized before banks and insurance companies, nationalization would surely come and should take the form of public corporations like the BBC or the London Passenger Transport Board. In 1938 too he forecast that death duties would encompass the end of stately homes, except for such of them as might be preserved as museums. All this was the shape of things to come.

In more mundane matters, too, he looked forward, welcoming Basic English and awaiting the all-electric house. Science always fascinated him and, as he told a convivial audience, 'I like the company of men of science: they are not excessively intellectual in their hours of leisure and they give good dinners'. In similar light-hearted vein, he could suggest that the Church Pastoral Aid Society would be better renamed Curates Unlimited or, addressing an audience of Free Churchmen, could draw the picture of a Lord Bishop a century earlier visiting dissenters 'with an air of determined affability... and perhaps an unconscious sniff', and evoke the prospect, a hundred years hence, of the Midland Commissioner for Cultural Development, a member of the Upper Proletarian House, descending in a magnificent motor on the Amalgamated English Ethical Societies, while comparing both images with his own easy relations with the Birmingham Nonconformists. All good Cambridge Union fun, but serious all the same. His close contacts with Free Churchmen in the city, such as Leyton Richards, Benson Perkins, Rossington and H. G. Wood, not only strengthened his position with the civic authorities but also gave him much personal satisfaction, not least because several of them shared his pacifist position.

For all these varied activities were overshadowed by the relentless approach of another war. From Hitler's first advent to power, Barnes had been torn between his hatred of the Nazis' methods and his deep desire to avoid an armed conflict with them. His attitude to Germany differed from his attitude to Russia. Russia was no immediate threat. The risk of war with Germany was real. So, much as he hated the sin, he felt that he had to show love for the sinner. Thus he denounced the brutality and injustice of Nazi policies, he deplored the neo-paganism which worshipped a German God, and he detested the Nazi persecution of the Confessional Church, little as he liked its theology. Nor did his criticisms spare other authoritarian régimes. He was particularly scathing over the *Te Deum* sung in Italian churches for the Abyssinian victory: 'We praise thee,

O God, for incendiary bombs and poison gas.' He joined in a letter of protest in *The Times* against the Austrian Government's trial of socialists for high treason. But he continued to plead that dislike of German policies must be subordinated to the search for a new and peaceful international system. Already in 1930 he had written to a German correspondent of his fear that the reactionaries would gain power in Germany. He had long thought that this would be the ultimate effect of the Versailles Treaty and refused to add his signature to that of Lloyd George in a letter to the press because 'I cannot associate myself with the man who was Prime Minister when the Treaty of Versailles was signed'. But his suspicions were not confined to the past. In 1932 he wrote in a private letter:

> France is the villain of the piece. Our own Foreign Office policy ties us to France, and Simon apparently is not willing to make a break with the past . . . The situation is less menacing now that France is so far from balancing her budget. May the confusion of her finances become worse confounded.

So when the Nazis did come to power, he had, as early as 1933, urged that there should not be a boycott of German goods but a move towards general disarmament. In 1935, he declared that competition in arms would end in war; even the risks of unilateral disarmament were worth taking. His strictures were directed particularly at the failure to abandon air bombing as a military option and this brought him into renewed newspaper controversy with Austen Chamberlain and Thelma Cazalet over the British Government's part in that failure. This was during the 1935 General Election, and Government spokesmen were naturally sensitive to criticism. Barnes had used the occasion of a memorial service to Arthur Henderson to accuse the British Government of causing the failure of the Disarmament Conference. When Thelma Cazalet attacked him for inaccuracy, he stood his ground, quoting at length from Philip Noel-Baker, who had been Henderson's secretary at the time. This brought in the big guns of Austen Chamberlain, who accused him of *odium theologicum* and of using his cathedral for party ends, and who asserted that the government had made clear that, if the reservation for police purposes was the only obstacle to air disarmament, it would be withdrawn; but it had not proved to be so. Barnes, who was by now confined to bed, wrote another long reply, in which he made effective use of Londonderry's admission in May 1935, that he had, as Air Minister, had 'the utmost difficulty at that time, amid the public outcry, in preserving the use of the bombing aeroplane'. Anthony Eden, as the responsible Minister, now intervened to accuse Barnes of 'episcopal error' and to claim that the British reservation had no effect on the course of the Disarmament Conference; its only importance had lain in party politics at home. Barnes then wrote a final letter to *The Times*, charging the British Government with withdrawing the reservation only conditionally and too late, and with acting from expediency rather than principle. The letter closed, 'Hence, the countries of Western Europe are building bombing planes against one another. The end must be disastrous'. So it was. During the election, the Labour Party made great play with the same theme, recalling Baldwin's remark of 1932 that 'the bomber will always get through', and after the election, incidentally, Londonderry lost his place in the government.

This controversy, also incidentally, arose before the Germans and Russians began to test their military aircraft in the Spanish civil war, and when Franco's forces did start to bomb Basque towns, Barnes was not slow to join in the protests. But he also argued more positively for world ownership of aviation, perhaps under the League of Nations. Meanwhile, from similar motives, he was calling for the international inspection and control of colonies. His belief in the beneficent virtues of the British Empire was now much less sanguine than it had been twenty or thirty years before. In December 1935, while he opposed the Hoare-Laval Pact, he urged the British Government to seize the opportunity for a new initiative over Africa as a whole. Despite his attitude over the North-West Frontier, in 1930 he was presciently writing: 'I believe it wrong for one nation to impose its will upon another. Yet, were we at once to withdraw from India, chaos accompanied by much suffering and injustice would arise.'

From the start at Birmingham Barnes had refused to take any part in occasions of a military nature, in which he even included gatherings interested in the welfare of ex-servicemen only rather than the community as a whole. As he told a correspondent in 1939,

My refusal to take part in any religious service of a military character is no new thing. Early in August 1914 I tried to give an address at such

346

a service; but I realised at once that for myself war could not be combined with the religion of Christ. Since that time I have never been at
any military function.

Thus he nailed his colours to the mast of absolute pacifism and took
a prominent part in many pacifist movements and societies. But he
took care not to become associated with what he saw as unwise
moves and often warned his friends not to overdo it and weaken
their case by fruitless repetition. If the same group always took
action, it would also run the risk of showing what a small minority
it was. Timing was important too: in 1931, for example, he advised
against letters to the press on pacifism when people were preoccupied
with the financial and economic crisis. Even in 1931 he still refused
publicly to advocate total and immediate unilateral disarmament,
although his willingness to do so increased as war drew nearer. He
also refused to approve statements that pacifists would give no
support to a war, since this would mean a refusal to pay taxes and
would be impracticable or indefensible. Nor, rather more surprisingly,
would he condemn shareholdings in firms such as ICI, International
Nickel or even Vickers, who were not exclusively engaged in armament manufacture.

But on the main issue he remained absolutely firm. 'War is utterly
demoralizing. Despite heroism and sacrifice, there go with it filth,
lies, cruelty and lust.' War preparations would make war inevitable.
It was to his mind essential to witness constantly to peace. So he
did consent to sign many pacifist collective documents. This was a
great age for manifestoes, deputations, round-robins and joint
letters to the press. Even though he distrusted *The Times*'s policy
and its unwillingness to print letters on pacifism any more than on
modernism, Barnes joined in the bombardment. As he wrote to
Margery Fry about a proposed telegram in 1936: 'It would be most
injudicious of me to add my signature to those of "leading Englishmen" who may sign. But as I am the only injudicious Bishop on the
bench, I suppose I had better do it.' His usual response was to say
that if certain like-minded people, such as Gilbert Murray or H. G.
Wells, agreed to sign, his own signature could be appended too.
Moreover, as he told Guy Rogers the same year: 'It looks as though
Europe is drifting into war and irretrievable disaster. Whatever we
can do to avert such a catastrophe is at the moment more important
than directly religious activities.'

347

Thus, he joined in August 1936, in a letter to *The Times* advocating a League of Nations Peace Plan; he signed in February 1937 the National Memorial on Peace and Economic Co-operation, in which a form of economic appeasement was advocated. Appeasement had not by then become a dirty word. In November 1936 he welcomed the Peace Pledge Union to Birmingham and the next January became President of the National Peace Council. In these activities he worked closely with Dick Sheppard; he was quoted as saying, 'What the Church of England needs to regain its position is a thousand Dick Sheppards' and on Sheppard's untimely death in 1937, he described him as 'the Mr Greatheart of the Twentieth century'.

In an Oxford University Sermon in October 1936, Barnes recalled the criticisms of his pacifist sermon there in 1915. At about this time, too, recalling the First World War, he wrote to a friend: 'I wish that you were a pacifist. Why not be one during the next war and thereby learn how valuable to religious understanding an experience of persecution can be?' Now at Oxford, taking the text 'Blessed are the peacemakers', he argued the futility of a war which would destroy, not save, European civilization. No blessing on war could be found in Christ's teaching. Was military service or conscientious objection the nobler service to Christ? Europe was already a veritable powder-magazine. How could Britain help to lessen international suspicion? By air rearmament and a policy of retaliation, which was contrary to Christ's teaching? Could we not build anew at Geneva, abandon economic nationalism and place crown colonies under the League of Nations? This sermon, which brought him numerous letters of support, was nevertheless promptly denounced by Duff Cooper, then Secretary of State for War, who said that Barnes's views would have disgraced a street-corner orator and that his suggestion about the colonies was impracticable and ludicrous. But the Bishop of Southwark and more than one newspaper rallied to Barnes's defence, affirming his right to express his views without sneers from Duff Cooper. This did not prevent the Colonial Secretary, Ormsby-Gore, from gratuitously taking the opportunity of a Commons debate, in February 1937, to suggest that it was no more reasonable to call Italian clergy in Malta nominees of the British Government than to say that he himself agreed with the Bishop of Birmingham's theology or politics. Jimmy Maxton objected that this was an attack on a public servant, and Ormsby-Gore then denied that he was officially condemning the Bishop.

When Germany reoccupied the Rhineland in March 1936, Barnes was among those who pleaded for an agreed solution, to which both Germany and her neighbours would contribute by moderate policies. He continued to denounce the dictators for their bombast, and in May 1937 he foresaw that their rake's progress would lead either to revolution or war. As he had written privately after a visit to Germany in 1936, 'the Government group are pursuing a policy of military preparedness that is only too likely to end in a drift to war. They do not desire war, but ultimately the military machine will become so efficient that the desire to use it will be irresistible'. In this context he spoke of 'the public-house politician and doss-house dreamer', a phrase reminiscent of H. A. L. Fisher's characterization of Hitler's Germany and Mussolini's Italy as the rule of the non-commissioned officers. But even so, by the beginning of 1938 a new note can be heard in Barnes's utterances. No longer does he attack German policies. His apprehension of the increasing risk of war has evidently led him to emphasize more strongly than ever the need for reconciliation and a peaceful solution before all else. For this reason, despite his dislike of sanctions and the implied use of force, he maintained his support of the League of Nations; the alternative was a return to the balance of power. But, despite his desire for reconciliation, he was not to be inveigled into the Anglo-German Fellowship. Indeed, when invited to join it, he replied that it was too much to the right for his taste and added ironically that it made much of a certain 'Baron von der Ropp, who spoke at this house to a small and highly critical audience on Herr Hitler's deeply religious and, as we understood, almost Christian attitude to life'. Pacifism, in short, was not to be a defence of fascism. He remained invulnerable to pro-Nazi propaganda and never, for example, had any contact with the members of the so-called Cliveden set. This may too have been one reason why he avoided the close clutches of Frank Buchman. Indeed, he constantly saw the strength of the pacifist movement as lying in the forces of the left, even if he was afraid that some left-wingers might be all too ready to use force against right-wing dictators. He described his position in a private letter:

I could not speak of the international situation without voicing the indignation which all of us must feel at the use of torture by the present Nazi Government; at the monstrous injustice of its treatment of the

349

Jews; and at the denial of freedom, even after due process of trial, as
in the case of Niemöller. One's indignation at the use of the bombing
aeroplane by the Fascists in Spain is profound; and I understand that
in Italy those suspected of liberal opinions are still sent to suffer and
die on the islands. The whole thing is horrible; and yet to speak of
such matters is to increase national tension and to bring nearer the
war which would be the supreme evil. Under such circumstances silence
is the only possibility.

There are still moments of optimism, as when he asserts his confidence that even after a war Christianity would return, with the
implication that in wartime it would inevitably be submerged. But
otherwise he reiterates his same themes: economic contentment is
needed if war is to be avoided; tropical regions should be shared;
rearmament and air-raid precautions make war inevitable; it is not
for the Church to argue, as Temple and others had done, that the
use of force was compatible with international law; the clergy have
higher duties than to become air-raid wardens or recruiting officers.
In this context he often pointed out that, while Article xxxvii of the
Church of England declared that service in war was lawful, it did not
say that it was right. But he also asked how young people could be
expected to accept membership of a Church which was powerless to
stop the mad course of events.

Throughout this period he strongly supported Neville Chamberlain's efforts to secure peace and refused, on the plea that he was not
privy to events behind the scenes, to join in any public action which
might possibly embarrass the Prime Minister. Indeed, after the
Austrian *Anschluss* he decided to keep silent altogether on international affairs. This was not only because he realised the harm
which could be done by a mistake based on inadequate information.
With unwonted realism, he told a correspondent who was urging
some public gesture: 'The existence of pacifism in England would
be taken as a sign of weakness by the dictators and lead them to
make increasingly extravagant demands.' Silence was therefore an
imperative duty. After Munich itself, he broke his silence and said
there could be no elation: the Czechs had paid a heavy price, the
tyranny of fascism and Nazism could not be condoned, and grave
anxieties and misgivings remained. But only the way of goodwill
was possible: he was thankful that war had been avoided, and while
there was peace, there was hope.

350

As events moved forward into 1939, however, he clearly fell into a mood bordering on despair. He still opposed the introduction of conscription. He still did what he could to evoke understanding for Germany, even going so far as to say at one point that German legislation on 'race hygiene' was on the right lines, as it provided for voluntary sterilization. He also rather surprisingly took an active part in 1938 in bringing to England pictures which had been shown in Germany as part of the Nazis' exhibition of 'degenerative art', presumably in order to show that there were still civilized Germans, capable of artistic creation, although the pictures themselves cannot have been to his taste. But increasingly he seems to accept war as inevitable and to be adjusting his thoughts to it. Thus by the end of 1938 he is already deploring the 'slovenly inadequacy' of air-raid precautions and asserting that the development of satellite towns would minimize the risk from air attacks; even now he tries to think constructively. He also accepts a request that the clergy should be approached to act as air-raid wardens, even though he refuses to sponsor the appeal himself; he would not use his position as a Bishop to enforce his private convictions. As he wrote about this time: 'My position here with the large majority of church people taking a different standpoint is not very easy and I ought not to seem to seek an open clash.' This is the voice of the peacemaker, not of the ecclesiastical controversialist. But he continues at the same time to try to arouse sympathy for pacifists and conscientious objectors. When the rape of Czechoslovakia actually took place he could do little more than express his sympathy for Chamberlain at the collapse of his policies and repeat his own convictions that war was madness and that there was no need for Europe to commit suicide.

In the few remaining months he did what he could to champion the cause of German refugees, both in public statements and by giving practical help to those known to him personally. In May he spoke in Convocation on the merits of Christian pacifism as a position incompatible with conscription or armaments manufacture. But he aroused no echo in his audience, especially as he provocatively coupled his remarks with an attack on the Pope for not dissociating himself from Mussolini's policies. Addressing the Diocesan Conference in sombre mood in July, he wondered whether a new Dark Age was coming and could only hope that suffering, if it came, would be for righteousness' sake. In the same month, he preached at St

Paul's on the text 'Ye shall hear of wars and rumours of wars: see that ye be not troubled'. But the sermon shows in every line how troubled he was. While he repeated that war was incompatible with Christianity and deplored Christian ministers avowedly acting as recruiting officers, the sermon was mainly a call for generosity to conscientious objectors and for the objectors themselves not to stand aloof, but to show themselves good citizens and above all to help to protect women and children, the sick and the old, if war should come. 'Christian pacifism can only maintain itself in Great Britain and spread in other countries if it is the creed of citizens whom none can despise.'

But by now the British people were no longer in a mood for appeasement, still less for absolute pacifism. For the rest, during that awful summer of 1939, Barnes could only watch and pray, helpless and desolate, while events unfolded: Mussolini's attack on Albania; the guarantees to Poland, Roumania and Greece; Hitler's denunciation of the Anglo-German naval agreement; the German-Italian 'Pact of Steel'; the abortive British negotiations in Moscow; and finally the Molotov-Ribbentrop treaty, which was the last sentence of the writing on the wall. Barnes spent his summer holidays at Seaton, and when he heard on the wireless, early on the morning of 1 September, that Hitler had actually invaded Poland, the news came almost as a relief from tension. He drove back to Birmingham the same day to take up the reins of a diocese at war.

CHAPTER IX

BIRMINGHAM
IN WARTIME, 1939-1945

Problems of a Pacifist and the
Bugbear of Big Business

Pacifist though he was, the Bishop was quickly into his stride in putting the diocese on a war footing. As early as 6 September, after consulting his Council of canons and rural deans, he issued operational instructions providing, among other things, for services to end early in the black-out, for congregations to stay put during air-raids rather than run out to the shelters, for clergy to wear distinctive armlets issued by the Diocesan Office and to take anti-gas courses, and for churches to be used if necessary as casualty centres. The clergy were also advised to study the national instructions on their legal position in wartime and on the pastoral care of the dying and wounded; they were asked to volunteer for work with troops stationed in the Birmingham area. These were all aspects of service to the public in times of danger which even a convinced pacifist could and should support.

Barnes's own views obtruded rather more noticeably in the guidance he issued on 15 September to his clergy about sermons in wartime. These hints were in fact based on some notes which he had received from a friendly incumbent and adapted for his own purposes. In them Barnes referred to the criticism in the First World War of 'the bellicose and unChristian character' of many sermons, which reflected the Old rather than the New Testament and showed 'that vindictive anger which to our present distress found expression in the treaties of Brest-Litovsk and Versailles'. This time he urged the clergy not to cast doubt on the sincerity of our national aspirations, but also not to speak as if our national policy had always been wholly good; to emphasize the constructive aspects of the Christian faith but not to slur over difficulties, such as undeserved suffering or the problem of evil; to repudiate the idea that Hitlerism could be conquered by force but to show that peace could only be built by international justice and goodwill; and to remind people that the best which could be given to the country lay in lives worthy of Christ but also that death was the gateway to eternal life. He ended:

> One last hint. Preach as little as possible: pray as much as you can. Before beginning to prepare a sermon, put down your newspaper, turn off the wireless and for at least a quarter of an hour read slowly some passage of the New Testament which reveals the mind of Christ. You are His minister.

This advice found its way into the newspapers and brought him grateful letters from all over England.

The same spirit informed his address at a civic service for the National Day of Prayer on 1 October. As he said, he spoke with great reluctance, but when the Lord Mayor invited those who governed the city to attend the Parish Church, the Bishop's absence or silence might be misconstrued. In any case, he believed in the value and power of prayer. Whatever happened, God's will would in the end prevail. Not physical force, but the unity and moral strength of a nation achieved lasting triumphs. Innocent suffering had a redemptive power. God would help us, in so far as we could rightly ask his blessing, for then the spiritual forces with us would be stronger than those against us. But our prayers might well not preserve us from suffering and sorrow; we might have to pass through deep waters. Yet our trials would not be in vain if we refrained from anger and hatred and selfishness. 'In brief, we need to be loyal to the spirit of Christ.' A month later, in a service to celebrate the centenary of the Birmingham Police Force, he gave expression to what was to be one of his main preoccupations during the war: the need for generous treatment of conscientious objectors. In this context he drew attention to the courageous suffering of Bible Students, 'bible-bugs as they are derisively termed', in German concentration camps, as revealed in a recent White Paper.

Christianity is a queer thing. It seems to die and yet you find its influence in the most unexpected places.

Even in his support of conscientious objectors, Barnes sought to temper mercy with justice. On the general policy, his line was clear and firm: genuine conscientious objectors should be recognized and accepted, conscientious objectors should not be victimized, and there should be no repetition of the cat-and-mouse tactics of the last war. Whenever he thought that any of these principles was being breached, he rallied vigorously to their defence, writing to Ministers, local authorities and the press to argue general propositions or individual cases, often at no little length. He also took up the cause of conscientious objectors in the House of Lords. The *Manchester Guardian*, true to its liberal traditions, was always receptive to his letters, but the *Birmingham Post* regularly printed them too, thanks to a particularly friendly and enlightened editor, E. W. Record, who cordially agreed that the Bishop's views should be heard in his own city, and no doubt also realised that they had some news-value. In this context Barnes took a close interest in the work of the tribunals, before whom conscientious objectors had to appear, and, although he publicly denounced some judges who showed prejudice and lack of sympathy, he was always ready to pay tribute to those who acted fairly. He realised that often the young men who appeared before the tribunals were inexperienced and inarticulate and could not hold their own in sophisticated argument, so that there might seem to be one law for the rich and another for the poor. He was therefore ready to suggest answers to awkward questions posed by tribunals, although in the process he was also drawn into defending one or two rather less attractive barrack-room lawyers. Thus he strongly supported the cause of the Jehovah's Witnesses, much as he disliked their theological opinions. But at the same time, while he supported the claim by objectors for exemption from services which they did not feel they could conscientiously render, he was clear that they should not gain any other privileges in the process. He was not prepared to encourage those who would do nothing to help their country in need. He himself, for example, saw no reason why they should not work in civil defence, although he recognized that some of them found even this objectionable to their consciences, as possibly releasing someone else for armed service. It was important to him that conscientious objectors should not earn a reputation for cowardice. He also held that conscientious objectors should gain no promotion in their civil employment at the expense of their fellows away in the forces; indeed, he regularly advised them to accept hard work, for example on the land, and to do it for the equivalent of service pay. For his view was that, while a real conscientious objection should be recognized, a man could not claim exemption just because he was a Christian. While he himself did not agree with them, he accepted that many genuine Christians found it compatible with their beliefs to serve in the armed forces. Thus, he refused to claim any special favours for the clergy as such. Unless they were genuine pacifists, they should be liable for service like anyone else. While he hoped to persuade others to accept his views, he constantly made it plain that he would not impose them. He did not expect others to wear his conscience on their sleeves.

Barnes had a personal interest in this problem. His younger son, then aged twenty, was a conscientious objector. This was obviously not the reason for Barnes's defence of conscientious objectors. His own pacifist convictions had been formed long before. Indeed, the boy's own attitude was much more their result. It was certainly not their cause. His son appeared before the East Anglian tribunal early in the war and his claim to objection on conscientious grounds was dismissed, largely, it seems, because he tried to be too honest in analysing his position and thus appeared to be more sophisticated than sincere. Barnes's comment at this stage was that if his son went to prison, it would be hard on him but good for the cause. 'I only wish I could go to prison instead of him.' But when his son appeared before the Appeal Tribunal in London, the verdict was reversed and he was authorized to take alternative employment, in agriculture or some other form of service. In the event, he joined the Friends' Ambulance Unit and in that capacity saw much more of the active and unpleasant side of the war than his brother in the Royal Artillery.

Thus Barnes sought to have the courage of his convictions, but, without betraying those convictions, to give a lead in practical matters. In diocesan affairs this leadership was mainly exercised through his War Emergency Committee, which met as often as necessary to deal with war-time problems as they arose. The Birmingham diocese, like others, had long worked through a structure of committees and other bodies, of which Barnes made full use and to which he made his own additions. Apart from the statutory Diocesan Conference and Board of Finance, there were, for example, Councils for Moral Welfare, Youth and Religious Education, with the Board of Women's Work, not to mention the interdenominational Birmingham Christian Social Council. If there was a meeting at Bishop's Croft on a Monday, the agenda would be marked 'Golf clothes permitted'. As Bishop and Visitor, Barnes had long taken great trouble over the affairs of Queen's College, bringing it through a bad period as a hostel loosely attached to the University to a status where it could form an integral part of the Faculty of Theology. To these institutions Barnes now added his War Emergency Committee, and, after the bombing, a Diocesan Reorganization Committee and a Church Rebuilding Fund were established. With the end of the war, the Emergency Committee was to grow into the Bishop's Advisory Committee, which consisted of the half-dozen most senior clergy of the diocese, acting jointly as the Bishop's General Staff, although Barnes would not have used that term.

But, despite these determined efforts to be as constructive as possible, Barnes could not conceal his distress and apprehension at the effect of another war. For this he drew not only on his personal experiences of 1914-18 but also on his historical reading about the collapse of Graeco-Roman civilization under the burdens of a series of wars. Now he saw a real risk that Europe was committing suicide, that the strength of religion was already declining and that civilization was descending into a new barbarism. Man's moral progress had not kept pace with his control over nature and his inventive discoveries had been put to destructive misuse. It was this concern for the long-term future of European civilization which led him, at Convocation in January 1940, to propose not only a motion, which was carried, urging Christians everywhere to work and pray for a just and durable peace, but also another calling on the Government 'to allow the free importation of foodstuffs into Germany in accordance with the precept "If thine enemy hunger, feed him" '. This second resolution failed to find a seconder and had to be withdrawn. Lang in correspondence with Barnes had accepted the resolution but then apparently tried to suppress the debate on it altogether. Garbett has recorded that, while disliking the resolution, he had to persuade the Archbishop not to deprive a minority of free speech. In the event, Lang argued volubly against it on the grounds not just that it was impracticable but also that the Germans were trying to deprive us of food from overseas and that blockade was legitimate under international law. Garbett commented on the debate that 'the

Archbishop made frequent speeches, often saying what had much better be left unsaid'. But the press was mainly critical of Barnes for misplaced sentiment. The *Daily Express*'s characteristic headline was 'Bishop wants food for Nazis'. Nevertheless, throughout the war he continued where he could to plead for relief not only for countries under German occupation but also for the German people themselves.

This incident, however, served to illustrate his almost total isolation from his fellow-bishops. Lang himself, as his biographer puts it, 'was in no uncertainty about the justice of the country's cause or of the Church's right to give it every spiritual reinforcement'. The same went for most of the episcopate. They had many of them reached the bench of bishops by conforming to majority opinion and were unlikely to change their ways now. Moreover, as the war went on and particularly under Winston Churchill, it came to be said that, to become a bishop, it was more important to have the MC than the DD. But there were exceptions. Temple, for example, although he found it easy to justify the use of force, was not prepared to exhort others to pray for victory. Bell was a prominent critic of the bombing of Germany, and it has often been said that his opposition to Allied policy in this respect cost him an archbishopric in 1942, 1944 or even 1955.

Barnes took his own line on both these questions. Early in the war, Canon Macnutt of Canterbury, on behalf of the Society for Promoting Christian Knowledge and with the approval of the two Archbishops, issued *A War Primer of Prayers* and sought the permission of individual bishops for its use in their dioceses. Barnes was perplexed, realising the value of many of the prayers to many churchpeople but finding himself unable to endorse them all. After consulting a like-minded archdeacon, Hartill of Stoke-on-Trent, he agreed on condition that a footnote was printed to the effect that 'the Bishop of Birmingham, in giving his permission, does not express his approval of any prayers which assume that participation in war is legitimate for a Christian or which pray for victory'. To Macnutt he added: 'I am sorry that my position as a Christian pacifist should make me a nuisance.' His own view was that, while he would not condemn those who prayed for victory, he himself could not pray for victory as such but only that 'Thy will be done' and that 'we should be made worthy of victory'. Indeed, at one time he even wrote that demoralization was more to be feared than defeat. Later, in May 1942, the Lord Chancellor, Simon, incidentally an old friend from Temple days, expressed his own concern and that of other members of the House of Lords that, when Barnes read prayers there, he did not pray for members of the forces. Temple took this up from Lambeth with Barnes, hinting that it should be possible to find an acceptable form of words. Barnes responded readily, recognizing that at that stage of the war pacifists 'cannot hope to make converts though we may easily cause needless dissension'. He realised the 'deep human longing' to pray for those serving in the forces and drafted a prayer to meet this, which he sent to Temple, pointing out: 'of course, it also prays for our enemies, but surely that is Christian'. In fact, there was no specific mention of enemies in the prayer, which was cast in general terms to cover 'those now serving by sea or land or in the air, especially those dear to us'. This may sound like the casuistry of an over-sensitive conscience, but it was a genuine attempt not to bruise unnecessarily the consciences and feelings of others. Temple, however, suggested some additions, and Barnes in turn some small changes to Temple's text; agreement was easily reached, as basically the two men thought much the same on this subject. Barnes's private comment to the Archbishop was: 'I do not think that I ought to pray for victory even though, being a very ordinary Englishman, I desire it.' Similarly, at various stages of the war, he worked closely with several Lord Mayors of Birmingham to ensure that civic services or other appeals were couched in a form which he personally could endorse but which would also elicit the fullest possible public response. The Lord Mayors concerned seem genuinely to have welcomed this help.

On the bombing of Germany, it has been suggested that Bell was alone among the bishops in his opposition to 'obliteration bombing'. This has been symbolized in the scene in Hochhuth's *Soldiers* where Bell is shown confronting Churchill on the subject. But this is fiction in more than one sense. Bell was a strong and sincere champion of his cause. But he was not alone. Bell was not a pacifist. Yet he had a special concern for German Christians, derived from his pre-war contacts with the German and other European Protestant churches. This naturally led him into efforts to alleviate the lot of the Christian man in the German street and thus of the German civil population as a whole. Barnes did not share the affection for the German church, whose theology he had always found conservative and uncritical, but he did share the concern for innocent victims of war and the desire to preserve international understanding after it. He had already given evidence of this in his motion on the blockade in January 1940, about which he had been in touch beforehand with Bell, who had himself at the same time submitted resolutions on moves for peace. In November 1941 Barnes joined in a call to end night bombing. He argued that this was not only Christian but might well work to the allies' advantage. When asked why, as a pacifist, he chose to single out night bombing from other forms of warfare, he answered that half a loaf was better than no bread, although afterwards he admitted that he had signed a useless appeal against his better judgement. None the less, in June 1942, after an early raid on Cologne, he warned his Diocesan Conference not to 'exult over Cologne'. In September 1942 he joined with other pacifists in a letter to the *Manchester Guardian* condemning 'four-figure' bombing raids. In December 1942, he shared a Birmingham platform with Bell himself to speak in favour of famine relief in Europe. In February 1944, in the House of Lords, he deplored the destruction of 'little houses' in Germany. In February 1945 with other Church leaders, he again wrote to the *Manchester Guardian* to condemn 'terror bombing'. After the war, at Convocation in October 1945, he was to second a motion by Bell, which was carried unanimously, deploring deportations from Germany. The two bishops worked on parallel lines, though from different points of departure, and both were equally unsuccessful.

Where Barnes for his part stood alone among the bishops was in his absolute pacifism. This was a fundamental belief derived from his understanding of Christ's teaching as a whole. In a statement of September 1940, setting out his reasons for remaining a pacifist in wartime, he wrote:

From Christ I have learned that God is good and that God's strength shall prevail. By His teaching I know that war is evil and that we must not do evil that good may come. The man or nation who renounces war must be ready to endure and to suffer. Such a man may perish miserably, but he shall not suffer or die in vain. Such a nation shall find its soul. The meek, not the mighty, shall inherit the earth. Peace and good-will shall win in the end. With war a new barbarism begins to spread over Europe: civilized progress will return when we begin to love our enemies and do good to them that despitefully use us.

He was reinforced in his convictions by the teaching of the early Christian fathers, notably Origen and Tertullian, and by the practice of the early Christian church. On these matters he drew heavily on C. J. Cadoux's *Early Christian Attitude to War*, a book which he constantly recommended to his correspondents. He was sometimes tackled on passages which suggested that neither Christ nor his immediate followers were pacifists, such as Luke xxii, 36–8, in which Christ is made to say 'He that hath no sword, let him sell his garment and buy one' and John xviii, 10, in which Peter cuts off the high priest's servant's ear with his sword. The first he regarded, even if it was rightly attributed to Jesus, as metaphorical teaching imperfectly understood; on the second he points out that in Mark there is no suggestion that it was Peter who drew the sword, whereas in Matthew Jesus says 'Put up again thy sword into his place: for all they that take the sword shall perish with the sword'. In fact, as Barnes saw it, 'the passage as we have it in Matthew is as strong a repudiation of force as we could desire'.

There are other ambiguous texts, which are argued in Cadoux's book. But, while Barnes could argue them too, his faith was not based on the niceties of textual criticism. He did, it is true, cause some irritation by claiming that Christ taught 'Blessed are the pacifists', even though 'pacifist' is undoubtedly the literal equivalent of 'peacemaker'. But at bottom he was concerned with the spirit rather than the words, and his interpretation of Christ's message of love was buttressed by the meditation and experience of a lifetime, a lifetime which had spanned the Boer War, the Great War and now the Second World War.

But despite the absolute nature of his pacifism, he remained careful in its expression. This was for two reasons. First, he held strongly that pacifists should do or say nothing which 'might encourage Hitler and his associates'. He therefore consistently refused to join in public pressure on the Government to modify its war policy, although he was willing, on appropriate occasions, to lend his support to private appeals. As in the First World War, his pacifism was still yoked to his patriotism, although they must have been a difficult team to handle in double harness. Secondly, he realised quite simply that to preach pacifism in and out of season

361

would be counterproductive. He remained in touch with the main pacifist bodies in the country, such as the National Peace Council, the Peace Pledge Union, War Resisters International, the Central Board for Conscientious Objectors and the Anglican Pacifist Fellowship; and he received constant requests to sign this or that memorial or manifesto or to take part in some protest or demonstration. Often these consisted of empty and repetitive verbiage or of cranky ideas without practical effect, such as foodless luncheons. Such things he was careful to avoid. For he had seen early in the war that the tide was flowing strongly against pacifism, and certainly when things were going badly for Britain in 1940 and 1941 he recognized the futility of action intended to stop the war or even to bring about a negotiated peace. Similarly, he advised his friends to avoid activities, such as house-to-house distribution of pamphlets, which would achieve nothing but irritation. As to his own participation, he pointed out to them that he was constantly going counter to general opinion in the Church and must therefore only act when he could really do good. Indeed, it was in some respects better that he should not be formally associated with too many pacifist organizations, so that, if a particular organization was discussed by the bishops, he could offer his judgement on it from an independent position. Moreover, he had to remind his importunate allies that he could only speak publicly as a bishop and would therefore seem to be committing the diocese to a view from which most of it dissented. This again would not only give offence, but simply be annoying and ineffective. As he said, he did not want to be accused of 'nagging' or 'classed as a perennial nuisance'. He maintained a burning desire for peace and international reconciliation, but he was not going to waste his fire. Persuasion is more positive than preaching.

In all these circumstances it is not strange that ecclesiastical affairs loom much less large in his mind and life in wartime than in earlier years. Not only is he at loggerheads with most of the other bishops. There is nothing new in that. Writing in December 1939 to the retired Bishop Nickson, he says:

It is delightful to hear from you again. I often think of you as I go to Bishops' meetings. I now sit at the very end of the table in the chair that Wynne Wilson occupied when you had gone. But he and you and the two Pearces with Burroughs of Ripon nearby are only memories, and I am beginning to find that I do not know by sight the new bishops who come along with such astonishing rapidity. They seem to me to be a lamentably undistinguished crowd, but I suppose that you would dismiss that view as the opinion of one who is merely *laudator temporis acti.*

But also, as Barnes saw it, the war was striking at religion itself. He wrote in the same letter, in apology for not visiting Nickson: 'while there was plenty of petrol there was much to do. Since the war there is a moratorium on Christianity but no petrol.' More sadly, he found himself out of sympathy with most of his old allies in Church affairs. Raven virtually alone of the modernists was also a pacifist. Otherwise, as he wrote in January 1943,

> I have been sorely troubled to find that modern churchmen in England have, for the most part, shown themselves as strongly nationalist and socially reactionary as liberal theologians in Germany. The world has no use for, and no need of, such a religion; it is not Christian.

Indeed, he was to tell a friend in 1945 that 'during the war certain articles in the *Modern Churchman* seemed to me so horrible that I resigned my membership of the Modern Churchmen's Union'. His own modernism was unaffected. Indeed, he described himself as 'more of a modernist than ever' and in 1948 he let himself be persuaded to rejoin the Modern Churchmen's Union. Whereas previously he had defined his position as ethical theism, he was now more inclined to speak of Christian humanism. But these two descriptions are in fact opposite sides of the same coin, both representing the binding relationship between God and man. Thus Christian theism represents the divine and human ethics the mortal side of the coin. Barnes did not of course think of humanism in the modern sense of a philosophy opposed to all religion, and to Christianity in particular. On the contrary, thinking, as he always did, back to the Reformation and looking for a new Renaissance in his own day, he saw humanism as a direct inheritance from the Christian humanists of the Renaissance, from his hero Erasmus or from the English humanists of Tudor times. So, too, when he spoke, as he sometimes did, of scientific humanism, he did not see it as a counterpoint to religious faith, but as a combination of new scientific knowledge with the Christian humanist tradition. As always, he was seeking a synthesis. In later life, perhaps, he was less inclined to discuss his theological position as such. He had reached it after thought and study as a young man and had set it out in his early teaching at Cambridge, the Temple and Westminster. At Birmingham he had applied it to ecclesiastical discipline. But now he was increasingly inclined to assume the theological background and to emphasize its ethical implications.

Not that he became in any way indifferent to theological distinctions. Thus, as a modernist, he still condemned conservative evangelicals, who acted like rebels, just as much as their Anglo-Catholic counterparts; he still advocated the admission of Nonconformists to the Holy Communion, on the authority of Mandell Creighton, who had held that membership of the Free Churches counted as confirmation; he still retained his interest in sacramental matters, opposing intinction, for example, as smacking of the sickroom; he still wanted to see women priests and would have ordained them if he had the legal power. But modernism had ceased to be his prime concern. It was merged in mightier matters. There was a moratorium on ecclesiastical controversy too. Indeed, the conditions of wartime, and of air-raids in particular, even led him to make a concession on sacramental practice:

> I personally do not believe that the doctrine of a spiritual presence in the consecrated elements of Holy Communion is either good theology or the teaching of the Church of England. Also, I am quite sure that God does not make any difference in His judgement on a man who has died if that man has had the Holy Communion shortly before his death. If a man at the point of death were to desire of me the Holy Communion, I should there and then have a short service which would consist of the Lord's Prayer and the shortened modification of the prayer of Consecration which is used when further bread and wine are required at a normal service . . . If, however, you will not follow me in these matters, I will not object to extended Communion. You may, while heavy air-raids continue, leave after your early Eucharist each day, under a linen cloth on the Holy Table, a small amount of consecrated bread and wine which could be used to give extended Communion to any parishioner who, being seriously injured, might ask for it. If not so used, it should be consumed early on the following day.

But this was not the only, or indeed the major, impact which air-raids made on his affairs. Already before the war Barnes had been expressing alarm at Birmingham's vulnerability to air attack and the inadequacy of air-raid precautions. This had in fact become a burning political issue in the city, with the Labour opposition at first condemning wasteful expenditure on what it called unnecessary provision for civil defence and then changing tactics to criticize the shortage of shelters. It had not been altogether the fault of the municipal authorities. The central Government had at first advised dispersing the population, a policy which could not easily be applied to the centres of large, industrial cities and which was in any case mainly dictated by reasons of economy in men, money and materials. After Munich there had been a change and the Government did offer some financial help with Anderson shelters in private premises and even with some public shelters too. Even then the City Council were reluctant to spend money on shelters. Local and central authorities each preferred, as is the usual way, to shift the burden to the other. The political attacks probably made it all the harder for the Council to lose face by changing their attitude. Things improved with the outbreak of war and, more particularly, with the formation of the National Government in May 1940. But there was still a long way to go, especially in the provision of safe public shelters. The Government's basic shelter plan has been described by the official historian of Civil Defence as 'the provision of widespread, but only moderate, protection', and it is evident from his account that the instructions issued in April 1940 to use two parts of lime to one of cement in mortar for surface shelters were intended 'to ease the pressing demands on cement', large quantities of which had to be diverted that summer to military purposes. Indeed, the War Cabinet issued specific instructions in May that year that defence works were to be given priority and there was undoubtedly a severe shortage for other purposes during that summer. Even so, a suggestion that the cement industry should work to capacity from April to September was not endorsed, and this of itself gives some credibility to the view that there was no all-out effort at cement production. Similarly, although a coupon system of rationing was set up in the summer, it did not last long, and the responsibility for allocation was returned to the industry. By November the Prime Minister was writing a minute to express his concern, not so much at the actual availability of supplies as at the progress of the production programme.

Meanwhile, it was obvious that Birmingham, with its numerous aircraft factories, would be a prime target for the Luftwaffe. When raids on Birmingham actually began in August 1940, it was, despite government policy, to the public shelters that the public flocked.

Barnes was soon receiving alarming reports from his clergy about conditions there: the overcrowding, the risk of flooding, the insanitary conditions, the behaviour of drunks and rowdies, the proximity to vulnerable targets and, above all, the vulnerability of the shelters themselves to anything like a direct hit. In these early raids of 1940, not only were people killed in Anderson shelters, but there were several deaths when a public shelter collapsed under a shop. This gave new impetus to the campaign for deep, bomb-proof shelters, which had been conducted, mainly by left-wing groups, since 1938; the pressure for such shelters was renewed in the Birmingham City Council, particularly from the Labour side, but official policy was still opposed to them, as requiring too much in the way of labour and materials.

One of the protagonists in the deep-shelter campaign was an unofficial body, of architects, surveyors, engineers and others, calling itself the ARP Co-ordinating Committee. Its Birmingham branch now decided to stage an exhibition there, designed to advertise the steel and concrete 'Haldane Shelter', so-called because it had been devised by Professor J. B. S. Haldane, chairman of the main London Committee. Barnes was invited to open this exhibition on 30 November. The invitation came from two prominent Birmingham Free Churchmen, Leyton Richards and H. G. Wood, who were both friends of his and pacifists, and he accepted it. In fact, the ARP Co-ordinating Committee had more communist than pacifist inspiration behind it. Simultaneously, and presumably not by coincidence, the *Daily Worker* as well as the *Daily Herald* had been giving publicity to the shortage of cement, as one cause of the lack of reinforced shelters, and suggesting that this shortage was deliberately engineered by the industry to keep prices up. But even if Barnes realised that political motives were at work, he could also see the objective need for better protection.

Before the exhibition opened, Birmingham suffered its worst week of air-raids of the war. In these four days of raids, from 19 to 22 November, the city lost 800 killed and over 2000 injured, more than a quarter of its casualties during the whole war. As Winston Churchill recorded, 'the life and spirit of Birmingham survived this ordeal' and, when he visited the city immediately afterwards, 'the spirit of Birmingham shone brightly and its million inhabitants, highly organized, conscious and comprehending, rode high above their physical suffering'. Yet, whether Churchill knew it or not, this was largely because the citizens were not aware how close they had come to a much worse disaster through the damage to the water supply and how this was probably only averted by the failure of the Luftwaffe to press home the attack on the following day.

All the same, these events made a powerful impression on Barnes, whose Cathedral had already suffered a direct hit the month before, while many other churches had been damaged, some destroyed. But his main concern was for the people in the shelters, several of which he had visited and talked to their occupants. Subconsciously, too, he may have wanted to serve Birmingham in wartime in one of the few ways which his pacifism left open to him. This may have been one reason why his criticisms were directed more at the central government than at the City Council. So Barnes used his speech at the opening of the exhibition, written incidentally on the back of his manuscript address at Neville Chamberlain's memorial service a fortnight before, to advocate the provision of better and stronger shelters and of steel and concrete Haldane Shelters in particular.

Why should they not be built? The answer of the Government is that there is no concrete available and that supplies of steel are short. To this answer strong objection is taken.

The cement industry is virtually a monopoly controlled by the Cement Makers' Federation. It seems established that this Federation has not expanded its pre-war plant adequately, nor is it producing what is called Portland blast-furnace cement. Such expansion and such production are urgently needed.

The monopolists, whose companies are now disquietingly prosperous, naturally desire to take no action which would injuriously affect their post-war profits. We know what would happen in Germany if opposition were forthcoming. The chief men of the cement ring would be taken by the Gestapo to a concentration camp. A few days later it would be announced that they had been shot in trying to escape. A month later adequate supplies of cement would be forthcoming.

It is a dreadful system, but dreadfully efficient. Britain is fighting that system. It cannot fight successfully if we deserve Mussolini's jibe that we are a pluto-democracy, that is to say, a democracy in which the financial advantages of wealthy groups prevail against the needs of the state.

The Government has power to take over the cement industry. Let it do so, working to capacity all existing plant, establishing, if need be, new works, and, in particular, supplying vast quantities of Portland blast-furnace cement which could be made and are urgently needed.

The fat was soon in the fire. On 3 December, Councillor Tiptaft, chairman of the Birmingham ARP Committee, complained that the Bishop and his pacifist friends were associating themselves with members of the Communist Party in an attempt to deceive the public, that they knew perfectly well that there was neither labour nor material available for deep shelters and that, if they could not help the national effort, they should not hinder it. Barnes promptly replied in the *Birmingham Post*, pointing out that, since he spoke, a Government spokesman had told the House of Commons that the cement industry was now controlled and that the policy of making blast-furnace cement and laying down additional plant was under consideration. He ended:

At the meeting we were appreciative of the local authorities: we recognized their difficulties. Imagine my surprise to read in your columns remarks made by Councillor Tiptaft yesterday. He declares that I have associated myself with 'members of the Communist party'. Does the ARP Chairman think that Communists alone are alive to the misery of present conditions? I repudiate the suggestion: it is most dangerous. He states that in asking for 'deep shelters' we are attempting to 'deceive the public'. We ask for Haldane shelters; and, whatever be my own reputation, Professor Wood and Mr Leyton Richards are not deceivers of the public, 'disturbing the minds of the citizens after the manner of Fifth Columnists'. Mr Tiptaft does no good by such innuendo. Those who speak in public of lamentable conditions of which all our poorer citizens are painfully aware, and whose object is an improvement of such conditions, ought not to be abused. Mr Tiptaft ought to regard us as his allies, not his foes.

But Tiptaft, with whom Barnes was to have friendly relations when he became Lord Mayor, was not the main foeman for his steel. The official historian of works and buildings in wartime asserts that the fear of a cement shortage for shelters

was exploited (if indeed it had not been created) for purposes of political propaganda by extremist agitators. Pamphlets and leaflets were disseminated attacking the Government, the 'capitalist system' and the 'Cement Ring', and the public were told that if they could not get their air-raid shelters the reason was that the 'Cement Ring' had deliberately restricted the output of cement in order to swell their own profits. A number of well-meaning persons, among them the Bishop of Birmingham and Professor J. B. S. Haldane, were credited with the belief that a monstrous crime against society had been committed and the subject was brought up more than once in Parliament. Since, as the cement companies claimed, the output of cement had been trebled between the wars and the price halved, while labour conditions had been greatly improved, these attacks were deeply resented; and a number of leading cement firms took action in the High Court, in order to clear the reputation of their industry.

That is the case for the companies. Whatever their exact motives, it was as early as 3 December that Messrs. Allen & Overy wrote to Barnes to say that they were instructed by the Cement Makers' Federation to issue a writ for slander. In acknowledging this the Bishop asked them to indicate the sentences to which objection had been taken, but the solicitors refused to be drawn.

Meanwhile, Barnes had put down a motion in the House of Lords 'to call attention to the present provision of air-raid shelters', and this was arranged for 18 December. While controversy continued in the Birmingham press, and even Ernest Canning, the industrialist who had given the Bishop so much support over church extension, was openly critical, the issue of the writ began to bring Barnes offers of support from many quarters. In particular, the *Financial News*, a Conservative newspaper which had been investigating the cement industry, put its information at his disposal, and several people with inside knowledge of the industry wrote confidentially to confirm the difficulty of obtaining supplies. His allies were not all communists. But he did keep in touch with Haldane, whom he found entertaining and had to stay at Bishop's Croft, since Haldane was also threatened with a writ, although in the end the cement makers did not proceed against him too. One barrel was enough for them, and a Bishop was a plumper bird.

The writ was served on him on 13 December and he put the matter in the hands of the same Quaker solicitor, A. W. Braithwaite of Waterhouse & Co., who had handled his son's appearance before the Conscientious Objectors' Tribunal. Perhaps partly with tongue in cheek, he wrote: 'I should like your advice *inter alia* as to whether things can be so arranged that I go to prison for contempt of court: such would seem to me the best way in which a Bishop should fight a multi-millionaire cement combine.' Braithwaite did not rise to this fly, and Barnes's hopes of being sent to prison, if such they really were, and Guy Rogers has recorded that Barnes would happily discuss how he could administer his diocese from Winson Green

Prison, were once again to be disappointed.

In the House of Lords Barnes first dwelt on the shortcomings of the shelters themselves, drawing on his own experience and on various public reports. 'I find myself, with great regret, forced to the conclusion that the Government's air-raid shelter policy has failed.' He went on to argue for the provision of Haldane shelters, which depended on the supply of cement. Here he justified his use of the word 'ring' by reference to evidence before the Select Committee on Estimates on 20 July 1938, where the same word was freely used and the Director of Army Contracts said that 'there was no effective competition outside'. Quoting the Government statement in the House of Commons on 3 December, he asked whether there had been conflict between the Government and the industry and ended with a renewed plea for safe shelters and for an end to the 'disastrous lack of cement'.

He was supported first by Lord Teynham, a naval officer who trenchantly criticized the lack of co-ordination over the provision of shelters and called for a programme for safe and well-equipped shelters in large cities, where they could be used as underground garages after the war, but did not mention the cement industry. From the Labour benches, however, Lord Addison did so, suggesting that the appointment of the head of the Cement Makers' Federation as Controller of Cement required justification and explanation. Replying for the Government, the Duke of Devonshire apologized that he could only give a sketchy reply, and sketchy indeed it was. He asserted that brick and concrete surface shelters had performed satisfactorily and that the Government were pressing ahead with improvements. On cement, he averred that the position was 'very greatly improved' but that to provide really safe shelters for the population of bombed areas a ton of cement per person would be needed and, with a shortage of labour and difficulties of distribution, that was out of the question. In withdrawing his motion, Barnes commented drily that the reply would arouse widespread misgiving.

The lawyers now set to work and Counsel's opinion was taken. The main question was whether Barnes should plead 'fair comment on a matter of public interest', which would mean fighting the action and could be expensive, or merely put in a plea on mitigation of damages, or settle the action out of court on the basis of some sort of apology. The plaintiffs, who were technically the sixteen member companies of the Federation, issued their statement of claim on 30 December, and it transpired from this that they were complaining of accusations that they were 'carrying on their business in a disloyal, inefficient, unpatriotic way' and that 'the Government would be justified in having the Directors of the plaintiff companies arrested and shot'. This seemed such an exaggerated version of Barnes's speech that Braithwaite advised an attempt to settle out of court. A letter was therefore prepared, amended slightly by Barnes himself, and sent to the plaintiffs' solicitors, who in reply asked both for a withdrawl of the 'defamatory allegations' and for payment of their costs, which they put at £200. The cement makers wanted their pound of flesh. Barnes did not like this much, as he did not want to 'hand bouquets' to the cement companies in open court, and he feared that to agree to pay costs would amount to acknowledging that he was morally to blame. Braithwaite more or less reassured him, and further negotiations followed, as a result of which a new form of words was sent to Allen & Overy. In return they sent a long draft statement, in which they proposed to say that the Bishop accepted that his charges were quite unfounded and desired unreservedly to withdraw them and apologize to the plaintiffs. Defending counsel was to make a statement in effect confirming this.

By now it was 5 March and in a letter of that date Barnes refused the proposed solution absolutely. He had had enough pussy-footing. He was not prepared to accept that his charges were unfounded or to withdraw them. On the contrary, the Government had accepted the policy he advocated. Moreover, on 20 December, the Parliamentary Secretary had said that instructions had been given to install the necessary plant for the manufacture of blast-furnace cement, that some plants were being brought back into operation and that the Minister had appointed a Committee to consider the provision of new cement works. This Committee had in fact been appointed on 10 January and held its first meeting on 14 January. Barnes wanted these facts brought out in court and was only prepared to withdraw any imputations not covered by them. He realised that this might involve him in heavy damages. 'But any financial sufferings would be widely deemed the result of persecution, and in the end the cement companies would suffer moral damage far more serious than that of which they now complain.'

Needless to say, this idea did not find favour with the cement companies, who decided to bring the matter to court and to seek damages. To this Barnes refused to file a defence. Meanwhile the

Cement Makers' Federation had evidently decided that their public image needed some burnishing. A series of self-justificatory advertisements was placed in the press, and the chairmen of several member companies, at their annual general meetings in April, took a markedly defensive line, at least one of them attacking Barnes by name and also referring by association to 'notorious Communists and other irresponsible and anonymous critics'.

The action for assessment of damages was to be heard early in May. Towards the end of April Braithwaite asked Barnes to draft a statement of regret and withdrawal of imputations. His Counsel, Constantine Gallop, was inclined to suggest that Barnes should appear in person to make the statement, as this would help to reduce damages. Braithwaite and Gallop must have been surprised to receive in return a draft statement of eleven pages, full of combative material and ending 'If the plaintiffs still persist, I suggest damages of one penny and no order as to costs'. Almost the only implied retraction was a passage that 'It is absurd to say that the Bishop urged the adoption of a system of concentration camps and murder, which he described as dreadful. He is known to be a liberal and averse from capital punishment.' This final statement incidentally represented a new departure from his previously known views. In his covering letter, Barnes added that he could not have his reputation for honesty as a public man imperilled and offered to make his proposed speech himself. Gallop presumably demurred, and there must have been some discussion by telephone. When the case was heard on 9 May, no such speech was made by the defence.

Valentine Holmes, KC, appeared for the plaintiffs. In his opening speech, he made much of Barnes's high reputation, in order to suggest that this made his statements more likely to be believed. Holmes then went over the lawyers' correspondence in some detail, to show that the plaintiffs were not out to make money, that they had been ready to settle for an apology, but that Barnes had neither withdrawn nor, as Holmes put it, been 'man enough to go into the witness-box' and defend himself. He then called Lord Wolmer, the former chairman of the Cement Makers' Federation, now Controller of Cement in the Ministry of Works and Buildings, whose evidence was to the effect that the cement companies had done their utmost to produce as much cement as possible in the national interest, without regard to their post-war profits. Cross-examined, Wolmer claimed that the Bishop's speech, if not refuted, would damage the cement companies pecuniarily, either during or after the war. Under pressure, he said that the Bishop 'ought publicly to grovel'. In his final remarks, Holmes sought to establish that Barnes had not tried to find out the full facts before making his speech. Gallop in reply admitted that any defamatory matter was unfounded and withdrew it with 'unqualified regret'. But, though constantly interrupted by the judge, he tried to explain why the Bishop made a distinction between his innuendoes defamatory of the companies and his description of the facts of the case. His task was not easy, as no defence had been entered and he could not call Barnes as a witness. But he tried to show that there was nothing defamatory in saying that the cement industry could be more productive and that, as there was no personal criticism of the plaintiffs or, if there was, it was withdrawn, there was no case for substantial damages.

It was a gallant effort. But Mr Justice Wrottesley gave judgement to the effect that the Bishop had made imputations against the loyalty, patriotism and decency of the plaintiffs. He called it a grave slander and suggested that even bishops, if they make mistakes, could apologize. 'Humility is a Christian virtue', and he could see no reason why the Bishop should not have recognized that the companies were working hard to help their country and, if he was prepared to apologize at all, should not have therefore agreed to the proposed statement submitted to him to be read in court. He assessed damages at £100 for each plaintiff company, or £1600 in all. Holmes announced that the damages would be given to the Royal Air Force Benevolent Fund. The plaintiffs were also awarded costs.

Barnes was not prepared to leave matters there. As soon as he heard the result of the case, on the same day he put down a further motion on air-raid shelters for the House of Lords. He also had recourse to his favourite device of a statement to the press. There was a side-skirmish with *The Sunday Times*, which had published a critical letter in which it accused him by misprint of saying that the cement companies were 'disgustingly' rather than 'disquietingly' prosperous. Otherwise, although the case had been fully reported, there was little editorial comment. But his main object was to show that, while he withdrew allegations reflecting on the credit and reputation of the plaintiffs, he had not withdrawn his assertion that the cement industry needed further expansion. His lawyers, having rejected his own first draft statement as likely to involve him in a further action, issued a bowdlerized version to this effect to the press. Barnes then brought this to the attention of his diocese, emphasizing that his object all along had been to improve conditions in air-raid shelters. There had been more heavy raids on Birmingham in March and April of 1941 and, with two thousand of its citizens dead and two thousand tons of bombs dropped on it in the war as a whole, it was, with Liverpool, second only to London in the weight of attack which it suffered. Barnes also made it known that, although he was receiving offers of financial help and was grateful, he did not want subscriptions organized. 'I will bear my own burdens.'

The second House of Lords debate took place on 17 June. Barnes started by arguing that there were still not enough bomb-proof shelters and that this problem was inseparable from that of cement supply. He went on to attack the cement 'ring' for keeping prices up and suggested that, as the chairman of the Cement Makers' Federation had become Controller of Cement though still paid by the industry, the 'ring' was in fact dictating government policy. He described the situation as impossible and called for Wolmer's appointment to be ended, for the cement industry's interests to be subordinated to the public good and for cement supplies to be increased so that enough bomb-proof shelters could be built. 'The Germans, we have been allowed to know, have been building such shelters in Berlin; if Berlin has them, why not Birmingham?' Wolmer, who followed him, denied that there was a monopoly or that there had been any attempt to restrict cement supplies. Prices had only been raised with Government approval. He himself did not see the cement companies' accounts. He merely carried out Government orders, and it was the custom for all controllers of industries to be paid by their industries and not the Government. Blast-furnace cement had not been in great demand, because Portland cement was preferred and there was always enough of it; the 1940 shortage had been exceptional and temporary. He ended with an attack on Barnes:

He has launched the gravest charges on the most flimsy evidence. He has in fact a complete lack of evidence. He brandished every sort of pamphlet issued by the Communists in front of Your Lordships' faces this afternoon as if they were authoritative documents. He has swallowed all this Communist propaganda without making any proper inquiry from those who could have given him the facts. I regret the attack and the statements that he has made very much indeed. I venture to say that it is not a righteous or a Christian act to accuse your fellow-countrymen of lack of patriotism when you have not got the slightest evidence in support of any charge of that sort.

The Duke of Devonshire, replying for the Government, relied mainly on Wolmer's riposte and for himself defended the Government's shelter programme. The Government did not believe that the Haldane shelter was the soundest type. But, without claiming that everything was perfect, he said that shelters existed for twenty-one million people and that it was of no service to attribute people's sufferings to governmental carelessness or the industry's rapacity. Relations between the Government and the companies were close and cordial.

In his own reply, Barnes repudiated Wolmer's charge that his statements had been untrue. When Wolmer jibed that he 'was given the opportunity of proving their truth in a Court of Law the other day; and he preferred to pay £1600 rather than go into the witness box to do so', Barnes, who had not previously mentioned the case, answered that his failure to defend had not been because he had not thought his speech substantially justifiable, but because in a defended case, costs 'which are a mere nothing to a multi-millionaire ring', could mount so rapidly. Our libel laws were the most severe in the world: 'American big business chiefs are reported to speak enviously of our "lovely law of libel". Equally, it is well-known that if and when a strong left-wing government in this country come into power the revision of the laws relating to libel and slander will probably be undertaken.' He ended, somewhat inconsistently, by saying that his one desire had been for better air-raid protection for the poor and, by refusing to defend the action, to draw attention to the scandal which he wanted to end. He had wanted to bear the cost himself;

but, against my publicly-expressed wish, friends unknown to me got together a fund and at my Diocesan Conference last week, nominally as a silver-wedding gift, announced that nearly £1100 had been collected. My Lords, deeply embedded in early Christian history is the practice of non-resistance. This practice will play its part in the great struggle of the future when democracy must save itself by conquering the individual and corporate aggrandizement which now threatens our social freedom.

This sorry affair did in fact have a happier ending. The diocese had already decided to mark the Barneses' silver wedding by having a portrait of the Bishop painted to hang permanently at Bishop's Croft. This was commissioned from Bernard Munns, who had already painted both Gore and Russell Wakefield for the same purpose. But, as the Archdeacon of Birmingham explained privately after the event, they had also decided to make a personal gift, quite independent of the law-suit. It was only when one subscriber asked for his contribution to be earmarked for payment of damages that the two purposes became mixed. The total subscribed came to £900 for the Bishop and £50 to Mrs Barnes. His figures in the House of Lords do not seem to have been up to his usual mathematical standard. Apart from £1600 damages, the law-suit had cost Barnes nearly £300 in costs and legal fees. But he did not apply the whole gift to meeting these expenses. The Munns portrait belonged to the diocese. For his own property he had a pencil sketch made of himself by Francis Dodd, RA, and it was, incidentally, a much better likeness than the Munns.

The gifts were presented on 29 September 1941, the anniversary of Barnes's consecration. In thanking the donors, Barnes said:

One makes mistakes at times. One's dreams and hopes fade as a great war sweeps like a torrent across the land where one would plant the standards of Christian moderation. Yet there remain friendship and sympathy and understanding, while at home for twenty-five years there has been a happy companionship for which I thank God.

So perhaps he agreed that the cement speech had been in some respects a mistake. On the credit side, he could undoubtedly claim that, whereas in the autumn of 1940, there had still been a shortage of cement, supplies were much easier by April 1941. Whether his intervention had contributed to this development neither he nor anyone else could say for sure, although he had certainly helped to bring the cement shortage to public notice. The Committee appointed in January had reported in April to the general effect that the cement industry's capacity would be enough for the rest of the war, but even their estimates did not include provision for bomb-proof shelters, which would have meant diverting too much labour and material from defence. Nor was anything done to manufacture blast-furnace cement in quantity during the war, although it would have probably been uneconomic to do so when adequate supplies of Portland cement existed. No attempt was made, moreover, seriously to deny that what amounted to a 'ring' existed: indeed, the Cement Makers' Federation had been formed in 1918 expressly to fix prices, and in 1934 there had been added a quota system, which penalized any firm delivering cement in excess of its quota. By common consent there was little competition in the industry, and it was virtually impossible for new firms to break into it. On the substance of the matter, therefore, Barnes had a good deal of right on his side. But on the other hand, as he himself recognized, he had not achieved much improvement in the actual shelter situation.

Moreover, in his impulsive sympathy for the people in the shelters he had allowed himself to use strong language and had done so largely on the basis of second-hand information. He had to work hard to collect more facts for his two speeches in the Lords. He also collected some dubious allies. His motives were humanitarian, not political, and he may not at first have realised the extent of communist sympathies behind the ARP Co-ordinating Committee. Even if he had, he might not have minded, for, as he said in 1944, 'if a public protest against some particular evil seems to me to be necessary, I make that protest although those who may be associated with it represent organizations or policies with which I should not be in sympathy'. But if he did not realise the communist connection, he soon must have done, especially when the Birmingham Young Communist League addressed their congratulations to their 'Dear Comrade'. By 8 March he was telling Braithwaite: 'If I am to contest the action, I do not see how I can avoid using the help of Mr Pritt and the National ARP Co-ordinating Committee. I do not wish to take this course because I am not a communist.' D. N. Pritt's services had been offered by Krishna Menon, who had also volunteered his own legal advice free of charge. All this was before Hitler's invasion of Russia brought the Soviet Union into the war on the Allied side, when charges of communist influence might not have been so freely flung around. Quite apart from this aspect, Barnes may have thought that he was cast in a less than heroic role when one of his reasons for not defending the case was to avoid escalating costs against wealthy opponents and when, after a first refusal, he had in the end accepted contributions to those costs. The risk of higher costs was one reason for returning to the charge in the House of Lords, although he incurred some criticism for sheltering behind parliamentary privilege there. Above all, he was conscious, as his correspondence shows, that the whole business was unlikely materially to improve the state of shelters in Birmingham before the air-raids expected in the coming winter. Luckily since the existing shelters would almost certainly have proved inadequate, those raids never came to pass and, apart from a few attacks in late July 1942 and one brief raid in April 1943, Birmingham was bombed no more.

But the cement case was a turning-point for Barnes none the less. Whatever his conclusions on his tactics, he was convinced of the justice of his cause. Many of his correspondents, and not only from the Left, congratulated him on his stand against powerful vested interests. Typical was a letter from Mervyn Stockwood, then a young incumbent at Bristol, who referred to the 'tyranny of the big combines and of the unscrupulous industrialist' and went on to say, 'it is a very great encouragement to some of us junior clergy to know that there are senior men in the Church who are courageously working for a more righteous social order'. As Barnes himself wrote to Lancelot Hogben, in declining Hogben's offer to raise a fund among the Bishop's former pupils,

> I have learned not a little of the methods of big business, especially when they are so closely associated with the Government that one does not know when one ends and the other begins. If we emerge from this war with our social system much as before we shall have a dreadful struggle to free ourselves from the grip of big business chiefs.

From now on big business becomes almost as much of a *leitmotiv* in his utterances as sacramental superstition had been at an earlier stage.

It was not surprising that in June 1941, he should complain that big business was destroying competition and controlling prices, and that it probably wielded more power than the Government. That was merely a comment on the cement case. But he went on from there to advocate State socialism, in order to achieve a redistribution of wealth after the war. He was careful to make clear that it should be a Christian socialism and, while inveighing against big business, to indicate that there was no moral objection to small businesses. Nor did he think it necessary that all shares in big business should be transferred to public ownership; control to him was more important than ownership. From the start of the war, he was already looking ahead to the political situation when it ended and voicing his views in public. Indeed, he saw the concentration of industrial power and the growth of cartels not just as social evils in themselves but as major causes of the war, which should be eliminated afterwards if peace was to be firmly established. He spoke in 1942 of socialism as inevitable: the State must control not only large-scale industrial production and distribution but also the use of the land. His wish to see the land nationalized was not new and was only partly inspired by the need to replan the bombed areas and, as he saw it, to move people out of big cities. His support for dispersal, too, was not only motivated by the dangers of air-raids on densely-populated city centres, wise though the policy had proved in Birmingham itself. He was an early advocate of new towns for their own sake, with new roads to serve them and a single system of nationalized transport. With this active interest in post-war reconstruction, he welcomed the series of meetings undertaken by Archbishops Temple and Garbett, with John Winant, the American Ambassador, to draw public attention to the subject and took the chair for them when they came to Birmingham. This archiepiscopal and ambassadorial crusade was by no means popular with the business world, who saw it as ecclesiastical interference in matters of no concern to the Church, even though most businessmen would equally readily have thought it quite normal to express their own views vigorously on religion. But it had a strong appeal to Barnes, who regretted that the established Church was all too often regarded as the mouthpiece of financial interests and wanted to see it freed from a link with any particular class.

But despite this advocacy of socialism as a political philosophy, he continued to hold it incumbent on him as a bishop to remain independent of any political party. He enjoyed helping to defeat the National Government on the Education Bill in the House of Lords in July 1944; but this was on a subject long dear to his heart and not a matter of party controversy. Indeed, he was still governed largely by his long-standing puritanism, as when, in November of the same year, he spoke and voted against the introduction of premium bonds into Palestine; although Fisher, then Bishop of London, also spoke against it, he did not carry his convictions into the lobby. Barnes also made an unsuccessful attempt in 1943 to promote a debate on the Paddington estate of the Church Commissioners, where the Church was accused of allowing brothels on its property; in fact, the

Church as ground landlord could do little to control the head lessees. Barnes thought that the true position should be brought home to public opinion, because 'left-wing secularism is growing and feeds on the belief that the Church as a landowner is indifferent to moral considerations'. He must, incidentally, have been a sore trial to the business managers in the House: more often than not, he intervened unexpectedly after the Government spokesman thought that he had tidily wound up the debate. Nor can Barnes have endeared himself to the official spokesmen of the episcopal bench, from whose utterances he often openly differed.

He was even less inclined to identify himself with the Communist Party than with the Labour Party. Although, after Russia entered the war in June 1941, he advocated study of the Soviet system for its lessons for post-war Britain, he had earlier condemned Russia's attacks on Poland and Finland and her annexation of the Baltic states, he refused to intervene in protest against the suppression of the *Daily Worker*, he was to speak out against the Soviet annexation of East Prussia, and at one time he was actually instrumental in having a victim of Defence Regulation 18B freed from gaol. When he told his diocesan conference in 1942 that it was not the business of left-wing clergy to press for a Second Front in order to bring about a series of socialist states in Europe, he drew upon himself the anger of Lord Beaverbrook, who linked him with the Duke of Bedford, another pacifist opponent of the Second Front, and commented: 'The Bishop, who lays up vast treasures in heaven, and the Duke, who has many possessions on this earth, are both against the Second Front.' While Barnes's post-war prognostications probably reflected accurately enough the ambitions of the voters who were to bring a Labour Government to power in 1945, he would have readily admitted that his own political instinct was not infallible. As he put it, 'I do not profess to know how the tides of thought and feeling which create or assuage political passions are generated'. Thus, he used to say that, when from the Peers' Gallery he had heard Churchill's famous 'blood, toil, tears and sweat' speech, he had thought it a piece of exaggerated rhetoric which would evoke no response in the nation, and he later spoke of 'a touch of unreality that marred a supreme moment in British history'. But then, like many Englishmen of his generation, and still more of his political persuasion, he had up to 1940 entertained a profound mistrust of Churchill's political judgement.

Nor did he confine his post-war aspirations to domestic politics. From early in the war he spoke out on the international system which should be established after it. Here again his main concern was to make sure that the tragedy of Versailles and the years between the wars should never again be repeated. At Neville Chamberlain's memorial service, he spoke of the 'Foreign Office record of tangled failure', leading up to the Second World War. He urged then that this time there should be no hard peace inflicted on Germany, no dismemberment of her territory and no occupation by a conscripted army, with all the bitterness which it would engender. The war and the horrors of the concentration camps were the responsibility of the Nazis, not of the German people, and there should be a peace of reconciliation. If colonies were not to be internationally administered, Germany and Italy must again have a share of them to govern. He aroused criticism by asserting that Italy's record of colonial administration in Rhodes was better than Britain's in Cyprus. Sadly, however, he realised that the days of Woodrow Wilson were past. In suggesting study of the Russian economic system, indeed, he had compared it favourably with that of the United States. This was partly because of the dominance of 'big business' in the American free enterprise system. But he was also deeply suspicious of its international effects. Who, he asked, for example, had sold Japan the oil which had made Pearl Harbor possible? Answer was there none.

More positively, from an early stage he was calling on western Europe to organize itself as an independent entity in world affairs. In April 1943, he spoke in favour of a united Europe, with a common currency and no tariff barriers. Few political voices were being raised at that time in favour of such ideas which, within ten years, were to become a commonplace. Moreover, speaking in the next year in the House of Lords on the preservation of cultural monuments in the battle zones, he emphasized the need for the new Europe to be a Christian Europe, as indeed most of the founding fathers of the Common Market were also devoutly to wish, although they would want it to be a Catholic Christianity. Later in 1944 he was giving his view that a Federation of Europe, which should certainly include Germany, should be provided with international organizations for manufacture, trade and transport. The business of Europe should not be 'big business'.

Nor were his interests confined to Europe. He continued to be closely concerned with India, where he appealed for the Congress leaders to be left free and for new negotiations with Gandhi, whom he saw as an apostle of non-resistance and someone who understood the true principles of Christianity. He even raised the possibility of American mediation between the imperial government and Indian representatives. With prophetic insight, he spoke in 1943 of his 'desire to see India freely choosing to be a member of the British Commonwealth of Nations'. In these years too he took an increasing interest in China, not least because his younger son was serving there with the Friends' Ambulance Unit. Barnes publicly welcomed the survival of the ancient civilization of China under Japanese assaults and affirmed his belief in her future. But at the luncheon where he spoke he confessed his total inability to use chopsticks.

Despite these preoccupations over the political and international future, Barnes could not and did not neglect the ecclesiastical present. He was still the administrator of a busy diocese and a member of a bench of bishops governing the national Church. He continued, too, to be much in demand as a speaker, addressing such varied war-time audiences as the Society of Chemical Industry, the Junior Chamber of Commerce, the Workers' Educational Association, several Rotary Clubs, the Co-operative Society, the Ear and Throat Hospital, the Birmingham City Transport Workers, a Religious Books Exhibition, or the Shakespeare Celebration of the Literary Association, quite apart from constant sermons and addresses to more strictly religious gatherings. His choice of subjects reflected his usual versatility. Addressing the Methodist Conference in July 1943, he warned them to beware of big business chiefs, but also to avoid following dexterous ecclesiastics. 'Follow Christ, as Wesley pointed the way, and God will bless you.' Just as he deplored what he saw as the prostitution of Christianity to nationalism, so too he regretted the divisions of the Church and the timorous failure of the clergy to face up to intellectual and moral challenge. For him, the first casualty of war was truth; but the second was social reform. 'What is wanted is not so much dogmatic Christianity as those essentials of the Christian faith which make for the Christian way of life.' In the same spirit, at Canterbury Convocation in January 1942, he deplored the reintroduction of controversial proposals on Prayer-Book reform in the middle of a great war.

He remained an austere moralist and spoke out again and again to denounce the effects of war on the moral standards of the community: the growth of dishonesty, the use of coarse language and the alarming rise in the divorce rate. True to his upbringing, he was particularly disturbed by the decline in Sunday observance and was relieved and happy when in April 1941 Parliament rejected the Government's proposal to open theatres and music-halls on Sundays. He implied that this proposal might be due to the strength of Jewish influence in the entertainment industry and for this was, not surprisingly, taken privately to task by Jewish leaders in Birmingham. But his concern was not with Sunday, or the Sabbath, as such. He remained apprehensive of the moral dangers of cinemas, which he thought should be under State control.

To counter the moral degeneration which he saw around him, he helped in 1942 to launch a United Birmingham Missionary Campaign, designed to recall the city to a Christian way of life and to restore Christian standards in Britain and Europe. This was a joint venture by the Anglican and Free Churches and, in the same spirit, Barnes suggested that after the war those Churches should unite in rebuilding places of worship in the city. For churches had suffered grievously from the bombing. By June 1941, eight of them had been destroyed and no less than one hundred and thirty-five damaged. Naturally enough, the civil defence services had had to give priority to saving lives, houses and industrial premises. As Barnes realised, this would impose a heavy burden on the diocese after the war; but he also recognized an ironical opportunity to replan on better lines than before. As he himself put it, the new church extension would be the best memorial to those who had died in the war.

Not only the physical pillars of the diocese were coming down. In September 1943, the Archdeacon of Birmingham resigned. Hopton was in his eighty-third year, had been Archdeacon since 1915 and for the past nineteen years had been a tower of strength in the diocese and, despite doctrinal differences, a real and loyal personal friend to Barnes. Barnes would, it seems, have liked to have Eric Abbott, later Dean of Westminster, as one of his archdeacons. Abbott had been one of the first to write and welcome Barnes's advice to his clergy on sermons in wartime, and his appointment would have provided fresh evidence of Barnes's readiness to promote those whose theological views differed from his own. But Abbott was fully occupied elsewhere and on this occasion the Bishop appointed a fellow-modernist in Geoffrey Allen, a former chaplain of Ripon Hall, then serving as secretary to the National Christian Council of China. Another development which must have given Barnes great pleasure was the foundation at last, through the generosity of the Cadburys, of the Chair of Theology at Birmingham University, for which he had long campaigned. Nor would he have minded at all that its first occupant was a Free Churchman; on the contrary, his own first suggestion was Reinhold Niebuhr and, when this was not adopted, he was delighted that the Professor appointed was his friend and fellow-pacifist, H. G. Wood.

There were some less happy problems of a personal kind. Barnes had always insisted on clergy living in their parishes, sometimes against the opposition of those who found cheaper or more comfortable quarters outside. But in wartime, and particularly under the bombing, several of them found it more congenial to absent themselves from the target area altogether. The Bishop had a good deal of acrimonious correspondence in his efforts to persuade these timid Timmies either to come back to share the fate of their parishioners or to resign their livings. Luckily they were rare exceptions to a general rule of devotion to duty.

One personality problem of particular concern to Barnes, because it touched both his diocese and his pacifism, was the case of Stuart Morris, the former Diocesan Secretary whom he would gladly have made Archdeacon of Aston in 1937. Morris had preferred to continue his work for the Peace Pledge Union, so much so that he had renounced his orders in 1939 'as a protest against the official attitude of the Church of England towards the war' and moved into the political arena. In May 1941, he stood as a Pacifist in a by-election at King's Norton in Birmingham and scored the surprising figure, immediately after heavy raids, of 1552 votes, nearly beating an Independent who stood on a platform of reprisals against Germany. This may partly have been due to Morris's local knowledge and warm personality; but he went on to pursue his political aims with more single-mindedness than discretion. In December 1942 he was arrested and charged under the Official Secrets Act with receiving documents from a government department. After a trial *in camera* Morris was sentenced to nine months' imprisonment, the judge describing his conduct as shocking. The trial was not reported at the time and the result was only made known by a Home Office statement nearly a month later. Barnes, who had kept in frequent touch with Morris over pacifist matters, gave evidence on his behalf but was not allowed to see or hear other testimony or details of the charge. While some of Morris's friends were inclined to accuse him of a schoolboyish delight in secret information, Barnes preferred to describe him as an idealist, who efficiently docketed any information which came his way but could be trusted not to misuse it. Morris's friends told the Bishop that his evidence had helped to lighten the sentence. Barnes himself thought that, without the special conditions of wartime, there might even have been no prison sentence. He considered raising the matter in the House of Lords but, much as he disliked secret trials and *ex parte* government statements, decided that further publicity would not help Morris. But after the war, when Morris was refused an American visa, Barnes again wrote in his support, though without success. The Peace Pledge Union were less generous to their General Secretary. They hastened to dissociate themselves from his actions and he had to resign his position, though continuing to work for the Union. Morris had a troubled life, but he was perhaps one of the geese in the Birmingham diocese whom Barnes persisted in regarding as swans.

But of course the most significant wartime changes in the personalities of the Church of England flowed from Lang's retirement in 1942 and Temple's early death in 1944 after barely two years at Lambeth. Barnes's relations with Lang had always been correct rather than cordial, and it was perhaps lucky that he did not have to pronounce an obituary on him at this time. Luckily too they had not crossed swords since the abdication in 1936; Lang had kept out of the cement controversy, and Barnes's attempt to put down a motion in Convocation at that time about the need for post-war industrial reform had been frustrated by illness. He was appointed one of the Royal Commissioners to confirm Temple's election as Archbishop of Canterbury. The appointment, though inevitable, was not unwelcome. Although Temple had of late moved closer to the establishment, he was a man of real intellectual power with strong social sympathies, a further illustration of the rule that few churchmen of his generation kept to the left both politically and theologically. He and Barnes had worked closely together during the First World War in particular, when Temple was editing the *Challenge* and Barnes writing regularly for it, and they had been colleagues for a time at Westminster. They had, in fact, regularly written to each other by their surnames without preamble or title, an uncommon enough practice among ecclesiastics of those days. In 1930 Temple would still write four pages in his own hand to Barnes from York; but despite this informality of manner the substance was critical and impatient of people who called themselves modernists. Temple's thesis then was that no one had questioned evolution or relied on miracles for many years, but myths had a spiritual value of their own which should not be ignored or rejected out of hand. Modernism as an intellectual attitude was indispensable to the Church, but it was harmful to the Church for modernists to form a separate organization, many of whose utterances seemed mainly negative. Already, like so many archbishops before and since, Temple was putting the unity of the Church in the forefront of his mind. But even so, in 1931 he was asking Barnes if he would write a book of 10,000 to 15,000 words on God and Evolution, although Barnes declined on the grounds that he was still busy with his Giffords. 'How I wish that I did not think so slowly and write with such difficulty.' Apart from their exchanges over prayers in the House of Lords, Barnes had little occasion for correspondence with Temple while he was actually at Lambeth. But Barnes gave full support to the Archbishop's call for a new Christian order of society. When Temple died he paid public tribute to his vitality, his sense of humour, his personal piety and modesty, his sympathy with those less fortunate than himself and his work for Church union. But he felt bound to mention also his theological conservatism, his lack of scientific qualifications and his limited knowledge of banking and finance. Finally, 'it must be confessed that his most noteworthy achievement, the creation of the Church Assembly, has disappointed expectations'. Writing privately in 1946 he was even more negative:

> When I first knew him, he was placidly critical, his attitude being substantially that of Streeter. As the years went on, a dreadful orthodoxy seems to have enveloped him. His extraordinary dexterity with words remained, but whether the ideas behind the words became increasingly valuable I doubt.

In short, *ichabod*. The glory had departed and Barnes would not have been alone in thinking that Temple was *felix opportunitate mortis*.

With Temple's successor Barnes was later to have much ado. He had known both Lang and Temple for a quarter of a century, as men as well as bishops. They all three belonged to much the same generation in the Church and had been through many controversies and experiences in each other's company, if not always in agreement. But Geoffrey Fisher belonged to a new school. Although he had an academic background and although he had been a bishop since 1932, his first years had been in the Northern Province, until he came to London in 1939, when wartime conditions made frequent contacts harder. So Barnes did not know Fisher nearly as well as his two predecessors and temperamentally the two men had little in common. Time was to show how little.

Meanwhile Barnes managed to live a personal and family life reasonably happily within the confines of war. The spaciousness of pre-war hospitality at Bishop's Croft soon disappeared, but they still managed to put up the occasional guest, even including archbishops. One by one the servants departed to other wartime jobs, until only a couple of faithfuls remained. During the bombing, the drawing-room became the air-raid shelter, much less secure than Haldane and his like would have recommended or than Barnes himself had demanded for others, while Mrs Barnes repaired to the roof to shovel away incendiary bombs and direct their extinction below. She used afterwards to explain her parents' longevity by pointing out that they had not had to live through two world wars. Barnes himself was active in visiting bombed churches and letting himself be seen where his presence could be most encouraging. Although he complained that he only had second-class priority on the telephone, he had a generous supplementary ration of petrol for his duties and still managed on his basic ration to repair to Seaton when he could, making clear that if there was an air-raid on Birmingham he would return at once. Holidays were fewer and shorter than they had been and visits to London on duty less and less comfortable or agreeable. But the Bishop took a masochistic pleasure in travelling third-class in gaiters on the early workmen's train and, when in London, he could still stay in one of his clubs and keep in touch with affairs by meeting his brother Sidney or one of his acquaintances for a meal or a talk. Sidney stayed at the Admiralty until the end of 1944, when he was made Director of Greenwich Hospital, and remained a shrewd and cynical judge of men and events. His main wartime achievement was to build the large redbrick Admiralty annex on Horse Guards Parade, which he liked to describe as 'my little wooden hut'; Winston Churchill was less complimentary, calling it a 'vast monstrosity'.

Looking as always to the future, Barnes was keen to put down more roots in Devon. In 1941 he took great pleasure in acquiring two farms at Cookshayes and Slade in the Widworthy valley, near Honiton and Axminster. Although the farms were nominally owned by his wife and sons jointly, it was he who played the greatest part in their management, and they provided an absorbing interest for the rest of his life. Some two hundred acres, with one farmhouse dating back to at least Elizabethan times, they then cost £4000. They fulfilled Barnes's need for close links with the countryside, but he also justified them as a hedge against inflation. As he wrote to his son at the time:

> In ten years' time, if the value of the one pound note should be one-third of what it is at present, the property should nominally be worth three times as much . . . I like to think of you being part owners of a Widworthy property. When times become normal again, visiting the farms and learning of difficulties and possibilities should give a touch of spice to visits to Seaton. At any rate, when the world seems lapsing into chaos, Cookshayes bears witness to centuries-old endurance.

But despite visits to London, country pursuits in Devon and the constant diocesan routine, Barnes's wartime life was one of growing isolation. He was driven back more and more on his own thoughts and his own reading. These were increasingly focused on the early history of Christianity, inspired partly by his need to assert the pacifism of the early Church and fed by his own abiding study of the Bible. He believed strongly, too, that Christianity had emerged in a world very similar to that of the present day: it had been a religion of the proletariat, which arose 'among provincials of the lower middle-class' in 'an agnostic State fashioned by war and permeated by great aggregations of wealth'. These parallels he was already seeking to apply to the period of post-war reconstruction. He read widely in these fields, but in books largely of his own choice, and he had little chance to discuss his ideas or conclusions with others working in the same field.

Few people can have welcomed the end of the war so whole-heartedly. On 8 May 1945 he greeted VE-Day with this statement:

> Thank God, fighting in the West has ceased. We can go forward with hope. At home we can now begin to rebuild our social life. Between

the nations reason can begin to prevail over passion. Stern and difficult times lie ahead. We grieve that bloodshed continues in the Far East, but we now have the first rays of dawn after the troubled night. Again I say: 'Thank God'.

He was over seventy years old, but the end of a world war was still for him a new beginning.

CHAPTER X

POST-WAR BIRMINGHAM
1945-1953

The Book on the Bible

The Bishop was not alone in Birmingham in looking for a new start after the war. The electorate, too, which in 1935 had returned twelve Conservatives for twelve seats, now in the 1945 election only gave them two out of thirteen. In Birmingham at any rate, even if not in the nation as a whole, this was a vote not so much against Churchill and his wartime leadership as against Chamberlain and the whole ethos of Conservative pre-war administration. This is not to say that it was a vote against appeasement. Indeed, appeasement was largely forgotten. People looked back far more to the unemployment and the class friction of the 1930s and were determined that if possible these things should not recur. They distrusted the ability of the Conservative Party, even under Churchill, to meet this requirement. Churchill had changed many things, not least the Conservative Party. But people were looking for bigger changes still.

So was Barnes. Not for him the nicely calculated less or more of political pragmatism. He was a radical in all things and his radicalism grew on him with the years. Despite his age he shared many of the aspirations of the new voters. As always, it was to younger minds and new breeds of men that he hoped to appeal. Policies in State and Church should be geared to the needs of the 'intelligent artisan'. The intelligent artisan was perhaps for him an idealized abstraction whom he would have had difficulty in recognizing or addressing if he had met him. Nor certainly would he have shared all his tastes and desires.

Nevertheless, it was the best interest of the young and the poor which he believed should be served. This aim had lain at the root of all his teaching for many years. Never was it to do so more than now, when in many ways a *tabula rasa* had, almost literally, been presented to him.

The city of Birmingham, and not least its churches, had suffered badly from the bombing. Eight churches were total losses and many others damaged. Several parishes had lost not only their places of worship but much of their congregations too. Many people had moved out into the suburbs or further afield, and would not be coming back. The parochial structure could not be reconstructed just as it had been. Churches in the centre of the city would need to be closed, pulled down or amalgamated. In fact, eight churches in central Birmingham were to be closed between 1945 and 1955. New incumbents should not meanwhile be appointed to livings which existed in little more than name only. In the outlying areas, more new churches, or rather church halls, would be needed than ever before. For the third time in just over twenty years Barnes was called to embark upon a new wave of church extension. This time, after a pause for reflection by a diocesan commission, it took the form of a Ten-Year Forward Movement, launched in 1946 under the chairmanship of the new Archdeacon of Aston, Michael Parker. This was not just a building campaign linked with an appeal for funds. It was an attempt to revivify the life of the diocese as a whole, by strengthening its administrative structure, raising the level of clergy stipends, increasing the number of candidates for ordination, providing new church buildings, including homes for the clergy, bringing church schools up to the standards of the new 1944 Education Act and thus helping, as Barnes himself put it, to 're-establish the Christian way of life' in Birmingham. All this seemed as if it might mean raising and spending something of the order of half a million pounds over the next ten to twelve years, but the immediate target was to be more modest. The Church could not do the job on its own. The diocesan and civic authorities had to work closely hand-in-hand. Co-operation between Anglicans and Free Churchmen could often also serve a common purpose. To Barnes's mind, too, developments in Birmingham should form part of a unified plan for reconstruction of the Midlands. For the task of the Church was to serve the people. Barnes quoted Rousseau: 'It is the people that make up the human race: what is not the people is so small a group as not to be worth the trouble of counting.' It was the same spirit as Ernest Bevin showed when, across a Foreign Office despatch recounting the views of the political and diplomatic élite, he would scrawl, 'What do the workers think?' In this spirit, too, Barnes was quite content, nay eager, for the clergy to be active in politics for social progress, provided they did not exploit the advantage of the pulpit to promote their own political views. They could not be silent, he told his Diocesan Conference, when, for example, idealism was opposed to 'big business' interests, when private ownership of land prevented slum clearance, when family life suffered from slow demobilization or when children were killed on bad roads while no motorways were built.

The wind of change blew into Barnes's own life too. Already before the war, under an Order in Council of 1937, the income of the bishopric, as of other sees, had been taken over by the Ecclesiastical Commissioners on their Common Fund, in place of the original endowment under which it had depended on the dividends from various investments, some of which had been passed or reduced in the economic crisis of the early 1930s. This had helped to stabilize matters for the Bishop. He was now glad to let the diocese know that, instead of his original official income of £4200 a year, which sounded so large but out of which he had had to meet all the expenses of a large house, the house would become the responsibility of the Ecclesiastical Commissioners and he would only be paid £2400. Even out of this he would pay a rent of £420 and a pension charge of £72, so that his net income would only be £1908 a year and on this he would pay tax. He was particularly pleased that the pension was to be funded, remembering the burden his predecessor had imposed on him for several years. It is true that, despite the egalitarian sound of the new arrangements, the Ecclesiastical Commissioners, in taking over Bishop's Croft, did a good deal to make it more habitable and convenient in the new servantless era. It's an ill wind . . .

Changes inevitably came too among his main colleagues in the diocese. Barnes had been lucky in working for so long with a largely unchanged team. But now the years began to take their toll. At the end of 1945, McGowan, Archdeacon of Aston, was appointed Bishop of Wakefield, where tragically he survived less than three years. In his place Barnes chose Michael Parker, whose appointment was another sign of the Bishop's tolerance of views other than his own. Parker had been a 'rebel', serving as curate to his brother-in-law, and thus refused the Bishop's licence to officiate. But after some years of unhappiness both he and his brother-in-law had rejoined the fold and Parker gave loyal service as Vicar of King's Heath. True, he shared many of the Bishop's social and pacifist views, and Barnes much enjoyed working with him, but he also had marked administrative ability, and the appointment fully justified itself: Parker went on to be Bishop of Aston and of Bradford. In the same way, when in 1946 the Roman Catholic Archbishop of Birmingham died, Thomas Williams, whom Barnes had known from Cambridge days, the Bishop did not let the religious divide prevent him from attending the funeral and paying public tribute; but then his quarrel had never been so much with Roman Catholics, who were open in their allegiance, as with the disloyal in his own ranks. In 1946, too, there died George Bryson, who had been chairman of the Diocesan Board of Finance for twenty-three years, and Hopton, who had resigned the Archdeaconry of Birmingham only three years before after twenty-eight years in that office. Bryson was succeeded by Stephen Lloyd, Neville Chamberlain's son-in-law and an executive of Guest, Keen and Nettlefold. Hopton's successor, Geoffrey Allen, after only two years as Archdeacon, was made Bishop in Egypt the same year, despite Barnes's protests to the Archbishop that Allen should be kept for an English diocese, which in fact he later attained. Also in 1946, R. D. Richardson, one of Barnes's examining chaplains and most stalwart Modernist supporters, was named as Principal of Ripon Hall Theological College at Oxford. Harvie Clark succeeded Allen as Archdeacon and Richardson as Vicar of Harborne and was to give Barnes strong support for the next six years. Although Barnes was sorry to lose both his Archdeacons within a year, he could enjoy pointing to the fact that Birmingham had become a training-stable for future winners on other courses, Indeed, he was later to claim that, whereas elsewhere clergy were reactionary, lacking in mental agility or apathetic, 'in this diocese, through the constant care that has been exercised, our clergy stand out well in the religious life of the country'; and he must have welcomed the letter from a clergyman leaving the diocese who wrote: 'The standards of scholarship and social service that obtain here have been a constant inspiration to me, as they are to many others.'

1947 was comparatively calm in this respect, though far from being so in others. But 1948 saw the retirement not only of Stuart Blofeld, an examining chaplain and the Vicar of Edgbaston, of quiet strength since Barnes came to Birmingham, and of Guy Rogers, the individual-istic Rector of Birmingham since 1925 and a self-styled rebel at heart, even though he might have been a bishop, but also of J. H. Richards from the Provostship of the Cathedral, recently restored at no little cost from its heavy bomb damage. Here again, to be Richards's successor Barnes sounded a former Birmingham incumbent, W. G. Arrowsmith, but his real preference was for Charles Raven, whose claims to a bishopric he had so often urged without success on the authorities. Raven shared his modernism, his pacifism and his social sympathies and would have been a most welcome colleague, quite apart from the fact that his time as Master of Christ's was running out and nothing else seemed to be on the cards. Indeed, Archbishop Fisher had rejected Raven's offer of his services out of hand. But Raven, whose first wife had died two or three years before, now relied on his daughter as his housekeeper; she did not, it seems, want to leave Cambridge for Birmingham, and ostensibly on these grounds he declined Barnes's invitation to become Provost. Nor Did Mervyn Stockwood then want to leave Bristol. Inpractice, the appointment now passed out of Barnes's hands. As part of a scheme to reorganize the Cathedral finances, so as to provide for residentiary canons, one of whom would also be Professor of Theology and another Suffragan Bishop, the Provost's House was to be completely rebuilt and part of it let profitably to an oil company. While this went on, the Provost would have nowhere to lay his head, so that the post was left vacant and the appointment lapsed to the Crown. The new Provost was not appointed until 1951 and, although Barnes was naturally consulted and agreed, the choice was not his. With his two new archdeacons and with the invaluable and experienced help of Bishop Linton, he was to play out his time at Birmingham.

The demands of administration were incessant and he did his best in response to them. Throughout his time at Birmingham, for example, he had always taken great pains in selecting subjects for discussion by the Diocesan Conference and in securing speakers to advocate progressive causes there. He also took a good deal of trouble over his own contributions on those occasions. In his correspondence, too, his collaborators admired the way in which, with a letter of a few short, pithy sentences, covering half a page, he could make the essential points on which others would have expended six sheets of foolscap. Indeed, journalists also used to complain that, since he made every word count, his remarks could not be summarized and had to be reported verbatim. During these years he was constantly to plead the pressure of diocesan reorganization as an excuse for refusing outside engagements. But, although teaching is endless repetition and he was nothing if not a teacher, his real reason for refusing must also often have been a wish, perhaps largely instinctive, to avoid occasions when he could only repeat himself. He was essentially an ideas-man; but he needed time, more time perhaps as the years went by, to keep his ideas fresh. Some time he had had during the war, or at least more time than either before or since. He had used it for reading and research into the origins of Christianity, and it was the result of these wartime lucubrations that he was now set to publish. He called his work *The Rise of Christianity*, but in the family it was always known as 'the Book on the Bible', or 'the B on the B' for short.

The book was first offered in 1944 to the Cambridge University Press, who to Barnes's chagrin refused it on the grounds that it was too one-sided for them. After some reflection and consultation, Barnes then sent it to Longmans, who had occasionally asked him to write something for them in the past. Towards the end of 1945 Longmans accepted it; but, what with paper shortage, the coal crisis and other difficulties of the time, it was not published until March 1947.

Priced at 15/–, this controversial book contained fewer than 350 octavo pages, divided into 334 numbered sections. It covers a wide range of thought and is correspondingly condensed. Christianity is first set against its historical background: evolution, early human religious expression, Middle Eastern conflicts, Judaism, Greek and Roman classical ideas, other aspects of Mediterranean culture, the mystery religions' contribution and the climate of contemporary thought, not least its credulity. Against this background, the Gospels and the other books of the New Testament are examined for their historicity, in order to reach conclusions about the life, death and teaching of Jesus. The method followed is essentially that of textual analysis of the books of the New Testament, sometimes known as source criticism, of the kind associated particularly with the work of such scholars as Burkitt and Streeter. But other contemporary writings are also brought under tribute and the author often calls in aid his own scientific training. The reliability of the Gospels and, still more, of the Pauline epistles as historical documents is analysed and called in question. The object is to reach the person of Jesus, behind the adornments with which He has been dressed by St Paul and His other early followers. The broad conclusion is that Jesus is certainly no myth. He lived, taught, suffered and died in history. But more can be known about His teaching than about His life, and His teaching is a better clue to His nature and His influence than any record of His life can ever now be. From this starting-point the main doctrines and rites of the Christian Church are examined in turn: the Fall and Atonement, Baptism and the Eucharist. From this examination the conclusion, again in very broad terms, emerges that their significance lies more in their exemplary moral influence than in any alleged supernatural or miraculous element. This leads on to a study of the early Christian community, showing how it held fast to high personal and civic virtues, which expressed themselves in purity of personal life and in socialist, pacifist and internationalist policies. A brief excursus at the end shows how the Church lost these prime qualities when it became institutionalized and identified with the official establishment.

In the course of his argument, Barnes came in effect totally to repudiate any miraculous element in the origin of Christianity, either in the circumstances of Christ's own birth and death or in actions which He performed. So too in the contemporary world. Barnes took his stand on the uniformity of nature, which was perfectly compatible with the creative activity of God. This did not exclude continuous divine activity, as, for example, in changes in genes in living cells or in exceptional cases of the influence of mind over body. But it did exclude 'finite-scale activities contrary to the normal ordering of nature' of the kind related in the New Testament. As some reviewers did not fail to point out, he had thus come a long way from the expressions of his personal faith in miracles some thirty years before. His stand now led him for example, to put particular confidence in the reliability of the Didache, in which there are no miraculous stories; and this led one critic to jeer that the Didache was a manual of church order, with no occasion to tell miracle-stories, and that one might as well 'praise the absence of limericks from Mrs Beaton's Cook Book'.

Such, in barest outline, is the content of a book which, as soon as it appeared, created a storm of controversy. Its sincerity was not questioned; but its methods and its conclusions were. One of the first reviews came in the *Spectator* from Charles Raven. Barnes was pleased with this review, and Raven welcomed the book as 'convincing proof that a man of outstanding intellectual integrity can give full effect to the work of critical scholarship and without shirking or minimizing its results can find it consistent to remain not only as a confessing Christian but as an Anglican bishop'. This verdict was fully in accord with Barnes's object in writing the book. But even Raven did not conceal that he differed from the author on many particular points. Other reviewers were more hostile. Many of them fixed on a passage in the Foreword:

> I personally find that the early Christian story as it can now be told explains why men, gaining understanding from prayer and sacraments, have, since the gospel was first proclaimed, worshipped Jesus the Christ as divine. I, too, so worship him: I have been at pains that the fact should not affect my historical enquiry.

This firm faith in the centrality of Jesus and acceptance of His divinity had run through Barnes's teachings since his earliest sermons. But captious, or orthodox, reviewers asked how this passage could be reconciled with the reductionist picture of Christ which emerged from the pages of the book itself. For them a divinity worthy to be worshipped depended on attributes which the author had either rejected or whittled away. As one put it, he had turned the New Testament into Hamlet without the Prince. In fact, Barnes had only gone as far as he did in his foreword under pressure from Longmans, who wanted something which 'might not only have a steadying effect on those whose views are different from yours, but would also be of the greatest comfort to those to whom your views are a relief but who . . . often tend to discard their personal devotion when they discard the traditional dogmas'. Barnes accepted this but added: 'I am somewhat anxious not to over-emphasize my own religious faith lest I should prejudice the appeal which I should like the book to make to the many who are acutely critical of Christianity as they know it.' This intellectual austerity did not disarm the stone-throwers. They emphasized the negative aspects of the book's conclusions and, although several of them recognized the positive religious assertions in the central chapter on 'Jesus and His Teaching', declared that these still did not balance the other side of the scale. 'Christians should say what they believe, not what they do not believe.' Barnes took the view that this was to misjudge the purpose of the book. He had written in the publisher's blurb that he had 'endeavoured to

present a scrupulously fair account of The Rise of Christianity . . .
Save for a single sentence in the Preface, Dr Barnes nowhere reveals
his own religious position', and he concluded: 'Modern Europe
needs a faith: can Christianity, as we must henceforth view it, supply
Europe's need? Dr Barnes's answer is a persuasive affirmative.'
Even so, to develop that affirmative would, in his view, have to be
the subject of another book, which in fact he never wrote. He saw
The Rise of Christianity itself as a companion volume to *Scientific
Theory and Religion*, since in his Gifford Lectures he had been
precluded by his terms of reference from dealing with revealed
religion as such. He was thus now taking on again where the Giffords
had had to leave off.

Two other general lines of criticism were advanced in many
reviews. First, he was accused, with some justice, of referring with
approval to 'modern critics', 'analytical scholars' and so on, without
identifying them and thus without giving the reader the opportunity
to judge how reliable or how universal the views of these critics and
scholars were. This was an old feature of Barnes's debating style and
by its very subjectivity undoubtedly detracted from the strength of
his arguments. But in the present case he could with justice plead
shortage of space and the need not to burden his pages with footnotes
and elaborate references. He did include a bibliography, but this
only helped to provoke the second general criticism, which was to the
effect that his reading and therefore his views were thirty years out of
date and that he was thus taking up an old-fashioned position more
negative than more modern scholars would adopt. In particular, it
was said that he had followed too much the devices and desires of
literary and textual criticism and had neglected the new emphasis on
'form criticism' and on the oral tradition behind the gospel writings.
This thesis was powerfully developed by C. H. Dodd in a pamphlet on
'Christian Beginnings', specifically published as a reply to Barnes's
book. Dodd's biographer says of this episode:

> One of his chief ambitions was to be a reliable historian and what this
> meant to him became very clear in an article which was perhaps the
> most outspoken and severely critical that he ever wrote . . . As always,
> Dodd tried to be fair to the book, acknowledging its constructive
> features. But in the main he found the Bishop's method of writing the
> history of the ancient world hasty and shallow. He likened it to a
> possible way of doing a jig-saw puzzle. 'The specific pieces of a jig-saw
> puzzle may look entirely meaningless, but it is unwise either hastily to

discard a piece, because you cannot think so queer a shape will fit anywhere, or to trim it to a better shape.' Patience, he claimed, would gradually bring the pattern of the whole to view. The historian, in his opinion, needs 'accurate information, command of critical method, patience, sobriety of judgement and the historical judgement which includes the power to enter with sympathy into the minds of men of another age'. Because these qualities seemed to be deficient in Bishop Barnes's incursion into the writing of history (his qualifications as mathematician were of the highest order) the results could not be taken seriously.

This is a partisan account, and Dodd was undoubtedly a leading scholar in the field. Others, too, commented adversely on Barnes's lack of imaginative ability to project himself into another period of history. But even on this showing, Dodd exposes himself to the charge, which he and others brought against Barnes, that in the last resort they all came back to believing what they wanted to believe. Some such subjectivities in Dodd's own pamphlet were pointed out by other commentators. As one fellow-professor said, 'he is tainted with Barthianism and wants direct interventions'. Form-criticism by its very nature is a rather shaky tool; textual criticism may sometimes cut too sharply but it can be more scientifically controlled.

As to the bibliography itself and the light which it shed on Barnes's background reading, he had explicitly introduced it as 'limited to comparatively recent works in the English language'. He had in fact read widely in other languages and, although he had studied such generally reductionist Frenchmen as Loisy and Guignebert, he by no means accepted all their negative conclusions. Moreover, his main objective was to present the contemporary sources to his readers and let them draw their own conclusions.

The experts of course attacked the book on many points of detail. But then Barnes would have answered that the book was not written for the experts, although he was quite prepared to challenge them on their own ground, as he did with T. W. Manson's anonymous review in *The Times Literary Supplement*. The book was written for the 'intelligent artisan' of the younger generation. This attitude sometimes led him rather far. For example, in a booklet called *The Bible and Modern Scholarship*, published the same year, the distinguished palaeographer Sir Frederic Kenyon uttered some direct criticisms of Barnes's book. In particular, he attacked Barnes's conclusions on the generally late date of the Gospels. Kenyon's argument was, briefly, that the Chester Beatty papyri, discovered in Egypt in 1931, were earlier than AD 250. They showed that by that time the New Testament text was firmly established. Moreover, the Rylands fragment of the Fourth Gospel, also found in Egypt in 1935, was written before AD 150. According to Kenyon, it would have taken time for these documents to reach Egypt from Palestine; therefore the texts must have been circulating in Palestine well before those dates, especially if, as was the case, as early as the first century the documents were in roll-form, which would make later interpolations harder. The Fourth Gospel was therefore written at latest early in the second century. The other gospels are recognized as earlier and might well therefore be first-century texts, written by eye-witnesses and contemporaries of Christ. In Kenyon's view, Barnes had ignored these later discoveries and had cast unjustified doubt on the Gospel stories, particularly their miraculous elements. Kenyon did not actually assert the truth of the miracles, even if he implied it. His case in short was that 'what we are entitled to claim is that the books which we know as canonical were produced within some fifty years of the first century and that the evidence for their text is in all essentials early and good'. But he was at pains to defend tradition as a guide to knowledge, and he seemed throughout to imply that the biblical narrative, miracles and all, was necessary for faith. This was the essential issue between the two sides. Which basis for faith was the more satisfying, with miracles or without?

Others sprang to Barnes's defence, asking why the texts need have taken so long to reach Egypt, why they need have been in roll form rather than in codices in which interpolation would have been easier, whether the Rylands fragment could not be from Q rather than the Fourth Gospel, whether, even if Barnes's dates were too late, the traditional dates were necessarily right and, above all, even if the Gospels did date from the first century, did this prove that the miracles really happened? One of Kenyon's sharpest antagonists was Basil Liddell-Hart, the strategist and military historian, who challenged the authenticity of the Rylands fragment itself and suggested that Kenyon was more anxious to be orthodox than objective. This is merely an example of the kind of detailed argument which developed. Only experts can adjudge the rights and wrongs of it. Barnes himself welcomed Liddell-Hart's support almost too readily and represented him as an intelligent and unprejudiced observer, while hinting that Kenyon, who was admittedly by now eighty-four years old, was no longer worth taking seriously. Even H. D. A. Major, normally one of Barnes's strongest supporters, had to point out in a private letter to him that 'Captain Liddell-Hart is a most remarkable all-round man, but papyri must be treated by a specialist'. This was true enough as far as dates and handwriting were concerned, but it still did not prove that a given hand at a given date was necessarily writing absolute truth. Opinion always enters in.

In short, the experts could foot-fault him in their own courts. As Bethune-Baker, one of his closest friends and allies, regretfully wrote to Mrs Barnes privately:

Neither I nor anyone else I know, who has had N.T. study and criticism as his life-long study and considered all the theories about Gospels and Epistles as they came along from time to time from all kinds of quarters, can accept his conclusions in the way in which they are put – without caveats all the way through and some definite dismissals . . . Mine is not a reverential attitude to any of the critics, but just that I myself have known a good deal about these things and feel that the Bishop had nothing to guide him and strayed often. There really is something in our Cambridge tradition in literary and historical criticism and of course he has never had any of it. 'Sense and science' is not enough.

Thus spake the Professor. But even he in the same letters spoke of 'my whole-hearted agreement in general as regards the action of God in the world by "natural" rather than "supernatural" means – so no use of "miracle" in the popular sense – any amount of it in the psychic, spiritual sphere'. So, whatever the foot-faults, there were aces too.

By no means all the criticisms came from experts on their own ground. Many reviewers fastened only on the statement that the early Christians were socialist, pacifist and internationalist and accused Barnes of transporting his own current prejudices into a past where they did not belong. Here again they may have been unable to see the beam in their own eye. Because some of them were conservatives, militarists and nationalists, they started with a prejudice which predisposed them to fault-finding, so that they could gird on their *apparatus criticus* with a vengeance. This was probably true, for example, of the hostile reviewer in the *Modern Churchman*, who caused the editor so much distress that Major consulted Barnes before publication. But Barnes encouraged him to publish it as submitted, even if he added some editorial comment elsewhere in the same issue.

For what really mattered to Barnes was the opinion not of pedants but of the public. The book brought him an enormous post-bag: letters ranging from the congratulatory, grateful and encouraging to the critical, abusive and mad; correspondents questioning points of scholarship and doctrine or seeking reassurance in their own religious doubts; the self-centred describing 'miracles' in their own experience or volunteering their own writings, poems or diagrams; and the self-interested seeking further articles or reviews or simply anxious to obtain free copies. They came from all over Britain, from the Commonwealth and the United States and from continental Europe, especially Germany and Switzerland. To them all, except the mad and anonymous, Barnes did his best to reply, usually expressing some pessimism for the immediate future but a confident optimism that his views would prevail in the long run. To quote but a single, not untypical, example, Barnes was particularly pleased with a letter from Sybil Thorndike, who wrote:

It has given me more than I can tell you – of stimulation, of new doors opening into most wonderful views, of real challenge too. It is such a brave book, and coming from a priest of the Church it is more than brave. It has been a releasing for me, and I am sure it must have been for many people. – Your last paragraph should be written round the walls of our churches and homes. Thank you deeply. I hope it will make me a better Christian.

That helped to make it worthwhile. So did the success of the book, which was not just a *succès de scandale*. As one reviewer put it, there was not much wrong with the book, except its price and the difficulty of finding a copy. The publishers could not keep up with the demand. As Barnes told Archdeacon Parker, who expressed sympathy with him over the criticism: 'We all have our troubles, but my publisher is surrounded with gold.' The book went to five impressions in little over a year and over eighteen thousand copies were sold by July 1948. The figure would have been much higher, had it not been for post-war restrictions and shortages. Unluckily, there were never enough copies on the market and this may have limited the book's influence. Barnes was also disappointed that it was not possible to arrange for an American edition or for French or German translations. As far as the United States and Germany were concerned, this was probably due to the fears of local publishers as to the reception which the book might receive from fundamentalist or Barthian theologians.

Seen from the perspective of thirty years, it is still a remarkable book. One can fault it sometimes for ignorance. There is, for example, little knowledge of Jewish thought and tradition. Comparative religion is virtually confined to parallels between Christianity and the mystery-cults. In this context, it was sad that the Dead Sea Scrolls were only discovered at Qumran in the year that the book was published. Barnes might well have concluded that some of the earliest features of Christianity, including even aspects of the Eucharist, reflected more accurately the ideas of the sect of the Scrolls than those of the adepts of Mithras. The teachings of the Scrolls would certainly have had a strong appeal for him, with their emphasis on both the intellectual and mystical sides of religion; and the position accorded to the Superior of the sect, as leader, examiner, spiritual director and, above all, teacher, would, incidentally, have tallied very closely with Barnes's conception of the functions of a Christian bishop. But even if he had known more about Qumran and its Teacher of Righteousness, he would still have believed that Jesus Christ was the unique Guide and Master. One can also fault the book for style or even taste. There is a certain conscious rectitude, often based on subjective criteria. There is an element of moral judgement, nineteenth-century in tone and more *a priori* than objective. There is an impatience with contrary opinions. One can fault it for method. There are over-simplifications which suggest leaps to hasty conclusions. The approach is sometimes by way of quasi-mathematical proof, on subjects not susceptible to such treatment. Too often, perhaps, passages are treated factually and literally, when more imagination might have suggested that they would be better seen through the glass of symbolism or imagery. The thought is occasionally anachronistic, with the judgements of later generations superimposed on ancient words and thoughts.

But, even if the book was not quite so objectively impartial as its author intended and claimed, the wish to discover the truth shines through every page. So do the acceptance of Christ's supremacy as the teacher *par excellence* and the determination to make his teaching prevail. Even the somewhat simplistic approach is justified by the need and desire to make the argument intelligible and attractive to the non-professional reader. Phrases which thirty years later seem stilted or archaic are being read after the rapid increase of a frankness or permissiveness which is not always for the better. More recent theological speculation has at the same time led to a much wider realisation than even thirty years ago that the Christian message need not and cannot be expressed in the old, crude, material and anthropomorphic language. The new approach is different: more philosophical and psychological, less mathematical and analytical. But Barnes was not just tilting at windmills: the adversaries were real, as the reaction to the book showed. Whatever else may be said, this remains an astonishing book to have been published by a man over seventy years old on a subject in which he had had no professional training and at a time when he was deeply involved in diocesan administration and had been isolated by wartime restrictions from contact with other minds of equal critical ability.

The adversaries were real. They were not just to be found in the ranks of the academics. They were massed in the upper echelons of the ecclesiastical establishment. To them the scandal was not that the views in the book could be uttered at all, but that they had been uttered by a man holding office as a bishop in the Church. But their attitude was dictated not so much by intellectual disagreement as by fear of the consequences. Thus Garbett: 'I do not think that in the whole course of my ministry anything has happened in the Church of England more likely to injure the work and influence of the Church than this miserable book.' Or Henson, who called it a 'melancholy book': 'Barnes's book will serve as a very serviceable weapon in the hands of non-Christians, who will rejoice to discover that their own negations are so powerfully echoed within the Church of England.' This echoed a frequent comment by the orthodox that, if Barnes was a spokesman of the Church, she needed to be saved from her friends: *non tali auxilio nec defensoribus istis*. Others called it 'a manual for hecklers'. Henson himself was so obsessed with the book that in his last letter to the Dean of St Paul's, written on the day of his death, he referred to it as 'a really scandalous production by Barnes of Birmingham'.

The Archbishop of Canterbury himself, however, at first seemed to be taking it quite lightly. Writing on 26 March to thank Barnes for sending him a copy, he said 'It is perhaps improbable that I shall be able to accept all that you say, but I am quite sure that it will have been written with great honesty of mind and sincerity of spirit'. But other counsels soon began to prevail. Garbett from the start was saying that 'something ought to be done about it ... Unless we take public steps to dissociate ourselves from Barnes, we shall be looked upon as failing in our duty'. The Bishops of Durham and Chelmsford wrote reasoned refutations of the book's argument in their diocesan magazines, but went out of the way to express friendly sentiments to the author. Not so the Dean of Winchester, Gordon Selwyn, who as long ago as 1927 had written privately to Archbishop Davidson asking him to disavow Barnes, and now sent a public letter to the press to express the hope 'that some means may be found by which Dr Barnes's errors may be clearly repudiated as incompatible with the character of a bishop's office'. Indeed, Selwyn, who was a cousin of Barnes's wife, carried Christian charity and family feeling to the point of cutting Barnes at the Athenaeum.

Fisher himself had also had second thoughts. On 13 May he wrote privately to Barnes to say that he had now read the book, which 'causes me the greatest disquiet about your position'. He went on to criticize two or three passages on the Incarnation and the Resurrection and drew the conclusion that 'you make fundamental departures from the doctrines held by the communion to which you belong'. From this he drew the further conclusion that 'the holding of your opinions and the holding of your office are incompatible, and for myself I believe that you ought in conscience to feel the same'. He warned Barnes that he might have to express his opinion openly but would not want to do so without first letting him know. Barnes replied to the effect that, properly understood, the passages in question were not inconsistent with the doctrine of the Church, although what he was writing was 'a simple account of the rise of Christianity, not a conspectus of Anglican theology'. He in turn concluded:

> I do not think that I . . . reach conclusions which make it impossible for me to hold the office of a bishop. That office I have now held for nearly twenty-three years, so that I am at the present time senior diocesan bishop of the province of Canterbury. My sense of unworthiness to hold such an office has grown with the years; but it does not proceed from defects of belief. Though the range of my knowledge has greatly increased, my Christian belief has not changed in fundamentals since I was ordained forty-five years ago.

In a follow-up letter he asked to be told if the Archbishop intended a public criticism, so that he could have a chance to reply, and suggested, rather strangely, that a debate in the House of Lords might be better than in Convocation. The Archbishop replied somewhat sharply that he was not intending to refer publicly to the book and had no reason to suppose that he would be put into the position of having to do so.

There matters rested as between Archbishop and Bishop until July. But behind the scenes there was plenty of activity. Fisher was subjected to a good deal of pressure and advice. In effect, there were four courses open to him: to ignore the book, to have Barnes tried for heresy, to debate the whole matter in Convocation, or to issue a unilateral condemnation.

The case for ignoring the book, argued by some leading members of the episcopal bench, was that any public action would exaggerate the book's importance and send up its sales. Worse than that, it might drive some prominent churchmen, who did not altogether agree with Barnes, to rally to his side in defence of freedom of speech. Fisher himself would probably have preferred to take this course and to rely on the fact that many of the lay reviews of the book had been critical. But he was under increasing pressure, not least from Garbett, to take some action, and there was the constant risk that his hand would be forced and the initiative removed from him by a hostile motion being put down for Convocation.

Judicial action, however, was soon seen to be out of the question. H. D. A. Major was to set out the legal position in an authoritative article in the *Hibbert Journal*. To show the 'freedom of doctrinal teaching possessed by the clergy of the Church of England' he cited first the Gorham judgement of the Privy Council in 1850 and its judgement on *Essays and Reviews* after its publication in 1860. These gave freedom to liberal clergymen, but by its judgements in the Denison and Bennett cases of 1855 and 1869 respectively the Privy Council had granted similar freedom to High Churchmen. Moreover, by the Amended Clerical Subscription Act of 1865, Parliament had introduced a new Declaration of Assent to the Thirty-Nine Articles 'as bare and general as it was possible to be, consistently with the retention of any expression of intent at all'. Major also quoted the legal decision of 1866 which allowed Colenso, also incidentally a Second Wrangler and Smith's Prizeman, to remain Bishop of Natal and the judgement of the King's Bench division which in 1901 confirmed Gore's appointment as Bishop of Worcester, despite the protest over *Lux Mundi*. Finally, he drew attention to the Modern Churchmen's Conference of 1921 which had led Archbishop

Davidson to appoint a Doctrinal Commission the next year. The Commission had not reported until 1938, but the liberating influence of the report had then been widespread. For example, it had recognized that belief in the Virgin Birth and belief in a normal birth were both held by members of the Church 'who fully accept the reality of our Lord's Incarnation, which is the central truth of the Christian faith'. Major therefore contended that Barnes was fully entitled to profess his views and remain a bishop. He added, *obiter*, that the doctrinal freedom of the Church of England was not paralleled by any similar liturgical freedom, but that was a different matter. Another of Barnes's supporters underlined the same general point, saying that Elizabeth I's reign had been notable for the introduction of tobacco, potatoes and thirty-nine other articles, and that the Thirty-Nine Articles thus reflected the spirit of comprehensive toleration which informed the reformed Church of England.

For Fisher the dominant consideration was that, although Barnes could be arraigned for heresy in an Archbishop's Court, as Bishop King of Lincoln had been brought before Benson's Court in 1888, an appeal would lie with the Privy Council. Even if Barnes were found guilty of heresy, and some of the leading authorities were by no means certain that the charge could be made to stick, he could exercise his right of appeal; this would mean that a lay court would pass judgement on orthodoxy in the Church of England. Fisher was adamant that the Church could not put itself in that position.

But there were still dangers in action in Convocation. Not only would a debate be divisive. It could all too easily lead to the Church being made to appear reactionary in suppressing liberal ideas and curtailing existing freedoms. Barnes himself could also be represented as a martyr and this too would tend to alienate the younger educated people from the Church. It was therefore necessary to proceed with caution and, as a first step, Fisher decided to arm himself with a theological critique of the book, which could be used to guide him both in framing a resolution for Convocation and in drafting testing questions which he might thereafter put to Barnes on his orthodoxy. The Archbishop was evidently still looking for a lever with which to prise the Bishop of Birmingham out of his diocese.

With no little subtlety Fisher decided to ask the Dean of Winchester to be one author of the proposed theological critique. Selwyn was a respected theologian; but, more importantly in this context, he was one of those members of the Lower House of Convocation most insistently demanding some form of public action against Barnes, but it would be difficult for him to put down a motion while engaged on the critique. As his co-author Fisher selected Hodgson, Regius Professor of Divinity at Oxford. He toyed with the idea of asking Raven, as Regius Professor at Cambridge, to join them in their work, since the omission of the Cambridge Professor might otherwise look like packing the jury. But as it seemed only too likely that Raven would take Barnes's side and most improbable that he and Selwyn could ever agree on a joint report, this idea was abandoned. Other possible third men were considered, but in the end Selwyn and Hodgson were left in June to go ahead together.

Although Fisher had already sounded some of the bishops about the possibility of action in Convocation, he now decided to do so rather more formally. The problem was whether Barnes should be present. Although some would have liked him to be there to see how seriously his colleagues saw the matter, Fisher thought otherwise. On 3 July, he wrote to Barnes to say that he was receiving constant letters and questions and wanted to consult his brother bishops on the question whether anything should be said in public. He could best do this at the regular private Bishops' Meetings and 'I think you will agree that for this purpose your absence is desirable'. He asked Barnes not to attend the session concerned. Barnes replied that, while he would have thought he ought to be present, the Archbishop's decision was final. He reminded him that, while others were more likely to receive letters of condemnation, his own were warm in approval and that a careful reading of the book should make clear that he retained all the essentials of the Christian faith. 'I believe that, though the presentation of the Christian faith in my book may be novel, it is valuable and true.' He saw Fisher on 28 July, but kept no record of their talk, apart from sending him a copy of *Should Such a Faith Offend?*

The Archbishop's mind was evidently already moving towards a simple statement in Convocation rather than a debate, which might be hard to control, on a resolution there. While he was prepared to admit, somewhat patronizingly, that Barnes had a simple, sincere and Quakerish Christian belief of his own, he also regarded him as having a stupid mind and a blind spot which prevented him seeing a great deal which was in the New Testament. Whatever the value of these judgements, more immediately relevant was his fear that Barnes was a fighter who would enjoy being made into a martyr.

All the more reason to avoid a debate.

Matters came to a head at the end of September. At almost the same time as Fisher received the promised report from Selwyn and Hodgson, he heard from Garbett that a resolution was to be put down for the Lower House of York Convocation. The Archbishop of York held that Canterbury should utter first and that the Upper House should retain the initiative. Selwyn, who regarded Barnes's book as a travesty of the Christian religion, was demanding a repudiation of it, whereas Hodgson, who considered it more from the philosophical standpoint, wondered whether a positive reaffirmation of faith by Convocation would not be more appropriate than a negative condemnation of the book. They also suggested that, if the Archbishop wanted to examine Barnes for orthodoxy, he should put to him questions as to his views on the inspiration of Scripture, the Incarnation, the Resurrection, the Trinity and the Sacraments.

Fisher thereupon drafted a long statement which he could make in Convocation and sent the draft to three or four bishops for their comments, with a view to seeking the approval of the bishops as a body later. Some doubts were expressed. Most thought that he was giving the book too much prominence and that he should either arrange for an open letter, to which he could reply with less risk of an effective come-back from Barnes than in Convocation itself, or he should at most append a short reference to the book to a more general presidential address to Convocation. Fisher, perhaps by now with some pride of authorship, decided that he had no other suitable subject on which to enlarge at Convocation; but he did shorten his draft a good deal, omitting not only various controversial points of doctrine on Christ's nature and life but also several comments on Barnes's motives.

The stage was now set for the meeting of the Convocation of Canterbury on 15 October 1947. Fisher only warned Barnes the night before of his proposed statement, of which he sent him a text, so that Barnes had not even brought the book to London with him and no copy could be bought in the bookshops. In his statement delivered to the joint opening session, Fisher referred to the distress and indignation which the book had caused among churchpeople, not least because it was written by a diocesan bishop. He gave credit to the Bishop's intentions, sincerity and devotion. But he warned against treating the uniformity of nature as an 'authoritative dogma', against relying on one's own spiritual perception alone and against the subjective treatment of evidence. 'The Bishop arrives at, or hints at, conclusions which are so much less than the faith of the Church as to be seriously inconsistent with its creeds and forms of worship.' 'The fact that a Bishop should publish a book which is so inadequate to the Church's doctrine as to be both implicitly and explicitly inconsistent with it cannot but disturb and shock us.' Then came the sentence which hit the headlines: 'If his views were mine, I should not feel that I could still hold episcopal office in the Church.' In effect, he was not going to push the contest to an issue; he left it to Barnes's conscience. This was very much the head-master's approach. Nor would he allow Barnes to reply in joint session, but only to make a personal statement in the House of Bishops later in the day.

When he did so, Barnes paid tribute to the restraint and Christian spirit of the Archbishop's remarks. He mentioned that most people had only been able to read reviews and not the book itself. He went on to speak of the increasing alienation of young people from the Church and their doubts arising from the incompatibility of the Gospel stories with their scientific knowledge. He quoted cases where science had won the battle with religion and Christianity had gained. 'A religion, like a man, must from time to time shed old garments.' In brief, belief in physical miracles had gone from the world. He emphasized that views such as his own on the uniformity of nature and miracles had long been held openly and not con-demned and he hinted that the Archbishop had quoted selectively from reviews of the book and had neglected favourable comment. Finally,

> we must come to terms with science and scholarship or face disaster. What I wrote in my book was most carefully thought out. Almost every sentence was weighed with anxious scrutiny. I believe that its conclusions, as they stand, are true, that from them we can see how Christianity arose. I also believe, and this is of supreme importance, that from their new insight and knowledge the rising generation will be led to worship Jesus the Christ as the Divine Lord of mankind, God's revelation on earth.

The Archbishop had been loudly applauded for his remarks, although at least one newspaper reported that he looked increasingly uncomfortable as Barnes's reply proceeded. Certainly, when Selwyn

'It's a fine state of ecclesiastical affairs when the Dean of Canterbury
believes everything he reads in *Pravda* and the Bishop of Birmingham
doesn't believe half he reads in the Bible.'

411

egregiously tried to promote a debate in the Lower House on a motion of thanks to the Archbishop, he found no support for further discussion and had rapidly to drop his motion. Indeed, he had learned that, if he went ahead, Guy Rogers among others would certainly have spoken in Barnes's support. After the headmaster had spoken for Canterbury, the headmistress thought it necessary to add something at York. Although Garbett had no responsibility or jurisdiction in the matter, he said that while there was no question of prosecution or other proceedings, it was right for the archbishops to dissociate themselves from the book. He added, like Fisher, that if he himself held such views, he could not continue as a bishop. Incidentally, he described the book as being of little importance. If so, it was certainly being given a great deal of attention.

Barnes for his part merely told reporters that he had no intention of resigning. In private, he added that he was following the advice once given to another bishop: 'much patience but no resignation'. It was not the first time in his career that resignation had been pressed upon him. He may have thought right back to the circumstances under which he left Trinity in 1915, when he had acceded to the pressure and been unhappy about it ever since. Now, however, in 1947 Osbert Lancaster published a cartoon in the *Daily Express* of one dignitary saying to another, 'It's a fine state of ecclesiastical affairs when the Dean of Canterbury believes everything he reads in *Pravda* and the Bishop of Birmingham doesn't believe half he reads in the Bible'.

Fisher's anathema with bell, book and candle brought Barnes a new wave of letters. Most of his correspondents were sympathetic. Although some called on him to resign, many were critical of the Archbishop's attempt to muzzle the Bishop. There was a good deal of feeling in the Birmingham diocese, in particular, even among clergy who by no means agreed with the book, that the Archbishop had mishandled matters by arraigning a senior bishop in so public a fashion, without giving him an immediate right of reply, and also that by his references to 'the unchanging dogma of the Church' Fisher was trying to suppress freedom of enquiry in a body which should be a living organism. The sales of the book were also boosted, in so far as the publishers could meet the demand.

In this situation the *Sunday Pictorial* seized the chance to give the book a wider readership by serializing it in its columns. The *Sunday Pictorial* then had six million readers and with the first extract from the book on 26 October published the result of a poll on the controversy, which showed 52% of those who replied as supporting Barnes, 32% against him and 16% neutral. Hugh Cudlipp, the editor at the time, has described in his book *Walking on the Water* what happened next. He says that, after the third instalment, he was visited by the Archbishop's chaplain who asked, on instructions, that the paper should also publish the other side of the case from the pen of another bishop. The paper could pick its bishop, and Cudlipp says that he picked Blunt, of Bradford and abdication fame, although the choice was published as being that of the Archbishop. Certainly, Blunt was more likely to be grist to the paper's publicity mill than to Fisher's, although the Archbishop at least gave his approval. Blunt had already had the good taste at his Diocesan Conference to compare Barnes with Jerry Cruncher and call him 'a resurrection man of dead theories'. Cudlipp says that Blunt was given 'a fat fee'. But it seems to have been generally agreed that he put up a pretty poor showing: letters to the Editor were critical of his triviality and of his 'scrappy, ill-prepared, dogmatic statement', and he himself was led to complain publicly that the newspaper had treated him unfairly. Barnes had no worries on that score.

Another confrontation over the book took place on the BBC Third Programme on 24 August 1948, when Barnes was challenged to a debate by Canon Alan Richardson, then at Durham and later Dean of York. This took the form of a set speech by Richardson, followed by a prepared reply from Barnes and then some impromptu exchanges. Richardson's opening statement was in effect an attack on Barnes's historical method and conclusions, designed to suggest that the miracle stories were true. It was more of a lecture than a speech. Barnes, who had plenty of experience of speaking on the wireless and had always found broadcasting a congenial medium, replied with a lighter touch: 'Religion is not like a caramel, the better for being wrapped up.' He made fun of Richardson's comparison of the resurrection of Jesus with carrying a chair out of a room as similar interferences with the course of nature: 'If the chair were to pick me up and carry me from the room, it would be a miracle, surprising and probably unpleasant.' He brought the discussion round to the value of the ethic of love rather than the raising of Lazarus. Richardson, in the subsequent exchanges, continued to try to justify miracles as historical and to accuse Barnes of an old-fashioned rationalist positivism. Barnes pressed him to justify some

413

of the more absurd passages in the Gospels, such as Matthew's description of portents at the crucifixion and resurrection. 'I asked whether you believed these statements. I gather that you don't, though you seem to be a little hesitant about the dead walking the streets.' He ended: 'My dear Canon, big words are of no use. Our faith will survive without miracles. The desire for them rests on a craving for the religious materialism of a pre-scientific age. Christianity is the revelation of God in Christ.' His Cambridge Union experience had stood him in good stead. Press comment and his post-bag alike suggested that he was thought to have wiped the floor with Richardson. Certainly Richardson refused to have any of the debate published beyond the two set opening speeches.

Fisher, for his part, despite numerous demands for further action against Barnes, had evidently decided that he had shot his bolt. No more was heard of an examination in orthodoxy. Fisher knew that he had no power to oust Barnes or force his resignation, which was obviously not going to come voluntarily. Garbett suggested that a private and personal appeal should be made to Barnes to resign, but without much hope of success and this move was not made. Again at Garbett's suggestion, supported by others, consideration was given to not inviting Barnes to attend the Lambeth Conference of 1948 or even the regular Bishops' Meetings. But no doubt it was concluded that pinpricks of this kind would only embellish a martyr's crown and indeed strengthen Barnes's determination to remain in office. Fisher also acted wisely in dissuading the hotheads from organizing a boycott of Barnes by clergy in his own diocese; there was no point in such action, still less in empty fulminations, if they were not to be effective. The Archbishop was rather less judicious in privately expressing sympathy with Birmingham clergy and attributing motives to Barnes; the headmaster should not discuss their housemaster with the boys. But in public he maintained the dignity of silence.

A more serious threat to Barnes's position was the Bishops' Retirement Measure introduced into the Church Assembly in 1948. This innocent-seeming proposal was managed by Mervyn Haigh, Bishop of Winchester, the same man who, as Davidson's chaplain in 1924, had evinced doubts about Barnes's elevation to a bishopric. It is clear that one motive behind the measure was to prevent the Church again being placed in the posture of impotence in which it had found itself in 1947. The measure followed a Clergy Retirement

Measure intended to weaken the parson's freehold on his living. Its long title was 'to make provision for the retirement of Bishops voluntarily or compulsorily where incapacitated by physical or mental infirmity, voluntarily where change of administration is desirable, and compulsorily in case of unbecoming conduct or neglect of duty, and for purposes connected with the matters aforesaid'. Nothing could have sounded more reasonable. But, in the section on unbecoming conduct or neglect of duty, wording was inserted to the effect that it could cover a 'question of doctrine, ritual or ceremonial' if the complaint was made 'by or with the approval of at least three diocesan bishops' and that the accused bishop could then be brought before a tribunal consisting of the rest of the House of Bishops. It was fairly clear against whom this was directed in the circumstances of the time and, given the line-up of the episcopal bench, what the upshot of any such case would be. An earlier form of the measure had included provision for action against a bishop's 'social and political opinions', but this had been dropped. Although limitations had also been inserted which would prevent its retrospective application, so that it could not have been used against Barnes for his book, he nevertheless realised that it could be applied to any liberal bishop in the future and fought hard against its passage through the House of Bishops.

Matters came to a head in February 1949, when the measure was reported to the full Church Assembly without any prominence on the agenda. Thinking that these tactics were designed to minimize its importance and give the impression that there was no opposition to it, Barnes asked that the voting in the House of Bishops should be made known. This Fisher refused to do, as the proceedings in that House were confidential. Barnes had at least made the point that the Bishops had not been unanimous. In fact, the minority had never been less than three and on the crucial vote it was six against sixteen. Even so, Barnes was not satisfied. He held that he attended the House as an appointee of the Crown, not on the sufferance of the rest of the episcopate; the Archbishop was only *primus inter pares* and could not impose silence. He therefore decided to bring the matter into the open with an address in his cathedral on 27 February. In this he spoke of the 'new Reformation of the Church of England' and warned that the measure could be used to frustrate the Crown's right to appoint bishops. This was a right which he had always strongly supported and he had for some time opposed the new-fangled idea of lay committees to assist the Crown's advisers in their choice. Now he said that, if Parliament knew what was intended, it would probably reject the measure and the King in Council would probably not confirm the condemnation of a bishop. But even so, a bishop condemned by his peers would be in an impossible position, especially as the evidence could all be heard in secret and he could be made to pay his own costs. 'All this could happen to a man for expressing disbelief in Jonah's whale or Noah's ark.'

All over the world the right of free speech is under attack. All over the world religious truth is menaced by repressive action. We must resist the entrance of such a menace into our own Church. I regret to have to speak in this way. My primary interest is in religion. I study theology earnestly as the handmaid of religion. I find ecclesiastical politics most distressing. But we are fighting what seems to be a desperate battle for liberal theology in the Church of England. I ought not to keep silent.

The press was generally sympathetic, although one paper suggested that Jonah's whale was the Bishop's red herring, and, briefed by Barnes, the *Modern Churchman* gave him strong support, sending copies of its editorial and his address to all members of the Ecclesiastical Committee of Parliament. After his broadside Barnes deliberately absented himself from the Church Assembly debate on the measure in June. But he was growing more confident, writing to Major:

I take it that Haigh and the Archbishop have received a warning that they will not be allowed to go forward with a measure designed to facilitate heresy-hunting . . . Modernism would appear to be more difficult to suppress than some ecclesiastics appear to think.

In November the Assembly decided that the measure was not the place or method for dealing with complaints against a bishop involving questions of doctrine; if at all, this should be handled by a revision of Canon Law. Ironically, an amendment to this effect was moved by Lord Selborne, who as Wolmer had been Barnes's chief opponent over cement. After this, all was plain sailing. When the amended measure was finally passed in 1950, Barnes could write:

Every clause in the Bishops' Retirement Measure which could have been used against a liberal churchman because of his writings has been eliminated. The Measure, as passed, was innocuous – from the point of view of the reactionaries, a waste of time.

416

Another tailpiece to the controversy over the book had been written at the time of the 1948 Lambeth Conference, when the Anglo-Catholic Council circulated a letter to all the bishops attending in which they protested at Barnes's inclusion. They made no headway and Barnes duly attended the conference and the numerous functions connected with it. This was before the days of residential Lambeth Conferences and involved renting a house in Hampstead for a month, although this had the advantage that they could entertain a number of London friends. The conference itself Barnes found disappointing. It was the first to be held for eighteen years and whereas in 1930 he had been a member of the committee on the Christian Doctrine of God and had helped to draft its impressive report, now he served on the Committee on the Christian Doctrine of Man, but took little active part in its work and was not attracted by its report, which contained some rather superficial pseudo-philosophy and which he found lacking in intellectual distinction. But he was in any case unlikely to be in sympathy with a gathering which declared that 'there are occasions when both nations and individuals are obliged to resort to war as the lesser of two evils'. As he pointed out, Lambeth Conferences produced their reports by majority voting, the votes were not announced and minority views were not represented.

The Book on the Bible furnished the last major theological controversy in which Barnes was engaged and the last occasion on which he was brought into public exchanges with an Archbishop of Canterbury. During these exchanges and in their preliminary correspondence, Fisher had treated him with courtesy, which Barnes had reciprocated. But from then onwards a marked change took place in Fisher's attitude towards him. The Archbishop, for example, knew quite well the import of the Bishops' Retirement Measure and may even have hoped that this would have succeeded better than his own words in Convocation in securing Barnes's departure from Birmingham. Privately, too, a new asperity began to enter into his correspondence. Thus, when in November 1948, Barnes asked him to come to a meeting to help the Ten-Year Forward Movement, he answered:

Even if the dates had been clear, I should not have felt able to commit myself to a visit to the Diocese of Birmingham at present. Much as I should like to encourage your people in the efforts which they are making, such a visit of an official kind to you as Bishop of the Diocese could not be reconciled with what I had to say in Convocation. Unless I explicitly reaffirmed what I said in Convocation, which would obviously be unsuitable, such a visit would appear to be a mitigation of what I then said.

This was, then, a personal ostracism of the Bishop. In fact, he ceased to tell Barnes of his planned visits to Birmingham. In September 1949, Barnes heard that Fisher was coming to the prize-giving of the University Medical School and offered him hospitality and the use of a car; the reply was 'Thank you for your offer of hospitality, but the St Johnstons are looking after me during my visit'. Mrs St Johnston was his niece. Or again in May 1950, he arranged, without telling Barnes, to attend the centenary of Saltley Training College. When Barnes wrote 'if we at this house can be of any assistance with hospitality or with a car, please command us', he answered 'thank you very much for your offer of assistance, but presumably Saltley Training College will take me to and fro'. As the headmaster could not sack his wayward housemaster, he preferred to ignore him and deal directly with the prefects. In the same way he took to sending curt enquiries about incidents reported to him as having occurred in the Birmingham diocese, shorn of any of the friendly expressions which his earlier letters had contained. 'It has been reported to me . . . It is more satisfactory to know the facts at first hand. I should be grateful therefore if you could let me know (a) . . . (b) . . .' 'Complaints have been made to me that . . . It is never satisfactory to have reports at second hand. I should be grateful . . .' 'With reference to my previous letter, I should be grateful if you would answer the two questions which I put . . .' 'I see that I must be more precise . . .I should be grateful if you would let me know whether you used this phrase or some such phrase and if so the context in which you used it, in so far as it may explain what you intended to convey by the phrase.' Again the accents are those of the headmaster, but this time he seems to be looking for grounds for expelling a recalcitrant pupil, even one who is also a distinguished scholar. When Fisher visited New Zealand in 1950, a stranger wrote to Barnes to say that, with 'a hard glint in his eye', the Archbishop had told an audience there that 'the bishops should have the power of asking people like yourself to vacate your office'. So the vendetta was pursued. Vengeance is mine, saith the Lord, although forgiveness or even

418

charity are usually thought to be more Christian virtues. Even when Barnes did resign, on health grounds, in 1953, Fisher did not refrain from commenting: 'You have suggested Ash Wednesday as the date of publication of your impending resignation. The date seems suitable and one might possibly add that the day seems suitable for such an act of discipline.'

Barnes had been associated with four Archbishops of Canterbury. They all obviously found him an awkward customer, as perhaps he was, but they handled him very differently. This reflects the differences in their characters and their backgrounds. In Barnes they were dealing with someone who was naturally out of tune with established authority, not so much from *esprit de contradiction* as because he was an independent thinker, whose sympathies lay with the underdog rather than the overlord. To meet this attitude, Davidson showed all the smooth self-confidence of one who for at least thirty years had embodied the ecclesiastical establishment; he had, too, the natural courtesy and modesty of a gentle Scotsman born in a leisured age. He was, moreover, an instinctive diplomatist, and it was perhaps this quality which led Barnes to say, somewhat wishfully, that Davidson 'quietly smoothed the way for the general acceptance alike of evolution and of biblical criticism'. Temple also belonged naturally to the establishment into which he had been born and, even though in everyday encounters he may not have seemed to have the humility of a simple Christian, and indeed had a highly sophisticated mind, he also had an ease of manner and a warm humanity, which carried him through and enabled him to deal gently with his colleagues, whatever he said of them behind their backs. Lang was a very different and more complicated character. He had had to establish himself and, although like Davidson he had a Scotsman's courtly turn of phrase, he was always very conscious of his worldly position. He too seems to have lacked real humility and, strangely enough, when it came to the point he seems also to have lacked that self-confidence and sureness of touch which come from genuine courage, so that on occasion he appeared bold rather than brave. It would have been natural, too, for Fisher, who came unexpectedly early to his office, to feel himself lacking in confidence when he compared himself with his predecessors. This alone might have tended to make him self-assertive and rigid, even if he had not been by training and temperament an administrator rather than a leader or teacher. Nor had he been a popular headmaster at Repton. He seems to have seen

419

people, including himself, primarily as parts of a machine and to have judged them by what they did rather than by what they were. It was not a happy formula for human relationships. Like Temple, Fisher was at home among -isms. But the human problem is to go behind the -isms to the 'is'. Temple could do this; Fisher apparently found it much less easy. This was no doubt his misfortune rather than his fault. But perhaps after all, to Barnes, Fisher never seemed quite as real as his three predecessors; he may have appeared to be more like a puppet operated by red tape.

A happier event than these conflicts was Barnes's silver jubilee as Bishop in September 1949. Even this was not unmarked by theological controversy, when the Birmingham Union of Lay Churchmen and the Birmingham Committee of the Church Union wrote to the press deprecating any special celebrations of the occasion. But this protest was ignored by most people in the diocese and the city, and the commemorative service at the cathedral was well attended. Bishop Linton presented the greetings of the diocese, acknowledging Barnes's 'generosity of spirit' and deliberately calling him a 'holy and humble man of heart'. Barnes in his reply, while saying that he would have preferred to let the anniversary pass in silence, expressed his gratitude and then spoke of his hopes for the future when 'sooner than most people expect the teaching of Christ will re-establish its influence'. The local papers all interviewed him and, while in these interviews he dwelt on some of the progress made in the past twenty-five years, they also gave him the opportunity to express his hopes for a more liberal and peaceful future. In its leader, with pardonable local patriotism, the *Birmingham Mail* declared:

The name of Birmingham is widely know in the world for many reasons, of which not the least honourable is that it is the See of Dr Barnes. Today after a quarter of a century the Bishop of Birmingham is unquestionably the outstanding figure in the Established Church. Since the death of William Temple, there is no one whose opinions and influence carry greater weight.

Since the Bishops' Retirement Measure was then still under consideration, the *Mail* went on to deplore any possibility that 'the disturber of thought should be silenced'.

Whatever may appear from the long-drawn-out discussion over the book on the Bible and its corollary in the Bishops' Retirement

Measure and other pinpricks, theological controversy was by no means Barnes's dominant interest during these last years at Birmingham. Indeed, he had written the 'B on the B' during the war and with its publication he seems to have thought that he had said his say and could stand by it. If he had lived longer he would on his own showing have liked in retirement to write an account of all these events through which he had lived in the Church of England. But now, with the end of the war and a job to do, he turned his mind to more immediately practical problems. Apart from diocesan administration, there were two main preoccupations which filled his mind and his utterances for the rest of his time as a diocesan bishop: peace and eugenics.

At first, his concern for peace showed itself in the continued pursuit of earlier aims. There should be no punitive settlement with Germany or Italy. They should be brought back into the European family. With this end in view, the policy of non-fraternization with Germans was deplorable and anyway would not work. He seconded the Bishop of Chichester's motion in Convocation deploring the expulsion of Germans from their houses and he denounced the Potsdam decisions on the division of Germany. He joined in a memorial to the Prime Minister for the rapid release of German prisoners of war. He called for the early withdrawal of our troops from Germany and the early abolition of conscription, which was in any case valueless for modern warfare. On more domestic concerns, he spoke in the House of Lords in support of the early release of conscientious objectors, although he received no help from the Archbishop of York.

All these themes were familiar. So was his caution over the overt actions which he was prepared to take. While he continued to assert 'I have always been a pacifist and my convictions have grown stronger with the years', he realized that some of the attacks on him on other subjects were motivated by dislike of his pacifism and he knew that his influence could be eroded by overplaying his hand. 'My diocese is most restive.' Although he did join the 'Save Europe Now' campaign, he warned George Bell in early 1946 against advocating too strongly the transfer of supplies to Germany. 'Food here is dreadfully short. People are almost in revolt.'

But soon his desire for reconciliation after the last war was overtaken by his fear of the next. The risk of another war was given an added new dimension by the existence of the atomic bomb, which emphasized the need to bring all war to an end. He was an early advocate of the peaceful uses of atomic energy, particularly to replace the degrading existence of coalminers, but he was convinced that the secret of the atomic bomb could not be kept. With the advent of socialism on the one hand and the neglect of religion and the menace of the atom bomb on the other, were we approaching a new era or the end of civilization? As early as November 1945, he was speaking to his Diocesan Conference about the possibility of war between America and Russia. From now on one of his overriding concerns was to promote understanding and friendship for Russia. It led him into some mistakes. It certainly brought him much misrepresentation.

Barnes was never a communist. Unlike the Dean of Canterbury, for whom none the less he entertained a warm personal regard and whom he often defended against his critics, he never allowed himself to be displayed as a red mascot. Indeed, one of his reasons for hating war was that it would spread communism and increase human degradation. At his Diocesan Conference in 1950, for example, he spoke of the battle being waged between Christianity and communism and described the Christian faith as something which 'should be preserved against communistic materialism'. But just as before the war he had refused to denounce German policies for fear of hindering chances of conciliation, so now he was to lean over backwards to avoid anything which might increase bitterness between Russia and the West. Indeed, he went further and did all he could to break down irrational suspicion of Soviet communism and to promote co-operation. There was no reason, he said, why social democrats and communists should not work together. 'Who is my neighbour? The reply comes back through the centuries: he is the hated enemy of my people, the Samaritan.' The British Government should not take a foolishly provocative line towards Russia, but should work to reconcile her with the United States. We disliked the Russian police state but Russia had cause to mistrust the West too. To disarm this suspicion the secrets of the atomic bomb should be made generally available. This of course was before the Soviet Union developed its own bomb.

When in this spirit in 1948 he refused to support action to secure the release of Russian wives of Western servicemen, lest it increase friction between the two countries, he was denounced by Vansittart in the House of Lords as representing the 'fine flower of appeasement'.

In the same spirit, he also refused to join in the popular clamour against the trial of Cardinal Mindszenty and indeed brought Michael Burn, who had recently been *The Times*'s correspondent at Budapest, to Bishop's Croft to talk to his clergy. But in January 1949, he dragged a fresh hornets' nest around his head by denouncing some ecclesiastical leaders for unwisely contrasting Christianity and communism and forgetting that Christianity had a communist beginning. When this statement was attacked, he defended himself by claiming that Lenin was primarily a social reformer, that communism was a politico-social movement for the welfare of the common man and that Christianity ought to be a religious movement with a similar object. He may have realised that this was a bit naïve, for he added 'I am not a communist, for I believe that our way of quiet development leads effectively, without revolution, to the welfare of the common man. But I desire from us friendly recognition of the greatness of Lenin's achievement, lest misrepresentation and suspicion lead to the culminating disaster of a third world war'. This did not appease his critics. It was supported in the *Daily Worker*. But the Lord Mayor of Birmingham called it 'rubbish' and even his fellow-pacifist H. G. Wood wrote that Barnes was 'darkening counsel by ignoring a distinction that should be familiar to everybody'. To cap the criticism, Winston Churchill remarked in the House of Commons that one of Mr Ramsay MacDonald's bishops, or perhaps his only bishop, had lately been eulogizing the humanistic virtues of Soviet communism, while all the time at least twelve million prisoners were being toiled to death as slaves in Soviet concentration camps. Churchill added that 'such an example of moral and mental obliquity on the part of a prelate' deserved at least the passing notice of thinking men, but, as that might be considered to reflect upon a member of the other House, he would avoid rebuke by not pursuing the topic or the prelate any further. No doubt fired by this, the President of the Cambridge Union wrote to ask Barnes to oppose a motion that Christianity and communism have nothing in common, but the Bishop declined the invitation.

His utterances on pacifism were by no means confined to expressions of friendship for Soviet Russia. He was deeply concerned at the hostility to China after the communists came to power there and the outbreak of war in Korea. 'We ought to treat the oldest continuous civilization of the world with sympathy and respect.' He seriously considered attending the Yugoslav Peace Conference at Zagreb in October 1951, but eventually refused because the international situation, by which he presumably meant Yugoslavia's relations with the Cominform, was too confused and his presence might be taken to imply that he had changed his views. But he did speak out in approval of the Vienna Peace Congress in September 1952, and drew upon himself the reproaches of the Secretary of the Church of England Council on Foreign Relations, who suggested that Barnes did not realise that the Congress had communist backing. Quite apart from these East-West aspects, he remained constant in his opposition to the manufacture or use of atomic weapons. As he wrote to a correspondent, he would not use the atomic bomb in any circumstances. 'To do so would be contrary to the teaching of Christ.' This contrasts with a letter from Garbett's chaplain to a correspondent who asked if Christ would take part in modern warfare: 'The Archbishop of York . . . finds it easier to picture our Lord taking an active part in modern war than it is to see Him standing aside passively while a desperate evil advances.' Barnes was dismayed when the Archbishops' Commission of 1948 concluded that use of the atom bomb might be justified against an unscrupulous aggressor. At the end of 1950, when a condemnation by the Church of atomic weapons had again been mooted, he wrote: 'All private efforts to move the Archbishops have been abortive. It is laymen of the political left who show what to me is the Christian spirit. I often wonder whether the Church will survive.' Nor was he concerned only with the horrors of atomic war. He deplored the use of bombs against villagers in the Malayan emergency, which Fisher had incidentally approved, and he denounced napalm bombing in Korea. He publicly opposed not only the rearmament of Germany but Britain's own rearmament programme too. He repeatedly called for an end to conscription and as late as August 1952 attended a tribunal for conscientious objectors to assess the quality of its work. He held aloof from the United Nations Association, because the Charter provided for the use of force in the last resort. These and many other examples show that, although in 1952 he ruefully wrote that 'from time to time I am told that I speak too frequently in favour of Christian pacifism', he maintained his absolute pacifism to the end and lost few opportunities of asserting it. But he also maintained his senses of humour and proportion: when the Dean of Canterbury asked for a 'Peace Bus' to be received by the Birmingham diocese, he declined because it would at once be named the Midland Red bus.

The other *leitmotiv* of Barnes's post-war utterances was his sustained interest in eugenics. This was of course not new for the champion of evolution. But it had been given fresh impetus by the march of events. In Britain's new economic situation he was concerned not only with the quality but also the quantity of the population. The quality must go up and the quantity come down. 'To be fruitful and multiply is no longer a divine command.' With the heavy cost of importing food, he saw the British becoming 'the paupers of the Western world' and he declared that a population of 25 million of first-rate quality was preferable to the 50 million then existing. Not only was Britain over-populated. The population contained too many bad stocks. There were great social and economic risks in too high a birth rate. The rise in illegitimate births in wartime, often from undesirable parents, was only one example of the decline in quality. But not only must the social environment be improved. Bad stocks were not just due to the environment. The belief that they were was 'orthodox Soviet genetics, associated with the name of Lysenko. But even I, in spite of the beliefs attributed to me, do not believe that the Soviet leaders are always right'. There must also be sterilization of the unfit and euthanasia, under proper safeguards, for children born defective. Euthanasia should also be permissible for the incurably ill, but that was another matter. Sterilization, euthanasia and birth control were better cures for over-population with tainted stocks than famine, pestilence or atomic war, with its mass murder and mutilation. 'Birth control, though unnatural, is not essentially more so than washing.' But he refused a request to speak in favour of it at the Cambridge Union.

These views, which formed the theme of many a discourse, did not go unchallenged. The orthodox were shocked. The future Cardinal Heenan called his remarks on population control 'insane and unChristian'. *The Times* took Barnes to task in a leader of September 1950, which was later endorsed by Fisher. It accused him of substituting the principle of utilitarianism for the Christian ethic of the sanctity of life. 'Apparently he finds nothing in history to caution him against the danger of well-intentioned discrimination between human lives – for which neither science nor Scripture provides a standard of judgement – degenerating into a general contempt for human life. The trouble is that, when supported by judgements of value and interpretations of science different from, but no less authoritative than, his own, the Bishop's proposals can yield conclusions as repugnant to his moral sense as some of his own conclusions are to the moral sense of others.' Others stated more specifically what *The Times* implied and accused him of advocating Nazi-like methods of population control. These critics were not only orthodox churchmen. They included J. B. S. Haldane. The former alliance of cement was broken. While Haldane as a geneticist had found Lysenkoism too much of a strain on his communist loyalties, he denounced Barnes for what he saw as socially prejudiced teaching and lack of charity towards the weak. 'They want to sterilize the poor.' In fact, Barnes would have been just as ready to eliminate undesirables in big business as in squalid slums. But, as he said at the time, 'genetics seem to give rise to controversy as vigorous as that which came from theological differences at the time of the Reformation'. Luckily, geneticists are not for burning.

Not content with improving the population at source, Barnes was saying as early as 1949 that immigration must be limited. While he welcomed the Welfare State in principle, he saw it as only too likely both to encourage the increase of 'slovenly, vicious, idle wasters' and to attract immigrants anxious to enjoy its benefits.

> We must not let the welfare state spoil rather than improve the quality of our population. You cannot gather grapes of thorns, or figs of thistles, as was said by a very great Teacher. What is to be done? We must limit immigration, whether from India, South Africa, the West Indies or East Europe. We must educate our citizens to have smaller families. Are populations to increase everywhere till an explosion comes and the miseries of atomic warfare end for a time the anxieties of starvation?

Thus pacifism and eugenics went hand in hand.

His concern with immigration and its eugenic effects inevitably led him on to problems of race. Indeed, he consistently laid greater weight on eugenic and racial factors in human standards and behaviour than it became fashionable to do a quarter of a century after his death. In February 1949, for the Galton Lecture to the Eugenics Society, he chose as his title: 'The Mixing of Races and Social Decay.' Starting from the premise that 'physical and psychical qualities are inherited by the same laws of inheritance', he surveyed in less than an hour a wide range of racial mixtures: English and German, Britons and Latins, East and West Europeans, Aryans and Jews, the various advanced civilizations, Europeans and Chinese in seaports, Eurasians and Anglo-Indians, French and Moslems, and finally black and white. The lecture contains some interesting asides: 'I always remember a saying of my Cambridge tutor, himself partially of Jewish ancestry – "A little Jewish blood is a good thing; too much is a mistake." One can hardly expect the Jews to accept the second part of this statement, which must not be taken too seriously: the first part expresses a widely held opinion.' 'The Norman Conquest stimulated the intellectual life of England and probably improved the English stock by diluting the Celtic, or pre-Celtic, strains within it.' 'There is in our industrial areas a superstition that it is "lucky to have an Indian doctor at child birth." ' There is an unspoken assumption throughout, as there had always been in his thinking and teaching, that European culture is superior to that elsewhere. But this is largely due to historical and environmental rather than inherent racial causes. He sums up his conclusions thus:

Racial intermixture cannot be avoided. A benevolent despot would prefer not to mix divergent civilizations or cultures. Such mixtures, even if they are not, as often, disreputable in origin, involve that different patterns of living impinge on one another to the disadvantage of each. At the beginning racial admixture is usually unsatisfactory: it leads to social decay inasmuch as the impalpable things such as the religious and moral strengths that are of highest value in culture, tend at the outset to disappear. But if economic conditions become satisfactory, if there are opportunities for social education and, more especially, if pressure towards wholesome living can be brought to bear, the future of a mixed race, as it becomes stable in its make-up, is by no means unpromising. Whether the mixed races now being fashioned in this world's turmoil will be great in human history, no man can say. Let us not be pessimistic: we are all hybrids.

This passage shows why, despite his long-term serenity, he was perturbed at the immediate situation around him. In Birmingham the wrong stocks were being mixed in the wrong places for the wrong reasons. As the flow of immigrants increased, his concern grew. In December 1950, he described the presence of West Indians in Britain as 'a social burden'. By September 1951, he was speaking of 'a disquieting increase of men alien to us in race and religion' in the Midlands and saying that 'alien immigration . . . is becoming a potential source of world-wide irritation and disorder'. By June 1952, he was even more outspoken, talking of 'semi-foreign areas', where foreign men – orientals, Jamaicans, Southern Irish – came to the city because they could almost always find work in its factories and asserting that 'in districts where there is a considerable foreign element in the population, neither moral standards nor social behaviour are satisfactory'. For remarks such as these he has been accused of lacking a constructive attitude towards coloured immigration. But in fact he was one of the first to draw attention to a problem at a time when it was still only a cloud the size of a man's hand: by 1951 there were only 51,000 immigrants in Birmingham, of whom 36,000 were Irish, 3000 Indian and Pakistani, only 500 West Indian and 3000 from the rest of the Commonwealth, whereas by 1961, long after his time, the whole dimensions had changed, with a total of 100,000, including 58,000 Irish, 10,000 from India and Pakistan, 16,000 West Indians and 5000 from the rest of the Commonwealth. Moreover, it was under Barnes's aegis that the Diocesan Conference in 1950 drew attention to the Christian duty of caring for coloured people and the Birmingham Protestant churches set up a joint co-ordinating committee for overseas nationals.

His Galton Lecture had one diverting sidelight. Barnes wanted to cite examples of successful racial mixtures and he wrote innocently to one peer, whose distinguished father was popularly supposed to be the product of an Eurasian union, to ask if this was true and if he might quote it. The response was an almost apoplectic letter and a threat to sue him for libel. The examples were omitted.

There was another aspect of eugenics in which Barnes took an active interest: artificial insemination for human beings. He had discussed it with Fisher before he took over at Canterbury and in return the Archbishop had asked him early in 1945 to join a committee with the Bishops of Derby and Oxford to consider the problem and report on it. Barnes was hesitant at first: while he had an instinctive repugnance for the idea, he had been, as he said, 'converted' to a belief in euthanasia and sterilization and feared that, if artificial insemination was condemned out of hand, this might later be seen as another example of the Church blocking the way of progress. But under pressure from Fisher and Rawlinson of Derby, he relented and agreed to serve. The Bishops interviewed the Minister of Health and some of his officials, as well as a judge and a doctor familiar with the problem. The upshot was a report which concluded that the Church should reserve judgement and not, for the present, publicly condemn artificial insemination by the husband, but that the use of a donor could not be approved, although if possible any public pronouncement should be avoided. Barnes went along with this but commented privately to a leading member of the Eugenics Society: 'You will realize how difficult it is for leaders of the Church to run counter to the almost unanimous opinions of the rank and file. I hope that no episcopal utterance, if and when it should come, will do harm by its unwisdom: more we cannot expect.' This was in 1945 and he never expressed his views in public. But in private he grew more and more convinced that artificial insemination, even by a donor, would be an inevitable and perhaps a desirable element in the positive genetic engineering to which he was increasingly attracted. As he told the British Medical Association in July 1950:

> It is already clear that possibly the most important medical research of the future will be concerned with the elimination from human stocks of genetic defects and with the production of human types finer than any that have yet appeared. It is among such human types that the finer kinds of religion and ethics will show themselves. I foresee a time to come when the great geneticist will be accepted as one of the leading agents of Christian progress.

Pacifism and eugenics were not the only threads in the tapestry of Barnes's thinking and teaching. There was the thread of personal morality. He continued to warn against drink, gambling, sexual laxity, dishonesty and the misuse of Sunday: 'One of the very few good results of the war is that beer has become weaker and dearer.' 'Millions of mugs spend their time and waste their money on football pools and greyhound racing.' 'The scales should not be weighted against Sunday schools and in favour of cinemas.' 'The destruction of an unborn child in a case of rape or to preserve the mother's life receives wide approval; but the use of abortion to protect a girl's good name after a moral lapse would lead to many abuses.' There was the thread of economic and social ethics. 'When wealth comes Christianity tends to decay.' 'Maldistribution of profits can still be justly criticized.' 'Capitalist industry demands a reservoir of a half-million unemployed.' If he had been present in the House of Lords, he would have voted against capital punishment, but this was largely because hanging was cruel; he was prepared to consider the painless extinction of murderers. There was the thread of education. Thus to schoolboys: 'Everybody ought to be able to swim, to ride a bicycle and to drive a car; cricket is good to be watched by elderly

429

gentlemen.' He particularly enjoyed his work on the Governing Body of his old school, of which he was Bailiff in 1947–8. As such, during his year of office, he had to give the keynote address at the Speech Day of each of the seven schools of the Foundation and, as he said, 'tried to put before the boys and girls a philosophy of life which should embody the Puritan ideals which have been of supreme value in the English tradition'. There was the thread of national politics, where he was not blindly partisan. 'It is right that the State should be responsible alike for the education and for the health of all its citizens.' But 'if the need for control of big business is conceded, the Labour Government has proved singularly conservative'. Nor was he an unqualified partisan of the National Health Service, having experience and respect for the contribution which private generosity had made to the voluntary hospitals. In reply to a correspondent: 'He himself has no great admiration for the House of Lords, as he dislikes the heredity principle. He would replace the House by a small Second Chamber of experts who could revise measures passed by the Commons. But he would add, in answer to your specific question, that he has never on any occasion seen any member of the House in the slightest degree under the influence of alcohol.' There was the thread of international relations, in which his pacifism was the binding factor. 'The teaching of the Roman Catholic Church and the need for cannon-fodder affirmed by the new Western religions of nationalism are producing overpopulation in Western civilization.' 'Everywhere a nationalist reactionary Christianity is being preached, with negligible or disastrous results.' 'In fact, an instinct emerging from our common humanity seems to be driving us to a world confederation of races . . . We need not expect to find the nations of mankind living resentfully under some super-Caesar: they will far more probably form a world-wide group of allied states.' There was the inevitable thread of ecclesiastical administration, in which as always were twisted his hopes for closer union with the Free Churches, expressed by his preaching to the Church of Scotland as the guest of the Lord High Commissioner, to the annoyance of the Episcopalian Bishop of Edinburgh, and his wish for a greater role for women in the Church, even though women had been disappointing in politics and in their attitude to war. 'When war threatens, the women, like the men, hover between apathy and easily-inflamed anger.' But not only women were to blame. 'Men with liberal sympathies have ceased to be ordained.' 'What you

430

term the "self-righteous complex" seems to me to dominate ec-clesiastics.' 'Ecclesiastics have a way of expressing themselves in terms so guarded that it is often difficult to know what they mean.' 'My episcopal colleagues, conscious that the Church over which they rule is steadily losing ground, become increasingly reactionary.' But sometimes more cheerfully: 'Whoever was the ass who invented the theory that I was not going to promote junior clergy in the diocese? I should have thought that most incumbents, when they lost their curates, said that I did nothing else.' Or, in refusing a Congregational invitation when he had an Anglican engagement, 'the lost sheep of the house of Israel should come first'. Some of his worst admin-istrative headaches at this time arose from the affairs of Ripon Hall, the modernist theological college at Oxford, where, as a member of the Governing Body, he laboured abundantly to pour oil on troubled waters. Finally, intertwined all through, was the thread of intellectual speculation. The interest in mathematics remained, even though in 1948 his 'Jacobian elliptic integrals are rusty'. It was supplemented by an informed interest in comparative religion and philosophy. 'I share the certainty with which Bishop Berkeley, supremely great as a philosopher, rejected the idea that the world in which we find our-selves is "a fortuitous concourse of atoms".' 'Lenin's defence of materialism, in so far as it is based on his attack on Berkeley's analysis of the foundations of knowledge, will not endure.' 'Confucius with his grave agnosticism, the Buddha with his doctrine of deliver-ance by suppression of desire, and the Christ, with his emphasis on the power and love of the living God, differ profoundly in their outlook. Yet these three leaders in their practical advice as to how men should outgrow the disorders of adolescent civilization are singularly close to one another.' 'My own endeavour to understand the universe leads me to the conclusion that the fundamental reality of the universe is a supreme Mind.'

These threads were all joined together in a single weave, remark-ably tight and consistent in its texture. Despite the occasional dark patch, the shuttle which wove the tapestry together was an enduring optimism: 'Remember that the kindness of God is overwhelmingly great and that the regret for wrong deeds should wipe out all anxiety, God's goodness being infinite.' 'Do not let the evil possibilities of the future worry you. Trust in God who can overrule the evil done by men.'

In May 1952 he gave one of his last set-piece addresses, a broad-

431

cast in a series called *When I Look Back*. He said that memory made him neither happy nor miserable. He spoke of his childhood when evolution was a newly-discovered fact and regard for Darwin unusual in Christian homes. Enlarged knowledge and material progress led to confident happiness in England before 1914. As a tutor at Cambridge, he had learned much from his pupils, particularly the Russians with their suspicion of Czarism and the Indians with their respect for Gandhi. The outbreak of war in 1914 had confirmed his pacifism, bringing much condemnation but many friends. Beauty, in church worship, on the stage or in the Italian hill country, had helped him to find the revelation of God. But the world of books and thinkers had also meant much to him. Prominent among the thinkers was Smuts, with whom he had talked of man's origin and who had given Robert Broom his chance as a palae-ontologist. Broom had become a friend, like himself enthusiastic for a smaller and better population, on which international co-operation in peace could be based. His own anxiety for the future of human civilization remained. Seldom had there been more need for Christian standards. But for half a century Christian influence had been failing. Young people found a lack of harmony between Christian tradition and scientific certainty. Hence his attempt to make an acceptable picture of the rise of Christianity. Of course, there had been hostility. But

> I can see that among thinking people some such liberal presentation of Christianity – modernism – call it what you will – has established itself. Yet the Christian religion is not dead. So look forward hopefully: to do so, one must at times turn back the pages and remember how the ebb and flow of life has come and gone. The mills of God grind slowly – but even in the past fifty years, one has seen the grinding going on.

It was an interesting summary of his intellectual and spiritual pilgrimage.

But although he was still in demand as speaker and lecturer, life in those closing years was not all high thinking. He had increasingly become a character in Birmingham. The prophet had achieved honour in his own country. As the historians of Birmingham say:

> Bishop Barnes continued to make pronouncements on secular affairs and he gave as good as he got in many a controversy right up to his

retirement. Though his support for euthanasia and eugenics worried some people, Birmingham loved him for his humanity, independence and healthy disrespect for established authority and precedent.

Another writer of the period speaks of 'Bishop Barnes, always odd man out'. He himself, when challenged on one of his sermons, wrote to *The Times*:

Many have similarly objected to my utterances in the past. I remain unrepentant. I have always conceived it my duty to apply Christian principles to current social and political issues. I still think it wrong to water down the Christian message to the taste of hearers who may resent it.

His clergy regarded him with affectionate respect, not untinged with amusement at some of his idiosyncrasies. One incumbent, whom he visited at a time when repairs in the church had not all been covered by a faculty, has recorded:

I trembled, what would his next question be? I must get him away from faculties at all costs. I talked about chromosomes, hormones, genes and ape-like stock, all the things he had been lecturing to us about in the last few months. Fortunately for me he rose at the bait and bit it.

Another tells of a car journey with the Bishop and both Archdeacons to visit new housing estates. It was a cold day and when asked to shut the window, the vicar said he had noticed that one Archdeacon's face was growing redder and redder and the other's bluer and bluer; the Bishop only commented that 'this was probably a reflection of their political attitudes'. The same writer mentions the 'sinister glee' with which Barnes enjoyed surprising people. Another relates how, when asked to ordain a man without a degree, Barnes merely replied, 'There is no notice over this diocese that rubbish may be shot here'. The rocking-chair from which he interviewed people became famous in the diocese. As one of his clergy said, 'one suspected he had adopted it as a means whereby he could intimidate his visitors'. But while they laughed, they loved. This was no case of *oderint dum metuant*. He could be intimidating, certainly. But there was genuine admiration, sometimes reluctant, for what one has called his 'steeliness of purpose'. At the same time, the word 'charm' appears in almost every account of him. Even his opponents recognized it and some even fell victims to it. Not that it was deliberately exploited. It was part of the full flavour of the man.

Family affairs were intertwined with diocesan. In May 1948 he married his elder son at St Peter's, Vere Street, although it took a little time to find a church where the incumbent was willing to let the heretic bishop officiate. Within three years, having become a grandfather at the age of seventy-five, he had christened his first two grandchildren at the same church. He made friends easily with the very young and took a keen interest in their fortunes, financial and otherwise. Meanwhile, Seaton and the farms continued to give him great pleasure. With the end of the war, too, he was keen to travel abroad again, although, less adventurous than his wife, who went to Belgium in 1946, he decided to wait until he could do so in comfort and safety. This was not until 1949, when they went to the Italian lakes and back through France. But 1950 was the *annus mirabilis* of his foreign travel, as he fulfilled his long-cherished desire to see the caves of Lascaux and feel himself directly in touch with the early men of whom he had read, studied and written so much. He found the caves far better than even he had expected. Then he could almost have said *nunc dimittis*. But in the autumn of 1952 he was to make one more, still more adventurous, journey, visiting his elder son at Beirut and travelling by Comet. It seems typical of his pioneering spirit that, although he could remember having his tonsils 'guillotined' without an anaesthetic, he made the first air journey of his life in the world's first jet passenger aircraft. Although he found the trip a strain and was pretty frail on arrival, he carried out a full programme for three weeks, visiting various parts of the Lebanon and even enduring the unaccustomed rigours of diplomatic cocktail parties. The highlight of his stay was a day-trip, by special permit through the military border-zone, into Israel, where the family picnicked at Capernaum on the shores of Lake Tiberias. It was a last glimpse of the Holy Land. His wife said later that she was sure that this Middle Eastern excursion shortened his life but she did not regret a minute of it.

Certainly his health did not long survive his return. He had had intermittent feverish attacks since the war, some more prolonged than others, and ever since his operation of the 1930s he had been troubled by shortness of breath. But he had always made good recoveries from the attacks, especially when he could escape to Devon to recuperate. Now, however, things took a more serious turn. It was clear to those about him that he was slowing down mentally and physically. He seemed somehow more transparent and perhaps the material world about him was growing more transparent too.

After coming back from Beirut in November, he fulfilled one or two engagements. He gave a last address to his Diocesan Conference, sharing with them some reflections on what he had just seen and heard in the Middle East, and he took a last confirmation at the cathedral, telling the young candidates something of the building's history and architecture and then giving them the simplest possible summary of his own Christian position. But when his doctors diagnosed heart-strain on top of his breathlessness, he recognized that he could not carry on. Strangely enough, one of his chief regrets seems to have been that he could not stay in office long enough to attend the Coronation. But once he had made his decision, he went smoothly forward with the business involved. His resignation was announced on 18 February 1953, to take effect on 1 May.

The announcement was greeted with many expressions of regret, and letters flowed in. Most were from friends and followers. But his colleagues were generous in their tributes too. Thus Bell of Chichester told him how much his presence on the bench had meant to his friends; Rawlinson of Derby wrote of the 'removal of a landmark'; and Hunter of Sheffield said that 'without you we shall be more monochrome than ever'. Of course, the announcement was also a signal for all the storms which had blown around Barnes's head in the past to be remembered again. But it is doubtful if he took much interest. He had to make his farewells to diocese and city by letters to the press.

The local press was indeed warm in its own farewell tributes. Thus the *Birmingham Gazette* wrote that 'it is to be hoped that the diocese will not be made to pay the price for its thirty years' association with this outstanding personality by being given a successor who is too orthodox and conventional', while the *Birmingham Post* commented: 'It may well be a case where final assessment, if there can ever be finality, will have to wait for the long perspective of history. His powerful intellect will start a train of thought that will go on shaping the future and, like John Huss, Wycliff or Roger Bacon, Dr Barnes may mean more to coming generations than to his own.'

It was left to Mrs Barnes to deliver their goodbye presents. From their own possessions they found mementoes, not only for the city and the see of Birmingham as such, but for most of the people and places with which they had had specially close connections. In return the City Council presented them with a water-colour of Bishop's Croft, while the diocese subscribed to a memorial in the cathedral.

With his bishopric Barnes resigned all his other appointments, including his position as the representative of Cambridge University on the governing body of King Edward's School, which he had held for nearly half a century, and his membership of the Council of Birmingham University. Now that he was no longer formally a member of it, the University could and did offer him an honorary Doctorate of Laws, like his brother Stanley before him, and, as he was too ill to attend the ceremony, took the almost unprecedented step of allowing it to be conferred *in absentia*.

In one matter he did take a personal interest. The Prime Minister's patronage secretary had been a close friend of his brother Sidney, who had died in 1952, and wrote Barnes a sympathetic letter on the announcement of his resignation. In reply, Barnes took the opportunity to suggest possible names for his successor. As he said in his letter, Raven would have been his first choice but was now too old. Failing him, he expressed a preference for Geoffrey Allen and the other names he mentioned were those of Mervyn Stockwood and Canons Marcus Knight and L. J. Collins of St Paul's. Two of these were indeed to become diocesan bishops, but not at Birmingham. Barnes's ideas were conveyed to the Prime Minister, but his advice was not taken. Nevertheless, when Leonard Wilson, Dean of Manchester and formerly Bishop of Singapore, was chosen as his successor, Barnes was genuinely pleased that someone who shared much of his liberal churchmanship, social sympathies and international interests was to take over from him.

One other happy note was struck before he left Birmingham. Fisher, who was in the city for a meeting of the British Council of Churches, made a point of coming to call on Barnes on the afternoon of 21 April. This was a graceful full stop to an unhappy chapter.

The rest of the story is not long to tell. Barnes and his wife went first from Birmingham to Seaton, until the house which their sons had found for them was ready in July. This was at Hurstpierpoint in Sussex, for they had come regretfully to the conclusion that Devon would be too remote for a permanent base. Ironically, their new home was not far from Piltdown, where Piltdown man had originated

436

and been accepted by Barnes and everyone else as genuine; it was during this summer of 1953 that Piltdown man was shown up as a fake, but, sadly, Barnes could no longer take much intellectual interest in him. He did take a gentle pleasure in his new house and garden, fed his love of nature with drives within sight of the Sussex downs and occasionally attended little Clayton church of Saxon origin near by. But his clock was fast running down.

He died quite suddenly on 29 November 1953. His wife said that, a few moments earlier, he had given her 'one of his special smiles'.

CHAPTER XI

EPILOGUE

*End of an Era
or Ahead of an Age?*

His ashes lie in his own cathedral, together with his wife's and below the memorial doors which bear his likeness.

One theme ran through the obituaries and the letters of sympathy: the contrast between the public and the private man, the warm and simple heart behind the hard and learned head. It is one of the pities of his life that he allowed so little of his private personality to appear in his public utterances. The private personality was, by common consent of those who knew him, unusually winning and attractive. He had too a happy sense of humour, to which he gave free rein in private talks and letters and on less formal public occasions. But on the main objectives of his life he was not concerned to be popular or amusing. He saw himself as a man with a mission: to help the truth of Christianity to prevail in the modern world. This was a matter of high seriousness, not to be lightly undertaken.

This was not the only seeming contradiction in his character. More than most men perhaps, he was a complex mixture: scientist and moralist, pacifist and controversialist, rebel and disciplinarian, revolutionary and traditionalist. The antitheses are all there, but they are often more apparent than real. He himself would have denied them all, seeing no conflict between science and morals, between respect for the law and freedom of thought, between the best of the past and the new knowledge of the present. A man of peace, he always held that he was no controversialist, that he was in this

438

respect more sinned against than sinning.

It has been written of the great Lord Salisbury by his grandson that 'he was a paradoxical mixture of scientific realist and religious mystic, of sceptical contemplative and combative man of action' and that 'he enjoyed the role of gadfly'. This could also have been said with truth of Barnes. The same writer, describing Salisbury's four sons, says of them: 'My father spent most of his life campaigning on behalf of losing causes; my Uncle William was generally odd-man-out among his fellow bishops; my Uncle Robert was a reformer whose reforms were rarely carried through; and my Uncle Hugh was noted for putting forward passionately and eloquently views with which hardly anyone agreed.' Some would have used similar phrases of Barnes's career, and there is a superficial plausibility in doing so. But would they be right? Is the faint aftertaste of failure which each of these judgements leaves in the mouth a true verdict on Barnes's life?

It has been often suggested that he was campaigning not so much for lost causes as for causes which had already been won: that everybody now believed in evolution and that nobody believed any longer in the inerrancy of the Bible. Even these statements were not true at the time, as is evident from the fierce reaction which Barnes's statements aroused. Disbelief in evolution and belief in fundamentalism both die hard. It could, for example, be said in 1955 that 'the vast majority of preachers still assume a background of pre-Darwinian if not pre-Copernican ideas' and it could be written of Jewish opinion as late as 1960 that 'there were even some concerned about the teachings of Darwinian biology, which were not compatible with statements that the world is exactly five thousand seven hundred years old'. But Barnes's purpose was not so much to teach the truth of evolution as such as to bring home to his hearers its implications for an ethical belief. The same is true of his approach to biblical criticism: historical truth was important, but far more important was its meaning for the religious values of modern man. This was why he came more and more to reject miracles, and here certainly he was not fighting again a battle already won. Not only could he find no historical evidence for the miraculous elements in Christian origins, not only did he find them incompatible with a scientist's view of the universe; he also believed that miracles and magic had been used to debase Christianity and to deform the Church. He would have echoed Goethe's line: *Das Wunder ist des Glaubens liebstes Kind.* 'Miracle is the best-loved child of Faith.' He would have agreed, too, with the ironical words which Dostoevsky puts into the mouth of the Grand Inquisitor: 'We have corrected Thy work and have founded it upon miracles, mystery and authority, and men rejoiced that they were again led like sheep.'

Some said that his science, like his theology, was out of date and focused on problems already solved. His own doctor brother used to say that Ernest was not a scientist, but a mathematician. But even he would not have denied that his brother used scientific methods of thought. Indeed, another commentator has said that 'if Barnes's biological knowledge was hardly so authoritative as his mathematics, that did not in any way justify those ecclesiastics who insisted that he had no claim to speak for science'. Certainly no holes to speak of have been picked in the strictly scientific parts of his Gifford Lectures, which represented a compendium of scientific knowledge at the time of their writing. He was not just stating known facts; he was asking questions too. He could not have been expected to foresee the debunking of Piltdown man, the discovery of the double helix or the uses to which atomic energy or electronic technology would be put. But his scientific enquiries were none the less speculative or forward-looking for all that.

More weight can perhaps be attached to the parallel criticisms of his approach to biblical history, that he was applying mathematical methods not always suitable to history or theology and that he was treading paths which had been well-worn by an earlier generation of scholars, while more recent travellers preferred different words. It is certainly true that he remained loyal to methods of biblical criticism familiar to him since he had first studied these matters early in the century. Even so, he had in fact read much more of the later material than his adversaries were prepared to admit. The difference, too, is partly a question of temperament. Barnes found himself instinctively closer to the rigorous approach of the earlier English scholars than to the often more subjective form of later German Protestant theology. Strangely enough, though, it is a modern German Catholic theologian, Hans Küng, whose conclusions he would have been more likely to share. Indeed, it was to Barnes's conclusions that his opponents really objected. Their attacks on his methods might well have been less harsh if they had agreed with his results.

Barnes was certainly a man of his own time. He was born a Victorian and he readily accepted much of the Victorians' conventional morality. His judgements and standards of good and evil varied little throughout his life. But he also accepted whole-heartedly the explosion of knowledge which came with the Victorian era and which was indeed to a large extent the product of its moral standards of hard work and devotion to truth. Nevertheless he certainly did not accept the way in which the Victorian standards of good and bad, of true and false, had been conservatively applied to solving many of the problems of Church and State. His own interpretation of those standards led him to be constantly a questioner, a reformer, a purifier and an innovator. This is perhaps why one obituarist declared that 'Barnes was a necessary event in the spiritual history of the twentieth century'.

At times he may have seemed like Cassandra making prophecies to which no one listened. But many of the questions which he raised and to which he offered answers were still being hotly debated a generation later. The ordination of women, remarriage of divorced persons in church, reunion with the Free Churches and the need for Christian endeavour to be concerned primarily with the poor were all causes which he advocated fifty years before the time when they had become burning but still unsolved problems. His views and teaching on the Christian attitude to such social questions as divorce, birth control or euthanasia, on which he was once a lone voice crying in the ecclesiastical wilderness, have come to be the conventional wisdom of an ever-growing number. A perceptive friend wrote after his death: 'Years hence he will be believed and understood by a generation that, maybe, will be as liberal-minded as he was.' The new theology, as exemplified by such works as *Honest to God* and *The Myth of God Incarnate*, has in some ways outpaced him, and he would not have liked all of it; but it has also followed the trail which he blazed and he would have fully endorsed its emphasis on the spiritual rather than the material. He would have rejoiced to know that the Lambeth Conference of 1978, in his own spirit but unlike some of its predecessors, declared the use of the modern technology of war to be 'the most striking example of corporate sin and the prostitution of God's gifts'. On a more mundane level, he would even have been pleased to know that twenty-five years after his death the Church of England was considering a Benefices Measure which would specifically empower bishops to ask prospective incumbents about their future intentions as well as their past practices.

441

More mundane was it to him, because his concerns were always ethical rather than ecclesiastical, practical rather than prelatical. He was in the tradition of the Cambridge Platonists of the seventeenth century rather than the schoolmen of the thirteenth. He was impatient of ecclesiastical institutions and of the concept of religion revealed by authority. For he was no preacher to the converted. His mission was above all to laymen. He would have welcomed the verdict given after his death that 'no single man in the twentieth century has done more to retain the informed laity of Britain within the Christian Church'. He might only have claimed that his influence had spread to other Protestant and English-speaking countries as well as Britain.

For him, Christianity, like Judaism and Islam, the other two world religions of Middle Eastern origin, was essentially a virile religion of prophecy and action. It was not, like the faiths which emerged in the Far East, a religion of reflection and contemplation. It was moreover to him an evolutionary religion in every sense, a religion which must look forward to the future and not be overburdened by the legacy of the past. Just as the first Christian message had been addressed to poor men, so too today should the poor be the first concern of Christian action; and the poor would be best served by the preservation of peace.

But his world was therefore not just the world of the Church. His intellectual, social and religious interests were integrated into a consistent programme of endeavour. It is hard to know just what he would have made of the world of the next generation: the world of the nuclear deterrent, the permissive society, the mass media, the sexual revolution, genetic engineering, the north/south gap, the colour question, public and private violence, international terrorism, and even 'black theology'. But these problems of tomorrow's world are all extensions of the challenges which he faced in his own day. He saw the causes and he often foresaw the effects. He could have been expected to face the new challenges with the honesty and courage attributed to him by many writers after his death. He might once more have shown himself despondent over the immediate future, but he would always have been confident for the longer term. For, while he may often have seemed the gloomy bishop, he was constantly the happy warrior, Mr Valiant-for-Truth.

No man is an island. Every man has his share of egotism. But here was a man who, more than most perhaps, fixed his eyes on the stars

442

and let idealism be his guide. He made no money. He sought no honours. He wasted little time. But he had a good mind and, what is more, a good heart. Mind and heart ranged over most of human life, seeking unity and harmony. He would not have welcomed the tendency of some recent thinkers to divorce Christian ethics from Christian theology. For he derived the ethics from the theology in a single whole. From the start his faith was based simply on his conviction that Jesus Christ was always close at hand. No one who saw him take Holy Communion up to the end of his life could have doubted that, overcrowded as that life had been, that was still his simple faith.

It cannot be said that he achieved all his ambitions. The Church of England has not rewritten its creeds, reformed its liturgy or re-organized its administration, as he would have wished. Nor has it strengthened its hold on the people. Nor indeed has pacifism become official policy. But then Barnes was not a clever politician, skilled at manoeuvring for short-term gains. Compromise was a word rarely on his lips and entirely foreign to his nature. Rather was his approach that of the prophet. As a prophet he could expect to be stoned; but he could also expect to be not without honour, save among his own colleagues. In January 1948, he foretold that 'in twenty years' time I shall be as orthodox as Colenso and Frederick Temple'. The combination was surprising and the forecast was not altogether fulfilled. But the gradual growth of his ideas on all manner of subjects, not least among the silent majority of laymen, shows that many of his prophecies, like Cassandra's, have come true. This is the monument which he would most have wished. It is a monument to a man who was not looking backwards from the end of an era, but peering ahead of his age.

SOURCES

The main sources for the book as a whole are

(a) Bishop Barnes's own papers, now in the author's possession, comprising:

(i) files of correspondence during the Bishop's years at Birmingham, 1924–53;

(ii) copies, in manuscript, typescript and print, of sermons and other addresses from his ordination onwards, i.e. 1901–52;

(iii) letters and other personal documents preserved by the Bishop from his entry to Cambridge in 1892 until his appointment to Birmingham in 1924;

(iv) copies of mathematical papers published in learned journals, mainly before 1914;

(b) Twenty-six albums, compiled by Mrs Barnes from the time of their marriage in 1916 until the Bishop's death in 1953 and now also in the author's possession. They include:

(i) press cuttings, not only from the *Birmingham Post*, *Mail* and *Gazette* but also from many national newspapers, in particular *The Times* and *Manchester Guardian*, from the church newspapers, including the *Church of England Newspaper*, the *Church Times*, the *Guardian* and the *Record*, and from a wide range of English and other language newspapers abroad;

(ii) reviews of the Bishop's books;

(iii) letters of congratulation or sympathy on significant occasions;

(iv) official reports (*Hansard*) of debates in the House of Lords in which the Bishop took part;

(v) service-papers, programmes, menus, invitations and similar documents related to ceremonial or official occasions, which the Bishop and Mrs Barnes attended.

CHAPTER I: *Birmingham, 1874–1892*

Most of the material for this chapter consists of family letters and papers and of personal memories. Mr Geoffrey Barnes of Southport has contributed the results of his researches into the background of the Barnes

445

family in Lancashire and Cheshire. The references to Barnes and Starkie in that part of England, and the connection with the Lancashire witches, have been supplemented from the *History of the County Palatine and Duchy of Lancaster* by Edward Baines MP (London: Fisher, 1836).

Jane Kerry, who married Starkie Barnes and became the Bishop's mother, wrote her own manuscript record of her early years, from which quotations are drawn. The late Dr Stanley Barnes also set down his private memories of his brother and of their childhood together.

The main source for the account of Birmingham in the mid-nineteenth century is the *History of Birmingham*, published for the Birmingham City Council by the Oxford University Press, of which vol. I by Dr Conrad Gill (1952) and more especially vol. II by Professor Asa (now Lord) Briggs (1952) have been used. Starkie Barnes's article on Birmingham appears in the 1880 edition of *Chambers's Encyclopaedia*.

The reference to the name Ernest in Samuel Butler's *The Way of All Flesh* is due to Ian Bradley, *The Call to Seriousness* (London: Jonathan Cape, 1976), p. 18.

The history of King Edward's School was written by T. W. Hutton, *King Edward's School, Birmingham, 1552–1952* (Oxford: Blackwell, 1952).

CHAPTER II: *Cambridge, 1892–1915*

Bishop Barnes's own sermons and writings show the development of his thinking and teaching during these years.

The account of his mathematical work is based mainly on a commentary which he himself wrote on the list of his published papers. It has been completed from the late Professor Littlewood's *A Mathematician's Miscellany* (London: Methuen, 1953), from *The Times* obituary notice (8 September 1977) on Professor Littlewood and from Dr J. C. Burkill's review of G. H. Hardy's *Collected Papers* (*Bulletin of the London Mathematical Society*, 7 [1975]), kindly communicated by Dr Burkill. The obituary notices of Barnes's mathematical work by Sir Edmund Whittaker and Professor W. N. Bailey appeared in the *Obituary Notices of Fellows of the Royal Society*, vol. 9, November 1954, and the *Journal of the London Mathematical Society*, vol. 29, 1954, respectively.

Other references to Barnes at Cambridge are drawn from the *Granta*, especially a profile under 'Those in Authority', 16 October 1897, and from the late Sir George Thomson's unpublished autobiography, in an extract kindly supplied by his son, Sir John Thomson. The late Professor A. V. Hill and the late Revd Sydney Clarke wrote privately to the author at some length with memories of their old tutor.

The quotations about R. V. Laurence and Lytton Strachey are taken from M. Holroyd's *Lytton Strachey* (Penguin edition), pp. 254–5 and 264.

The reference to Senrab as Barnes spelled backwards is to be found in Roy Harrod's *Life of John Maynard Keynes*, p. 68.

For Barnes's later years at Cambridge the mainly unpublished diaries of A. C. Benson, now in the possession of the Master and Fellows of Magdalene College, Cambridge and the subject of a study by Dr David Newsome, Headmaster of Christ's Hospital, provide numerous sidelights.

In the comparison with Bertrand Russell, quotations have been made from *The Life of Bertrand Russell* by Ronald W. Clark (London: Jonathan Cape and Weidenfeld & Nicolson, 1975). For the 'Russell Case' at Trinity and its connection with Barnes's own departure from Cambridge, the minutes of the College Council and the Statutes of Trinity College are valuable sources. Use has also been made of G. H. Hardy's *A Mathematician's Apology*, with foreword by C. P. Snow (Cambridge: Cambridge University Press, 1967) and the same author's *Bertrand Russell and Trinity* (Cambridge, 1942). Barnes's own account of these events is contained in a letter of 5 May 1942, to D. A. Winstanley, then Vice-Master of Trinity.

An account of some of the families to whom the Wards were related is set out in Lord Annan's celebrated essay on 'The Intellectual Aristocracy' in *Social History – A Tribute to Trevelyan*, ed. J. H. Plumb (London: Longmans, 1955).

CHAPTER III: *The Temple, 1915–1919*

The principal sources for this chapter are again Barnes's own sermons and letters, as well as his diaries and account books. Contemporary press cuttings collected by Mrs Barnes have also been used.

Quotations are made from:
(a) W. R. Inge, *Diary of a Dean* (London: Hutchinson, n.d.), p. 38.
(b) H. D. A. Major, *Life and Letters of William Boyd Carpenter* (London: John Murray, 1925), p. 54.
(c) R. H. Tawney, *The Radical Tradition* (London: George Allen & Unwin, 1964), Pelican edition, 1966, p. 42.

The Davidson papers at Lambeth Palace Library and A. C. Benson's diaries have afforded helpful background material.

The illustrated guide to the Temple Church by David Lewer, ARIBA (London: Pitkin, 1971) contains useful historical information.

CHAPTER IV: *Westminster, 1920–1924*

Apart again from Barnes's own papers and the cuttings collected by his wife, the Davidson papers at Lambeth Palace Library have provided material for this chapter, particularly on the background to the appointment of the new Bishop of Birmingham in 1924. The MacDonald papers

447

now in the Public Record Office at Kew have also thrown light on this appointment, notably in connection with W. E. Moll's nomination to the Deanery of Carlisle.

The Benson diaries have again shed light on Barnes's private attitude.

On Dean Inge's links with the ex-Kaiser, the source is *Diary of a Dean*, p. 162.

Bishop Gore's approach to religious and social problems is fully documented in G. L. Prestige's *Life of Charles Gore* (London: Heinemann, 1935).

R. H. Bainton's *Erasmus of Rotterdam* (London: Collins, 1970) shows the parallels between Barnes's thinking and that of the Renaissance Christian humanist. He was called 'the Erasmus of our day' in F. A. Iremonger's *Men and Movements in the Church* (London: Longmans, 1928), p. 126.

The *Church Times* and the *Modern Churchman* were the ecclesiastical journals most involved in the controversies of this period.

Valuable texts are to be found in the report of the 1920 Lambeth Conference (London: SPCK, 1920).

CHAPTER V: *Birmingham, 1924–1929*

With this chapter the main source becomes Barnes's correspondence as Bishop, faithfully filed during his lifetime and sorted after his retirement by his secretary, Miss N. M. V. Owen, now Mrs Edward Parker.

Mrs Barnes's albums increasingly reflect the volume and variety of the Bishop's utterances and activities.

Barnes's first book, *Should Such a Faith Offend?* (London: Hodder & Stoughton, 1927), was published during this period and several passages are quoted from it.

Most of the controversial correspondence was reported at length in the local and some national newspapers at the time. But, although Bishop Bell, in his *Randall Davidson, Archbishop of Canterbury* (London: Oxford University Press, 1938) and especially in chapter LXXXI, on the Archbishop and Bishop Barnes, has recorded Lord Davidson's side of the exchanges, Barnes's own share has never appeared in book form.

The Davidson and later the Lang papers at Lambeth Palace Library continue to illustrate the background to the two Archbishops' personal approaches to these problems.

The *Report of the Royal Commission on Ecclesiastical Discipline* in 1906 gives an important statement of the legal position on sacramental and ritual questions.

The Prayer-Book controversy was fully reported in the press at the time and the voting details in Parliament are to be found in *Hansard*.

The Emerson quotation is from Ralph Waldo Emerson's *Intellect*.

CHAPTER VI: *Birmingham, 1929–1931*

For the St Aidan's case, Barnes's correspondence and contemporary press cuttings contain full accounts, although the letters have again not been previously published in book form.

Archbishop Lang's consultations and other activities behind the scenes, including minutes of his conversations with Sir Lewis Dibdin and the Revd G. D. Simmonds, are fully documented in the Lang papers at Lambeth Palace Library.

References in other books are to be found in:

(a) J. G. Lockhart, *Cosmo Gordon Lang* (London: Hodder & Stoughton, 1949), p. 379.

(b) F. A. Iremonger, *William Temple* (London: Oxford University Press, 1948), pp. 490–2.

(c) W. R. Inge, *Diary of a Dean*, pp. 144 and 161.

(d) Alec Vidler, *Scenes from a Clerical Life* (London: Collins, 1977), chapter V, pp. 57–75. His reconsidered judgement is in 'Bishop Barnes – A Centenary Retrospect', *Modern Churchman* XVIII/3 (1974).

(e) Malcolm Muggeridge, *Chronicles of Wasted Time* (London: Collins, 1972–3), vol. I, chapter 4, pp. 131–3.

The retrospective tribute by Bishop Henson is included in the foreword to volume II of his *Retrospect of an Unimportant Life* (London: Oxford University Press, 1943).

The quotation from George Eliot on Savonarola is from *Romola*, chapter XXIV.

CHAPTER VII: *Birmingham, 1930–1934*

In addition to Barnes's regular public utterances and private letters, the main material for this chapter comes from his Gifford Lectures, published as *Scientific Theory and Religion* (Cambridge: Cambridge University Press, 1933).

Increasingly during this period, he used the Birmingham diocesan *Monthly Messenger* as a vehicle for his teaching, particularly for reproducing his addresses at Diocesan Conferences.

Bernard Shaw's comments are to be found in the preface to *The Adventures of the Black Girl in her Search for God* in *Prefaces by Bernard Shaw* (London: Constable, 1934), pp. 615–16.

Canon Richardson's book, to which the Bishop wrote a foreword and which he later defended, is *The Gospel of Modernism* (London: Skeffington, 1933).

The exchanges between Sir Thomas Inskip, as Attorney General, and Mr Aneurin Bevan in the House of Commons on the Incitement to

Disaffection Bill took place on 30 October 1934.

The *Report of the Lambeth Conference 1930*, published by the SPCK, contains the section on the Christian Doctrine of God, to whose drafting Barnes contributed substantially.

CHAPTER VIII: *Birmingham, 1934–1939*

The quotations from the Bishop's statements are taken either from press reports or from his personal letters.

The House of Lords debates on the A. P. Herbert Marriage Bill took place on 28 June and 7 July 1937 (*Hansard*, vol. 105, no. 81 and vol. 106, no. 87 respectively).

J. G. Lockhart in his *Cosmo Gordon Lang*, p. 401, asserts that the Archbishop was not privy to Bishop Blunt's speech which led to the abdication crisis. The Lang papers in Lambeth Palace Library throw little light on this aspect of the matter. Apart from contemporary press reports, Barnes's part in the affair is mentioned in Frances Donaldson's *Edward VIII* (London: Weidenfeld & Nicolson, 1974), p. 266, and, without Barnes's name, in Alistair Cooke's *Six Men* (London: Bodley Head, 1977), p. 72.

The growth of Birmingham and the efforts at church extension to meet this growth are documented in Lord Briggs's *History of Birmingham*, vol. II (London: Oxford University Press, 1952), H. J. Black's *History of the Corporation of Birmingham*, vol. VI (General Purposes Committee, Birmingham Corporation, 1957), and C. R. Elrington's contribution to the *History of Warwickshire* (Victoria Histories of the Counties of England, vol. VII) (London: Oxford University Press, 1964).

Changes in the personalities and organizations of the Birmingham Diocese are recorded in the annual numbers of the *Diocesan Kalendar*, as well as by references in the *Monthly Messenger*.

Dr Stanley Barnes wrote an account of the Birmingham Hospitals Centre in his book of that name (Birmingham: Stanford & Mann, 1952).

There is a reference to the Bishop's pre-war pacifism in T. E. B. Howarth's *Cambridge Between Two Wars* (London: Collins, 1978), pp. 175–6.

CHAPTER IX: *Birmingham in Wartime, 1939–1945*

Barnes's pacifism during the war was given full expression in his public utterances reported in the press and in his letters to private correspondents, in which he often included counsels of moderation.

The comparison between the attitudes of Barnes and Bishop Bell to the treatment of Germany in wartime was first made in the author's letter to the *Observer* of 9 March 1969. It was occasioned by a report in the *Observer* of 2 March that year of an article by the Venerable Lancelot

Mason in the March 1969 issue of *Crucible* (the journal of the Church Assembly Board for Social Responsibility). There is a further reference in Professor Donald MacKinnon's article in *Crucible* for July 1969.

Air attacks on Birmingham and the Government's shelter policy are described in Basil Collier's *The Defence of the United Kingdom* (1957) and T. H. O'Brien's *Civil Defence* (1955), both volumes in the *Official History of the Second World War* (HMSO and Longmans). The story as it directly affected Birmingham is told more fully in Anthony Sutcliffe & Roger Smith's *History of Birmingham, Vol. III, 1939–1970* (London: Oxford University Press, 1974), chapter II. Sir Winston Churchill's comments on Birmingham are in vol. II of his *Second World War, Their Finest Hour* (London: Cassell, 1949), p. 333.

Wartime policy on cement is fully recorded in C. M. Kohan's volume on *Works and Buildings* in the *Official History of the Second World War* (HMSO and Longmans, 1952), and his reference to Barnes's comments and the subsequent libel case is on p. 171. The High Court case (*Alpha Cement Limited and Others v. Right Reverend Ernest William Barnes the Lord Bishop of Birmingham*) was listed as 1940 A. No. 2597. It was heard before Mr Justice Wrottesley on Friday, 9 May 1941 and full shorthand notes were taken by the Association of Official Shorthandwriters, Ltd.

References to a cement 'ring' are in the *Report from the Select Committee on Estimates, 1938* (meeting of 20 June 1938), pp. 233–4. Bishop Barnes's two motions in the House of Lords were on 18 December 1940, and 17 June 1941 (*Hansard*, vol. 118, no. 7 and vol. 119, no. 49 respectively). Relevant answers to questions in the House of Commons were on 3 December 1940, 19 December 1940, 14 May 1941 and 20 May 1941 (*Hansard* columns 419, 1259, 1196 and 1400 respectively). The report of the Committee on Cement Production was issued as a White Paper, Cmd. 6282 in May 1941.

Sir Winston Churchill's description of the Admiralty annex is in *Their Finest Hour*, p. 331.

Some account of the difficulties of Christian pacifists in wartime, without reference to Barnes, is in F. W. Dillistone's *Charles Raven* (London: Hodder & Stoughton, 1975), pp. 343–50.

CHAPTER X: *Post-war Birmingham, 1945–1953*

The effect of wartime damage on Birmingham and the reply by the Ten-Year Forward Movement are recorded in Sutcliffe & Smith's *History of Birmingham*, vol. III, chapters VII and VIII, notably pp. 258–9.

The same authors mention Barnes's attitude to coloured immigration on p. 365, his good relations with the City Council and the Nonconformists on pp. 259 and 263 respectively, and the affection in which he was held in Birmingham on p. 265, among other references.

The Rise of Christianity was published by Longmans in March, 1947.
The account of Professor Dodd's criticism of the book is taken from
F. W. Dillistone's *C. H. Dodd* (London: Hodder & Stoughton, 1977),
pp. 225–6. Sir Frederic Kenyon's pamphlet *The Bible and Modern Scholarship* was published by John Murray in March 1948. Captain Liddell-Hart
wrote about it to *The Spectator* in the same month.

Bishop Henson's comment on the book written on 27 September 1947,
the day he died, to Dr W. R. Matthews is in *Retrospect of an Unimportant
Life*, vol. III.

Dr Major's article on 'Criticism and Conscience' appeared in the
Hibbert Journal for April 1948.

The proceedings in the Convocation of Canterbury on 15 October
1947, are reported verbatim in the *Chronicle of Convocation 1947*, no. 2,
on pp. 173–5 and 187–91. Comments on this incident can be found in
W. R. Matthews's *Memories and Meanings* (London: Hodder & Stoughton,
1969), pp. 308–10.

Extracts from *The Rise of Christianity* were serialized in the *Sunday
Pictorial* on 26 October and 2, 9, 16, 23 and 30 November 1947. Bishop
Blunt's articles appeared on 7, 14 and 21 December and his complaint of
unfairness on 28 December. The Editor's comments are in Hugh Cudlipp's
Walking on the Water (London: Bodley Head, 1976), pp. 177–80.

Some of Archbishop Garbett's comments on the book and the controversy to which it gave rise are contained in C. H. Smyth's *Cyril Forster
Garbett* (London: Hodder & Stoughton, 1959).

The advice 'much patience but no resignation' was given to Bishop Boyd
Carpenter by H. D. A. Major.

The first part of the broadcast debate with Canon Alan Richardson was
published in *The Listener* of 2 September 1948.

Archbishop Fisher's unpopularity at Repton is attested in the *Lyttelton-
Hart-Davis Letters* (London: John Murray, 1978), pp. 13 and 16.

Sir Winston Churchill's criticism of Barnes's remarks on Christianity
and communism was made in the House of Commons on 26 January 1949.

Archbishop Garbett's views on Christ as a combatant were described
in a letter of 1 August 1950, from the Rev J. A. P. Kent, his chaplain, to
Mr Albert Thornton.

Bishop Barnes is described as 'always odd man out' in Alan Jenkins's
The Forties (London: Heinemann, 1977), p. 179.

Comments on Barnes by his clergy are mainly derived from private
letters to the author, although one or two stories were published by the
late Canon W. S. Power in *The Real Thing* (London: Thomas Dixon,
1970).

The remaining material in this chapter is based on the Bishop's personal
correspondence and other private information.

CHAPTER XI: *Epilogue*

The references to Lord Salisbury and his sons are from Lord David Cecil's *The Cecils of Hatfield House* (London: Constable, 1973), pp. 240, 229 and 304.

The survival of pre-Darwinian, if not pre-Copernican, ideas was noted in C. E. Raven's 'E.W.B. – The Man for the Moment', *Modern Churchman*, March 1955, p. 16. The similar description of Jewish thought is in Abba Eban's *An Autobiography* (London: Weidenfeld & Nicolson, 1977), p. 286.

The quotation from Dostoevsky is from Constance Garnett's translation of *The Brothers Karamazov* (Everyman's Library edition, 1950, vol. I, p. 263).

The comparison of Barnes's mathematical and biological knowledge is also from Raven's 'E.W.B. – The Man for the Moment', p. 19.

Barnes was described as a necessary event in the spiritual history of the twentieth century in Sir Henry Self's obituary notice in the *Modern Churchman*, March 1954, p. 24. The same writer (p. 14) refers to his influence on the laity of Britain.

BIBLIOGRAPHY

I. E. W. BARNES'S OWN WORKS

A. BOOKS

Should Such a Faith Offend?	Hodder & Stoughton	1927
Scientific Theory and Religion	Cambridge University Press	1933
The Rise of Christianity	Longmans	1947

B. CONTRIBUTIONS TO PUBLISHED BOOKS
(title of E. W. Barnes's contribution in brackets)

Report of the Archbishop's Committee on the Teaching Office of the Church (Supply and Training of Ordinands)	SPCK	1918
Outline of Literature, ed. John Drinkwater (The Story of the Bible)	Newnes	1922
The Christian Faith, ed. C. F. Nolloth (Modern Psychology: Its Bearing on Religious Teaching)	Murray	1922
Liberal Evangelicalism (The Future of the Evangelical Movement)	Hodder & Stoughton	*c.* 1923
Great Modern Sermons, ed. H. D. McKeehan (Religious Revivals)	Revell (New York)	1923
Harvest Thanksgiving Sermons (Harvest at a Village Church)	Clarke	*c.* 1923
Immortality, ed. J. Marchant (Science and Immortality)	Putnam	1924
Easter Sermons, ed. F. J. North (Man's Nature and Destiny)	Clarke	*c.* 1924
Advent and Christmas Sermons, ed. F. J. North (A Christmas Sermon)	Clarke	1925
British Preachers 1925, ed. J. Marchant ('Follow Me Yourself')	Putnam	1925

The Inner Life (Essays in Liberal Evangelicalism) (The Rise and Growth of Man's Spiritual Consciousness)	Hodder & Stoughton	*c.* 1925
Ascension and Whitsuntide Sermons, ed. F. J. North (The Gift of the Holy Spirit)	Clarke	1926
Christian World Pulpit, vol. CXIV (The Uniformity of Nature and the Freedom of Man)	Christian World	1928
Science and Religion (series of broadcast talks on this subject)	Howe	1931
The Gospel of Modernism by R. D. Richardson (Foreword)	Skeffington	1933
The Church and the Twentieth Century, ed. G. L. H. Harvey (Foreword)	Macmillan	1936
Letters of a Prisoner for Conscience Sake by Corder Catchpool (Foreword)	Allen & Unwin	1941
Christianity and Life (Science)	Birmingham, Carrs Lane Church	1942

C. SELECTED OCCASIONAL PUBLISHED PAPERS

(It is not feasible to give a complete list of sermons, addresses, articles or reviews published or reprinted in periodicals or privately reproduced as offprints. The more significant sermons were often published in the *Modern Churchman* and in other Church papers. The following list is intended to be a representative selection indicating the range of signed published work over the years.)

Spiritualism and the Christian Faith (booklet)	Longmans Green	1918
'Movements of Thought in the English Church' (review of several books)	*Edinburgh Review*	January 1923
'English Modernism' (article)	*The Pilgrim,* vol. 3, no. 2	January 1923
'Heredity and Predestination' (Lloyd Roberts Memorial Lecture)	*Manchester University Medical School Gazette*	1930
'Science and Religion' (broadcast talk)	*The Listener*	22 Oct. 1930

'A Finite Universe?' (address to schoolmasters)	*School Science Review*	March 1931
'Man' (Presidential address)	Birmingham & Midland Institute	1932
'The Reformation and the Scientific Movement of Today' (conference paper)	*Modern Churchman*	October 1932
'The Old Testament and the Modern Man' (conference paper)	*Modern Churchman*	October 1934
'Man the Adolescent' (Foundation Oration, University College, London)	*Hibbert Journal*	July 1946
'The Basis of the Christian Faith' (broadcast debate)	*The Listener*	2 Sept. 1948
Religion Amid Turmoil (Rede Lecture)	Cambridge University Press	1949
'Mixing of Races and Social Decay' (Galton Lecture)	*Eugenics Review*, vol. XLI	1949
'Welfare and Population' (address)	*Eugenics Review*	April 1950
'Overpopulation' (Cavendish Lecture)	*West London Medical Journal*	July 1951

D. MATHEMATICAL PAPERS

'A New Proof of Picard's Theorem'	*Messenger of Mathematics*, vol. 27, pp. 16–17	1897
'The Theory of the Gamma Function'	*Messenger of Mathematics*, vol. 29, pp. 64–128	1899
'The Theory of the Gamma Function'	*Quarterly Journal of Mathematics*, vol. 31, pp. 264–314	1899
'The Genesis of the Double Gamma Function'	*Proceedings of the London Mathematical Society*, vol. 31, pp. 358–81	1900
'The Theory of the Double Gamma Function' (abstract)	*Proceedings of the Royal Society*, vol. 66, pp. 265–8	1900
'The Theory of the Double Gamma Function'	*Philosophical Transactions of the Royal Society*, Series A, vol. 196, pp. 265–387	1901

456

'A Memoir on Integral Functions' (abstract)	*Proceedings of the Royal Society*, vol. 69, pp. 121–5	1901
'A Memoir on Integral Functions'	*Philosophical Transactions of the Royal Society*, Series A, vol. 199, pp. 411–500	1902
'On the Value of the Fourier Series'	*Messenger of Mathematics*, vol. 32, pp. 108–12	1902
'On the Coefficients of Capacity of Two Spheres'	*Quarterly Journal of Mathematics*, vol. 35, pp. 155–75	1903
'The Generalization of the Maclaurin Sum Formula and the Range of its Applicability'	*Quarterly Journal of Mathematics*, vol. 35, pp. 175–88	1903
'On the Expression of Euler's Constant as a Definite Integral'	*Messenger of Mathematics*, vol. 33, pp. 59–61	1903
'The Classification of Integral Functions'	*Cambridge Philosophical Transactions*, vol. 19/III, pp. 322–55	1903
'The Theory of the Multiple Gamma Function'	*Cambridge Philosophical Transactions*, vol. 19/III, pp. 374–425	1903
'The Asymptotic Expansion of Integral Functions of Multiple Linear Sequence'	*Cambridge Philosophical Transactions*, vol. 19/III, pp. 426–39	1903
'On Functions Generated by Linear Difference Equations of the First Order'	*Proceedings of the London Mathematical Society*, Series 2, vol. 2, pp. 280–92	1904
'The Linear Difference Equation of the First Order'	*Proceedings of the London Mathematical Society*, Series 2, vol. 2, pp. 438–69	1904
'On the Homogeneous Linear Difference Equation of the Second Order with Linear Coefficients'	*Messenger of Mathematics*, vol. 34, pp. 52–71	1904
'The Maclaurin Sum-formula'	*Proceedings of the London Mathematical Society*, Series 2, vol. 3, pp. 253–72	1905

'The Asymptotic Expansion of Integral Functions of Finite Non-zero Order'	*Proceedings of the London Mathematical Society*, Series 2, vol. 3, pp. 273–95	1905
'The Asymptotic Expansion of $G(x, \theta) = \sum\limits_{n=0}^{\infty} \dfrac{x^n}{\Gamma(n+1)\,(n+\theta)}$, and the Singularities of $g(x, \theta) = \sum\limits_{n=0}^{\infty} \dfrac{x^n}{n+\theta}$,	*Quarterly Journal of Mathematics*, vol. 37, pp. 289–313	1905
'The Asymptotic Expansion of Integral Functions Defined by Taylor's Series'	*Philosophical Transactions of the Royal Society*, Series A, vol. 206, pp. 249–97	1906
'On Certain Functions Defined by Taylor's Series of Finite Radius of Conveyance'	*Proceedings of the London Mathematical Society*, Series 2, vol. 4, pp. 284–316	1906
'On the Asymptotic Expansion of the Integral Functions $\sum\limits_{n=0}^{\infty} \dfrac{x^n\,\Gamma(1+an)}{\Gamma(1+n)}$ and $\sum\limits_{n=0}^{\infty} \dfrac{x^n\,\Gamma(1+n\theta)}{\Gamma(1+n+n\theta)}$,	*Cambridge Philosphical Transactions*, vol. 20/IX, pp. 215–32	1906
'On the Binomial Theorem for a Complex Variable and Complex Index'	*Quarterly Journal of Mathematics*, vol. 38, pp. 108–16	1906
'On the Use of a Factorial Series in an Asymptotic Expansion'	*Quarterly Journal of Mathematics*, vol. 38, pp. 116–40	1906
'The Asymptotic Expansion of Integral Functions Defined by Generalized Hypergeometric Series'	*Proceedings of the London Mathematical Society*, Series 2, vol. 5, pp. 59–116	1906
'On Generalized Legendre Functions'	*Quarterly Journal of Mathematics*, vol. 39, pp. 97–204	1907
'On Functions Defined by Simple Types of Hypergeometric Series'	*Cambridge Philosophical Transactions*, vol. 20/XI, pp. 253–79	1907
'A New Development of the Theory of the Hypergeometric Functions'	*Proceedings of the London Mathematical Society*, Series 2, vol. 6, pp. 141–77	1907

| 'A Transformation of Generalized Hypergeometric Series' | *Quarterly Journal of Mathematics*, vol. 42, pp. 136–40 | 1910 |

II. OTHER RELEVANT WORKS

A. DICTIONARIES

Dictionary of National Biography	Oxford University Press	
Fontana Dictionary of Modern Thought, 2 vols., ed. A. Bullock & O. Stallybrass	Collins	1977
Oxford Dictionary of the Christian Church, ed. F. L. Cross	Oxford University Press	1971 edition
Dictionary of Christian Theology, ed. A. Richardson	SCM	1969
Dictionary of the Bible, 5 vols., ed. J. Hastings	Clark (Edinburgh)	1900
Encyclopaedia of Religion and Ethics, 16 vols., ed. J. Hastings	Clark (Edinburgh)	1908
Dictionary of Christian Biography, ed. H. Wace & W. Piercy	Murray	1911
Concise Encyclopaedia of Living Faiths, ed. R. C. Zaehner	Hutchinson	1971 edition
Encyclopaedia Judaica, 16 vols.	Macmillan (New York)	1971

B. OFFICIAL PUBLICATIONS

Official Reports (Hansard), House of Lords and House of Commons	SPCK	1924–53
Chronicle of Convocation (Record of Proceedings of the Convocation of Canterbury)		
Acts of the Convocations of Canterbury and York (since the reform of Convocation in 1921)	SPCK	1948
Report of the Royal Commission on Ecclesiastical Discipline		1906
Book Proposed to be Annexed to the Prayer-Book Measure 192– (the 'Revised Prayer Book')	Oxford University Press	1927

Report of the Commission of Enquiry into the Properties and Revenues of the Church	SPCK	1924
Lambeth Conferences: Encyclical Letters from the Bishops, with the Resolutions and Reports	SPCK	1920 1930 1948 1978
Doctrine in the Church of England (Report of the Commission on Christian Doctrine Appointed by the Archbishops of Canterbury and York in 1922)	SPCK	1938
Birmingham Diocesan Monthly Messenger & Birmingham Diocesan Annual Kalendar		1924–53

C. HISTORY

E. Baines, *History of County Palatine and Duchy of Lancaster*	Fisher	1836
R. H. Bainton, *Penguin History of Christianity*, 2 vols.	Penguin	1964
I. Bradley, *The Call to Seriousness*	Cape	1976
A. Briggs, *History of Birmingham*, vol. II	Oxford University Press	1952
E. Carpenter, *Cantuar*	Cassell	1971
D. Cecil, *The Cecils of Hatfield House*	Constable	1973
O. Chadwick, *The Victorian Church*, 2 vols.	Black	1966–70
O. Chadwick, *The Secularisation of the European Mind in the Twentieth Century*	Cambridge University Press	1975
W. S. Churchill, *The Second World War, vol. II: Their Finest Hour*	Cassell	1949
B. Collier, *The Defence of the United Kingdom (Official History of the Second World War)*	HMSO and Longmans	1957
D. L. Edwards, *Leaders of the Church of England, 1828–1944*	Oxford University Press	1971
G. Eliot, *Romola*	Blackwood	1863
P. Ferris, *The Church of England*	Gollancz	1962
C. Gill, *History of Birmingham*, vol. I	Oxford University Press	1952
R. Harrod, *Life of John Maynard Keynes*	Macmillan	1951

History of Warwickshire (*Victoria Histories of the Counties of England*, vol. VII)	Oxford University Press	1964
T. E. B. Howarth, *Cambridge Between Two Wars*	Collins	1978
T. W. Hilton, *King Edward's School, Birmingham*	Blackwell	1952
A. Jenkins, *The Forties*	Heinemann	1977
P. Johnson, *History of Christianity*	Weidenfeld & Nicolson	1976
C. M. Kohan, *Works and Buildings* (*Official History of the Second World War*)	HMSO and Longmans	1952
R. Lloyd, *The Church of England 1900–1965*	SCM	1966
T. H. O'Brien, *Civil Defence* (*Official History of the Second World War*)	HMSO and Longmans	1955
J. H. Plumb, ed., *Social History: A Tribute to Trevelyan*	Longmans	1955
Z. Steiner, *Britain and the Origins of the First World War*	Macmillan	1977
A. Sutcliffe & R. Smith, *History of Birmingham*, vol. III	Oxford University Press	1974
M. Swartz, *The Union of Democratic Control in British Politics During the First World War*	Oxford University Press	1971
R. H. Tawney, *Religion and the Rise of Capitalism* (Holland Memorial Lectures, 1922)	Pelican	1938

D. THEOLOGY AND RELIGION

(A fuller bibliography is appended to *The Rise of Christianity*)

C. F. Andrews, *What I Owe to Christ*	Hodder & Stoughton	1932
F. C. Burkitt, *The Gospel History and its Transmission*	Clark (Edinburgh)	1906
C. J. Cadoux, *The Early Christian Attitude to War*	Headley	1919
J. Carter, ed., *Dare We Believe?*	Christadelphian (Birmingham)	1949
G. Faber, *Oxford Apostles*	Penguin	1954
T. R. Glover, *The Jesus of History*	SCM	1917
C. Gore, ed., *Lux Mundi*	Murray	1890

461

J. Hick, ed., *The Myth of God Incarnate*	SCM	1977
F. J. A. Hort, *The Way, the Truth, the Life*	Macmillan	1897
J. S. Huxley, *Evolutionary Ethics* (Romanes Lecture)	Oxford University Press	1943
H. Küng, *On Being a Christian*	Collins	1977
C. S. Lewis, *The Screwtape Letters*	Collins	1979
R. D. Richardson, *The Gospel of Modernism*	Skeffington	1933
J. A. T. Robinson, *Honest to God*	SCM	1963
B. H. Streeter, ed., *Foundations*	Macmillan	1912
B. H. Streeter, *The Four Gospels*	Macmillan	1926
B. H. Streeter, *Reality*	Macmillan	1926
W. Temple, *Christianity and Social Order* (with foreword by E. Heath)	Shepheard-Walwyn and SPCK	1976
E. Underhill, *Mysticism*	Methuen	1911
E. Underhill, *The Mystic Way*	Dent	1913
G. Vermes, *The Dead Sea Scrolls in English*	Penguin	1962
H. B. Wilson, ed., *Essays and Reviews*	Parker	1860

E. MATHEMATICS AND SCIENCE

W. N. Bailey, 'On Two Manuscripts by Bishop Barnes'	*Quarterly Journal of Mathematics*, vol. 10, no. 39	Sept. 1959
R. Broom, *The Origin of the Human Skeleton*	Witherby	1930
W. C. Dampier-Whetham, *History of Science*	Cambridge University Press	1932
C. Darwin, *The Origin of Species*	Murray	1859
C. Darwin, *The Descent of Man*	Murray	1871
A. S. Eddington, *The Nature of the Physical World*	Cambridge University Press	1928
A. Einstein, *The Theory of Relativity*	Methuen	1920
R. A. Fisher, *The Genetical Theory of Natural Selection*	Oxford University Press	1930
J. G. Frazer, *The Golden Bough*	Macmillan	1922
G. H. Hardy, *A Mathematician's Apology* (with foreword by C. P. Snow)	Cambridge University Press	1967

J. E. Littlewood, *A Mathematician's Miscellany*	Methuen	1953
W. W. Rouse Ball, *History of Mathematics*	Macmillan	1908
J. Arthur Thomson, *Science and Religion*	Methuen	1925

F. BIOGRAPHY AND AUTOBIOGRAPHY

N. Annan, *Leslie Stephen*	MacGibbon & Kee	1951
B. Askwith, *Two Victorian Families*	Chatto & Windus	1971
R. H. Bainton, *Erasmus of Rotterdam*	Collins	1970
G. K. A. Bell, *Randall Davidson*	Oxford University Press	1938
R. Clark, *Life of Bertrand Russell*	Cape and Weidenfeld & Nicolson	1975
H. C. Colles, *Walford Davies*	Oxford University Press	1942
H. Cudlipp, *Walking on the Water*	Bodley Head	1976
T. Cullen, *The Prostitutes' Padre*	Bodley Head	1975
F. W. Dillistone, *Charles Raven*	Hodder & Stoughton	1975
F. W. Dillistone, *C. H. Dodd*	Hodder & Stoughton	1977
G. Faber, *Jowett*	Faber & Faber	1957
M. Fitzgerald, *Herbert Edward Ryle*	Macmillan	1928
P. Fitzgerald, *The Knox Brothers*	Macmillan	1977
'Gentleman with a Duster', *Painted Windows*	Mills & Boon	1922
G. H. Hardy, *Bertrand Russell and Trinity*	Cambridge University Press	1942
H. H. Henson, *Retrospect of an Unimportant Life*	Oxford University Press	1942-50
W. R. Inge, *Diary of a Dean*	Hutchinson	n.d.
F. A. Iremonger, *Men and Movements in the Church of England*	Longmans	1928
F. A. Iremonger, *William Temple*	Oxford University Press	1948
R. C. D. Jasper, *Arthur Cayley Headlam*	Faith Press	1960
R. C. D. Jasper, *George Bell*	Oxford University Press	1967
J. G. Lockhart, *Cosmo Gordon Lang*	Hodder & Stoughton	1949
H. D. A. Major, *Life and Letters of William Boyd Carpenter*	Murray	1925

W. R. Matthews, *Memories and Meanings*	Hodder & Stoughton	1969
M. Muggeridge, *Chronicles of Wasted Time*, 2 vols.	Collins	1972–3
W. S. Power, *The Real Thing*	Dixon	1970
G. L. Prestige, *Life of Charles Gore*	Heinemann	1935
W. Purcell, *Fisher of Lambeth*	Hodder & Stoughton	1969
E. Richards, *Private View of a Public Man*	Allen & Unwin	1950
R. Ellis Roberts, *H. R. L. Sheppard*	Murray	1942
B. Russell, *Autobiography*, 3 vols.	Allen & Unwin	1967, 1968, 1969
E. H. Ryle, ed., *Arthur Christopher Benson*	Bell	1925
C. Scott, *H. R. L. Sheppard*	Hodder & Stoughton	1977
C. H. Smyth, *Cyril Forster Garbett*	Hodder & Stoughton	1959
J. A. Spender & C. Asquith, *Life of Lord Oxford and Asquith*, 2 vols.	Hutchinson	1932
A. Vidler, *Scenes from a Clerical Life*	Collins	1977
A. W. Ward, *Bibliography and Memoir*	Cambridge University Press	1926
J. Ward, *Experiences of a Diplomatist*	Macmillan	1872

INDEX

A comprehensive index would double the size of the book. Nor would it be profitable to give repeated page references for all the causes, doctrines, ideas and theories which are integral to the subject and intertwined with each other. The same applies to ecclesiastical and political parties and persuasions and to countries discussed as political entities rather than geographical expressions.

This index therefore covers:
(a) events;
(b) institutions;
(c) people;
(d) places, except those visited or mentioned only incidentally;
(e) publications.

A

Abbott, Very Revd. Dr Eric (b. 1906; Dean of Westminster, 1959–74), offered Archdeaconry of Birmingham, 383

Abdication of King Edward VIII (1936), E.W.B.'s part in crisis, 332–5

Abelard, Peter (1079–1142; theologian), 135, 292

Aberdeen University, awards E.W.B. honorary degree, 214; Gifford Lectures at, 308–9

Abyssinian War (1935), 344–5

Acocks Green, Birmingham, 157

Acton, 1st Lord (1834–1902; historian), 56, 73, 82, 109, 141

Acts and Monuments (Foxe), 196–7

Adam Smith, Sir George (1856–1942; Principal of Aberdeen University, 1909–35) and Lady, 309

Addison, 1st Viscount (1869–1951; politician), 370

Admiralty, 21, 49, 387

Agar-Ellis, Revd. J. J. (Trustee of St Aidan's, Small Heath), 240–72

Ainger, Canon Alfred (1837–1904; Master of the Temple, 1894–1904), 78, 118

Albania, invasion (1939), 352

Alexandra Theatre, Birmingham, 154

Allen & Overy, Messrs. (solicitors for plaintiffs in cement libel case against E.W.B.), 369–71

Allen, Rt. Revd. Geoffrey (b. 1902;

Archdeacon of Birmingham, 1944–7; later Bishop in Egypt, Principal of Ripon Hall and Bishop of Derby), 383, 393, 436

All Saints, Small Heath, 226, 237

Altrincham, Cheshire, E.W.B.'s birthplace, 18, 23

Amended Clerical Subscription Act (1865), 406

Amritsar massacre (1919), 101

Andrewes, Bishop Lancelot (1555–1626; Cambridge Platonist), 29

Andrews, Revd. C. F. (1871–1940; missionary), 25, 91

Angell, Sir Norman (1872–1967; economist), 64

Anglican Evangelical Group Movement, 175

Anglican Fellowship, 56, 79

Anglican Pacifist Fellowship, 362

Anglo-Catholic Congress (1922), 164; (1925), 175

Anglo-German Fellowship, 349

Anglo-German Naval Agreements (1935–7), 352

Anglo-Hellenic Society, Athens, address to, 323

Annan, Noel, Lord (b. 1916), 73

Anschluss of Austria (1938), 350

Ansell, Edward (Ansell's Aston Ales), 232

Antigua, E.W.B.'s limerick on, 289

465

Record [*contd.*]
references, 132, 194
Record, E. W. (1873–1943; journalist),
editor of *Birmingham Post*, 355
Reform Act (1867), 13
Registrar of Birmingham Diocese, *see*
Ekin
Religion and the Rise of Capitalism
(Tawney), 58
Renan, Ernest (1823–92; theologian), 23,
141
Repertory Theatre, Birmingham, 154, 289
Repton School, Archbishop Fisher as
headmaster of, 419
Rhineland, reoccupation (1936), 349
Ribbentrop-Molotov Pact (1939), 100, 352
Richard II, King (1367–1400), 154
Richards, Revd. Leyton (1879–1948; Non-
conformist minister), and cement, 366–8;
mentioned, 344
Richards, Very Revd. J. H. (1869–1952;
Archdeacon of Aston, 1920–37; Provost
of Birmingham, 1937–48), married by
E.W.B. to deceased wife's sister (1939),
331; other references, 157, 180, 337, 394
Richardson, Very Revd. Alan (1905–75;
Dean of York, 1964–75), broadcast
debate with E.W.B. on *Rise of
Christianity*, 413–14
Richardson, Canon R. D. (b. 1893;
Principal of Ripon Hall, 1948–52), 294,
393
Richmond, Sir Bruce (1871–1964; journa-
list), editor, *Times Literary Supplement*,
112, 131
Riemann, G. F. B. (1826–66; math-
ematician), 33, 311–12, 314
Ripon, Bishop of, *see* Boyd-Carpenter,
Burroughs
Ripon Hall, Oxford, centre of 'modernist'
teaching, 122, 134, 157, 383, 393, 431
Rise of Christianity (E.W.B.), origins, 388;
summary, 395–6; reviews and criticism,
396–403; assessment, 403–4; official
reactions and Fisher's attitude, 404–9;
his denunciation in Convocation and
E.W.B.'s reply, 409–12; serialized in
Sunday Pictorial with Blunt's comments,
412–13; debated by E.W.B. with
Richardson on BBC, 413–14; other
references, 63, 421
Robertson, Revd. F. W. (1816–53;
preacher), E.W.B.'s debt to, 109
Robinson, Rt. Revd. J. A. T. (b. 1919;
Bishop of Woolwich, 1959–69; Dean of
Trinity, Cambridge, 1969–   ), 67–8

Rogers, Canon T. Guy (1876–1967;
Rector of Birmingham, 1925–48), 340,
347, 369, 394, 412
Rolland, Romain (1866–1944; writer), 140
Ropp, Baron von der, Nazi propagandist,
349
Rosenthal, Revd. G. D. (d. 1938), local
leader of 'rebels' in Birmingham
Diocese, 166–72, 181–2, 209–10, 226,
228, 241, 279
Rossington, Revd. H. J. (1870–1957;
Unitarian minister), 344
Rotary clubs, addresses to, 382
Roumania, guarantee to (1939), 352
Rouse Ball, W. W. (1850–1925; math-
ematician), E.W.B.'s Cambridge tutor,
30–1
Rousseau, Jean-Jacques (1712–78; phil-
osopher), cited, 91, 391
Royal Air Force, and Incitement to
Disaffection Bill, 304; Benevolent Fund
profits from cement case, 373
Royal Army Medical Corps, 71
Royal Artillery, 59, 356
Royal Astronomical Society, 34
Royal Commission on Ecclesiastical Disci-
pline (1906), *see* Ecclesiastical Discipline
Royal Holloway College, 70, 308
Royal Institute of Public Health, address
to, 175
Royal Military Academy, Woolwich,
E.W.B. instructor at, 34
Royal Society, E.W.B.'s Fellowship, 34;
other references, 25, 89, 110; *see also*
Proceedings
Ruskin, John (1819–1900; writer), 82, 95
Russell, Bertrand, 3rd Earl (1872–1970;
mathematician), comparison with
E.W.B., 61–3; prosecution and ex-
pulsion from Trinity, 63–7; and contra-
ception, 298; mentioned, 27
Rylands Library, Manchester, fragment of
Fourth Gospel, 400
Ryle, Rt. Revd. Herbert (1856–1925;
Bishop of Winchester, 1903–11; Dean
of Westminster, 1911–25), E.W.B.'s re-
lations with, 122, 138; presents E.W.B.
for consecration, 149; death, 182

S

St Agatha's, Sparkbrook (Rosenthal's
church), 166, 209, 279
St Aidan's, Small Heath: the case of
'Notley and others [the Trustees] v.
Bishop of Birmingham': background,

INDEX

St Aidan's [*contd.*]
236–8; initial moves, 238–41; legal proceedings, 241–52; Lang's decision and correspondence with E.W.B., 252–67; E.W.B's final comments, 267–9; legal, theological and ecclesiastical implications, 269–82; other references, 180, 231, 284

St Alban's, Bishop of, *see* Furse

St Anne's, Duddeston, return from 'rebellion', 184, 227

St Bartholomew's Day (1913) sermon, 61, 208

St Edmundsbury and Ipswich, Bishop of, *see* Whittingham

St Gregory's, Small Heath, first 'rebellion', 172–6, 237; second 'rebellion', 250

St Joan (Shaw), 289

St John's, Sparkhill, E.W.B. confirmed at, 26

St Johnston, Mrs, 418

St Jude's, Birmingham, return from 'rebellion', 282–3

St Mark's, Washwood Heath, dispute over 'rebel' nominee, 177–9; implications, 179–82; other references, 173, 237–8

St Mary's, Tyne Dock, and St Aidan's, 238, 254

St Matthew's, Southsea, 170; *see also* Cornford

St Paul's Cathedral, Bullock-Webster's brawl in (1927), 194–7, 199, 206

St Paul's, Dean of, *see* Inge, Matthews

St Peter's, Vere Street, 434

St Sepulchre's, Old Bailey, E.W.B.'s first sermon, 48

Salisbury, 3rd Marquess of (1830–1903; Prime Minister, 1885–6, 1886–92 and 1895–1902), 439

Saltley, Birmingham, and St Mark's, Washwood Heath, 173, 177; Training College visited by Fisher, 418

Salvation Army, *see* Booth

Sancroft, Archbishop William (1617–93; Archbishop of Canterbury, 1678–90), 253

Sanday, Revd. William (1843–1920; theologian), 135

Sankey, John, 1st Viscount (1866–1948; lawyer and politician), 82, 307

Savonarola, Fra Girolamo (1452–98; reformer), 58

Sceptical Essays (Russell), 65

Schiller, F. von (1759–1805: dramatist), 82

Schuster, Sir Arthur (1851–1934; physicist), 74

Schuster, Lady (née Caroline Loveday) (1867–1962), 74

Schwarbrick, Thomas (fl. c. 1715; organ builder), 155

Schweitzer, Albert (1875–1965; philosopher and missionary), at Westminster Abbey, 143

Scientific Theory and Religion (E.W.B.), discussed, 308–19; and *Rise of Christianity*, 398; and *Principia Mathematica*, 62; *see also* Gifford Lectures

Scotland, Church of, 430

Scott, C. P. (1846–1932; journalist; Editor, *Manchester Guardian*, 1872–1929), 74, 132

Screwtape Letters (Lewis), 55

Seaton, Devon, E.W.B.'s holiday home, 321–2, 352, 387–8, 434, 436

Selborne, 3rd Earl of, *see* Wolmer

Select Committee on Estimates (1938), 370

Selwyn, Very Revd. E. G. (1885–1959; Dean of Winchester, 1931–58), and *Rise of Christianity*, 405, 407–12

Senrab, Colloquies of (Strachey), 49

Shackleton, Sir Ernest (1874–1922; explorer), 23

Shaftesbury, 7th Earl of (1801–85; philanthropist), 14

Shaw, George Bernard (1856–1950; writer), 199, 287, 296, 299

Sheffield, Bishop of, *see* Hunter

Shelley, P. B. (1792–1822; poet), 82

Sheppard, Very Revd. H. R. L. (1880–1937; Vicar of St Martin's-in-the-Fields, 1914–27; Dean of Canterbury, 1929–31), 125, 204, 348

'Sheppard v. Bennett', *see* Bennett

Sherlock, Thomas (1678–1761; Master of the Temple, 1704–53; Bishop of London, 1748–61), 116

Sherlock, Dr William (?1641–1707; Master of the Temple, 1685–1704; Dean of St Paul's, 1691–1707), 116

Shore, S. R. (Trustee of St Aidan's, Small Heath), 240–72

Short History of Mathematics (Rouse Ball), 30

Should Such a Faith Offend? (E.W.B.), discussed, 206–9; other references, 223, 408

'Shropshire Lad' (Housman), 42

Simmonds, Revd. G. D. (1899–1961), and St Aidan's, 238–72

Simon, John, 1st Viscount (1873–1954; lawyer and politician), 38, 345, 359

483

Y

Z